BEWITCHED

BEWITCHED

WAYNE MILLER

CREATION
HOUSE
A STRANG COMPANY

BEWITCHED by Wayne Miller
Published by Creation House
A Strang Company
600 Rinehart Road
Lake Mary, Florida 32746
www.strangbookgroup.com

Unless otherwise noted, all Scripture quotations are from the King James Version of the Bible.

Scripture quotations marked NIV are from the Holy Bible, New International Version. Copyright © 1973, 1978, 1984, International Bible Society. Used by permission.

Unless otherwise noted, Greek and Hebrew definitions are derived from Kenneth Wuest, *Word Studies in the Greek New Testament* (n.p.: B & H Academic, 2000) and A.T. Robertson, *Word Pictures in the New Testament* (Grand Rapids, MI: Eerdmans, 1980).

Design Director: Bill Johnson

Cover design by Rachel Lopez

Library of Congress Control Number: 2010931340
International Standard Book Number: 978-1-61638-197-4

First Edition

10 11 12 13 14 — 9 8 7 6 5 4 3 2 1
Printed in the United States of America

Contents

Dedication

I DEDICATE THIS BOOK to those who are on a spiritual journey. The journey began when we were in Egypt where we were in bondage to sin, to Goshen where we were saved and began our spiritual journey, to the wilderness where the carnal man rules, and finally to Canaan where the spiritual man abides. I dedicate this book to those who have gone from the outer court, to the holy place, to the holiest of all.

To those who stand boldly at the foot of the cross where the gospel is not diluted, who dare to capture and embrace the reality of a Spirit-filled life. To those who are freed from the bondage of sin and the chains of legalism. To those who refuse to come under the spell of the enemy, who will not be bewitched. I dedicate this writing to all those would dare to capture the walk of the Spirit.

Foreword

I N THE FALL of 1981, I was a recent high school graduate in search of a purpose in life. I enrolled at East Coast Bible College because it was just assumed that when you are a son of a pastor, you ,follow in your father's footsteps and go into the ministry. I remember at orientation I was introduced to a fellow freshman by the name of Wayne Joseph Miller. The introduction was not intentional, but rather accidental. What an impression he made that day. I sat in a room filled with other nervous rookies to college life when I heard a booming and hearty laugh echo off the block walls. As I looked to see what was making such a clamor, I was shocked to behold a red-headed giant of a youth sitting with a grin from ear to ear. As I sat there bored and uninterested, wondering what I had gotten myself into, it was obvious that this guy was having the time of his life and was completely comfortable with this studious environment and awfully glad to be there.

Soon after that I tried out for the college basketball team where I again found this jolly giant. We spent that year on the same basketball team, which by the way, was crowned conference champ and made it to the Final Four. The friendship and bond that was formed back then has only strengthened over time. Through these many years I have shared some of life's fondest moments with Wayne Miller and have found him to be more massive in spirit and heart than in body. There are few people that have the passion for Christ and enthusiasm for ministry that he does. This was not a passing fancy with him, but a zeal that never wanes.

He has proven to be a man of God and a champion of faith. His success as evangelist was unparalleled as he crisscrossed this nation declaring the soul-saving message of the Lord Jesus Christ. As a pastor, his faithfulness, dependability, and leadership have been unmatched or unequaled. He has led his church on multiple building campaigns and expansions, and he (along with his dear wife Debbie) has grown a church that is a beacon of light and serves as the epitome of what a New Testament church stands for.

These qualities are sought after and envied by every minister; but in my humble opinion his greatest assets are his thorough knowledge of the Word of God (developed by relentless and intense study) and the mighty anointing of the Holy Spirit that has rested heavily upon his life. These properties never stagnate but continue to grow and intensify with each passing day. One cannot help but be envious of a man that is so advanced.

Through the help of God, he has put to paper and chiseled out a masterpiece through which the souls of men will be able to breathe the sweet air of freedom. Even though man has grown and evolved culturally, domestically, scientifically, and of course economically, he is still in many ways deprived and living in the dark ages spiritually. Many are still trying to use the crude instrument of works to carve their way to salvation when the way has already been provided through the blood of Jesus.

This preacher's preacher proves that the blood is the only price that could pay the penalty of sin. He goes to great depths and details to outline for us in no uncertain terms that the cross stands alone and needs no help or support. When we add to the wonderful work of the Wonder Worker, we dilute His power by subtracting and taking away from all that He has purchased for us through the redemptive process. No longer do we need to live under the bondage of legalism and works. Just as Adam's attempt to cover himself with fig leaves to justify his sin proved to be insufficient, so are our efforts.

Bishop Miller reinforces the call to righteousness and true holiness by proving how shallow self-help methods are in covering sins. He attacks the shallow belief that you can live as you choose while you profess to be under grace. Grace is no license to sin. The statement "The grace of God is more than that which justifies us, forgives, and makes us righteous in His sight; it is God's power at work in us giving us victory over sin" is at the heart of this writing.

—Bishop Roy Lee Tucker
Pastor of the Praising Place
Church of God

Introduction

IMAGINE THAT YOU came into the local church one Sunday morning and your pastor or the Sunday school teacher made the following statement: "It is no longer necessary for you to be saved by grace through faith. There are additional things you have to do in order to be saved." It is as though Calvary is not enough to deliver men from the lordship, control, and power of sin. What if someone said, "It is no longer necessary for one to be filled with the Spirit or rely on God's sanctifying, enabling grace? We need to abandon the Holy Spirit and the grace of God and make a flesh attempt to serve God." How would you respond?

Who would have ever believed that they were being bewitched? Or that they had fallen under a demonic spell? Salvation has been turned into nothing more than a course in self-improvement and not a work of a sovereign God accomplished by Jesus' sacrificial atoning death on the cross.

The ultimate deception is thinking that by abandoning the Holy Spirit and the sanctifying, enabling grace of God and returning to a flesh attempt to serve God, we can obtain the same results through the flesh as we did by walking in the Spirit and relying on God's sanctifying, enabling grace.

What started in the Spirit and the grace of God has got to be maintained by the Spirit and God's sanctifying enabling grace. Any teaching or influence that would seek to tear you away from these two foundational truths needs to be identified as demonic and Satan's attempt to place you under a demonic spell.

While many enjoy coming up under the title of Pentecostal, it is evident that many people are not filled with the Holy Spirit. Yes, many have been baptized by the Holy Spirit into Christ; but where are those who have been baptized by Christ into the Holy Spirit? I believe that at salvation the Holy Spirit takes up His abode in the heart and life of the believer—that is the indwelling of the Holy Spirit. It is not the empowerment for service.

It is the Holy Spirit who came as the high sheriff of heaven with a warrant for our arrest, slapped the handcuffs on us, and drew us to the foot of the cross. He takes the victory that was accomplished for us at the cross, tomb, and resurrection and makes it real in us. It is the Holy Spirit that gives us the desire to serve God. He puts the *want to* in the life of the Christian. When you lose your *want to*, you are in trouble. With salvation comes a desire.

It is the Holy Spirit who enables us to obey God. All perfection in the Christian life comes from Him. Through the presence of the Holy Spirit we are free from sin. Only the Holy Spirit of God can change us, work miracles, and fill us with the Holy Ghost. It is the presence of the Holy Spirit that puts a glow on our countenance. How many have lost their glow because they have neglected the presence of the Holy Spirit? Through His sanctifying, enabling presence we find a liberty that keeps us from becoming entangled with the yoke of bondage. Through Him our spiritual life goes from buds to blossoms, then from fruit to fire. Through Him we are able to order our behavior through the life-giving principle of the Spirit.

The grace of God is more than that which justifies, forgives, and makes us righteous in His sight; it is God's power at work in us giving us victory over sin. Too many are treating grace as a license to do as they please instead of serving God and their fellow man. Grace is not a license to sin. Too many are treating God's grace as a cover-up for their mistakes rather than living an overcoming, victorious life. In the Book of Jude, Jude, the servant of Jesus Christ, spoke of those who turn "the grace of our God into lasciviousness" (v. 4). Here the word *lasciviousness* comes from the word *aselgei,* which means "to prepare oneself for every pleasure." It is unbridled lust. Man has given himself over to sensuality. He has thrown off all restraints and begun to reveal just how out of control he is. He performs every impurity and still lusts for more. Sensuality does not satisfy; it only creates a greater appetite. A bad man will usually try to hide his sin, but the man who falls into lasciviousness does not care who he shocks in public just so his desires are gratified.

Even Jude, in his defense for the faith, spoke of those who would turn the grace of God into a license to sin. People in the church are more concerned about what they can get by with instead of what they can live by. We want to see how close to the world we can get without calling it sin instead of seeing how close to God we can get and overcome a lifestyle of sin.

Paul said the believer is "in Christ Jesus" (1 Cor. 1:30). We have entered into a union with Christ. He is the atmosphere in which we inhale and exhale from day to day. We have died with Him, been buried with Him, and been resurrected with Him to walk in newness of life. Our life is now Christ's own resurrected life. In one way we live in Him; in another way He lives in us. Paul said, "Nevertheless I live; yet not I, but Christ liveth in me" (Gal. 2:20). In a real sense, to be in Christ is to be a limb or organ of Christ's body, dependent on Him, subject to His will, and dedicated to His purposes. Freedom from condemnation, victory over sin, and fellowship with God comes through our union with Christ and the indwelling presence of the Holy Spirit.

Chapter 1

Bible Christianity

IT IS HAS been said that Christianity without the supernatural is not Christianity at all. There is no such thing as a powerless, lifeless Christianity. John Rice, in his book *The Power of Pentecost*, made the statement that "any Christian that is not content to have the soul-winning power of the Holy Spirit upon him is complacent and lives in sin, with God's dear face turned away from him."[1]

The Christian life is rooted and grounded in the Holy Spirit. It is not enough for us to say that we have the Spirit; the Spirit must have us. The question is not "When are we going to get more of God?" The question is "When is God going to get more of us?" It is only then that He can share with us the abundant and victorious life that is ours in Christ.

The Christian life is not about a flesh attempt to serve God, but is a Spirit-led relationship. It is not about a struggle with the flesh; it is about being borne along by the Spirit. There is life in our Christian experience because of the presence of the Holy Spirit. The Christian life from start to finish is all supernatural. There is nothing dull about the Christian life. If there is anything dull about it, it is what we have made it to be instead of what Christ intended. There is no such thing as a lifeless and dead Christianity. Is Christianity really Christianity without the supernatural? Hollis Gause, in his book *Living in the Spirit*, said, "For years we have tried to separate Christianity from Pentecost and Pentecost from Christianity. The truth is real Christianity is Pentecost and Pentecost is Christianity."[2]

When we understand that the New Testament has nothing good to say about the flesh, we know that those who are in the flesh cannot please God. We know that our flesh is at war with God, and because of that fact the carnal mind refuses to be marshaled by God's law. For this reason, it is impossible for the flesh to obey God.

For too long in the church we have attempted to get the old nature to obey the laws of God, and as a result we give birth to a legalistic mentality. Legalism is when we base our righteousness on anything other than the redemptive work of Jesus Christ that He purchased and accomplished for us on the cross at Calvary.

The condition of Romans 7:7–25 is past—trying to make the old nature obey the laws of God, which has produced nothing but frustration and defeated living. We now have a new set of goals and a new set of desires that the Holy Spirit has imparted to us. We have turned our backs on our flesh that was dominated by sin and have turned our faces to the Spirit as the Spirit of life in Christ Jesus. Though at times we may battle the sins of the past, we are enabled now by the Spirit of God to conquer the flesh and walk in the Spirit. If we cannot conquer ourselves and learn how to possess our vessels in sanctification and honor, we will never conquer the cities in which we live.

Such was the feeling of Christ in the Gospel of John when He said, "Verily, verily, I say unto you, He that heareth my word, and believeth on him that sent me, hath everlasting life, and shall not come into condemnation; but is passed from death unto life" (John 5:24). It was not the intention of Jesus that believers would be condemned with the world (1 Cor. 11:32).

Paul wrote to the church at Rome, "For sin shall not have dominion over you: for ye are not under the law, but under grace" (Rom. 6:14). In Romans the sixth chapter, sin was personified as a person having dominion, lordship, and control over the individual. For us to continue in sin is contrary to our new nature and our new position in Christ. At Calvary, Christ died once and for all for our sin. At the cross we die to sin. Either we die to it or we will die in it. If we have been identified with Christ's sacrificial atoning death at the cross, we are to be dead to sin but alive to God. We should be as dead to sin as a dead man lying in a funeral home is to this world. How can we embrace the cross and continue in a life of sin?

As the sanctifying Holy Spirit applies the redemptive benefits of Christ's sacrifice at the cross, we are delivered from the flesh. His sanctifying presence and activity does what the law can never do or accomplish. The answer to man's sinfulness is the sanctifying influence of the Holy Spirit. My fleshly existence is placed under holy control. Heaven's will is now my *want to*. The Spirit sanctifies my human existence.

Paul said to the church at Rome, "There is therefore now no condemnation to them which are in Christ Jesus, who walk not after the flesh, but after the Spirit" (Rom. 8:1). This does not mean that we have arrived and reached a point of perfection. Whereas the Holy Spirit does not condemn us, there are times that He does convict us. We must choose to repent and forsake sin. I hear many make the statement, "I don't want to go to a church where I am made to feel condemned." They have never understood that condemnation is for the sinner, but conviction is for the child of God.

Thank God the Holy Spirit still convicts. Paul showed in Romans the seventh chapter that without grace, there is defeated living, misery, and bondage. Condemnation is a legal term in the judgment of God. God's answer to condemnation is justification. In justification condemnation is resolved. There is no penal servitude. There are those who are in Christ Jesus that go on doing penal servitude as though they have never been pardoned and never been liberated from the prison house of sin.

Paul's frustration in trying to measure up to the law of God in his own strength is expressed in verse 24: "O wretched man that I am! Who shall deliver me from this body of death?" Then Paul pointed back to his triumphal note when he said, "I thank God through Jesus Christ our Lord. So then with the mind I myself serve the law of God; but with the flesh the law of sin" (7:25). As sinners we deserved condemnation in our sinful state, but God offered us pardon in Christ. This is Paul's gospel. Only at the cross is there safety. Those who are in Christ can live a consecrated, crucified, and baptized life.

There is no reason for us to live under condemnation. We need to quit beating ourselves up over our past. The devil is doing a good enough job. He does not need our help. There are many people who continue to punish themselves for the mistakes of their past. God help us if our past has more mortgage and influence over us than our future. When the devil reminds you of your past, remind him of his future. Many cannot look forward without looking backward and reviewing the mistakes of their past. Many are problem conscious rather than triumph centered. Many condemn themselves over their struggle with temptation.

Christ has borne the penalty of the law at Calvary to satisfy the mercy and justice of God. The judgment that should have fallen on us for our sin fell upon Him at the cross. He was condemned that we might be saved. He was cursed that we might be blessed. In chapter 8 of Romans the dilemma that is expressed in Romans 7:13–25 is resolved. In the original Greek, verse 1 of chapter 8, translates, "Therefore, now there is not even one bit of condemnation to those who are in Christ Jesus." And then he continues, "Who walk not after the flesh, but after the Spirit."[3]

To Paul the spirit of a man is dead and dormant until it is aroused by the Holy Ghost of God. To walk after the Spirit is a lifestyle of dynamic Christian living. We are delivered from the power of sin and led onward to final glorification in Christ. To walk after the Spirit is to seek and to submit to the Holy Spirit's direction and enablement and to concentrate our attention on the things of God. We do not get ahead of Him nor lag behind Him, but stay in step with Him. To stay in step with the Holy Spirit is more important than staying in step with the times. It also means weed pulling. We need to reach down and pull up weeds that do not belong in our lives and replace them with seeds of truth that will one day reap a bountiful harvest. Those who make the things of the Spirit of God their chief love and concern can expect eternal life and communion with God.

The Holy Spirit has triumphed over the flesh and placed it under holy control. The flesh is still subject to the law of sin, but Christians are not living their lives by the dictations of the flesh. They are walking according to the Spirit. We are not going to come into condemnation but into the glory with Christ. Christ has liberated us from the power of the evil nature and made us partakers of His divine nature. Everything the devil stole from us in the garden we get back at Calvary. The divine nature is what motivates us toward obeying God's commandments.

We can boldly declare: "What the law could not do, in that it was weak through the flesh, God sending his own Son in the likeness of sinful flesh, and for sin, condemned sin in the flesh" (Rom. 8:3). The law could not change me, work miracles, or fill me with the Holy Ghost. It could not bring me into the presence of God. It placed demands on my life but gave me no power to live up to them. What the law could not accomplish because of the weakness of my flesh, God sent His own Son "tabernacle" in a tent of flesh and through the power of the Holy Spirit conquered and mastered sin.

To be in Christ is to be in Him receptively. It is the state of our commitment to Him. The judgment which the world anticipates happening at the end of the age has for the believer already occurred. The judgment was resolved at the cross when our sins were forgiven. We live in justification not condemnation. In justification God acquits us of our guilt, He puts us in position of one who has never broken the law; He declares us to be righteous in His sight. He looks upon us as He would look upon His own Son. In justification we have peace with God (Rom. 5:1). The word *peace* means to bind back together that which has been separated.

We have access in this grace wherein we stand and we rejoice in hope of the glory of God. Spiritually speaking we live on the tiptoes of expectancy. At the cross Jesus with one hand took the hand of fallen humanity and with the other hand He took hold of the hand of God the Father. In the person of Christ, God and man were reunited. Paul affirmed the fact when he wrote the church at Rome: "For if, when we were enemies, we were reconciled to God by the death of his Son, much more, being reconciled, we shall be saved by his life" (Rom. 5:10).

Whereas the New Testament has nothing good to say about the flesh, the believer does have an obligation to the Holy Spirit. There is a debt that we owe to the Spirit. "The law of the Spirit of life in Christ Jesus hath made me free from the law of sin and death" (Rom. 8:2). Paul here refers to the Holy Spirit as the "Spirit of life." The Nicene Creed invites us to confess: "We believe in the Holy Spirit, the Lord, the giver of Life."[4] He was the giver of life in creation (Gen. 1:2). He is the giver of life in the new birth (John 3:5). He is the giver of life in progressive sanctification. He has brought to an end the tyranny of the reign of the flesh and is delivering us and bringing us into that perfect love which is the fulfillment of the law (Rom. 8:4). He is also the life-giver in the resurrection.

Jesus Christ came to meet the tyrant on his own ground in his own realm— in the flesh. The verb *condemned* means that Jesus pronounced the doom of sin.[5] Jesus deposed sin from its lordship, domination, and control in the lives of men. In His own body, on the very territory of sin, God doomed sin in the person of His Son. By Jesus' life of perfect obedience and through His death and resurrection, the reign of sin over mankind has been broken. Sin is now a defeated power, a dethroned tyrant. Romans 8, verse 2 reassures us that the Holy Spirit has liberated us from sin. Luther said, "He wrote His Law with living fire in our hearts. The Law itself is not a doctrine, but life. It is not a word but reality, not a sign but fullness."[6]

The Holy Spirit has offered us new possibilities in Christ. As a believer we need to recognize our opportunities and act on them. New obligations have been imposed on those who have died and risen with Christ. We owe something to the One who has set us free so "that the righteousness of the law might be fulfilled in us, who walk not after the flesh, but after the Spirit" (Rom. 8:4). Because of the Holy Spirit, the Christian is no longer under obligation to live under the dominion of sin. When we were joined to Christ, from that point on the Holy Spirit forbade us to live under an obligation to the flesh. The Christian has been lifted from the plane of the earthly to the heavenly. Christians are those who live their lives not dominated by the sin nature but by the Holy Spirit.

By the provision of the Holy Spirit, God wishes us to live unique lives. Walking in the Spirit produces two blessings for believers: 1) The Holy Spirit enables and obligates the believer to put to death the deeds of the flesh. Redemptively we have been set free from all connections to the old way of life. There is no legitimate claim of loyalty to the flesh. 2) It offers to us the assurance that we are the children of God.

> But now we are delivered from the law, that being dead wherein we were held; that we should serve in newness of spirit, and not in the oldness of the letter.
>
> —ROMANS 7:6

In the believer's death with Christ on the cross, Christ has discharged us from the law, just as a woman was discharged from the law that bound her to her husband. The Christian is now more alive than ever. Now the power of the sin nature has been broken in the heart and life of the believer. The believer is not under the law anymore and neither is the believer subject to it. Man was bound by law to his wife just as she was bound to her husband. As long as they lived they were under the authority law of marriage. If the woman left the man for another man, she committed adultery (Matt. 5:32). But if the husband died, she was free to remarry because she was no longer a wife. It is death that broke the marriage relationship. Being bound to the law was captivity. It was only through death that the bound wife could be set free. In the Greek the violent death at Calvary that Christ died is brought out. It was necessary for both Christ and the believer to die.

Under the law we were united with sin; when we died in and with Christ at Calvary, we were liberated from the law. In rising with Christ to newness of life, we are united with Him in a new bond of faith and love. So the body of Christ is the body of Jesus that was put to death on the cross. In and with

His body, I died and became identified with His death through faith. I was raised from the dead that I might become a part of the church, the new bride of Christ. The old marriage was fruitful to death (Gal. 5:19–21), so the new union is fruitful to God (Gal. 5:22–23). Seeing that we have been released from the law, we serve God in the newness of the Spirit and not the oldness of the letter.

In the Old Testament Christ was married to unfaithful Israel. In the New Testament sinners are bound by the power of sin and the chains of the law. Christ died, freeing Him of His Old Testament relationship with Israel. At the same time the believer died, freeing him from the law and sin. Death allows a new marriage to take place. The blessed relationship will be fully consummated at the marriage supper of the Lamb (Rev. 19:7–8).

In Paul's illustration it was the husband that died and it was the wife who was free to marry again (1 Cor. 7:39). The church is represented by the wife and the husband represents the law. When the church died to the law through her identification with Christ at the cross, by her being identified with Christ's resurrection, she arose from the dead and was free to be married to Christ. The only way she could marry again was to come back from the dead. When we trusted Christ, we died to the law; but in Christ we arose from the dead and now we are married to Christ to live a new kind of life. Being bound to the living Christ is freedom in the Holy Spirit. Serving God in newness of the Spirit is perfect freedom

The purpose of this is "that we should bring forth fruit unto God" (Rom. 7:4). The spiritual man was delivered from the law. When we were unsaved, we were under the authority of the law. When we trusted Christ as Lord and Savior, we were united to Him. We died to the law. The law did not die, but we did.

We no longer look to the Old Testament law and sacrifices for salvation and acceptance before God. We have been separated from the old covenant of the law and have been united to Christ. We now look to Christ for salvation and believe in Him to receive His Spirit and grace. We have received forgiveness, and there has been a recreation of our new nature so that we can "bring forth fruit unto God" (v. 4).

Paul said, "That being dead wherein we were held" (v. 6). The actual translation of the Greek says, "Having died to that in which we were constantly held down."[7] The believer was constantly held by the evil nature. We rendered habitual bondslave obedience. The law cannot exercise authority over a dead person. Death meant deliverance. We were delivered that we might serve. We died to the law to be married to Christ. We were delivered from the law that we might serve Christ.

Paul wrote to the church of Colossians: "Blotting out the handwriting of ordinances that was against us, which was contrary to us, and took it out of the way, nailing it to his cross" (Col. 2:14). This referred to the Law of Moses and the commandments which pointed to right conduct but could not give us power and life to obey God. Salvation through the Old Testament covenant has been nailed to the cross and abolished (Gal. 3:13). God has established a better covenant through Christ and by the Spirit. In that day when a man could not pay his taxes, he, his wife and children, and everything that he owned could be sold into slavery to pay his debt. The governor came by and nailed handwritten ordinances to the doorpost of his home. The only way he could be pardoned was if the governor came by, took his pen, and blotted them out with an X, rendering the debt paid in full.

I owed a debt that I could not pay. Christ paid a debt that He did not owe. Handwritten ordinances were nailed to the doorpost of my life. The law was spiritual; I was carnal and was sold under sin. On His way to the cross, Jesus stopped by my house, took down the handwriting of ordinance from the doorpost of my life, and took it to a place called Calvary. There He nailed it to an old rugged cross. He shed His blood, blotted out my debt, and rendered my sin debt paid in full. Thank God, Jesus paid my sin debt.

The Christian is more alive than ever before. Satan seeks to gain control over him. The power of the evil nature has been broken in the believer. Before salvation he was constantly held down by the law's grip and control. Paul uses the imperfect tense to show the absolute control of the evil nature over the unsaved person.

Paul then says "that we should serve in newness of Spirit" (Rom. 7:6). Paul is saying that we have been discharged from the law, having died to that which we were constantly held down. We were habitually rendering the obedience of a bondslave.[8] The difference between Christian service and the service we rendered in the old life of sin is that the Holy Spirit energizes us as we seek to obey and serve the Lord. Under the law no enablement was given. God's commandments were written on stones and were read to the people. But under grace, God's word was written on fleshy tables of the human heart (2 Cor. 3:1–3). The believer is no longer under the law.

The phrase "newness of Spirit" (Rom. 7:6) comes from the Greek word *kainos*, which means "new" when it comes to quality and is used in contrast to that which has become worn and that which has seen service. It has to do with that which has become affected and marred from age.[9] It is that which has become old through age. Serving God in the newness of the Spirit is perfect freedom.

The believer now serves in the newness of the Spirit. There is a new attitude and a new motive. He can serve now in the power of the Spirit as he experiences the energizing presence and control of the Holy Spirit. Now the gospel bids me to fly and gives me wings. Wings in scripture speak of supernatural power.

Paul said "not in the oldness of the letter" (v. 6). The word *old* comes from the Greek word *palaios*, which means "that which is old in point of use, worn out, useless."[10] The law that was fulfilled at the cross is looked upon as outworn and useless, so that it may be set aside.

As we yield our members to the Spirit (6:12–17), He applies to us the death, burial, and resurrection of Christ. He puts to death the things of the flesh and reproduces the things of the Spirit. By the Spirit we are to "reckon… [ourselves] to be dead unto sin, but alive unto God" (v. 11). We are to become instruments available to the Spirit. The word *reckon* comes from the Greek word *logizomai* which means that we are to take into account the fact that we have been discharged from the evil nature and that it has no power over us anymore.[11] The divine nature of God has been imparted to us and we have been given the power to say *no* to sin. We have now been given the desire and the power to live our lives according to the Word. If we do not count on the fact that the divine nature has been implanted into our soul, we will go on trying to live our lives in our own strength. All that does is exhibit the effects of a powerless Christianity. If we believe that we possess God's divine nature, we will cease from viewing the Christian life as a flesh attempt; we will avail ourselves of the life that is supplied by God's divine nature. We must see the power of the sinful nature as broken and the divine nature imparted. It is then that we must order our lives according to this principle.

Rick Renner, in his book *Merchandising the Anointing*, said there are two types of imbalances in the church today: first of all the devil would love for us to settle for a gospel that is powerless to change a life. This indeed is another gospel. Jesus did not just preach and teach, he healed the sick and cast out devils. The church was born in the power of the Spirit and must be maintained in the power of the Spirit. Are we the church if we do not have the operation and demonstration of the Spirit of God in our midst? This imbalance can be found in much of our denominational world.

The second imbalance is that we cannot allow our desire to see the miraculous to take the place of the teaching ministry of the Word of God. Miracles, wonders, and signs have no converting power. Only the Word has converting power. Even though miracles and wonders and signs do confirm what the Word of God has said, we need a foundation of God's Word to support that supernatural move. It is then that we become preoccupied with the sensational and the spectacular.[12]

According to the New Testament, from the time that we are born again there is supposed to be a pursuit on our part for the spiritual things of God. How is the chase? If we do not start pursuing the things of the Spirit of God, we will destroy our profession that we are the Pentecostal church before a world that is lost. The whole purpose of being Pentecostal is to rekindle in our hearts a renewed passion to know Christ more and more. As God with His finger carved the Ten Commandments on tablets of stone, God wrote His laws on the walls of our hearts with His finger. When God's Word is written on the walls of our hearts, we will live this Christian life.

Have we lost our passion today to experience New Testament Christianity? We must go by the cross, the tomb, and the resurrection, and then we can go up into the upper room and get what God has for us—power. You cannot get to Pentecost without going by Calvary. The rock was first smitten, and then there was flowing of the water. The olive was crushed, and then there was flowing of the oil. A Pentecost without a cross is fanaticism.

We see professed Christians all around us experiencing a drought of the worst kind. Yet there seems to be little alarm, little burden, little crying out to God for the rains of revival. The church is not an organization but an organism that is 1) growing spiritually 2) with life and the power of God operating in their souls and 3) reproducing for the kingdom of God on the Earth. Without these elements being present, you are either dead or on your way to being dead. Somebody needs to stop the funeral.

We need to compare our powerlessness with Christ's promises. Must Christians hide their light under a bushel? Has our salt lost its savor? We are living in a day when powerless Christianity has become the norm. Why is there little Holy Spirit being manifested in the life of the church today? Why has the command of Christ and the apostles to be filled with the Spirit become an optional lifestyle?

The Full Life Study Bible gives us a test whereby we can be able to determine whether or not our baptism in the Holy Ghost is of God.[13] In order for our baptism in the Holy Ghost to be of God, it must be examined in light of the Scripture. Our experience does not prove the Word, but the Word must prove our experience in order for it to be of God. We should be able to read the Word and know whether or not our experience is of God. When John wrote his first Epistle, he said, "Beloved, believe not every spirit, but try the spirits whether they are of God: because many false prophets are gone out into the world." (1 John 4:1). There are biblical principles to prove and to test whether or not an assumed or professed baptism in the Holy Spirit is of God. Paul wrote to the church of Thessalonica: "Prove all things; hold fast that which is good" (1 Thess. 5:21).

First of all, a genuine baptism in the Holy Ghost will cause us to love, magnify, and glorify God the Father and the Lord Jesus Christ more than ever before. Any assumed baptism in the Spirit that draws our prayers, worship, and adoration toward anything or anyone else other than God and the Lord Jesus Christ is not of God.

Second, a genuine baptism in the Holy Spirit will increase our consciousness of sonship with the heavenly Father. It will lead to a greater awareness of the presence of God in our lives. We will be more conscious of the work, guidance, and presence of the Spirit in our daily lives. Every day we ought to be conscious of the operation and presence of the Holy Spirit in our lives. There should be an increase of a heartfelt cry, "Abba, Father" (Rom. 8:15; Gal. 4:6). Any assumed baptism in the Spirit that does not result in a greater fellowship with Christ and a more intense communion with God as our Father is not of God. Any assumed baptism that does not increase our awareness of His presence, strengthen our desire to obey His leadings, and reinforce our goal to live before Him in such a way as to not grieve, quench, or resist Him, is not of God.

Third, a genuine baptism in the Holy Spirit will cause a greater love and appreciation for the Scriptures. A real anointing will get us into the Word. The

Holy Spirit is the Spirit of truth (John 14:17), who inspired the Holy Scriptures (2 Tim.3:16), and will deepen our appreciation and love for the truth of the Word of God. Any assumed baptism that reduces our hunger to read and abide in the Scripture is not from God. We cannot lay the Word of God aside and go on with the Holy Spirit. If this is the case, then we are no better than the New Age movement.

Fourth, a genuine baptism in the Holy Spirit will deepen our love and concern for other followers of Christ. Luke, the first century historian, gives us a list of the daily practices of a Pentecostal church:

> And they continued stedfastly in the apostles' doctrine and fellowship, and in breaking of bread, and in prayers. And fear came upon every soul: and many wonders and signs were done by the apostles. And all that believed were together and had all things common; And sold their possession and goods, and parted them to all men, as every man had need. *And they, continuing daily with one accord in the temple, and breaking bread from house to house, did eat their meat with gladness and singleness of heart, Praising God, and having favour with all the people. And Lord added to the church daily such as should be saved."*
>
> —ACTS 2:42–47, EMPHASIS ADDED

The Greek verbs of this passage show a continuous or repeated action in past time.[14] They kept being filled with awe, kept sharing everything in common, kept selling their goods when individual needs arose, and the Lord continued to add to their fellowship those who were being saved. They were not on and off Christians. There was a consistency in their everyday conduct. There was a deep abiding awareness of God's presence in their midst.

Christian fellowship and communion can only take place in the spirit as the Holy Spirit binds us together with cords that cannot be broken. Any assumed baptism that diminishes our love for all who sincerely seek to follow and obey Jesus Christ as Lord and Savior is not of God.

Fifth, a genuine baptism in the Holy Spirit comes after we have turned away from sin and have begun to faithfully obey Christ. It will only be maintained as we continue to be sanctified by the Holy Spirit. Mortification in the spirit takes place when the Holy Spirit and the Word come together to destroy every root of indwelling sin and every area in our lives that is unlike the Lord Jesus Christ. It is only then that we are led by the Spirit. If we are not free from sin and if we are walking according to the flesh, then it is a sure sign that our professed baptism is not of God. We are delusional to think that we can embrace God's power in our lives without embracing righteousness.

Sixth, the baptism in the Holy Spirit will intensify our displeasure with habitual, sinful enjoyments and pleasures of the world that are not considered to be godly. If our love for this world supersedes our love for God, it cannot be the baptism of the Holy Spirit. Paul said, "We have received, not the spirit of the world, but the spirit which is of God" (1 Cor. 2:1).

Seventh, a genuine baptism in the Holy Spirit will give us a greater desire and power to witness about the Lord Jesus Christ. When the world sees the transformation in our lives through our relationship with the Holy Ghost, it will open the door for evangelism. The purpose of Pentecost is not the tongues, but that we would be witnesses for Him.

Eighth, a genuine baptism in the Holy Spirit will cause us to be more receptive to the Spirit's operation and the gifts of the Spirit within the life of the church. There will be manifestations of the Spirit to edify the church and bring glory to God.

In the Book of Galatians alone we see the operation of the Holy Spirit in the life of the Galatian believers.

1. He arrested their hearts and drew them to the foot of the cross. He made real in them what Jesus accomplished for them at the cross, tomb, and resurrection.
2. He enabled them to serve God.
3. He gave them the desire to obey God.
4. He changed them. Change is a normal part of the walk of the Spirit. All living things change, and if you are not changing you are dying whether you are a preacher, layman, or church. There was an outward manifestation of Jesus in their lives.
5. He worked miracles through them.
6. He filled them with the Holy Ghost.
7. He brought perfection in the Christian life.
8. He gave them victory and liberty over sin.

9. He produced fruit of the Spirit.

10. He put a glow upon their countenance.

The church in the language of scripture has two things: 1) We have miscarrying wombs in the fact that we have aborted the promises of God in our lives and have not carried it to term. We have not given birth to it in the Spirit. 2) We have dried up breasts in the fact that we have not nurtured our young. Who have we nurtured in the kingdom of God today? Are we in the business of mentoring new converts? Could the reason why many of our new converts do not stand be that we do not pray them through to the baptism of the Holy Ghost? If it had not been for the baptism of the Holy Ghost, the early church in that first century would have fallen back into Judaism.

In his book *Merchandising the Anointing*, Rick Renner states that every Christian is going to have to regain a passion for two things: to get all the teaching ministry of the Word of God we can get and to get all of God's power that we can get.[15] Having been a pastor for many years I have found many who have a passion for the Word of God, but they have no desire to experience the power of God. While some have a real hunger and thirst for God's power they are not the slightest bit interested in the teaching ministry of the Word of God. It takes both to ride the train. Many have fallen into spiritual boredom because of it. Because we have not kept our minds renewed by the Spirit and by the Word, we have become bored with church, worship, and prayer.

This kind of Christianity has produced little stability in the lives of men and women. There does not seem to be a passion for personal holiness. Many are falling prey to just experiencing the emotional side of Pentecost. They are all about fire but no fruit.

A holy unrest needs to come into the church, a distress of the soul, an unquenchable thirst for God's presence and power. It is not Christianity if it:

1. Does not produce salvation, healing, deliverance, wholeness and prosperity.

2. Does not produce joy unspeakable and full of glory.

3. Does not produce power for Christian living and victory over sin. We are not just sinners saved by grace, but saints redeemed from the power of sin and raised up to live above the grip of it.

4. Does not produce progress in soul winning and making disciples (pupils, learners, worshipers, witnesses and reproducers).
5. If it is not based on the New Testament. The Word must prove our experience to be of God.
6. If it does not honor Christ.
7. Does not demand the new birth.

Once we have trusted Christ as Savior and Lord and have experienced the new birth, God's Holy Spirit takes up residence on the inside of us and we have become new creatures in Christ. Once we have been sanctified by the blood, Word, and the Spirit (instantaneously and progressively), we should be manifesting the same power that the early church exemplified. We need to be demonstrating first century Christianity again. We need to be seeing the same vibrant, joyous experience. The power of the Holy Ghost should be manifesting itself in our worship. We should be seeing communities transformed by revivals like those that took place under the preaching of the apostles.

Gibbon, a first century historian, did a survey on what made the early church grow. He prophesied to the church when it was in the grip of apostasy and told them what they must do to embrace first century Christianity. In the first six months after Pentecost, sixty-five thousand joined the church.[16] There was a movement of God's power in the life of the church that made it alive and made it a place for desperate people to come to receive a miracle from God. Gibbon first of all mentioned their zeal and passion. They were torn up about Jesus Christ. The talk of the death, burial, resurrection, ascension, and soon return of Jesus Christ dominated their conversation everywhere they went. The early church was on a mission to reach the world. They were very confident in their eternal security. They were zealous and bold; they prayed for the sick and moved in the gifts of the Spirit. They evangelized in a demonstration of the Spirit's power that showed a pagan world that Jesus was Lord (I Cor. 2:4) How much of our conversation is about Jesus Christ and His imminent return? What has happened to the reproductive power of the Holy Spirit in the life of the church? Why are many of our churches singing about having the power, and yet many of them have gone all year and never had a soul saved?

Many of those who were converted to Christianity turned from past sins, became reliable workers, fair in business, honest in labor, modest in behavior, and faithful to both spouse and family. So it was not just miracles that caused an impact, but it was a different kind of morality that helped commend the Christian faith to a world that was bent on destruction.

The unity and discipline of the local church was a factor. Believers were locally organized under spiritually qualified elders who cared for them, teaching and supporting them in their newfound faith. Along with miracles came relationships and pastoral oversight.

Modernism has rejected New Testament doctrine. How sinful, wicked, barren, and full of poison has this wicked belief become that rejects the authority of the Bible, deity of Christ, and salvation by the blood. I am convinced that the apostate church is not in the world, it is in the pew. It is the church that has seen it all, heard it all, experienced it all, and now nothing excites them any more. What about those who give lip service to the doctrines of the New Testament but do not reproduce themselves in the life and power of the fruitfulness of New Testament Christianity? Many won't go to the regions of the damned because modernists have robbed them of their confidence in the Bible.

Today we are trying to create an interest in the life of the church, when in the Book of Acts the Holy Ghost in the life of the church *was* the interest. The anointing is for the lost. For too long we have prostituted the anointing and have made it our toy instead of our tool to build God's kingdom. Should we not be producing biblical Christianity in our lives? Should we not be seeing the same results the New Testament church produced?

Much of our effort in these last days involves restoring apostolic Christianity along with the genuine beliefs and practices of the original apostolic church. Much of what our fathers have told us about an awakening of biblical spirituality has been relatively shallow. *Christianity Today* recorded that 20 percent of born-again Christians believe in reincarnation, while 26 percent believe in astrology. George Barna reported that of those who are classified as born-again Christians, 45 percent of them believe that if people are good enough they can earn a place in heaven.[17]

Wade Clark Roof, in his book *Spiritual Marketplace*, states that "half of those who are born again believe that all religions are equally good and true, while half of them have no involvement in the conservative Protestant church. Even a quarter of them believe in communicating with the dead." (Necromancy is conjuring up the spirits of the dead.) Roof believes that we are living in a pragmatic generation that emphasizes experiences of people in place of truth—if they can experience it, it must be truth whether it is biblical or not.[18] We are substituting feelings for objective reality. There is a strong tendency to seek self-centered spirituality over the structured demands of organized religion. With self-fulfillment as a standard, we pick and choose. Like a salad bar, we pick from any belief system that offers to us comfort and meaning.[19]

Pluralism is on the rise in our country, teaching that all roads lead to heaven. It teaches that we can dibble or dabble in this or that religion and still make heaven our home. Universalism teaches that in the end all are destined to be saved. So why not go ahead and live your life the way you want to? It needs to be remembered that in the Old Testament Israel did not totally forsake the worship of Yahweh. They took a little bit of this religion and combined it with that religion and came up with their own religion.

Chapter 2

Living in the Spirit

If we live in the Spirit, let us also walk in the Spirit.
—GALATIANS 5:25

IF THE SPIRIT is the source of your life, let the Spirit also direct your course. In the original language it tells us "in view of the fact that we are being sustained in spiritual life by the Spirit, let us go on ordering our conduct through the Spirit."[1] The Galatians began their Christian lives in reference to the Spirit. There was a new divine life residing in their souls that was supplied by the Spirit.

A new law now regulates the believer's life. Life is now governed by the Spirit. Spiritual life is not a visit from a force, but a resident tenant in the soul. It is the Spirit that creates life and keeps imparting it.

The Christian is supposed to be living in the Spirit. You received your divine life from the Spirit indwelling and taking up His abode on the inside of you. This spiritual life is the motivating force that produces the fruit of the Spirit. The Christian is supposed to be Spirit-led, spiritually driven, and spiritually motivated. There is life because of the presence of the Holy Spirit.

When Paul said, "Walk in the Spirit," he used the word *stoicheo,* which means "to walk in a straight line, to conduct oneself."[2] The Galatian believers had divine life residing in their beings. They were to conduct themselves under the guidance, impulses, and energy of that life. We have the responsibility to live the highest kind of Christian life possible, and grace makes it a possibility.

The active execution of the sinful nature is followed by an active expression of new life in the Spirit. Here Paul combines the combination of the Greek indicative (we live) with the imperative (let us keep in step), also found in verses 1 and 13. The indicative describes God's gift to us: freedom in Christ and life in the Spirit. The imperative expresses our responsibility: to protect our freedom from the slavery of the law and to use our freedom to serve one another in love and keep in step with the Spirit. To keep in step is a military command to make a straight line or march in ordered rows. The Spirit sets the line and the pace for us to follow. This requires an active concentration and discipline of the whole person. While we constantly see many paths before us, we reject them to follow the Spirit. While we are constantly hearing the drum beats of this world that seek to slow down our pace in God, we tune them out to listen to the Spirit.

As we depend on the Holy Spirit for power, we desire to live the Christian life to the fullest. We have not been positioned in some valley or dry place. We have been positioned in fullness. We are to step out in faith and live that life. This will bring all the resources of grace to the aid of the saints. It will put in operation all the activities of the Spirit on our behalf.

Staying in step with the Spirit involves worship, praise, prayer, meditation, study of God's Word, and fellowship with God and His people as they participate in His kingdom. Freedom in living in the Spirit is fulfilling the law of Christ. The Holy Spirit will produce His own fruit in the life of the believer as he yields to Him and cooperates with Him in His work of sanctification.

"Let us not become conceited, provoking and envying each other" (Gal. 5:26, NIV). This verse of scripture along with verse 15 clearly indicates that the community life of the Galatian churches had been torn apart by pride, which caused provoking and envying. In their concentration on keeping the law, the Galatian believers had become very competitive in their spiritual walk. There was a strong attempt on their part to outdo each other. The word *provoke* means "to challenge to a contest." Some felt that they were so spiritually superior that they wanted to prove it in a contest. This attitude caused those who were spiritually inferior to become resentful of those who made them feel that way. Both attitudes were caused by pride that could not tolerate rivals.

C. S. Lewis says the devil laughs when he sees us overcome with pride: "He is perfectly content to see you become chaste and brave and self-controlled provided, all the time, he is setting you up in the Dictatorship of Pride—just as he would be quite content to see your chilblains cured if he was allowed, in return, to give you cancer. For Pride is spiritual cancer: it eats up the very possibility of love, or contentment, or even common sense."[3] The Bible Gateway commentary goes on to say, "The only treatment for the cancer of pride is radical surgery: we must crucify the pride of the sin nature and be led by the Spirit, who alone has the power to overthrow the dictatorship of pride."[4]

And the LORD said unto Cain, Why art thou wroth? and why is thy countenance fallen? If thou doest well, shalt thou not be accepted? and if thou doest not well, sin lieth at the door. And unto thee shall be his desire, and thou shalt rule over him.

—GENESIS 4:6–7

Cain stood at the door of the tabernacle of worship. He was told to offer his sacrifice as Abel did or he wouldn't be accepted. Sin desired to have Cain, but Cain had to master it. If the believer depends on the Holy Spirit to give him both the power and the desire to do the will of God, he will be able to resist and to conquer the lust of the flesh. The believer has the responsibility to refuse the dictations of the flesh by conducting himself in the power of the Holy Spirit. He has to remain under the Holy Spirit's control. The believer has been liberated from the enslavement to sin. He has been freed to choose the right and refuse the wrong. The Holy Spirit is the agent that places our fleshly Adamic nature under holy control. Being under the control of the Holy Spirit, the child of God will be able to say no to sin. What many have referred to as being the devil, is nothing more than our flesh that has not been brought under subjection to the Holy Spirit of God.

The Galatians were making a false assumption to think that by them observing the law that it would bring them into spiritual perfection. Their churches were torn apart by conflict. They were biting and devouring each other (Gal. 5:15). Their devotion to the law had not enabled them to be devoted to each other in love. Because they were not loving each other, they were breaking the law. Where could they find the motivation and power to resolve their conflicts and renew their love for each other? Many who are members of churches where there is strong biblical teaching are torn apart by conflict. What went wrong? How can they be devoted to each other one minute and then become so divided? How can the church of the living God be empowered to really love?

Paul's answer is the Spirit of God. "This I say then, Walk in the Spirit, and ye shall not fulfil the lust of the flesh" (Gal. 5:16). Paul's use of the double negative in the Greek could be expressed in English by saying, "You will absolutely not gratify the desires of your sinful nature." The fulfillment of the promise is dependent on us walking in the Spirit. The command to "walk in the Spirit" is Paul's response. Walking in the Spirit involves choosing a way of life in which every aspect of life is directed and transformed by the Spirit. A walk of the Spirit is when the Christian does not get ahead of Him nor lag far behind Him, but stays in step with Him.

The Christian life also involves weed-pulling. The Christian reaches down and pulls up weeds that do not belong and replaces them with seeds of truth that one day will reap a harvest. Walking in the Spirit demands active determination to follow the direction of the Spirit in the power of the Spirit. Those who follow the Spirit's direction in the Spirit's power will not carry out the evil intentions of their sinful nature. It is the Holy Spirit who suppresses our sin nature and puts our fleshly nature under Holy control. Walking in the Spirit brings transformation and empowerment and can take people who are biting and devouring one another and turn them into people who are serving each other in love. The Christian life begins with the Spirit (Gal. 3:3; 4:6, 29). The only way to continue the Christian life is by the power and operation of the Spirit. The Spirit is not only the source of the Christian life but also the power to sustain it.

"This I say then" (v. 16) is Paul's statement that was intended to counteract the erroneous impression held by the Galatians from the Judaizers who were suggesting that without the restraining influences of the law, they would fall into sin. Paul is admonishing the Galatians to continue to govern their lives by the impulses of the Holy Spirit, not by trying to measure up to the law of God in their own strength motivated by the terrors of the law.

So the secret to victory over sin is not a flesh attempt to serve the law, but it is our submission and subjection to the Holy Spirit. The moment sinners place their faith in the Lord Jesus Christ, the Holy Spirit takes up residence in their being for the purpose of ministering to their spiritual needs and enabling them to live a Christian life.

In his admonition to "walk in the Spirit" (v. 16), Paul used the word *stoicheo* which means to walk about; an act of conducting one's self or ordering one's manner of behavior.[5] We are to conduct ourselves as the spiritual children of Abraham. The Holy Spirit suppresses the activities of the sin nature as the saint trusts Him to do so and cooperates with Him in the work of progressive sanctification. Again, let us not get ahead of Him nor lag far behind Him, but let us stay in step with Him. Let us reach down and pull up weeds in our lives that do not belong there and replace them with seeds of truth that will one day reap a bountiful harvest.

> This I say then, Walk in the Spirit, and ye shall not fulfil the lust of the flesh. For the flesh lusteth against the Spirit, and the Spirit against the flesh: and these are contrary the one to another: so that ye cannot do the things that ye would.
>
> —GALATIANS 5:16–17

A more accurate translation of the original Greek says, "But I say, through the instrumentality of the Spirit habitually ordering your manner of life and your will, in no wise execute the passionate desires of the flesh."[6] The flesh has a constant desire to suppress the Spirit, and the Spirit has a strong desire to suppress the flesh. There is a mutual opposition here. When the flesh presses hard upon the believer, the Holy Spirit is there to oppose the flesh and give victory over sin so the believer will not obey the flesh. Every time the Holy Spirit places a course of conduct upon the heart of the believer, the flesh opposes the Spirit in an effort to prevent the believer from obeying the Spirit. The flesh wants to prevent the believer from doing what the Spirit is telling him to do. What many of us attribute to the devil is nothing more than our flesh that is not submitted to the Holy Spirit.

The reason why the battle still rages is because the totality of our being struggles to determine whether we will wholly surrender to the flesh (sin nature) and return to the dominion of sin, or whether we will yield to the dictations of the Holy Spirit and continue under the dominion of Christ. The battle is within the Christian himself. This conflict with the Spirit and the flesh will continue until the day God calls us home. When the saint subjects himself to the control of the Holy Spirit, he will find that this is the secret of living a life of victory over sin.

"Ye shall not fulfil the lust of the flesh" (v. 16). In this statement Paul used the word *epithumia* for lust. It means a strong impulse, desire, or passion. The word translated *flesh* is the Greek word *sarx*. Evil desires, impulses, and passions are constantly arising from the evil nature as smoke rises from a chimney[7]; the power of which was broken when the believer was saved. The sin nature through the flesh is constantly attempting to control the believer as it did before salvation was wrought in his being.

The flesh and the Spirit are lined up in conflict, face to face, and a spiritual duel is going on. "So that you cannot do the things that you would" (v. 17). Here Paul uses the present active subjunctive, which means, "So that you would not keep on doing the things that you would."[8] You are either going to yield yourself to sin or to the Holy Spirit. You are going to have to cooperate with the Holy Spirit in the work of progressive sanctification, which is the way to the life and power of God. You are going to have to trust in the Holy Spirit to give you victory over sin. Because of the presence of the Holy Spirit, you are freed from sin.

The choice lies with the saint. The more we say no to sin the easier it will be for us to say no. The more we say yes to the Holy Spirit, the easier it will be for us to say yes to Him. It will become our habit. The Spirit will keep on suppressing the activities of the sinful nature and any control which it might attempt to exert over the saint.

Even though the Galatians began their Christian lives by the Spirit (3:2–3), they soon turned to the law to direct their lives. They felt that their commitment of the law was the way to identify and direct their behavior as God's people. They failed to realize that it is the Holy Spirit that identifies them as God's people and that it was through His ministry that their conduct was directed. In chapters three and four, Paul assures his readers by them being indwelt by the Spirit, they were clearly establishing their identity as the spiritual descendants of Abraham as well as the children of God. Paul had complete confidence that the Spirit is more than adequate to direct their moral behavior. It is the presence of the Spirit that identifies us as the church in this world. Where you find the Holy Spirit you find the church, and where you find the church you find the Holy Spirit. He is the only sure guide for Christian behavior. The Spirit is the only source of power to love in a way that fulfills the law.

Here Paul is confident in the promise of the Spirit's victory over the sinful nature. It is the Holy Spirit that suppresses our sin nature. If we abandon the Holy Spirit and return to a fleshly attempt to serve God, we must realize that the flesh cannot overcome the flesh. Like the Galatians, the Christian who abandons the Holy Spirit will find himself surprised by how fast sin will overtake him. If the Spirit's direction is continually defeated by the sin nature, there is no good reason to live by the Spirit or to have confidence in the Spirit's directive power.

The conflict spoken of in verse 17 of chapter 5 had been going on in them: "For the flesh lusteth against the Spirit, and the Spirit against the flesh: and these are contrary the one to the other: so that ye cannot do the things that ye would." Paul is saying that there is a constant warfare against the sinful nature by the power of the Spirit. They were living a victorious life over sin (4:19).

Paul is dealing with our confidence in the Spirit. He is describing the war between the flesh and the Spirit and the results of that war. The Spirit and the flesh (sin nature) are two hostile forces that are opposition to each other. The sin nature desires what is contrary to the Spirit, and the Spirit desires what is contrary to the flesh. They are in conflict with each other. As Christians, we will never reach a point that we do not have to contend with the flesh. We will have to contend with it until the day God calls us home.

The apostle Paul writing to the church at Rome said, "Because the carnal mind is enmity against God: for it is not subject to the law of God, neither indeed can be. So then they that are in the flesh cannot please God" (Rom. 8:7–8). Paul is telling us that our flesh is hostile toward God and at war with Him. The flesh refuses to be marshaled by God's law. It refuses to line up, and Paul says because of the flesh we are going to find it impossible to please God. I wonder what the Lord feels like when He walks the aisles of our churches and finds people that are so busy yielding to the flesh and the sin nature that they are literally at war and hostile toward Him. When they cannot submit to the preached word because they have a mentality that refuses to be marshaled by God's law and they refuse to line up with truth, surely, it must break His heart.

Every Christian feels this conflict between the two natures. When a Christian is totally committed to the Lord and chooses each day to walk in the Spirit, they will find themselves engaged in a fierce, intense battle between the Spirit and the flesh. The day we became born again and placed our faith in a crucified, buried, and resurrected Savior, hell declared war on us. We became an upstream swimmer in a downstream world. We don't go along with the tide, we go against it. Many Christians feel ashamed to admit that they are experiencing such a conflict. They feel that a mature Christian should somehow be above this kind of struggle.

Paul is honestly portraying the reality of the warfare in the life of a Spirit-led Christian. He is not painting a picture of defeat but one of victory. If you have sworn your allegiance to the Spirit in this war, you will not use your freedom as an occasion to please the flesh or indulge in the sinful nature (Gal. 5:13). Nor will you gratify the desires of the sinful nature (v. 16). The result of this fierce conflict is that you will not do those things that you want to do (v. 17). You will find yourself doing what the Spirit desires you to do.

Paul gave us a whole chapter in Romans 7 to describe his frustration in trying to measure up to the law of God in his own strength, separate and apart from the life-giving presence of the Holy Spirit. He admits his defeat in Romans 7:14–25 and the frequent experience of defeat in the Christian experience. Our common experience of moral failure should not be justified by Paul's explanation of life in the Spirit.

Paul is presenting a reason for confidence in the Spirit's power to guide Christian behavior. The Christian who walks by the Spirit is involved in a war that determines the direction of every choice and every action. Christian freedom does not mean that we are left without direction in our morality to do whatever we want. When we march under the Spirit's orders, we can fulfill the direction of the Spirit. In the war for true Christian freedom, victory is only possible for those who continually renew their allegiance to the Spirit in the war against the flesh. They do not do whatever they want, but what the Spirit would have them to do.

> But if ye be led by the Spirit, ye are not under the law.
> —Galatians 5:18

The Galatians had lived their Christian lives in dependency upon the Holy Spirit, before the Judaizers made their way into the church. By them participating in the story of the Holy Spirit the following things happened: 1) The power of the sin nature was broken; 2) The divine nature of God had been implanted into their souls; 3) The Spirit had taken up residence in their hearts and lives; 4) The Holy Spirit wrote God's laws in their hearts so that they would desire to obey Him in love. (See Hebrews 10:14–17 and 2 Corinthians 3.)

Those who are living their Christian life in the power of the Spirit and are fighting each day against the influence of the sinful nature do not need to be supervised and restrained by the law. No one has to spy on them to see whether or not they are living the Christian life. What many Christians blame on the devil is nothing more than their flesh that is not submitted to the control of the Holy Ghost.

Paul speaks of life in the Spirit as a passive submission: "If you are led of the Spirit" (Gal. 5:18). The verb used here for *led* suggests pressure and control. A donkey and a colt were *led* by the disciples to Jesus (Matt. 21:2). The soldiers arrested Jesus and *led* Him away (Luke 22:54). The soldiers arrested Paul and *led* him away (Acts 21:34; 23:10). Paul has already described the control of the law in similar terms in chapter 3 of Galatians: We were held prisoners by the law, locked up (v. 23); the law was put in charge to lead us (v. 24); even though the law exercised control, it could not give life or transform our character (v. 21); the law controlled by locking up all who were under sin (v. 22); and we were subject to guardians and trustees (4:2).

Paul gives us an alternative when it comes to control: the control of the Spirit. Life began with the Spirit (3:3); the children of promise are born in the power of the Spirit (4:29); and the Spirit produces a transformation and a radical change in our character (5:22–23). The one that submits to the control of the Spirit is not under the control of the law.

When the Spirit is leading you to forgive your brother or sister who has wronged you instead of taking on resentment or hatred toward them, you are under the control of the Spirit. It is then that you are not under the command of the law that says, "Thou shalt not kill" (Exod. 20:13), but you made a decision to forgive. When your conduct is guided and empowered by the Spirit, your conduct will *fulfill* the law, so you will not be under the condemnation and supervision of the law. Life by the Spirit involves active participation in the story of the Holy Spirit, not passive in obedience. Such a life will experience freedom from the control of the sinful nature and the control of the law.

The human body is in itself not sinful. It is either controlled by sin or by God. Paul in writing to the church at Rome said:

> Let not sin therefore reign in your mortal body, that ye should obey it in the lusts thereof. Neither yield ye your members as instruments of unrighteousness unto sin: but yield yourselves unto God, as those that are alive from the dead, and your members as instruments of righteousness unto God. For sin shall not have dominion over you: for ye are not under the law, but under grace. What then? shall we sin, because we are not under the law, but under grace? God forbid. Know ye not, that to whom ye yield yourselves servants to obey, his servants ye are to whom ye obey; whether of sin unto death, or obedience unto righteousness.
>
> —Romans 6:12–16

The Christian is to obey his new Master and to ignore the old one. No man can serve two masters (Matthew 6:24). You cannot worship a God you do not serve. Neither can you remain in Egypt and worship. You have to come out in order to worship. One of the compromises that Pharaoh offered to Israel was to "stay here and worship" (Exod. 8:25–26). If Israel would have offered sacrifice in Egypt they would have been stoned. Molech, which was calf worship was strong in Egypt and it would have caused the Egyptians to stone Israel if they sacrificed a bullock to their God.

If our bodies are controlled by the Holy Spirit, we are walking in the Spirit. I have been amazed at those who have been in the ranks of Pentecost for many years but in their personal walk have still not captured the meaning of a walk in the Spirit. To walk in the Spirit means not get ahead of Him nor lag far behind Him, but stay in step with Him. It means to reach down and pull out the weeds in your life that do not belong there and replace them with seeds of truth that one day will reap a bountiful harvest. When we are governed by the flesh, we will fulfill the desires of the flesh and of the mind. The solution is to not yield to the flesh, but to surrender to the Holy Spirit. It is not a flesh attempt to serve God but a Spirit-led relationship. It is about being borne along by the Spirit.

The flesh and the Spirit have different appetites. The old nature is like the pig and the raven, always looking for something unclean to feed upon. A pig is an unclean animal that enjoys wallowing in filth. The pig can never stay out of mud holes. When Noah released a raven, it never came back to the ark and found plenty of dead flesh to feed on. The new nature is like the sheep and the dove, always yearning for what is clean and holy. A sheep is a clean animal that avoids garbage and drinks from clean refreshing water. When Noah released the dove, it found a clean place to settle down and returned with an olive branch in its claws, indicating a new beginning. If the church desires for the Holy Spirit to rest upon them, they are going to have to realize that the Holy Spirit rests on purity, not on the garbage dumps of this world.

Isaac and Ishmael were unable to get along. In fact Ishmael did not have any problems until Isaac showed up. The flesh knew the moment the Holy Spirit showed up that trouble had come to town. Remember it took Abraham getting together with a bondwoman to give birth to Ishmael. Abraham and Sarah got together to give birth to Isaac, who was a child of promise. If we are going to give birth to children of promise, we must find the operation of the Holy Spirit in our lives.

There are two ministries of the Holy Spirit that are performed. First, the Holy Spirit enables us to fulfill the law. "That the righteousness of the law might be fulfilled in us, who walk not after the flesh, but after the Spirit" (Rom. 8:4). There are many who feel that because we are not under the law but under grace that the rules no longer apply. In the new covenant, rules are still a part of our nature and do apply. It is the Holy Spirit and the grace of God that enable us to live up to the law of God. The law finds nothing to condemn in a person who is being led by the Holy Spirit. This is the blessed moral freedom of a person who is being led by the Holy Spirit. He is in such a condition of spirituality and morality that the law has no power to censure, condemn, or punish him. I believe that it still takes holiness and righteousness under the law combined with worship of God under David to produce the glory in Solomon's temple. While many have a passion for worship, not everyone has a passion for living right. There are many who are so strict that they squeak when they walk, but they have no passion for worship. It takes both to ride the train.

Second, the Holy Spirit enables us to overcome the flesh. "For what the law could not do, in that it was weak through the flesh, God sending his own Son in the likeness of sinful flesh, and for sin, condemned sin in the flesh" (Rom. 8:3). The law made no provision to change me, work miracles, or bring me into the presence of God. God sent Jesus from heaven to earth to show me how the Christian life was to be lived, so that one day I could go from earth to heaven. Jesus was made in the likeness of sinful flesh as an offering for sin. He conquered and mastered sin in His flesh through the power of the Holy Spirit. What the law failed to do, God accomplished through His Son Jesus Christ. Through the power of the Holy Spirit, our flesh can be placed under holy control. It is not an issue of whether we have the Holy Spirit, but does the Holy Spirit have us?

"But if ye be led of the Spirit" (Gal. 5:18). There is a continuous force in the present tense of *agesthe*. Paul was actually saying, "You are being led." One translation says, "If you are willingly being led by the Holy Spirit."[9] As long as we are being led by the Spirit of God, we know that we are not under the bondage of the law. All who belong to God possess or receive the Spirit of God and share in His life. It is the Spirit that identifies a Christian from an unbeliever. When we have the Holy Spirit we possess the mind of Christ (1 Cor. 2:16). It is the Holy Spirit who enables us to understand the scriptures.

Then Paul said that "ye are not under the law" (Gal. 5:18).The Judaizers felt that if the Galatians were not under the restraining influences of the law, they would have no form of restraint. They would find themselves yielding to the impulses of the evil nature. Paul is introducing a highway of freedom that is higher than a road that leads to the statutes of the law and those of the sin nature. Paul is introducing a highway that is characterized by faith and a dependency upon the Holy Spirit. According to Paul, if they were led by the Spirit of God, they would not be living their lives by the principles of legalism. The Spirit and the law are contrasted. These two methods of living the Christian life are here opposed to each other. The flesh made the law weak. This is the blessed freedom of a person who is led by the Spirit of God. It is then that he lives in such a condition of spirituality and morality that the law had no power to censure, condemn, or punish him. When the Holy Spirit works within the believer, He allows him to live a righteous life that is the fulfillment of God's moral law.

It is the Holy Spirit who differentiates God from everything that is not of God. All who belong to God possess and receive the Spirit of God and share His life. It is the Spirit who distinguishes believers from unbelievers. If we possess the Holy Spirit, we have the mind of Christ (v. 16). It is the Holy Spirit who makes spiritual truth understandable.

The law does not enable the believer to overcome the flesh. It provokes it more to sin. "The strength of sin is the law" (1 Cor. 15:56). The law made no provision for mercy, pardon, and forgiveness, but by the law came the knowledge of sin. We can pile on all the rules and regulations we want to, but all we will do is create rebellion. It is amazing to me that the one tree that God told Adam and Eve they could not eat from was the one tree that tripped them up—even though Adam and Eve had access to all the trees of the Garden. Our fleshly nature is not going to be dictated to.

Chapter 3

Paul's Greeting

Paul, an apostle, (not of men, neither by man, but by Jesus Christ,
and God the Father, who raised him from the dead;) And all
the brethren which are with me, unto the churches of Galatia:
Grace be to you and peace from God the Father, and from our
Lord Jesus Christ, Who gave himself for our sins, that he might
deliver us from this present evil world, according to the will of God
and our Father: To whom be glory forever and ever. Amen.

—GALATIANS 1:1–5

ON THE DAMASCUS Road, Saul ("asked for") of Tarus's name was changed to Paul the Apostle whose name meant "small." He had been a persecutor of Jesus Christ and even held the clothes of those who stoned Steven. He was blinded by a flash of light and heard a voice and yet saw no man. Paul became a traveling preacher and teacher, explaining the scriptures to the Greeks, starting new churches, and settling conflicts wherever they arose. He was jailed and ran out of town many times for angering religious and civil leaders. Together with Simon Peter, and James the Just, he is considered to be one of the most noble of the early church leaders.

Thirteen epistles, or letters, in the New Testament are attributed to Paul. His conversion drastically changed the course of his life. Throughout his missionary journeys, through his activities and writings, his beliefs changed the religious thoughts throughout that Mediterranean world. His leadership and influence and legacy led to the formation of many communities and churches. He shared the name of Saul, the first King of Israel, a fellow Benjamite. He was of the tribe of Benjamin, a Hebrew of the Hebrews; as touching the Law, a Pharisee (Phil. 3:5).

He violently persecuted the church of God prior to his conversion. He was possibly a member of the Sanhedrin and was well respected by everyone in

Judaism before he came to believe that Jesus, by the resurrection of the dead, was actually the Messiah (Rom. 1:3–4).

What do you do with this man called Paul the Apostle? Put him in jail and he will sing his way out. When he was stoned in Lystra and left for dead, he was caught up into the third heaven and walked with God in His walled garden. He came back to his body, and he got up and went right back into the very city that stoned him and preached the gospel. He was persuaded that the present sufferings he was going through was not worthy to be compared with the glory that one day will be revealed in him (Rom. 8:18). He got on board a ship, and for fourteen days the sun did not shine, and the stars hid themselves in the blackness of the night. The ship was falling apart, and all hope was gone that they would be saved. He got in a prayer meeting, and an angel of the Lord came on board the ship and told him "to be of good cheer, Paul: for as thou has testified of me in Jerusalem, so must thou bear witness also at Rome" (Acts 23:11). Suddenly they heard the water beating the shore, and hope replaced hopelessness.

The church at Galatia was founded by Paul during his first missionary journey (Acts 13:4–15:35). Paul addressed this letter to cities that were located in the southern region of Galatia (Pisidian, Antioch, Iconium, Lystra, and Derbe). He addressed his letter to a group of churches in Asia Minor. Those who lived in this area were known for their worship of nature.

When Paul was in Cyprus, his missionary team consisted of Paul, Barnabas, and John Mark. Paul here performed his first miracle where he blinded a sorcerer by the name of Elymas. He was called by his Gentile name for the first time. There he won the deputy to Christ. (Acts 13:4-12)

At Antioch and Pisidia (Acts 13:13–50), Paul preached six points and gave an invitation. The points were as follows: 1) Exodus deliverance, 2) wilderness wanderings, 3) conquest of Canaan, 4) the rule of Saul and David, 5) ministry of John the Baptist, and 6) crucifixion and resurrection of Christ, the seed of David. His invitation was: "Be it known unto you therefore, men and brethren, that through this man is preached unto you the forgiveness of sins: and by Him all that believe are justified from all things, from which ye could not be justified by the Law of Moses" (Acts 13:38–39). While many Gentiles and some Jews received his message, the Jewish leaders rejected it and attempted to run the apostle Paul out of town. Paul then stated that it was his intention to turn to the Gentiles. Paul said, "It was necessary that the word of God should first have been spoken to you: but seeing ye put from you, and judge yourselves unworthy of everlasting life, lo, we turn to the Gentiles" (13:46). The Gentiles were glad and glorified the word of the Lord (Acts 13:48). The Jews were filled envy and spoke against those things (Acts 13:45.)

At Iconium many came to believe in the gospel, but Paul's preaching seemed to stir up the Jewish leaders who began to cause trouble (Acts 13:51–14:5). There Paul learned that many of the Jews formed a plot against their very lives. Then Paul and Barnabas left for Lystra.

At Lystra, a man that had been crippled from his birth was healed. The crowds at Lystra sought to worship Paul and Barnabas. They called Paul Mercury, and Barnabas they called Jupiter. There was an ancient myth that two Greek gods by the name of Zeus and Hermes who were disguised as mortals came to this area. Everyone within the city turned them away except an elderly couple. Later a flood overtook the city and drowned everyone except this elderly couple. The priest of Jupiter in this city was determined not to repeat the past, began to worship the team by the sacrifice of animals and flowers.[1] Paul being filled with shock, ripped his clothing and declared to them, "Sirs, why do ye these things? We are also men of like passions" (Acts 14:15). When Paul refused this honor, he was stoned and left for dead. Many believed that Paul actually died there. It was at that exact time that He was caught up into paradise and walked with God in his walled garden (2 Cor. 12:1–9). Paradise was a Persian term. Whenever a king desired to bestow an honor on someone, he invited him to come up and walk with him in his walled garden. There the King walked with Paul in intimate fellowship. Paul came back to his body, got up, went right back into the very city that stoned him, and preached the gospel there.

On his second missionary journey (see Acts 15:36–18:22), Paul went through northern Galatia (16:6). On his third missionary journey, he visited the disciples in north Galatia (18:23). Luke uses the word *disciples* rather than *churches* with Paul's visit to north Galatia. There the missionary team confirmed the souls of the disciples, exhorting them with the Word of God. There they ordained elders in each church and commended them to God.

According to Kenneth Wuest, in 278–277 B.C., the Gauls left their home in southern Europe and settled in northern Asia Minor. In 232 B.C. their state became known as Galatia. Under the reign of King Amyntas (35–25 B.C.), Galatia was a Roman province. The term *Galatia* was used in two different ways: geographically, it referred to the northern part of Asia Minor where the Gauls lived. Politically, it referred to the Roman province. There were large differences between northern and southern Galatia in respect to language, occupation, nationality, and social order. The northern section was populated by Gauls with little commerce and few roads.[2]

In south Galatia the situation was different. It was full of flourishing cities. There was a constant flow of commerce. In days gone by, it was the ancient highway along which the Asian monarchs kept up their communications with the western coast of Asia Minor.

Dr. Henry Clarence Thiessen, chairman of the Department of Bible, Theology, and Philosophy at Wheaton, states some important facts.

1. Paul always used provincial names of districts.
2. Luke does not seem to tell us much about the finding of the church in South Galatia (Acts. 13:14–14:23).
3. Does it not seem strange for Paul to write a weighty letter to a church whose details are practically passed over by Luke?
4. Is it not strange for Judaizers of Palestine to pass by the most important cities of Iconium and Antioch in south Galatia, where there were a good many Jews and Jewish Christians on whom to do their mischievous work?[3]

Paul established churches around capitals of Roman provinces and linked those centers together by chains of churches along principal roads. He made the capitals of Pisidian, Antioch, Corinth, and Ephesus centers of church life. These were also centers of imperial administrations, and each group was surrounded by dependent churches.

Many Jews lived in these cities. The Galatians were noted for their violence, fickleness, and their love for new and curious things. Paul visited Galatia on two of his missionary journeys (Acts 13:51; 14:8, 20). On Paul's second journey he was forbidden by the Holy Spirit to preach there. "Now when they had gone throughout Phrygia and the region of Galatia, and were forbidden of the Holy Ghost to preach the word in Asia" (Acts 16:6).

In Galatia there was a native, national spirit that was joined to the power of the priesthood in Oriental temples. Galatia was a city that was one of stagnation, ignorance, and superstition. By nature they were fickle, fond of change, and could not be trusted. In Paul's first visit in the morning they attempted to worship him and in the afternoon they attempted to murder him (Acts 14). The Galatians were heathens and their religion was one of the grossest kinds. They worshiped the mother of the gods whose name was Agdistis. They were mentioned by historians as being a tall and valiant people. They walked about destitute of clothing. In their arms they carried a sword and a buckler. They were irresistible and victorious.[4] Many of Paul's converts had shaken off the influences of magic and superstition when they came to Christ. Greece and Rome had offered a level of education that revolted against superstition.

Paul noted two important things in his greeting: First of all, Paul had a God-given authority that accompanied his ministry (vv. 1–2), his message (vv. 3–4), in his motive (v. 5). Second, in His message, he focused on the person of Jesus Christ.

The twelve apostles of Christ were given authority from Christ to do the following: a) preach the gospel, b) heal the sick, c) cleanse the lepers, d) raise the dead, and e) cast out devils (Matt. 10:7–8). Authority is the hallmark of an apostle.

Order is another hallmark of an apostle. The church of the living God is an organism. To be an organism we have to have the following: 1) growing spiritually, 2) power of God is flowing through our lives, 3) reproducing for the cause of Christ in the earth. We are a part of an organism that is struggling to stay alive in these last days. There needs to be order in the body of Christ today. That order will be restored when we:

1. Make disciples instead of trying to build churches.
2. Covenant relationships that can help develop us and cause us to grow.
3. Jesus spent three years discipling 12 men.
4. If we don't know His ways, how can we know His power?

According to Ron McKenzie, in his book *Being Church Where We Live,* "When a church has an apostolic vision, they will train people up and send them out into the business world."[5] The kingdom of God expands as Christians extend the kingdom of God into areas of life where they have authority. Authority is an essential aspect of any kingdom. Christians should seek positions of authority to help the kingdom of God to expand. The idea has developed that politics and business are not proper activities for Christians. Some believe that the two areas have been handed over to the devil. Even when Christians get involved in politics and business there has not been any serious attempt to apply biblical principles to these activities, and this has caused the kingdom of God to be severely weakened. The church has retreated from the world, and many believe the kingdom of God will not be established until Jesus returns. This is false doctrine. This view has caused many Christians to sit around and wait for Jesus to return, while we leave the world in the hands of Satan.[6]

Jesus performed many of His miracles right inside the marketplace. All of the apostles were marketplace apostles. The real church of Jesus Christ is not a building or a denomination. It is a people from every tribe, tongue, and nation who have taken up their cross and followed Jesus. Many Christian people live their lives in the marketplace, in the business of everyday life. Jesus is a great example of this. He did not build an organization; He built people and met them where they lived and carried out their day-to-day activities.

There were two areas that caused the Galatian believers a problem at the time of Paul's writing: 1) the problem of doctrinal purity, and 2) purity in their conduct. False brethren came into the church and sought to pervert the gospel of Christ (1:7). They were insisting that while salvation was through faith in Christ, works were necessary in order for them to be saved. At the very time of Paul's writing, the Galatian believers had already begun to yield to this legalistic teaching (1:6, 3:1). Paul began to attack every attempt they made to mix law and grace. Abraham was declared to be righteous by faith 430 years before the Mosaic Law had been given. Paul set before the Galatians the truth about the role of the Holy Spirit in progressive sanctification and the richness the Holy Spirit brings into a life that is totally yielded and surrendered unto Him.

By Paul identifying himself as the one that is doing the writing, "Paul an apostle," He put his own name and apostleship here because both his message and apostleship were under attack by the Judaizers. He needed to vindicate these against those who were quick to deny them. They questioned the validity of his apostolic call, which led the Galatians to question it.

In Paul's day, it was customary for Greek and Hebrew letters to begin with a formal salutation. Formal salutations included the name of the one doing the writing, the one whom he is addressing in the letter, and a personal greeting.

Paul introduced himself as an apostle. The word *apostle* comes from the word *apostolos,* which means "one that is sent." Here we have a compound word: first we have the word *apo,* which means "from." Second, we have the word *stello* meaning "sending someone with a commission to represent the sender." Paul was an appointed representative with an official station; one who was given authority to represent another and divinely commissioned to preach the gospel and plant Christianity. An apostle was a messenger provided with credentials. They had received unique authority from Christ to represent Him in the earth. "As my Father hath sent me, even so send I you" (John 20:21). The word *sent* means "to furnish the credentials and the power to represent one, given the power of attorney to use his name, to transact business in his stead, and to carry out the work as if he was there to do it himself." Many times they were sent into areas to establish churches. In Galatians chapter 1, Paul sees himself being personally commissioned by Christ Himself. Paul knew that even though there were apostles before him, he never saw himself in an inferior position (Gal. 1:17). His authority came directly from Jesus Christ and from the Father above who had raised Jesus Christ up from the dead. Paul could not have received any higher source for his apostleship. When Paul used the phrase *of men* he used the word *apo,* which was a word that meant "from." It is where we get the word *source.* The word *men* comes from the word *aner,* which is used to describe an individual man. The word that Paul used was *anthropos,* which means "a race of men." If Paul was referring to an individual man, he would have used the word *aner.* Paul was denying that his apostleship came from a human source or a human channel. Jesus Christ was both the source and origin of his apostleship. It was the risen Christ who commissioned Him. If anyone sought to challenge Paul's message, after the Lord had commissioned him, they were challenging the Lord Himself. Jesus said, "He that receiveth you receiveth me" (Matt. 10:40). So Paul was sent forth with apostolic power for apostolic ministry. He was the apostolic representative of Christ. There will be no unity in the body of Christ, church of the Living God, until each member "submits one to another" (1 Pet. 5:5). This submission includes us acknowledging the authority that God has given to the apostles.

When Jesus was alive on the earth, he selected twelve disciples who later became His apostles. As an apostle, they were given delegated authority to deal with specific problems. God has called special people to do specific tasks.

While Jesus ministered on earth, He had many disciples and from them He selected twelve apostles. There were three conditions for being an apostle:

1. He had to be an eyewitness of Jesus' ministry.
2. He had to be an eyewitness of Jesus' resurrection. In 1 Corinthians 9:1 Paul states that he had seen the Lord, which was a token of His apostleship.
3. He had to be personally commissioned by Christ. Paul saw the risen Lord on the Damascus Road and had been commissioned by Him (Acts 9:1–18; 1 Cor. 9:1).

Many believe that there are no longer apostles in the church having apostolic power for apostolic ministry. After Jesus' resurrection He led captivity captive and gave gifts unto men. These gifts include: 1) apostles, 2) prophets, 3) evangelists, 4) pastors, and 5) teachers. These gifts have been placed in the body for the equipping of the saints and the work of the ministry (Eph. 4:11).

Many times we fail to recognize the office of the apostle because we are looking for the wrong kind of authority. Remember, Jesus chose the foolish, ordinary men of his day as apostles to confound the wise (1 Cor. 1:27). Leadership is not about being on a power struggle, it is about brokenness and humility. The church has become institutionalized because it has become all about the hierarchy. We must remember that the office of the apostle and the prophet are the foundation stones of the true church. They are foundational, not the top floor. "Being built upon the foundation of apostles and prophets, Jesus Christ Himself being the chief cornerstone, in whom the whole building, being fitted together, grows into a holy temple in the Lord, in whom you also are built together for a dwelling place of God in the Spirit" (Eph. 2:20–22). We will never become a habitation of God in the Spirit until the offices of apostle and prophet come together and perform their function.

The gift of apostleship was never given to draw attention to personalities of men. It was given for us to live out a function and purpose in the kingdom of God. The gift of apostleship was given to us by God for us to perform a living function in the body of Christ.

True apostles will not be forceful in asserting their spiritual authority that has been bestowed on them by Christ. They will be humble and submissive to Christ and the rest of the body. There will be no long-ranger mentality, which is outdoing your own thing. There will be a focus on being in covenant relationship with a pastor along with spiritual fatherhood. We must remember, that we do not grow in isolation or alienation. We only grow in the context of relationships. There will be no unity until there are strong ties of relationships. When someone flows in an apostolic anointing, the fruit of it will be true unity. You may operate in the apostolic and the prophetic, but your gift will never be complete until you submit to the pastoral. Most dangerous people in the world are prophets who have no pastors. A real anointing will make someone accountable.

Many times God revealed His revelations to the apostles. In Paul's generation God revealed to him the mystery of the Gentiles being included in God's plan for the ages. Paul's generation went from the transition between the age of law into the age of grace. In our generation, we are seeing the transition between the age of grace into the age of the kingdom, which includes the marriage of the Lamb to His bride, the church.

The Lord's apostles will lead the way in this revolution. True apostles will never draw attention to themselves, but will always point men to Jesus Christ. Jesus did not come to be a magician; many times He refused to perform a miracle when it was demanded of Him. I believe the church would accomplish so much more if we were not worried about who got the credit. He came to usher in the kingdom, and we must have this same mentality in the life of the church.

Then Paul says, "And all the brethren which are with me" (v. 2). Paul did not have a feeling of superiority over his brethren. He was one with them in Christ. He was united with them in their belief in the truth. He was a passionate laborer in his work of being a pioneer in the faith and in his attempt to bring edification to the church at Galatia.

Then Paul addressed the church of Galatia: "Unto the churches of Galatia" (Gal. 1:2). The word *church* comes from the Greek word *ekklesia,* which means "called-out ones." It was an assembly summoned for legislative business. Paul's love for the church was evident, and his greatest desire was to see them glorify Christ (4:12–19). Unfortunately, this affection was not being returned to him. Paul was not content to lead men and women to Christ and then abandon them, and neither is it the mission of the church to do so. Many times we fail to realize that the great commission is not about just making converts but also making disciples. A disciple is a pupil, learner, worshiper, witness, and a repro-ducer. Teaching young Christians how to live in this world for Christ is the great commission (Matt. 28:19–20). When is a convert genuinely converted? A New Testament conversion is when one repents of his sin, turns his back on a life of sin, and sets his face toward heaven like a flint. A disciple is a pupil, learner, worshiper, witness, and a reproducer. There is a process to making a disciple. It does not occur overnight. For the rest of my life, I will be a disciple of the Lord Jesus Christ.

The fact that Christ affirmed Paul in his divine appointment may be a strong source of encouragement to us in our work for God. We may not be an apostle, but each of us has been given a work from God to do. We must be careful about it becoming just another job. It seems in our day and hour that it is easy to forget what it means to be called by Christ to serve as a priest in His house and adopt the attitude, "What a wearisome thing it is to serve the Lord (Mal. 1:13). If we believe that God has given us this work to do for Him, then we can overcome every situation and obstacle that has confronted us. Paul viewed each task as having been given to him by God Himself, and for that reason he was able to endure. Paul knew that his God-given task was to bring the good news to a lost and dying world. His work to him was very sacred and precious. For that reason Paul was able to endure many hardships.

Christ's confirming Paul in his office of apostleship can become a great source of encouragement to us in our place of labor. If we have been given a task to do for God, we should not view it as just another job. This could lead to great discouragement. If God has given us a task to perform then it should become a great incentive for us to overcome the greatest of obstacles. Where God guides He provides. Where He leads He feeds. If the task we have undertook is from God, then God will give us the strength to bear up under the load. We view every assignment as a God-given opportunity. Each task can be viewed as sacred if we believe that it has been given to us by God. This outlook enabled the apostle Paul to endure many hardships while he labored for the souls of men. Jesus was able to drink from the bitter cup because knew that it had been handed to Him by the Father (Matt. 26:39).

In the gospel of Luke, we see Jesus in the Garden of Gethsemane. Luke records, "Being in agony, He prayed more earnestly (Luke 22:41). Here Luke used the word *agodia* where we get the word *agonize* from Jesus entering into the arena of the gladiators. It was here where Satan made one last attempt to kill Him before He made it to the cross. He made one last effort to destroy God's plan of redemption. The capillaries in Jesus skin begin to dilate, and His sweat became as great drops of blood. He drank the bitter cup the Father had handed over to Him. Then "an angel appeared to Him from heaven, strengthening Him" (Luke 22:43). It was in the garden where Jesus won the battle and defeated Satan.

In verse 3 he gives his salutation: "Grace be to you and peace from God the Father, and from our Lord Jesus Christ." *Grace* and *peace* are typical forms of greeting in the Greek and Hebrew. But it is much more than that. It sums up the total work of salvation accomplished by God through Jesus Christ. Paul is talking about sanctifying grace through the enabling ministry of the Holy Spirit. Paul is praying that the Galatians might be the full recipients of the work of the Spirit in their lives.

Grace is God's unmerited favor. We can't work for it, we can't earn it, and we don't deserve it, but God bestows it on us anyway. Grace has been defined as "God's redemption at Christ's expense." It is a thing of sheer beauty. It comes from the Greek word *charis*, which means beauty and charm. If the Christian life has grace in it, it must be a lovely thing. It also means undeserved generosity of a gift that man can never earn or deserve.[4] Grace is more than what justifies us, forgives, or makes us righteous in His sight. It is God's power at work in us to give us the ability to overcome sin. It is also grace that determines our level of ministry. The experience of grace by faith results in peace, a sense of harmony and completeness in our relationship with God and with one another.

The word *peace* comes from the Greek word *eirene* and means to "bind back together two that have been separated." It is a heartfelt peace that is the result of the ministry of the Holy Spirit. Paul, being a Jew, no doubt knew the Hebrew word *shalom*, which means more than just the absence of trouble. It means a sense of harmony and completeness in our walk with God that defines our relationships with each other. It means everything that is to a man's highest good, everything that makes his mind pure, his heart glad.[7] We need to know that peace of God that passeth all knowledge and understanding is able to keep our hearts and minds in Christ Jesus." Thank God the peace of God is on patrol in the town of man's soul and stand outside the door of our heart and mind and want let anything in that would upset us. We need peace of mind because we have been reconciled to God. We need to be able to lay our head on the pillow and know that it is well with our soul. We need to have peace with our enemies. Many are not at peace with others because they are not at peace with themselves. Where there is no grace there is no peace.

The word *from* comes from the Greek word *ek,* a prepositional phrase. It is a word for source. God our Father and the Lord Jesus Christ are the only sources of these blessings.

In three brief phrases Paul outlines the basic structure of His Christ centered message. First, he focuses on "Christ, who gave himself for our sins" (vv. 3–4). From the very beginning Paul stated the message of the gospel. Paul's message centered on a person—Jesus Christ the Son of God. The main theme of his letter was victory over sin that was accomplished through and by the cross. This is no time to substitute the efforts of the flesh for what Jesus accomplished for us at the cross. Jesus death at the cross was what gave us right standing with God. The Galatians were falling back on works for acceptance. The Judaizers offered a bloodless religion. The right doctrine of the substitutionary atonement taught that our Lord took our place, that He died for our sins, and that He gave Himself as a sacrifice that would satisfy the just demands of God's holy law. Christ paid a price that He might deliver sinners from bondage. The sacrificial death of Christ is God's final answer to the fall of man. Jesus Christ, the Son of God, paid a price in that He gave Himself to die on the cross. No one took His life, He willingly gave it.

Secondly, Paul stated that purpose of the cross is to "rescue us from the present evil age" (v. 3, NIV). Liberty in Christ is the dominant theme of Galatians. Christ died to set men free. The present age is controlled and held in the grip of destructive, demonic forces. Man is delivered from sin and this present evil age by the sacrifice of Jesus on the cross. When the law did not offer us a way of escape, only the cross of Christ can set prisoners free (v. 23). Because of the cross, Christians can enjoy the freedom that is ours in Christ.

Paul said, "That he might deliver us" (v. 3). The word *deliver* comes from the Greek word *exaireo,* which means to pluck out, to rescue, to draw out.[8] The word denotes a rescue from this present evil age. The gospel is a rescue team. It is an exodus from the state of bondage. Believers are delivered from the evil that dominates today's society. Paul wrote to the church at Colossians of Father, "who hath delivered us from the power of darkness, and hath translated us into the kingdom of his dear son" (Col. 1:13). By His strong arm, as by a mighty Conqueror, we have been transferred from arbitrary tyranny of darkness (bondage, misery, unhappiness, unholiness, and ignorance of the truth) to a well-ordered sovereign kingdom. Darkness refers to the rule of Satan and his demons over the unsaved.

Paul said that we have been delivered "out of this present evil age" (v. 3, NIV)—out of this age that is evil. Jesus found it existing when He came the first time. He will also find it existing when He comes back the second time. There are two Greek words used in the New Testament translated "evil." *Kakos* means that one is content to perish in his own corruption. *Poneros* means evil, active opposition against the good.[9] Man is not content to perish in his own corruption; He wants to pull and drag down everyone else right along with him. Satan is called the "poneros one." He knows that he is going to hell but is not content to go by himself, he wants to pull everyone else down with him. Even the world around us is attempting to do the same.

In this world we will experience tribulation (John 16:33). Because Christ has chosen us out of this world, the world hates us (15:19). We are persecuted by the world (Matt. 5:10–12). The word *persecuted* came from the Greek word *dioko*, which means to run one off as one might chase a dog out of a garden—pursuing with hostile intent, to molest and harass an individual.[10] The same hostility that the Jews used on Jesus, the disciples would see used on themselves. In this world we will suffer (Rom. 8:22–23). Through the allurements of the world, Satan can seek to destroy the life of God and the passion for the things of God in the lives of believers (1 Pet. 5:8). Believers need to know where to draw the line. "Wherefore come out from among them, and be ye separate, saith the Lord, and touch not the unclean thing; and I will receive you. And will be a Father unto you, and ye shall be by sons and daughters, saith the Lord Almighty" (2 Cor. 6:17–18).

Christ's death has transferred the Christian from Satan's power to the power of God. Satan is the god of this present world. Jesus said, "Now is the judgment of this world: now shall the prince of this world be cast out" (John 12:31). Jesus interpreted the cross in terms of the end of Satan's dominion and the beginning of His triumph over the hearts of men. The verb translated "to be cast out" is always used in John's writings to describe being cast out of a holy place or society.[11] With this verb John also used the word *exo*, which means to clean out. The casting out of Satan from heaven is equated with the purging of heaven.

Ever since the death, burial, and resurrection of Christ, the kingdom of the devil began to hemorrhage. Jesus does not have to come back a second time to win a battle that was already won. Once was enough. We are the mop-up crew here to clean up all the mess in light of His sacrificial atoning death. The situation created by the fall of Adam was reversed. Adam and Eve were driven by God out of the Garden of Eden Because of disobedience, having submitted themselves to the prince of this world. Now by the perfect obedience of Jesus on the cross, the prince of this world will be cast out.

Thirdly, Paul affirms that "it is according to the will of God and our Father" (Gal. 1:3). The Father planned our rescue and sent a rescue team in the person of Christ to deliver us from the bondage, lordship, and control of sin. Paul told the church at Colossae, "Who has delivered us from the power of darkness, and hath translated us into the kingdom of His dear Son." (Col. 1:13). When the fullness of time had come, He sent His Son to accomplish our rescue (Gal. 4:4–5). The Father has sent the Spirit of His Son into our hearts to let us know that we are no longer slaves, but children of the Father (4:6–7). Our salvation is the accomplishment of the Father's plan and is an expression of His grace and peace.

Then Paul reveals His motive. With God's amazing grace in full view, it is time to sing a doxology to God: "To whom be glory forever and ever. Amen" (1:5). It is time we put the amazing back into grace that glorifies God and not the human efforts of men. It was Paul's motive to glorify Jesus Christ. False teachers were not ministering for the glory of God but for their own glory.

So Paul sums up in one sentence the meaning of the work of Jesus Christ, "who gave himself…to rescue us" (1:3–4, NIV). The love that Christ gave was reflected in His sufferings, but it conquered and arrested the hearts of men. More men and women have been drawn to Christ through and by the cross than were ever drawn to Him because of His miracles. He was never more glorious than He was hanging on an old rugged cross. His love still rescues men from the bondage of sin.

The offence of the cross has left our preaching and because of it our gospel has been watered down and diluted. When we take the offence of the cross out of our preaching, we have said good-bye to the power of God. It was the cross that opened up the door for the Holy Spirit. Paul told the church at Corinth: "The preaching of the cross is to them that perish foolishness; but unto us which are saved, it is the power of God" (1 Cor. 1:18). For this reason many have said good-bye to sound doctrinal preaching and have turned aside to another gospel. This other gospel does not and will not produce the same results as the true gospel does.

In a day when God's amazing grace has been turned into nothing more than a cover up or a license to sin or to do as one pleases, I still proclaim that the grace of God is more than that which justifies us, forgives us, and makes us righteous in His sight. It is God's power at work in us that gives us the power and ability to overcome sin.

The salvation that was offered to us at the cross is received by faith aside from any merit of our own. We cannot through our works earn what Christ has purchased for us.

Chapter 4

Another Gospel

I marvel that ye are so soon removed from him that called you into the grace of Christ unto another gospel: Which is not another; but there be some that trouble you, and would pervert the gospel of Christ.

—GALATIANS 1: 6–7

THE FACT THAT Paul was willing to confront the Galatian believers was proof of two things: 1) that he loved them, and 2) it expressed his commitment to the gospel. Paul's rebuke was one of tenderness and gentleness (6:1). Many within the church avoid confrontation. We would rather take flight than stand and fight when there is a need to confront. Many times we are accused of being judgmental.

In many of Paul's letters he always took the time to give thanks. In his writings to the Galatians there is no record of Paul giving thanks. He moves right into the rebuke. This was a strong indication of how serious the problem had become. Paul offers a defense of the gospel with a tone that is sharp, intense, and urgent as he deals with his erring opponents (1:8–9; 5:12). His rebuke covers almost the entire part of his letter. (1:6–4:12). First of all, he gave the reason for his rebuke (1:6). Secondly, he restates the rebuke in (3:1–4, 8–10). Thirdly, we find Paul rebuking them for their foolishness (3:1–3). Fourthly, we find him rebuking the Galatians for being negligent and not following his instructions (4:9). Fifthly, he rebukes the Galatians for their gullibility (1:6; 3:1; 4:19–20). His rebuke came from a heart of love

Paul views his friends with affection as "brothers" (1:11; 3:15; 4:12, 28, 31; 5:11, 13; 6:1, 18). He uses this word nine different times. Here he uses the word *adelphos*. He refers to them as "dear children, for whom I am again in the pains of childbirth until Christ is formed in you" (4:19, NIV). Here Paul finds himself having to travail in prayer all over again that the beauty of Christ that was once attached to their Christian experience will be restored to them, until there is an outward expression on an inward relationship so the beauty of Christ could be clearly seen. As a wise pastor he knows that "the corrections of discipline are the way of life" (Prov. 6:23, NIV). Solomon told us that true love cares enough to confront. "Better is open rebuke than hidden love. Wounds from a friend can be trusted, but an enemy multiplies kisses" (27:5–6, NIV).

Paul had received a report that the Galatians were being infiltrated by false teachers who professed Jesus while trying to place the converts of Galatia under the requirement of the Law of Moses. Paul was astonished that the Galatians were quick to abandon the gospel that had been brought to them. They were receiving the message of the Judaizers with the same zeal as they received Paul's message of the cross. He sees them turning aside to another gospel (*eteros*), one not of the same kind or quality. Really they were turning aside to a gospel that was not a gospel at all.

The Galatians had come under a demonic spell and fell into a world of spiritual foolishness. This foolishness had grown so fast inside the Galatian church that Paul said, "I marvel that you are soon removed from him that called you into the grace of Christ unto another gospel" (Gal. 1:6). This is the first reason for Paul's anxiety. The Galatians were deserting the grace of God. The word *marvel* comes from the word *thaumadzo*, which means wonder, astonishment or amazement.[1] This is a continual amazement to Paul that many were so silly and so gullible to the charlatans of his day. Paul was amazed that the Judaizers had gotten such a stronghold in the church. He is almost amazed that this seduction could happen so quickly. The verb indicates that they were in the process of deserting and had not fully turned away.[2] They had not yet decisively carried out their desertion. They were just starting to turn around and leave. Paul's letter was intended to arrest them before they had gone too far.

The Galatians were turning away from the teaching and reality of the ministry of the Spirit. The present tense of the verb indicates that the Galatians had already begun this attempt. They were starting to depend on self-effort alone in an attempt to obey a legalistic system of works.[3] The Galatians had begun their Christian life in dependence upon the Holy Spirit, now they were depending on self-effort alone to continue the work of sanctification in them, which the Holy Spirit had begun.

The Judaizers insisted they had to conform to the Law of Moses. They abandoned the Holy Spirit and the grace of God and went back to a flesh attempt in conforming to the Law of Moses, while still trying to live a Christian life. They were going about it in the wrong way. They were failing to live a Christian life. The flesh was not producing the same results that they had seen while they were depending on the Holy Spirit. By them depending on self-effort to live up to the law, the Spirit had no opportunity to minister to their spiritual lives. This mechanical set-up of spiritual machinery which God had installed had become ineffective by reason of the monkey wrench of self-dependence which the Galatians had thrown into it. Many of the Galatians were turning away from the doctrine of grace toward legalistic teaching. Through the bewitchment of the Judaizers in the church and through their abandonment of the Holy Spirit, they had lost the glow upon their countenance as well as the beauty of Christ.

Two words are very important in this verse of Scripture: The word *removed*, from the Greek word *metatithesthe*, which is a compound word of *meta*, denoting a change, and *tithimi*, describing a position. It denotes a positional change. It can mean to transfer or depart. It can mean a change in one's opinion about something. It is a word that is used in a military sense to describe rebellion against authority, insubordination, revolt, and defection. This change took place in a very short period of time. Paul was saying, "You are transferring yourselves and you're doing it quickly."[4] Paul was shocked and amazed that after he had preached the gospel and the Holy Spirit had laid His mark on the Galatian believers, they would turn aside to another gospel.

Paul identifies the type of teaching that was going on and called it "another gospel" (1:6). The word *another* comes from the Greek word *heteros*, which means one not of the same kind or quality. It had a qualitative difference.[5] False prophets and false teachers had invaded Galatia with a gospel of a different kind. Paul was saying that "which is not another; but there be some that would trouble you, and would pervert the gospel of Christ" (Gal. 1:7). Paul was saying that there is not another gospel like this one. Here Paul uses the word *allos*, which means "something of the same kind." Paul was saying that the gospel they preach is not like the gospel we preach. It is not a gospel like ours at all.

Paul mentions "another gospel" (v. 6) using the Greek word *eteros* meaning one not of the same kind or quality. Paul said it "is not another" (v. 7) meaning there is not another gospel like this one. It stands in a class by itself. Paul was not going to allow his gospel to be served alongside other gospels, buffet style. This gospel that had become so attractive to the Galatians Christians was really no gospel at all. It was a perversion of the gospel of Christ to be carried about by those who are seeking to cause confusion. It was Paul's desire that his readers would reject the false and embrace the true.

French Arrington, in his book *The Ministry of Reconciliation,* makes reference to "another Jesus" and "another spirit" mentioned in (2 Cor. 11:4). This was preached by false apostles, which led to a different kind of gospel in the life of the church. It introduced a different spirit into the church. It was not the Holy Spirit who brought liberty to the heart and life of the believer, but a satanic spirit that sought to restore the shackles and chains of legalism. Corinth was not only listening to these false apostles but they were "putting up with this disguise of the gospel." The teachings of these false apostles are just as deadly today as they were then.

Arrington noted that this kind of Jesus was stripped of His saving grace.[6] They viewed Christ as nothing more than a miracle worker. He was not viewed by them as someone who reconciled the world unto Himself. He was declared to be nothing more than a social reformer. They felt that He was not an example of morality or a spiritual man. This was a complete rejection of Jesus as crucified Lord. The result of this was a different gospel and a different religious experience, which was not of the Holy Spirit.

Many are bowing to the Jesus of the culture instead of the Jesus of the Bible. Jesus becomes to them anything that they want Him to be. The Jesus of the Bible was never tolerant of a life of sin in the sinner or the religious leaders of the nation.

Many in the church prefer the kind of gospel that makes them happy not holy. They are looking for a gospel that will give them a change of circumstances, not a change of character. They want a gospel that makes them feel good instead of living good. Many are attempting to disobey the Word of God and yet do the will of God. If you cannot discern the voice of God through the preached Word, how can you discern the voice of the Holy Spirit telling you to leave your local church?

Many are content to go to a church that is totally seeker sensitive instead of being Spirit-led. Many of our Christian churches in North America no longer have services where Holy Ghost conviction strikes the heart of the sinner. There are many of our churches that no longer have altar calls for those who desire to repent. Seldom is the word *judgment* spoken when national calamities devastate our productivity or prosperity. Many of our sheep are being blinded by willing ignorant shepherds.

Paul then spoke of false ministers that would "trouble you" (Gal. 1:7). The word *trouble* comes from the Greek word *tarasso*, which means the Galatians had become mentally shaken up. It speaks of a shaking, tossing, anxious, excited disturbance that had occurred in the church. The present tense of the participle means that the Judaizers were still in Galatia at the time of Paul's letter, and Paul wrote to combat them while they were in the midst of their activity.[7] They had made a royal mess of the gospel. They took the doctrine of grace and mutilated it with all their new additions.

The deserting and perverting of the Judaizers was doing something to the Galatian Christians. The word *trouble* carries with it the idea of perplexity, confusion, and unrest. The word *trouble* speaks of the feelings of the disciples when the ship was tossed in the midst of the storm (Matt. 14:26). It describes the feeling that King Herod had when he heard that a new king had been born (Matt. 2:3). Grace always leads to peace (Gal. 1:3), but these believers had deserted the grace of God.

Then Paul said that they had perverted the gospel of Christ (v. 7). The word *pervert* comes from the Greek word *metastrepho*, which means "to reverse, turn aside, turn about, bend, or change."[8] They were adding new revelations to the message of the cross of Christ, and as a result they were bending it, changing it, twisting it to the point that they were reversing it. Paul said the Galatians were perverting the gospel of God. The word *pervert* that is found in verse 7 is used three times in the New Testament (Acts 2:20, James 4:9; Gal. 1:7). By the Galatian believers substituting the gospel of Christ and going back under the Law they were perverting the gospel of Christ (1:7, 5:4).

The Judaizers felt their message completed Paul's message. They did not view their version of the gospel as heresy. After all, they did not deny the deity of Christ, the cross of Christ, or the resurrection of Christ. They subtracted nothing from Paul's message; they just added to it.

Here Paul rebuked the Galatians for their desertion. How could the Galatians, after receiving the message of the cross and after they had received the Holy Spirit into their lives (3:1–5), turn aside to another gospel that is empty of power? The One they were deserting was the One who had called them by the grace of Christ. Paul was called by God's grace (1:15). The Galatians were called by God's grace (5:8). Then Paul blames the confusion on those who perverted the gospel. He pronounced condemnation on those who tamper with the truth of the gospel.

From the example of the Galatians, we come to understand that not every search for spirituality is in reality a quest for God and His power. Sometimes in a desire to be spiritual, it can become a way of not only finding God, but also a way of running to hide from Him. The perversion of the gospel is being trapped by a message that promised spiritual perfection but instead turns away from God.

God had called them by His grace and saved them from their sins. When Paul beheld the Galatians moving from grace back into the law and abandoning liberty for legalism, he knew that he had to strike while the iron was hot. They were doing it quickly, without consulting Paul, who was their spiritual father in the Lord. They were not depending on the teaching ministry of the Holy Spirit to guide them into all truth. They were going back to Old Testament practices to avoid persecution by the Jewish people (6:12–15). Paul was no man-pleaser. His ministry did not come from man (1:1), nor did his message come from man (v. 12). Why should he seek to please men when his heart's desire was to please Christ?

The Galatians were not simply changing religions or changing churches, but were actually abandoning the grace of God. They were abandoning the very God of grace. They were deserting the God of grace for the Judaizers who would bring them back into bondage. For them to desert grace for law is to desert the God who saved them.

The grace of God is the dominant theme in this letter. Salvation is a gift of God's grace. We are not only saved by grace, but we are kept by grace. Our stance in grace is the foundation for the Christian life (Rom. 5:1–2). Grace is what enables us to be victorious in the Christian life (2 Tim. 2:4). Grace is what enables us to suffer without complaining. Grace is what turns suffering into glory. When a Christian turns away from God's grace, he has to depend on his own resources. This leads to failure and disappointment. This is what has caused much of the frustration in the Christian life. It is then that we are void of God's resources and we began to depend on our own. When you fall from grace (Gal. 5:4), you lose the beauty of the Lord Jesus Christ, and the glow upon your countenance. The word *fallen* comes from the word *ekpipto*. Here it refers to a ship that is not under control. When the Galatians placed themselves back under the law, they were denying the sweet and sure control of God's grace. As a result they were nullifying and making of no effect the very grace of God. They had begun their Christian lives in the Spirit, but now they were attempting to live this Christian life in the strength of the flesh while trying to obtain the same results.

Paul went as far as to say, "But though we, or an angel from heaven, preach any other gospel unto you than that which we have preached unto you, let him be accursed" (v. 7). Paul uses here a very strong language. The word *accursed* is the Greek word *anathema* which means let him be condemned to hell fire and damnation. It means that they are dedicated to destruction. In a spiritual sense they are alienated from God by their sin.[9] It does not matter if it is preacher, an angel from heaven, or Paul himself. The true gospel is the final test of authority. Many have never understood this in the church. Our experience is not the standard. Our experience does not prove the Word of God, but the Word of God proves our experience and testifies that it is of God. Even the authority of a messenger from heaven or the authority of Paul himself must be tested by loyalty to the gospel. Paul held himself accountable to this divine mandate.

When leadership does not operate in their giftedness and calling, many times the church will drift into compromise and will become divided. As leadership goes so goes the church. Sometimes leaders in a church become lords over God's heritage, and there is an abuse of power. Sheep cannot be driven; they must be led. It is sad to say that there is not always freedom in every church to grow in faith and love.

When there is submission to authority and the powers that be ordained of God, the abuse of power and spirits of control can be avoided. Leaders in the church should lead with humility and must be willing to be accountable. If leadership is not willing to be accountable, then how are we going to get the church to follow the Lord in divine alignment? The laity of the church needs accountability to be able to grow in their relationship with the Lord.

In verse 9, Paul pronounced a curse on those who preached another gospel. Paul had no tolerance for anyone who would seek to pervert the gospel of Christ. How do we respond to this in a day when pluralism (all roads lead to heaven or in the end all are destined to be saved) seems to be progressively growing and confronting the church? When there seems to be a tolerance and respect for people of other religious persuasions, it should not lead us to compromise the true gospel of Christ in any way.

When the truth of the gospel was at stake, Paul drew a line in the sand and refused to compromise. He would not yield in his defense of the "truth of the gospel" (2:5, 14). He wanted to protect the freedom of the Galatian believers. When anyone departed from the truth of the cross of Christ, Paul did not hesitate to forcefully confront him as he did, Peter.

Paul was not trying to win the applause of men, but he desired God's affirmation. "For do I now persuade men, or God? or do I seek to please men? For if I yet pleased men, I should not be the servant of Christ" (1:10). Paul was not preaching to please men. Paul had been accused of preaching a gospel that did not require Gentiles to follow Jewish customs. He had just pronounced a judgment on anyone who preached a perversion of his gospel and held himself bound by that same standard. By doing so he considered himself to be cleared of any accusation of trying to please men. If preaching to please the hearts of men would have been his ambition, it would have indicated that he was not a true servant of Christ. One thing I have discovered in the church that I have pastored for more than twenty years, you can water down your gospel to make friends and lose the respect of your congregation. If I am faithful to the charge that God has given to me to preach His Word, it is for sure that I will have my enemies, but I will maintain the respect of my congregation. When Paul was in sin his life was swallowed up in the will of Satan. Through his identification with Christ's sacrificial atoning death the chains that bound him to the service of Satan have now been broken. Now His Lord and Master is Jesus Christ, and his life is wrapped up in the sweet will of God.

Paul was totally submitted to the lordship of Christ. Here he rebuked the Galatians who were quickly turning their backs on the One who had called them and turning to a different gospel. True servants of Christ will not win popularity contests with people who heap to themselves teachers having itching ears that will tell it like they want to hear it and will preach it like they want to hear it preached (2 Tim. 4:3), as if this were cafeteria religion. They would rather have the praise of God than the praises of men. True servants of Christ are marked by their loyalty to the Christ. They have an undivided heart and a single eye of devotion. There are men and women who have suffered because of their defense of the gospel. They resisted any temptation to renounce their faith in Christ. They boldly declare as Martin Luther did: "Here I stand. I can do no other. God help me."[10]

Paul waged war against the deceptive fraudulent teachers because the truth had come under attack and because he loved those he had led to Christ. Like a father who loves and guards his daughter until she walks the isle to give herself away to her bridegroom, Paul watched over the Galatian believers lest they be ensnared by sin. The gospel the Galatians were turning to was very inferior to the gospel that they had already received through the apostle Paul.

Dake's Bible gives us a list of things that the gospel the Galatian believers turned to could not do.[11] With another gospel the law cannot justify or put us in right relationship with God (Gal. 2:16; 3:11; 5:4).Justification was the watchword of the Reformation. It was this message that liberated Martin Luther from religious bondage and fear. Romans explains what it means to be justified by faith (Rom. 1:17). Galatians explains how the just shall live (Gal. 3:11). Hebrews tell us that it *is* by faith (Heb. 10:38).

No amount of observance of the law can make a person right with God. Anytime we base our righteousness on anything other than the redemptive work of Christ at Calvary, it is legalism. We have to fling ourselves at the feet of the mercy and grace of God to be saved. We have to come to Him, not by any merit of our own but by the merits of His blood that was shed for us on Calvary. "I do not frustrate the grace of God: for if righteousness come by the law, then Christ is dead in vain" (Gal. 2:21).

Justification is when one is acquitted of his sin and placed in the position of one who has never broken the law. God declares him to be righteous in His sight and now looks upon him as He would look upon His own Son. As a result we have peace with God; we have access into this grace and rejoice in hope of the glory of God (Rom. 5:1–2). It is an act, not a process. If we were justified by works it would have been a gradual process.

Paul said "It is God that justifieth" (Rom. 8:33). It is not by doing the works of the law that makes the sinner get in right standing before God, but by putting his faith in Jesus Christ. All the law did was reveal sin, not redeem from sin. God in His grace has put our sins on Christ, and Christ's righteousness has been put on our account (2 Cor. 5:21). Real justification leads to a changed life.

Another gospel brought only a curse (Gal. 3:10). Everyone is cursed who doesn't consistently obey and perform all the things written in the law. If you choose the law, you must rise and fall based on your decision. No man has ever succeeded nor will he ever succeed in keeping the law. If you don't, you place yourselves under a curse. (Deut. 27:26). Salvation could never come by obedience to the law because the law brings a curse, not a blessing. The law cannot justify the sinner (Gal. 2:16), nor can it give to him righteousness (2:21). The law cannot give the gift of the Spirit (3:2), nor can it guarantee the spiritual inheritance that is ours in Christ (3:18). If the law cannot give life (3:21) or liberty (5:1), then why go back to the law?

Another gospel is not one of faith (Gal. 3:12). For the Christian to abandon faith and grace for law and works is to lose everything existing that he can experience in his daily fellowship with the Lord. Paul could never forget that the peace, the liberty, and the right relationship that we possess cost the life and death of Jesus Christ.

Another gospel cannot give an inheritance (3:18). The word *promise* is used eight times in these verses (vv. 14–22). It refers to God's promise to Abraham that in Him all the nations of the earth would be blessed (Gen. 12:1–3). This promise to Abraham was given about 2,000 B.C.; centuries later came the Law of Moses in about 1450 B.C. The Judaizers believed that the giving of the law changed the original covenant of promise. The covenant finds its consummation in Jesus Christ. The way to peace with God is the way of faith which Abraham took. We must look to Jesus in faith.

Another gospel will not make sin sinful (Gal. 3:19). "Wherefore then serveth the law? It was added because of transgressions, until the seed should come to whom the promise was made; and it was ordained by angels in the hand of a mediator." Where there was no law, there was no sin. A man cannot be condemned for wrongdoing if he does not know that he has done wrong. So the function of the law was to define sin. The law could define sin, but it could not do anything to cure it. A doctor can be an expert in diagnosis but may be helpless when it comes to clearing up the trouble. When the law was given at Sinai, there was thunder and lightning, and the people trembled with fear. Even Moses was shaking in his shoes (Heb. 12:18–21). It was very dramatic in comparison to when the covenant was given to Abraham (Gen. 15). The Judaizers were very impressed with the drama that accompanied the giving of the law.

Paul felt the giving of the law was inferior to the covenant God made with Abraham in two ways. First, the law was temporary. It was added until the seed should come (Gal. 3:19). The word *added* implies that the law was not a central theme in God's redemptive plan; it was supplementary and secondary to the enduring covenant made with Abraham. It marks the beginning point of the Mosaic Law. The word *until* marks its point of ending. The Mosaic Law came in effect at some point in history and was in effect until the promised seed, Christ, appeared. So there is a contrast here between the permanent validity of the promise and the temporary nature of the law. The promise was made long before the law and will be in effect long after the law was fulfilled in Christ. The law was in effect for a relatively short period of time and was limited in both directions by the words *added* and *until*.

Paul's temporal framework for the law is a major theme in his argument for the superiority of the promise fulfilled in Christ over the law. The Jews believed there were two things that would last forever: the law and the temple being the dwelling place of God. They emphasized the eternal, immutable nature of the law. Paul believed that Christ, not the law, was the Eternal One.

Let's take a look at the definition of the word *seed* (v. 16). The Jews have been convinced that the term *seed* referred to the physical descendants of Abraham, the Jewish people. Therefore they believed that it was absolutely necessary to belong to the Jewish nation in order to receive the blessings promised to Abraham. In Jewish literature it referred to the nation of Israel. The term *seed*, Paul explains, is not plural but singular. Therefore the covenant designated one person to be the recipient of the promise, which was Christ. Rabbis believed it stood for a specific individual. Paul believed that Christ is the sole heir and channel of God's promised blessing. Since Christ is the heir of that promises, only those who are in Him are recipients of these blessings (v. 29).

Just as the seed is one (v. 16) so "ye are all one in Christ" (v. 28). So the emphasis of the oneness of the seed in verse 16 prepares the way for the emphasis on the unity of all in Christ (v. 28). Now the people of God are identified by their union with Christ. Christ, who is the seed of Abraham, ushers in through Himself a new community of all believers that is not dependent on racial and gender divisions. Whereas the law made a division between Jews and Gentiles, Christ being the promised seed of Abraham, is the center whereby Jews and Gentiles find their unity.

Legal documents that are signed and dated take priority over other documents. A will can annul or change the previous contract. So lawyers search to make sure they have documents with the latest date, which override all previous documents. The date of the Abrahamic covenant was 430 years before the Mosaic Law. Because the Mosaic Law came 430 years after the Abrahamic covenant, they should be distinguished from each other, and the terms of the

Abrahamic covenant could not be changed by the Mosaic covenant. Those who seek inheritance by the law have failed to realize that because the law was given 430 years after the promise given to Abraham, it could not annul or be attached to the promise as a condition for inheriting the promised blessings

So the time of the confirmation of the promise to Abraham and that of giving of the law stands in contrast to the claim of the rabbis that Abraham knew and even kept the minute detail of the Mosaic Law. This Jewish tradition that the Mosaic Law was inseparable from the Abrahamic covenant is what influenced the Galatians believers to keep the Mosaic Law to inherit the blessings promised to Abraham.. If the inheritance depends on the law, then no longer does it depend on a promise. But God in His grace gave it to Abraham through a promise. So the inheritance cannot be received as a payment for keeping the law. This is an argument developed by Paul to drive home his rebuke for the foolish error of viewing something as a payment that had already been received as a gift.

The promise that God made to Abraham was an irrevocable trust agreement that is described in terms of the beneficiary of the trust (v. 16), the date of the trust (v. 17), and the conditions of inheritance (v. 18). A temporary law (Law of Moses) cannot be greater than a permanent covenant that was given to Abraham. In the Abrahamic Covenant there are no ifs and nothing was conditional. All of it was grace. The blessings of the law was dependent upon the Israelite meeting certain conditions. Through the death and resurrection of Christ, the law was done away and now its righteous demands were fulfilled by the Spirit (Rom. 8:4). An agreement according to the law depended on two persons: the person who gave it and the person who accepted it. It depended on both sides keeping it. If you break the any law then the whole agreement becomes undone. But a promise depends on only one person. The way of grace depends on God and on God alone. It is better to depend on the grace of an unchanging God than on the helpless efforts of men.

With another gospel the law demanded a mediator. The law was given through and by the mediation of angels. A mediator does not represent just one party, but God is one. There is a contrast here in the plurality of participants in a process of mediation and God who dealt personally with Abraham. In fact, Israel "received the law by the disposition of angels" (Acts 7:53). It was a well-known Jewish tradition that God gave the law through the agency of angels (Deut. 33:2; Ps. 68:17; Heb. 2:2). The law was given to Israel, passing from God to angels to Moses. Many of the rabbis in Paul's day believed that because God was holy, it was impossible for God to deal with fallen humanity. When God made His covenant to Abraham, it was done without a mediator. A mediator is one who stands between two parties and helps them to agree. The covenant of promise was permanent, and no mediator was required, so the covenant was greater than the law.

The presence of angels in the mediation of the law that was given to Moses was understood by the Jewish people to mean the great glory of the law. There is a difference in a promise that is directly given by God to Abraham and fulfilled in Christ, the seed of Abraham, and the law given through numerous intermediaries.

The churches of Galatia were becoming law centered. The law had to be put back into its rightful place. Its purpose was negative: to point out the transgressions. Its time was limited in the fact that it came 430 years after the promise and lasted until Christ came on the scene. Even though the law was given through angels to Moses, it failed to do two things: 1) it did not provide direct access to God, and 2) it did divide Jews and Gentiles. People who were preoccupied with the supreme value of the law must have been stunned when told it did not cancel out the Abrahamic covenant. How could Paul speak against the law?

The Galatians were being persuaded that if they identified themselves and observed the rituals of the Jewish people, they would experience new levels of spiritual life and blessing; and if they became members of the Jewish community, they would be guaranteed intimacy with God. But the Galatians had already entered into an experience with the Spirit (3:1–5), which was the fulfillment of the promise (v. 14). It was Paul's argument that the law had a mediated origin. The law did not provide direct access to God. Only by the promise being fulfilled of the Spirit being poured out on those who are in Christ are we guaranteed direct access to God (4:4–9).

Paul said to them, "God is one" (3:20). The law was mediated through angels and Moses to the Jewish people. The Judaizers felt that the blessings of God were only for the Jews. Their view limited God's blessings only to the Jewish nation. They implied that God was the God of the Jews only. But God is the God of the Gentiles as well as the Jews (Rom. 3:29–30). The promise was to all nations. The bestowal of the Spirit on Gentiles who had not become Jews could not be refuted.

So Moses, being a mediator of one, ushered in a law that brought a division between Jews from Gentiles; the one new community promised to Abraham (Gal. 3:8) was found in Christ, not Moses. Christ is the mediator of the unity of all believers in Christ—Jew and Greek, slave and free, male and female. At the cross Christ broke down the wall that had divided them.

Paul knew that the law had an important place in God's plan of redemption. It was an essential step toward the fulfillment of God's promises in Christ. It was not the final goal of God's plan. It was good in that it offered to us a standard of righteousness. Christ is the beginning, end, and center of God's plan. The law prepared the way for the coming of Christ (3:19). It was the worship of their own law that led Israel into self-righteousness, religious works, and caused them to reject Christ. This was the position of the Judaizers in the Galatian churches. They were promoting the law as the way to live for God. It was their position that set the law in direct opposition to the promise; it contradicted the gospel.

With another gospel the law could not give life. Paul said, "For if there had been a law given which could have given life, verily righteousness should have been by the law" (3:21). Even though the Law of Moses governed the lives of the people, it did not provide them spiritual life. If life and righteousness came through the law, Jesus Christ would not have had to die on a cross. By *life* Paul means living in right relationship with God. The law did not enable the Israelites to live in a right relationship with God. The law was unable to impart life to the sinner and place him in right standing before God.

With another gospel the law could not give righteousness (2:21). If righteousness was gained through the law, Christ died for nothing! "Is the law then against the promises of God? God forbid: for if there had been a law given which could have given life, verily righteousness should have been given by the law" (3:21). This is like telling you that just by believing in the cross of Christ you will not be able to live in a right relationship with God By you keeping the law you will be able to live in right relationship with God. That is what the Galatians were being told by the false teachers. Believing the gospel has been proven to be the only way to receive life in the Spirit and righteousness (3:1–18).

The law was a schoolmaster to bring us to Christ (3:24–26). Paul said that "the law was our School master to bring us to Christ, that we might be justified by faith" (v. 24). The law was put in charge to bring us to Christ. The law was our disciplinarian until Christ came. Here Paul speaks of the child's guardian. The word that Paul used was *pedagogue,* a household servant called a child conductor. Usually he was an old and trusted slave who had long been with the family and had a good character. Being in charge of the child's welfare, it was his duty to see that the child took on the qualities and characteristics of true manhood. His duty was to take the child to school and deliver him to his teacher and then later bring him home.

In the time of the apostle Paul, the pedagogue was different from the teacher (*didaskolos*). The pedagogue supervised, controlled, and disciplined the child, while the teacher instructed and educated him. So the function of the law was to lead him to Christ, to show him that by himself and through his works he could not merit salvation. Once he came to Christ he was not under the bondage of the law, but he was under grace.

In many Roman and Greek households, well-educated slaves took the children to and from school and watched over them during the day. Sometimes they would protect, prohibit certain behaviors and sometimes they would even discipline. The slave was not the child's father; he was the child's guardian and disciplinarian. Josephus tells us of a pedagogue who was found beating a family cook when the child under his supervision overate. The pedagogue himself was corrected with the words: "Man, we did not make you the cook's pedagogue did we? but the child's guardian. Correct him; help him!"[12]

The use of the term *pedagogue* finds reference in the Hellenistic world. He was to supervise and discipline the conduct of children. He did not educate the child; he was only supposed to control the behavior of the child through consistent discipline. The law was given to perform a role of discipline and supervision over the Jewish people. This role came to an end when Christ came.

The work of the guardian was to prepare the child for maturity. Once they came of age he or she no longer needed a guardian. So the law was preparation for the nation of Israel until the promised seed came in the person of Jesus Christ. It demonstrated that God's people could then be justified by faith (v. 24). The Jewish people learned under the constant discipline of the law how impossible it was to keep the law. The law constantly beat them down like a stern disciplinarian. It pointed out their shortcomings and failures. The pain of that discipline was designed to teach them that they could only be declared righteous by God through faith.

Verse 25 draws a conclusion that destroys any argument that Christians ought to live under the supervisory control of the law. It tells us that now that faith has come, we are no longer under the supervision of the law. The Judaizers were telling the Galatian believers that their new life in Christ should come under the supervisory discipline of the Mosaic Law. For us to live under the supervision of the Mosaic Law is to live as if Christ had not come. Now that Christ has come we will live as Paul said, "by faith in the Son of God" (Gal. 2:20, NIV). Living by faith in Christ sets us free from the supervision of the law.

Here Paul is speaking from the first person plural (we). Because the Jewish believers have placed their faith and have been delivered from the supervision of the law, they are now walking in true freedom. If Jewish believers are not under the supervision of the law, then why place Gentile believers in Christ under the supervision of the law. No wonder Paul called them foolish. They had received the Spirit by believing the gospel, but now they are trying to make progress in their spiritual life by observing the law. Their attempt to observe the law as if they were now under its supervision is not progress.

Paul now turns to the privileged position of the Galatian Christians. "For ye are all the children of God by faith in Christ Jesus. For as many of you as have been baptized into Christ have put on Christ. There is neither Jew nor Greek, there is neither bond nor free, there is neither male nor female: for ye are all one in Christ Jesus. And if ye be Christ's, then are ye Abraham's seed, and heirs according to the promise" (Gal. 3:26–29). Union with Christ is the main emphasis in each verse: Faith in Christ Jesus (v. 26), baptized into Christ...clothed...with Christ (v. 27), one in Christ Jesus (v. 28), and belonging to Christ (v. 29).

How foolish it is to think that by observing the law one could enhance their privileges when Christians already enjoy their union with The illustration is drawn from a household where sons were treated as slaves until they received the full rights of sons at the age of maturity. Imprisonment under the law (vv. 19–25) has been replaced by new relationships in Christ. These relationships are spiritual (vv. 26–27) and social (vv. 28–29).

Under the law there were differences and distinctions, especially between Israel and other nations. Jesus did not come to divide but to unite. Jews were children of God because of their nationality, and Gentiles were sinners. Now Gentile Christians are all sons of God through faith in Christ Jesus. This declaration would have been shocking for the Jews to hear. In Jewish literature "sons of God" was a title of the highest honor, used only for the members of righteous Israel who were destined to inherit the eschatological blessings.

But now Gentiles, who were rejected, outsiders of the covenants of promise, sinners by nature, those who do not serve the law, are called sons of God. This is a new creation (6:15). How could a Gentile ever be called a child of God? Paul gives the answer—through faith in Christ Jesus (3:26). Since Jesus is the Son of God (2:20), all who are by faith in Christ are also sons of God.

This was good news for the Galatian Christians. In society, slaves were considered to be pieces of property. Women were kept confined and disrespected. Gentiles were constantly being sneered at by the Jews. The law perpetuated these distinctions, but God through His grace declares all men to be on the same level. This results in a new horizontal relationship with one another. All racial, economic, and gender barriers have been removed in Christ.

Unless the church expresses this equality and unity in Christ in its life and ministry it is not being faithful to the gospel. Gentiles were regarded as being second class because they were not Jews. The gospel of Jesus Christ does not justify racial superiority. The radical affirmation of unity and equality in Christ is a deliberate rejection of the attitude expressed by the synagogue prayer in which the worshiper thanks God for not making him a Gentile, a slave, or a woman. This attitude of superiority contradicts the truth of the gospel.

Any expression of social class superiority (free over slaves) or gender (men over women) violates the truths of the gospel. There is neither Jew nor Greek, slave nor free, male or female, for you are all one in Christ Jesus (Gal. 3:28). Divisions and prejudices that seem to be prevalent in the world have been abolished in Christ.

We are children of God because we have been united with Christ in baptism. Baptism in the Spirit identifies the believer with Christ and makes him part of Christ's body (1 Cor. 12:12–14). Water baptism is an outward symbol of an inward work. As a result we are clothed with Christ. When there is genuine faith in Christ, baptism becomes a symbol of our union with Christ. Paul desires for them to renew the sense of belonging to Christ. The ceremony of initiation into Christ and the Christian community points to the solid foundation for their new relationship as children of God. Baptism pictures our vital union with Christ by faith. Baptism was a Jewish rite. If a man wished to accept the Jewish faith, he had to do three things: he had to be circumcised, he had to offer sacrifices and be baptized, and he had to partake in ceremonial washings to cleanse from the defilement—very common in Jewish practice.[13]

Barclay stated that the Jewish baptism involved the following: The man had to cut his hair and his nails. He undressed himself completely. A baptismal bath contained forty-two hogsheads of water. Every part of the body had to be touched with water. He had to make a confession of faith before three men, called fathers of baptism. While he was in the water, parts of the law were read to him. Words of encouragement were addressed to him. Benedictions were pronounced upon him. When he emerged he was a member of the Jewish faith.[14]

The Galatian baptism led to them being clothed with Christ. The phrase "to put on Christ" (Gal. 3:27) refers to a change of garments. The believer laid aside the dirty garments of sin (Isa. 64:6) and by faith has received the robes of righteousness in Christ. Changing clothes had a different meaning as well. When a Roman child came of age, he took off the childhood garments and put on the toga of adult citizenship.[15] The believer in Christ is not just a child of God, he is a son of God. The son of God has an adult status before God.

Why go back to the law and become a child of the law again? This is drawn from the metaphor of them robing again after baptism. The candidate for baptism was clothed with a white robe, symbolic of the new life into which he had entered. His life becomes clothed with Christ.[16] It is a picture of our complete identification with Christ. In the Old Testament there are frequent references to being clothed with righteousness, salvation, strength, and glory. In the New Testament Paul uses the metaphor of putting on clothing to mean taking on the virtues of Christ (Col. 3:12; 1 Thess. 5:8). Being clothed with Christ portrays our participation in His perfections by faith.

The title "sons of God" and the two ceremonies of baptism and being clothed with Christ point to the new reality of our new relationship with God in Christ. With the coming of Jesus Christ, the nation of Israel moved out of childhood into adulthood. The long preparation was over. The glory to the law could not be compared to what was being revealed in Christ. The law could reveal sin and to a certain extent control behavior. But the law could not do for the sinner what Jesus Christ was able to do. It could not justify the guilty. It is only through faith in Jesus Christ that we are declared justified, righteous before God.

The law separated man from God and could never offer a person oneness with God. There was a fence around the tabernacle that told the common man to stay out. There was a veil between the holy place and the holy of holies.

Before Christ came, Israel was imprisoned by the law. It was the law that separated Israel from Gentile nations (Eph. 2:12–18). It had governed every aspect of their lives. The law was preparing Israel for the coming of Christ. The demands of the law reminded Israel they needed a Savior. Even the types and symbols in the law were pictures of the coming of the Messiah. In the Old Testament we have preparation for Christ. In the Gospels we have presentation of Christ. In Revelation we have the appropriation of Christ.

When the Savior came, there was no need for a guardian. It is a shame that the nation of Israel did not recognize the Messiah when He appeared. Their rejection of the Messiah caused God to destroy the temple. The Jews defiled it, God abandoned it, and Rome came in and destroyed it. Today it is impossible for a devout Jew to practice Judaism. He has no altar, no priesthood, no sacrifice, no temple, and no king (Hosea 3:4)—all of which have become fulfilled in Christ.

When Paul put his faith in Christ, he saw the turning point in his life. Before that time he lived under the supervision of the Mosaic Law. But after he put his faith in Christ, his life was lived by faith in Christ, under the supervision of Christ. He had immigrated to the kingdom of Christ (Col. 1:13). Our new life in Christ is not under the supervision of the law; it is under the rule of Christ by His Spirit. Freedom in Christ from the supervising rule of the Mosaic Law empowers us to live for God (Gal. 2:19).

With another gospel Christians were bound by the law (Gal. 3:19–25). The scripture says that the whole world is a prisoner of sin (v. 22). The law condemned us all. Literally Paul was saying that the scripture imprisoned us all under sin. So the purpose of the law was to reveal to us that we were all were sinners, and that placed all sinners under God's judgment. The law placed the Jews on the same level as Gentiles. So the law reduces all to the level of sinners; the law prepares the way for the gospel. The law has a negative purpose; it makes us aware of our sin. It cannot set us free from the bondage of sin. The promise of blessing comes only through faith in Christ.

So being identified with the Jewish people by circumcision and observance of Mosaic Law did not keep them from being sinners or bring them into the arena of righteousness, blessing, and life; rather, it left them imprisoned under sin. The law was given to Israel 430 years after the promise of God to Abraham to show that all humanity was held under the bondage of sin, and what God had promised us through faith in Jesus Christ might bestowed (v. 22). Now we see how the law and the promise work in harmony to fulfill the purpose of God. The law puts us under the curse; the promise lifts us up in Christ. We were left without an exit under the condemnation of the law so that we might find our freedom only by faith in Christ. The law imprisons all—both Jews and Gentiles—under sin to prepare the way for all believers in Christ for the promised blessings to Abraham.

The law has been personalized as a jailor and a disciplinarian (3:23–25). Even though the law placed on the same level with the Gentiles and identified us as sinners. It was only temporary in God's plan of redemption. The law was God's jailor on the stage of history. "Before this faith came, we were held prisoners by the law, locked up until faith was revealed" (v. 23, NIV). In verse 22 it says that the whole world was declared to be a prisoner of sin. In verse 23 Paul says "We were held prisoners by the law." The law is related to both Jews and Gentiles without distinction. All are condemned as sinners by the law. The Jews in a large sense were held prisoner by the law for a period of time. When we read the law of the Old Testament we can see how every aspect of Jewish life was restricted, restrained, and confined by the law. In this sense the law was a jailor over the Jews.

Every person born into the human race is under the condemnation of the law given in Scripture. The law makes it clear that everyone is a prisoner of sin in order that the salvation that was promised by God can be received only by faith in Jesus Christ (v. 22). This was the universal function of the law. The condemning sentence of the law against humanity can never be overturned. It stands as a permanent indictment of the sinful rebellion of the whole world against God.

The Mosaic Law was given not only as a permanent standard for all humanity but also a temporary system to supervise a particular people. It was a complex system of laws that were set up to guide the Jewish people. When Israel came out of Egypt, they had no king, no palace, no throne, and no laws to govern them. They did not even have the identity of being a people. He brought them to Sinai, cut a covenant with them, and made them the people of God.

The lockup was meant to be only temporary. Verse 23 begins and ends with clear reference to the time when imprisonment within the system of Mosaic Law would end. "Before this faith came, we (the Jewish People) were held prisoners by the law, locked up until faith should be revealed" (3:23, NIV). The function of the law as a jailor was not permanent; it was limited to a certain period of history.

Another gospel makes us servants, not sons (Gal. 4:1–3). Paul is describing the slave condition of the sons while they were still minors. Jesus Christ was sent by the Father to liberate the slaves and make them sons of God (v. 4–5), and then Paul describes the full rights of sons (v. 6–7). *Wilmington's Guide to the Bible* states that there is a difference between being a child and being adopted. Adoption is one of the blessings of the Christian experience. 1) Childhood refers to my condition in God's family whereas adoption speaks of my position God's family. 2) Through the new birth I enter into God's family, but adoption allows me to enjoy God's family. 3) The circumstances of childhood are private, but my circumstances in adoption are made public. 4) While a child is under guardians, an adopted adult in God's family has full liberty.[17]

One of the reasons God sent Christ into the world was "to redeem them that were under the law, that we might receive the adoption of sons" (v. 5). Paul is giving us a portrait of a young boy in a wealthy home. The boy is the legal heir and future master of the entire estate. As long as he is a child, his life is just like that of a slave. He is subject to guardians and trustees. They supervise him, discipline him, and control him. Their orders regulate and control his behavior. He is under their authority until the time set by his father, when he will be free from their control and enjoy his full rights as heir and master of the family estate.

The word that Paul used for adoption means to "place in the family as an adult son." It has to do with our standing in the family of God. We are members of God's family with all the privileges of sonship. He can draw upon His Father's wealth and can exercise all the wonderful privileges of sonship.

Paul has already used the image of a jailor (3:23) and a disciplinarian (vv. 24–25) to describe the supervisory function of the law. Then he uses another method. The Jewish Christians must have been astonished that their history under the Mosaic Law had been compared to being imprisoned by a jailor and controlled by a disciplinarian. Paul would not have accepted this before his conversion. The Jews had been redeemed from slavery in the Exodus. When God set them free, He called them His "son" (Exod. 4:23).

The giving of the law began with the announcement of freedom for God's people. "I am the LORD your God, who brought you out of Egypt, out of the land of slavery" (20:2, NIV). If God had redeemed them out of slavery, how could their whole existence under the Mosaic Law until Christ be defined in terms of slavery? The Gentiles had been told that only those who unite with the Jewish people under the law could participate in the freedom God gave his offspring. So Gentiles couldn't see them being slaves any more than the Jews could.

Even in the best of homes, sons who were loved by their fathers and destined to be heirs of his estate went through a period of supervision. It was appropriate for immature heirs to be subjected to the care of guardians. Obedience to the guardians was evidence of their love for their fathers. Once they had entered into the age of maturity, it would have been inappropriate for sons to be kept under the supervision of guardians. It was not a mark of disloyalty for sons to eagerly anticipate the day set by their fathers when they would no longer be subjected to guardians but would enjoy their full rights of sonship. When that day came, love for a father would find free expression from the heart of a mature son.

Even the Jewish people, the rightful heirs of God's promises to Abraham, experienced slavery for a period of time. "When we were children, we were in slavery under the basic principles of the world" (Gal. 4:3, NIV). Paul continues his series of images representing slavery under the law (NIV): "held prisoners by the law" (3:23); "under the supervision of the law" (3:25); "subject to guardians and trustees" (4:2). So the basic principles of the world were equivalent to the Mosaic Law. The Mosaic Law was given by God; it was not God's last and ultimate revelation. All that was necessary was its ABCs of God's revelation. It wasn't proper for an elementary student to be kept forever at the level of education that kept him in slavery.

In chapter 4:8–10 Paul viewed the Gentile Christians' attempt to observe the Mosaic Law as a return to slavery under the "weak and miserable principles" (v. 9, NIV). The pagan Gentiles were not enslaved by the Mosaic Law; Jews were not enslaved to pagan idolatry. Jews and Gentiles were enslaved to something less than the immediate knowledge of God enjoyed by Christians. Even the Jews were caught in the universal condition of slavery. They were in a common condition of helplessness; all alike are completely dependent on the liberating grace of God.

Slaves were set free to enjoy the full rights of sons only because God acted in history. "When the time had fully come, God sent his Son" (4:4, NIV). It was a time set by the Father (v. 2). There is a whole string of references to God's time schedule: "until the Seed" (3:19); "before this faith…up until faith" (v. 23); "Now that faith has come…we are no longer" (v. 25). When God sent His Son, the former period of universal slavery ended, and a new era of freedom had dawned. God's redemptive work must be understood in the framework of His actions in history. God gave a promise to Abraham, 430 years later God gave the law through Moses, and at a time God selected, He sent His Son. Through this framework in history we come to understand the redemptive plan of God.

The Galatian Christians were confused because they failed to understand the structure of the redemptive work of God. In their attempt to inherit the blessings promised to Abraham by keeping the Mosaic Law, they failed to understand that the Mosaic Law had been given 430 years after the Abrahamic promise and could not change the terms of the promise or a condition for inheriting the promised blessing (vv. 15–18). By them attempting to make progress in their spiritual lives by observing the law after believing the gospel, they failed to understand that the supervision of the law ended when faith in Christ came.

"God sent his Son, born of a woman, born under law, to redeem those under law" (Gal. 4:4–5, NIV). Here we have the essence of the gospel story: the incarnation and the birth of Christ, His perfect life of obedience under the law, and His redemptive death on the cross.

First of all, "God sent his Son" was a reference to the prophetic mission of Jesus. The prophets of old were sent by God. Jesus was sent by the Father for a special redemptive mission. The word *sent* means He was furnished with the credentials and power to represent the One that sent Him. He was given the power of attorney to use His name. It means that Jesus was there to transact business in the stead of the Father. He was there to carry out the work as if the Father was there to do it Himself. Before the incarnation, the preexistent Son was commissioned by God to set slaves free and make them children of God. Jesus told about the wicked tenants of the vineyard in a parable (Mark 12:1–12), where the owner of the vineyard (God) first sent messengers (prophets), who were killed by the tenants (Jewish leaders); then he sent his own son (Jesus), who was also killed.

When Paul talks about "born of a woman," he points to the incarnation and the full humanity of Jesus. The Son of God was sent to be one with us in our humanity. He was the God-man. He was God's Son, and He was the son of Mary. He was "born under the law," a Jew under the obligation to keep the requirements of the Mosaic Law. He was circumcised eight days after his birth. He celebrated the Passover just before His death. Every detail of Jesus' life was under the direction of the law. He was perfect in His obedience to the Father, He was born of a woman, and He fulfilled the requirements of the law. As God's Son, Jesus took our place to offer perfect obedience to God on our behalf.

He was "born under law" is also meant to experience the curse of the law against all who fail to observe all that the law requires. Although Jesus did fulfill all the requirements of the law, he still experienced all the conditions of sinful humanity under the curse of the law. He was subjected to temptations, suffering, loneliness, and on the cross, a God-forsaken death.

When Galatians says, "To redeem those under law, that we might receive the full rights of sons" (4:5, NIV), Paul gives a two-fold purpose of the Son's full participation in our humanity: His perfect fulfillment of the law and the curse of the law on our behalf. Christ is uniquely qualified to fulfill these two purposes. As the Son of God, He is able to give the position and rights of sonship to sinful people. Because of His incarnation He is able to represent and redeem all humankind. He rendered perfect obedience to God and bore the curse of God against the disobedient. He set us free from the obligation to keep the law and the curse of lawbreaking. Calvin said that when Jesus put the chains on Himself, He took them off the other; and when he took the obligation and curse of the law upon Himself, He set us free from both the obligation and curse of the law.[18]

In verse 5 we find two verbs, *redeem* and *receive*, which present both sides of our relationship with God. God has already acted in human history to set us free; for our lives to be changed we have to respond in faith. It is then that we receive the adoption of sons. Adoption of sons was defined by Roman law and widely practiced in Roman life. Several Roman emperors adopted men that were not related to them by blood in order to give them their office and authority. When a son is adopted, he is in all legal respects equal to those born into the family. He had the same name and the same inheritance, the same position and the same rights as natural born sons. God sent His Son, who was and is the Son of God, in order that we, who are not His children by nature, might be His children by adoption and receive the full rights of sonship. We have the same name, inheritance, position, and rights as the One who is Son of God by virtue of His divine nature.

Then there is a shift in Paul's image from a son who is treated like a slave until He reaches a certain age (vv. 1–2) to the picture of a slave who becomes a son of adoption (v. 5). The second picture focuses on the nature of sonship itself. We are adopted as God's children by the sending of the Son of God.

No matter how wealthy a father may be, the child could not enjoy his wealth. In the Roman world, the children of the wealthy were cared for by slaves. No matter how wealthy a father was, the child was still under the supervision of a servant. The servant was commanded by the master of the house, and the child was commanded by the servant.

This was the condition of the Jews under the law. The law was the guardian that disciplined the nation and prepared the people for the coming of Christ. When the Judaizers led the Galatians back into legalism, they were leading them back into religious bondage and spiritual infancy and immaturity. The Jews were like little children, in bondage to the elements of the world. The word *elements* means "basic principles," or what we would call the ABCs, so that they would be ready when Christ comes. Then they would get the revelation that He is the "Alpha and Omega…the first and the last" (Rev. 22:13) and He is everything in between that too. He is the climax of God's revelation to man (Heb. 1:1–3).

So legalism is not a step toward maturity; it is a step back into childhood. The law was not the final revelation to man; it was in preparation for that final revelation in Christ. Under the law, the Jews were children in bondage, not sons enjoying liberty.

The world was getting ready for the birth of a Savior. The Roman world at that time was in great expectation, waiting for a deliverer. Old religions were dying; philosophies were empty and powerless to change men's lives. New mystery religions were invading the empire. There was religious bankruptcy and spiritual hunger everywhere. Greek was the predominant language. God was preparing the world for the arrival of His Son.

The Roman Empire helped prepare the world for the birth of the Savior. A road system connected all cities with Rome. Roman law protected the rights of the individual, and Roman soldiers guarded the peace. Latin and Greek were known across the Empire. Christ's birth was not an accident; it was an appointment. Jesus came in the "fullness of time" (v. 4), and He will come again when the time is ready.

Paul portrays Christ as both God and man. As God, Jesus "came forth" (John 16:28). As man, He was "made of a woman" (Gal. 4:4). It was the promise of the coming Redeemer that He would be the "seed of a woman" (Gen. 3:15). Jesus fulfilled that promise. (See Isaiah 7:14 and Matthew. 1:18–25.)

So Paul has told us who came: Jesus Christ, God's Son. He told us when He came and how He came. Now he explains why He came: "to redeem them that were under the law" (Gal. 4:5). The word *redeem* means to "set free by the paying of a price." A man could purchase a slave in any Roman city. There were about 60 million slaves in the Empire. The owner could keep the slave for himself or set him free. Jesus came to set us free. So, to go back to the law is to undo the very work of Christ on the cross. He did not purchase us to make us slaves, but sons. Under the law, the Jews were nothing but children; but under grace, the believer is a son of God with an adult standing in God's family.

When we experience regeneration, which is the recreation of the new nature, we become a child of God. As a result, we enter into God's family. We are placed under guardians and we cannot come into our inheritance. Under grace, by adoption we become sons of God. We enjoy all the rights and privileges of the family. We know the liberty of an adult son and become an heir of the Father.

Then Paul describes the way that children experience their full rights: "Because you are sons, God sent the Spirit of his Son into our hearts" (4:6, NIV). There is a shift from the first person (we) to the second person (you), which shows that the adoption under the law was received by the Gentile converts. The confession of faith on the part of the Jew is not the confession of faith on the part of the Gentiles. Gentiles were not under the law the same way the Jews were. Paul's point is that the Gentiles were set free from the tyranny and curse of the law by the Father sending His only Son. By the Gentiles placing their faith in Christ, they have entered into a new relationship, which involves the full rights of sons and daughters of God. Now their lives are to be lived under Christ and not the law.

There is a parallel between God sending His Son and God sending the Spirit of His Son. By the act of God sending His only Son we became secure in our position in being sons and daughters of God. We receive the gift of adoption by faith. By God sending the Spirit of His Son into our hearts it enables us to enjoy a new relationship with God the Father. By us receiving the Spirit of adoption we have received the Spirit of God in our hearts and lives. You do not have to go through a series of steps, recite special prayers, or meet extra conditions. God sent the Spirit of His Son into our hearts because He adopted us into His family. Adoption and reception of the Spirit are two separate stages in the Christian life. The Spirit of His Son emphasizes the unity of the experience of adoption and the experience of the Spirit.

"God hath sent forth the Spirit of his Son into our hearts, crying, Abba, Father" (4:6). *Abba* is the Aramaic word for father. It was a word that was used by a child having intimate conversation with the father in the home. When a child addressed his father as Abba, he was expressing affection, confidence, and loyalty. Jesus addressed the Father as Abba in His prayers and encouraged and taught His disciples to do the same. Even in Greek-speaking churches the Aramaic word for Father was heard as believers called out to God in prayer. The Spirit of Jesus was assuring them within their hearts that they were the children of the Father.

To know that God is our Father is the result of God sending the Spirit of His Son to speak to us and to convince us that in spite of our fears, guilt, and doubts, the Father of Jesus is our Father too. To know God as our Father is being aware that our lives have been transformed as we enter into an intimate relationship with Him. The Spirit of God gives off an inward witness as we pray to God from our hearts.

When Jesus addressed His Father as Abba in the Garden of Gethsemane, He was expressing confidence, trust, and willing obedience. "Abba, Father… everything is possible for you. Take this cup from me. Yet not what I will, but what you will" (Mark 14:36). So if the Spirit of His Son is moving us to call God, Abba, then we will be expressing the same confident trust and willing obedience of the Son to the Father. All that Jesus said and did flowed out of His relationship with the Father. His sense of identity (who He was) was not based on His ministry (what he did), but He did what He did because He knew who He was. So the witness of the Spirit within us is that God is our Father and we are His children.

Jesus used Abba for the name of God the Father in His prayers. We can use the term Abba in our prayers because His Son gives us the right to do so. It is the activity of His Spirit within us who calls out, "Abba, Father." We call God Abba through the Son in the power of the Spirit.

Then Paul says, "So you are no longer a slave, but a son." (Gal. 4:7, NIV). The witness of the Spirit within us convinces us that we are the children of God. Sons and daughters are no longer held prisoners by the law (3:23). We are no longer under the supervision of the law (v. 25), and no longer subject to guardians and trustees (4:2). We have been freed from the control of the law. We are under the direction of the Spirit, and do not need the law to guide and discipline us. We are directed by the power of the Spirit.

There is a contrast here between a servant and a son. Like the prodigal son, the Galatians wanted the Father to accept them as servants when they were sons (Luke 15:18–19). The son has the same nature as the father, but the servant does not. The son has a father while the servant has a master. The son is rich while the servant is poor. The son has a future while the servant does not.

The promise of the Spirit is the promise of the inheritance. In Galatians 3:14 the blessing of Abraham came upon the Gentiles, and they received the promise of the Spirit. What greater inheritance could there be than the presence of the Spirit of God, the Spirit of His Son, within our hearts? The Spirit of His Son assures us that we are the children of the Father, and He also makes us like His Son. In Gethsemane when Jesus prayed "Abba, Father," He was expressing complete trust in his Father and expressing His willingness to endure the cross in obedience to the Father. He was looking ahead with confidence and obedient trust to both the cross and Resurrection.

When we are sure of our adoption by the witness of the Spirit within, we will be living in the power of the inheritance, who is making us less and less like this world and more and more like Jesus Christ. Everyday as we die to self, something of His cross will be seen in us. As the Spirit of Jesus lives His life through us, something of His resurrection will be seen in us. Then one day we will be like Him. Our greatest inheritance is not the abundance of things the Father gives us, but the character of His Son which the Spirit of His Son is forming within us.

In the Jewish world after a Jewish boy turned twelve, the first Sabbath following his birthday his father took him to the synagogue, where he became a son of the law. The father would utter a benediction, "Blessed be thou, O God, who has taken from me the responsibility for this boy." The boy prayed a prayer in which he said, "O my God and God of my fathers! On this solemn and sacred day, which marks my passage from boyhood to manhood, I humbly raise my eyes unto thee, and declare with sincerity and truth, that henceforth I will keep thy commandments, and undertake and bear the responsibility of my actions toward thee."[19]

Paul used the word *stoicheia*, which means the line of things that came to be known as the ABCs, and then any elementary knowledge of the law. Paul's world was haunted by the belief in astrology. If a man was born under a certain star, they believed that his fate was settled. Men lived under the tyranny of stars and longed for release.

Barclay stated that under Roman law a boy was an infant in the eyes of the law; he might be the owner of vast property but he could not make legal decisions. He was not in control of his own life. Everything was done for him. He had no more freedom than a slave, but when he entered into manhood, he entered into his full inheritance.[20] So Paul governed his life by the slavery of the law and was still a child. When he learned the way of grace, he became a mature man in the Christian faith. In our hearts we cry "Abba, Father!" so we know that we are sons, and all the inheritance in grace is ours.

When the Galatians were under the tyranny of the law, everything was ready. Christ came and released them from that tyranny. So now men are no longer slaves under the law; they have entered into their inheritance. The childhood that belonged to the law had passed; the freedom of manhood had begun.

For the Galatian Christians to live under the direction of the law was sheer folly. "You foolish Galatians!" (3:1, NIV), How did you receive your new nature to start with? Then Paul asked them, Can you add anything to your new nature? Paul admonished. You are sons and daughters not slaves. Why turn to the law for guidance when you have the direction of the Spirit? The tragedy was that believers who had entered into a love relationship with the Father by the operation of the Spirit were now acting like slaves. Garments in Scripture are descriptive of thinking, mentality and attitude. Sons can be indentified by dressing differently that slaves. While we profess to be sons we hold to the mentality of slaves. They were relating to God by attempting to keep the law rather than worshiping and serving Him in the power of the Spirit. It is like the elder brother in Luke 15:29; he served his father faithfully, yet he never called him father or related to him as a son. He thought and acted like a slave:

"All these years I've been slaving for you and never disobeyed your orders" (Luke 15:29, NIV).

The result of sonship is the inheritance: "Since you are a son, God has made you also an heir" (Gal. 4:7, NIV). The Galatian believers had been told that they were going to have to be related to the descendants of Abraham through observance of the law to inherit the promises made to Abraham. Paul demonstrated how through faith in Christ, we have been made children of God and also heirs of God.

Another gospel will bring us under bondage (Gal. 4:9). "But now, after that ye have known God, or rather are known of God, how turn ye again to the weak and beggarly elements, whereunto ye desire again to be in bondage?"

Why would the Galatians abandon their liberty for bondage? When they trusted Christ they were delivered from superstition and slavery. Now they were abandoning their liberty in Christ and going back into bondage. They were dropping out of the school of grace and enrolling in the kindergarten of the law. They were destroying the good work the Lord had done in them.

The phrase the "weak and beggarly elements" tells us they were giving up the power of the gospel for the weakness of the law, the wealth of the gospel for the poverty of the law. The law never made anybody rich or powerful; all it did was reveal man's weakness and spiritual bankruptcy. No wonder Paul was weeping over them.

Paul refers to elementary things that were based on law as weak and poverty stricken. It was weak because it was helpless. It can identify and define sin and convict a man of sin; but it made no provision for forgiveness, mercy, and pardon for past sin or strength to conquer future sin. It was poverty stricken in comparison to grace. The law could deal with only one situation at a time. Every situation required a new law. *Grace* here is translated from *poikilos*, which means "many colored or variegated." There is no situation in life that grace cannot match. It is sufficient for all things. That is why God told the Apostle Paul, "My grace is sufficient for thee, and my strength is made perfect in your weakness" (2 Cor. 12:9).

Another gospel will give us a religion of days, months, and years (Gal. 4:10). Evidently the Jewish calendar had been instituted in the Galatian churches, which emphasized the observance of special times. Sabbaths were each week, the months were the new moons; the seasons were the annual feasts like Passover, Pentecost, and Tabernacles. Years were sabbatical years. Days were divided into sacred and secular. The thought was when men observed the sacred days they were liable to think they had discharged or fulfilled their duty to God.

They were led to believe that if they observed these holy days and festivals that it would draw them closer to God. What foolishness! They had already received adoption as children of God. They were already praying Abba, Father in the Spirit. When people who are known by God and are known of Him start depending on their observance of holy days for their relationship with God, it is a return to the weak and beggarly elements that characterized their lives in paganism To make religion a thing of special days is to make it an external thing. For the real Christian everyday is God's day.

It was Paul's fear that men who had once known His grace would slip back into legalism. Those men who had once lived in the presence of God would confine Him to special days.[21]

Another gospel cannot give the new birth (Gal. 4:28–30). There is a physical birth that makes us sinners and a spiritual birth that makes us children of God. Isaac was born by God's power. God waited twenty-five years before He gave Abraham and Sarah a son. Isaac was "born after the spirit" (4:29). And the Christian is born of the Spirit (John 3:1–7). Isaac came into the world through Abraham (who represented faith). Sarah represented grace. So He was born by grace through faith as is true of every Christian. Isaac's name means "laughter," and he brought joy to his parents. He grew and was weaned. After we are born we must grow (1 Pet. 2:2; 2 Pet. 3:18). Along with maturity comes weaning, where we must lay aside childish things (1 Cor. 13:11). It is easier for us to hold on to our toys we played with in our spiritual childhood than to lay hold of the tools of a mature believer. A child never enjoys being weaned, but he can never become a man until it happens.

Isaac was persecuted (Gen. 21:9). Ishmael caused problems for Isaac just as our old nature causes problems for us. Ishmael represents the flesh. Ishmael created no problems in the house until Isaac was born, just as our old nature created no problems for us until the new nature entered into us. In Abraham's house we see the same problems and same basic conflicts as Christians face today.

You have Hagar (law) versus Sarah (grace)—law versus grace. Ishmael versus Isaac—flesh versus the Spirit. The Judaizers taught that the law made the believer more spiritual, but Paul said it only released opposition of the flesh. There was no law strong enough to change or to control Ishmael, but Isaac never needed any law.

By Paul using the illustration of the two wives (Hagar and Sarah), he is revealing the contrast between the law (flesh) and grace (by the Spirit). He proves that the believer is not under the law but is under the freedom that comes through God's grace. By using the example of Hagar he proves that the law no longer has power over the Christian.

Hagar was Abraham's second wife. Abraham did not start with Hagar but with Sarah. God began with grace. When Adam and Eve sinned in the garden, He provided them with coats of skins for a covering (Gen. 3:21). He gave them the promise of a victorious Redeemer (v. 15).

God's covenant with Abraham was one of grace, not law. When God delivered Israel from Egypt, it was on the basis of grace, not law. For the law had not yet been given. When it came to Hagar, the law was added (v. 19). Hagar had a temporary function, and then moved off the scene, just as the law performed a special function and then was taken away (Gal. 3:24–25).

Hagar was a slave. Five times in this section she is called a bondwoman. Sarah was a free woman, and her position was one of liberty. Hagar's position was one of a servant. The law was given as a servant. It served as a mirror to reveal man's sins (Rom. 3:20). It served as a school monitor to control men to lead them to Christ. The law was never meant to be a mother.

Hagar was never meant to bear a child. Abraham's relationship with Hagar was outside the will of God. It came about as a result of Abraham's and Sarah's unbelief and impatience. When Abraham got together with Hagar (slave), He gave birth to a legalist by the name of Ishmael.

Hagar was trying to do what only Sarah could do; it failed. Isaac was born as an heir to Abraham (Gen. 21:1), but Ishmael could not share in the inheritance. The Judaizers were trying to make Hagar mother again. Paul was in spiritual travail for his converts that they might become like Christ. No amount of religion or legalism can give the dead sinner life. Only Jesus can do that through the gospel.

It is impossible for law and grace, the flesh and the Spirit, to stay together without compromise. Hagar and Ishmael were not asked to make occasional visits to the home. The break was permanent. The Judaizers were trying to reconcile Sarah and Hagar and Isaac and Ishmael. This reconciliation is contrary to the Word of God. It is impossible to mix law and grace or faith and works, God's gift of righteousness with man's attempt to earn righteousness.

Hagar never married again. God never gave the law to any other nation or people, including His church. For Judaizers to impose the law upon the Galatian Christians was to oppose the very plan of God. In Paul's day the nation of Israel was under the bondage of the law, while the church was enjoying liberty under the gracious rule of Jerusalem which is from above (Gal. 4:26). The Judaizers wanted to wed Mt. Sinai and the heavenly Mt. Zion (Heb. 12:22), but to do this would be to deny what Jesus did on Mt. Calvary (Gal. 2:21). Hagar is not to be married again.

Abraham might have seemed cruel to send away Ishmael. It was the only solution to the problem. A wild man can never live with a child of promise. Think of what it cost God when He gave His Son to bear the curse of the law to set us free. Abraham's broken heart meant Isaac's liberty. God giving His only Son meant our liberty in Christ.

Another gospel will demand circumcision (Gal. 5:2–3). The Judaizers wanted the Galatians to believe that we are missing something, and that they would become more spiritual if they practiced the law with its demands of spiritual disciplines. The law comes in as a thief and robs the believer of the Spiritual riches he has in Christ. It puts him back into bankruptcy, responsible for a debt he is unable to pay.

Circumcision was an issue of covenant, purification, the cutting away and the removal of that which is unclean. It typified the Abrahamic covenant. At the time the Book of Galatians was written even though many of the Jews bore the physical mark of circumcision, it had almost lost its meaning. To impose circumcision upon the Galatians would have been to rob them of all the benefits they had received in Christ. To submit to this ordinance would put them under obligation to obey the whole law.

Another gospel, if the law was observed, cancels grace (Gal. 5:4). If you decide to live under the law, then you cannot live in the sphere of God's grace. The Galatians had been bewitched by false teachers (3:1) and had disobeyed the truth. They had been removed to another gospel (1:6–9) and had turned back to the elementary things of the old religion (4:9). They had become entangled with the yoke of bondage, and as a result they had "fallen from grace," and this robbed them of all the good things Jesus Christ could do for them.

The Jews believed that the law was the greatest thing in their national life.

God had given it to Moses, and the Jews' lives depended on it. But Abraham was the founder of their nation, and to him the greatest promise was given. Paul asked them how Abraham obtained favor with God. He did not gain it by the law. He lived 430 years before the law was given to Moses. Abraham gained it by an act of faith. It was faith that saved Abraham, not law. It is faith that must save every man. When God told him to get out of his father's house to a land that He would show him, as an act of faith Abraham left and trusted everything to God. The real son of Abraham makes the same surrender of faith to God.

While it is true that the law was given by God, its purpose was to tell man what sin is. The law made no provision for mercy, pardon, and forgiveness. "By the law is the knowledge of sin" (Rom. 3:20). If there is no law, a man cannot break it, and there can be no such thing as sin. The law drives a man to the grace of God. Man has to throw himself at the feet of the mercy and love of God. It teaches us that the only thing that can save us is the grace of God. Paul's central theme is the glory of God's grace and for us to realize that we cannot save ourselves.

Paul told the Church at Galatia, "But God forbid that I should glory, save in the cross of our Lord Jesus Christ, by whom the world is crucified unto me, and I unto the world" (Gal. 6:14). Paul said he was not going to boast in works, good deeds, or human accomplishments. Jesus Christ is mentioned forty-five times in the Book of Galatians. One third of the passages pertain to Him. The person of Jesus Christ captivated Paul. It was Christ who made the cross glorious to him. Legalists don't glory in the cross, because they do not glory in Christ. The false teachers were not ministering for the glory of Christ, but for their own glory. The Judaizers were not busy winning lost people to Christ. They were stealing other men's converts and bragging on their statistics. Paul experienced the power of the cross and went from being Saul of Tarsus to Paul the Apostle. The cross ceased to be a stumbling block to him and became the foundation stone of his message.

Liberty in Christ is a dominant theme of Galatians. The Judaizers presented another gospel that said you don't have to be saved by grace through faith; you still have to conform to the Law of Moses. They wanted to lead Christians out of liberty of grace and take them back into the bondage of the law.

The Galatian believers were ignoring the substitutionary character of the atoning death of Jesus Christ. They were falling back on works as the grounds of acceptance. The Lord Jesus took our place at Calvary and gave Himself as a sacrifice that would perfectly satisfy the demands of God's holy law, which the human race had violated. It was His death on the cross for our sins as He became our sin offering, the suffering Servant of Isaiah 53 that Paul had on his mind.

To Paul the cross meant liberty from self (Gal. 2:20), liberty from the flesh (5:24), and liberty from this world (6:14). So Paul knew the person of the cross, the power of the cross, and the purpose of the cross. The cross was a fence that separated me from this world and the world from me. My prayer is *Lord, hide me in the cross.*

Chapter 5

Christ Revealed in Paul

But when it pleased God, who separated me from my
mother's womb, and called me by his grace, To reveal his
Son in me, that I might preach him among the heathen;
immediately I conferred not with flesh and blood.

—GALATIANS 1:15–16

WE ARE ALL familiar with the story of the apostle Paul. Saul was breathing out threats and slaughter against the disciples of the Lord. He went to the High Priest and desired letters from him that if he found any Christians, he could bring them bound to Jerusalem. As he came near to Damascus there shined around about him a light from heaven. He heard a voice and saw no man. "And he fell to the earth, and heard a voice saying unto him, Saul, Saul, why persecutest thou me? And he said, Who art thou, Lord? And the Lord said, I am Jesus whom thou persecutest: it is hard for thee to kick against the pricks. And he trembling and astonished said, Lord, what wilt thou have me to do? And the Lord said unto him, Arise, and go into the city, and it shall be told thee what thou must do" (Acts 9:4–6). The Great Shepherd of our souls laid hold of the big bad wolf and arrested his heart on the Damascus Road.

We know that he spent three days in darkness. Ananias came to him to pray for him that he might receive His sight and be filled with the Holy Spirit. As he laid his hands on him, the scales fell from his eyes. After having been baptized in water, he became one of the mightiest of all Christian teachers.

What was it that changed Saul of Tarsus to Paul the Apostle? What changed him from being a follower of tradition to a servant of Jesus Christ? We know that "beyond measure [he] persecuted the church" (v. 13). We know that he advanced in Judaism and that he was zealous in the tradition of his fathers. Tradition played a powerful role in the life of a former Pharisee who was now teaching the Christian tradition. Whenever Paul spoke of his conversion, it always was with the emphasis that it was God who did the work.

There was no doubt at this time that Paul was under attack. His opponents were saying that his message was one of human origin. They were saying that the message that Paul preached was not the same one that was being preached by the apostles at Jerusalem. Before Paul's conversion his life was dedicated to destroying the message he was now preaching. He was advanced in Judaism; he was now persecuting the church of God beyond measure and was trying to destroy it. He even held the clothes of them that stoned Stephen. He was very zealous in his attempt to destroy the church (Gal. 1:13–14).

Wherever Paul went, the false teachers dogged his every move. No sooner than he would plant a new church the false teachers began to trouble the church by perverting it. They not only discredited his message but also challenged his authority.

Once we have come to believe and obey the gospel, we should never allow anyone to cause us to compromise or back off from what we have believed. We should allow no one to cause us to pervert the gospel of Christ. If we have been called to preach this glorious gospel, we should be able to declare that our message has come from Jesus Christ through the writings of the New Testament. I should be ready at all times to give a defense for what I believe. We need to be ready to take the charges off what we believe.

How is Paul going to prove to the Galatians that the revelation he is now bringing is a direct revelation from God? His conversion was an act of God. God had called him by His grace. Paul declared to King Agrippa that "he had not been disobedient to the heavenly vision" (Acts 26:19).

It was God "who separated me from my mother's womb, and called me by his grace" (v. 15). The word *separated* comes from the word *aphorize*, which means "mark off from a boundary line."[1] The simple verb is *horizon*, which means "to place limitation upon, to fix limits around." The noun *horos* speaks of a "boundary, limit, or frontier."[2] Pharisees were separatists who held themselves off from others. Paul considered himself to be a spiritual Pharisee who was separated to the gospel of God. "Paul, a servant of Jesus Christ, called to be an apostle, separated unto the gospel of God" (Rom. 1:1). It was like a physical separation of a child from his mother's womb. Paul was devoted to a special purpose from before his birth. The preposition that was used revealed a starting point. Paul is stating that he was set apart and devoted by God to be an apostle before He was born. Being a separate person means being with God, for God, and near God. It means living in faith and obedience for His glory and the manifestation of His Son.

Each believer has been set apart by God's grace in order that God might reveal His Son in them. It was Christ's death that transferred us from Satan's power to God. "Who hath delivered us from the power of darkness, and hath translated us into the kingdom of his dear Son" (Col. 1:13). We have been separated from sin and from this present evil world. "Who gave himself for our sins, that he might deliver us from this present evil world, according to the will of God and our Father" (Gal. 1:4). The word *deliver* comes from the word *exaireo* which means "to pluck out, to draw out, to rescue, to deliver."[3] The gospel has rescued us from a state of bondage. It denotes not only a removal from but also that we have been rescued from the characteristics of this present evil age. Paul is talking about things that now exist in this age, not things that are to come in the future.

What did Paul mean by evil age? The word evil comes from the word *poneros* which means "evil, active opposition against the good." The world is not content to know that it is going down alone; it wants to pull the child of God down right along with it.[4] So the death of Christ has to do with more than just the forgiveness of our sins but also deliverance from this present evil world. The believer has been delivered from the evil that dominates the societies of this world. John saw the whole world lying in the grip of the wicked one. "And we know that we are of God, and the whole world lieth in wickedness" (1 John 5:19). Because the whole world lies in the grip or control of the wicked one, we are going to have to make a clean break from this world.

Satan controls this world with his host. Paul said to the church at Ephesus, "For we wrestle not against flesh and blood, but against principalities, against powers, against the rulers of the darkness of this world, against spiritual wickedness in high places" (Eph. 6:12). If you will notice that four different times Paul used the word *against*, which comes from the word *pros* which means "an eyeball to eyeball, forehead to forehead confrontation."[5] Our battle is not with one another, but with:

1. Principalities—*archas*: chief rulers in the system of Satan

2. Powers—*exousia*: spirits that have been deputized to carry out the will of the chief rulers

3. Rulers of the darkness of this world—*pneumatica ponerios*: demonic spirits that are placed in rank and file that are committed, organized, and disciplined and set against our lives. Satan's kingdom has organization, commitment, and discipline. (How can the church move in an awesome display of God's power when Satan's kingdom possesses things that we don't?)

4. Spiritual wickedness in high places—a host of demonic spirits in the heavenlies. Satan has organized the world into a political, cultural, economic, and religious system that is hostile toward God and His people.

The world refuses to submit to God's truth which exposes wrongdoing. Believers stand against a satanic world system. Jesus interpreted the cross as both the beginning of the end of Satan's dominion and also the beginning of His triumph over the hearts of men. Ever since the death, burial, and resurrection of Christ, the kingdom of the devil has begun to fall apart. The cross is a magnet that draws people to Christ. The cross attracts more people to Christ than the exemplary life that Jesus lived. While living in this world, the believer enjoys the powers of the age to come. This is the victory of the cross.

The world and the church are two different groups of people. The world is energized by Satan who is the prince and power of the air. The church belongs to God and is energized by the Holy Spirit to bring glory to God in the earth. While we live in this world we are "strangers and pilgrims on the earth" (Heb. 11:13). We are strangers in the fact that this world is not our home, but pilgrims in the fact that we know where we are headed.

We are told by the apostle Paul in Romans, "be not conformed to this world" (Rom. 12:2). The word *conformed* refers to "the act of an individual assuming an outward expression that does not come from within, nor is it a true representation of his inner heart and life." The verb is in the present imperative. Paul is forbidding the continuance of an action that is going on. We are to stop allowing this world to control the way we think. It was a command to cease from doing something that was already in process in the church and Paul said, "Stop it!"[6] Here Paul commands us to stop allowing the world to squeeze us into its mold. We are not to adopt the form, fashion, or dress of this world, and we are not to allow our appearance to nullify our profession. Many times we put on a mask and a costume that hides the Lord Jesus living in our hearts.

The first gospel message that was preached after the Pentecostal outpouring of the Holy Spirit contained these words: "Save yourselves from this untoward generation" (Acts 2:40). Peter kept on exhorting his Jewish audience to save themselves from this "untoward generation." The word *untoward* is the opposite of being straight. This was a generation that was turning away from the truth. The apostles looked upon the nation of Israel as a crooked generation that was under condemnation. The nation had only about forty years left before Rome would come and destroy their temple and scatter the people. It seemed that history was repeating itself. During the forty-year wilderness journey, the new generation saved itself from the older generation that rebelled against God.

Paul said in writing to the Church at Rome, "I am not ashamed of the gospel of Christ: for it is the power of God unto salvation" (Rom. 1:16). Before Paul's birth God had plans for him and called him by his grace. Paul's experience reminds us of young Jeremiah. "Before I formed thee in the belly I knew thee; and before thou camest forth out of the womb I sanctified thee, and I ordained thee a prophet unto the nations" (Jer. 1:5). Then there was John the Baptist, who was filled with the Holy Ghost from his mother's womb. The idea of a child's destiny being fixed by God before birth was beautifully illustrated by Samson (Judg. 16:17). Salvation is by God's grace through faith, not through man's efforts. Grace and called go together. Whoever God chooses through His grace He calls through His Word.

Paul was called by God to reveal His Son to the Gentiles. And after obeying the gospel, he "spent some days with the disciples who were at Damascus and immediately he preached Christ in the synagogues, that He is the Son of God." (Acts 9:19-20). Paul said, "To reveal his Son in me" (Gal. 1:16). The word *reveal* comes from the Greek *apokalupto* which means to disclose something by removing that which conceals it.[7] The Lord Jesus had been hidden from him in times past, but now God had revealed the Lord Jesus Christ to Paul: *en emoi* which means "to me and through me." Paul in writing to the church at Ephesus said, "to me, who am less than the least of all the saints, this grace was given, that I should preach among the Gentiles the unsearchable riches of Christ" (Eph. 3:8).

Paul was preaching a message that came to him by revelation of Jesus Christ. To obtain this revelation he did not consult with men. He believed it, preached it, and practiced the gospel of Christ that came to him by revelation. The gospel he preached along with his missionary journeys found their source and origin in God. The first years of His labor were proof of that very thing.

What came to Paul as a revelation of Christ became a revelation of Christ in Paul as the Spirit produced His fruit in the soil of Paul's heart. The purpose of that revelation was the unveiling of Christ. God revealed Christ to Paul, in Paul, and through Paul. His faith in Christ brought an inward experience of reality with the Lord. God called Paul so that He could reveal the Lord Jesus to the world through him. God revealed the Lord Jesus Christ to Paul and through him to a world that was lost. Paul here is making the distinction between the call and the revelation. The revelation was an inward one that was apprehended by his senses given to Paul on the Damascus Road.

We are to live in fellowship with God and be a witness of Jesus Christ before a world that is lost. It is the work of the Holy Spirit to make us more and more like Jesus Christ. "They took knowledge of them, that they had been with Jesus" (Acts 4:13). Only the Holy Spirit of God can produce the beauty Jesus Christ in the heart and life of the believer.

Paul goes on to say "that I might preach him among the heathen; immediately I conferred not with flesh and blood" (Gal. 1:16). Paul did not make a trip to Jerusalem to visit the apostles to check in with them about what to preach. In fact, he did not consult with any man. Instead, he went to Arabia, then he returned to Damascus. The Jews believed that Gentiles were dogs. Paul's calling was to the Gentiles. The Galatians were not only his spiritual children, they were the fruits and the seal of Paul's apostleship. Paul's apostleship was to those who were not descendants of Abraham, Isaac, and Jacob. Paul preached to the Gentiles the "unsearchable riches of Christ" (Eph. 3:8). God chose Paul not only to save him, but to use him to win others. Election is not only a privilege, it is also a responsibility. God chose Paul to preach among the Gentiles the same grace that he had experienced. This was evidence that Paul's conversion was of God. A prejudiced Jewish rabbi would never decide to minister to a despised Gentile.

Paul was not dependent on men for His commission, nor was he subject to their control. After Paul's Damascus Road experience, he went to Arabia. He spent three years in Arabia (Gal. 1:17). He did not consult with anyone to learn their opinion or to obtain instruction from them. Pagans used this term to consult with soothsayers. Paul was saying his commission came from

God and was not affected in any way by human intervention. He did not ask anyone for guidance or advice.

We know that after three years he went up to Jerusalem to see Peter and remained with him for fifteen days (v. 18). He saw James on the trip but no one else. After this he went to the regions of Syria and Cilicia. He was unknown to the faces of the churches of Judea. They had heard about him but had never personally met him. They knew that he had formerly persecuted them, but now he preaches a faith that he once tried to destroy.

It seems like the right thing for Paul to have done after his conversion on the Damascus Road would be to go and introduce himself to the church at Jerusalem. But, if he had gone to Jerusalem, his ministry might have been identified with that of the apostles to the Jews. This could have been a hindrance to his work among the Gentiles.

Chapter 6

Judaizers

*From henceforth let no man trouble me: for I bear
in my body the marks of the Lord Jesus.*
—GALATIANS 6:17

THIS LETTER CONTRASTS the Judaizers, who were motivated by pride and a desire to escape persecution, and Paul, who suffered for the true gospel and boasted only in Jesus Christ. What a rebuke! Paul was telling them that if your religious celebrities have any scars to show for the glory of Christ then let them be shown. Otherwise they should stop bothering him.

The time has come that we need to beware of religious celebrities who still live in the ivory tower and know nothing of the battlefield of this world, the flesh, and the devil. They have no marks to show for their obedience to Christ. Paul was out on the front lines waging war against sin and holding up the bloodstained banner of Jesus Christ, taking his share of suffering.

Judaizers were identified by the false gospel they preached. The test of a man's ministry is not his popularity, miracles, or signs and wonders (Matt. 24:23–24), but by his faithfulness to God's Word. We are not to encourage those who bring a false doctrine (Matt. 24:11). Christ had committed this gospel to Paul (1 Cor. 15:1–8); and he in turn committed it to faithful men.

The gospel teaches that all we need to be saved was done by Christ on the cross. The Judaizers believed they must be circumcised and observe dietary laws. This type of thinking destroys the gospel. It is another gospel, but really no gospel at all. It makes salvation more a work of self-effort than a work of a sovereign God.

Barclay stated that the Jews who had accepted Christianity believed that all God's promises and gifts were only for the Jews. They believed that no Gentile could be admitted into those privileges. If Christianity was God's greatest gift to men, how come the Jews were the only ones to enjoy it? There was one type of a Jew that believed that the Jews were His chosen people. How could they say that God loved only Israel? They believed that God would judge Israel in one measure and have another measuring stick to judge the Gentiles.[1]

They believed the best of snakes crushed was the best of Gentiles killed. They believed that God created the Gentiles to be fuel for the fires of hell. They believed that it was illegal to help a Gentile mother in her sorest hour, because she was bringing another Gentile into the world. When the Jews saw Paul bringing the gospel to the despised Gentiles, they were appalled and infuriated.

They believed that if a Gentile wished to become a Christian, he had to become a Jew first. They believed that anyone had to be obedient to the law to be saved. For Gentiles to be saved, they had to be circumcised and take the whole burden of the law upon them. There was a big battle in the early church over what one needed to do to be a Christian. To Paul that was opposite of all that Christianity meant to say that man's salvation was dependent on his ability to keep the law and could be achieved by his own efforts. To Paul salvation was by grace.

Paul presents three men in this sixth chapter who were marked: the legalist (vv. 12–13), the Lord Jesus Christ (vv. 14–16), and Paul himself (vv. 17–18).

"From henceforth let no man trouble me" (v. 17). Paul used the Greek phrase *kopous parecheto* which means "let no man trouble, annoy or bother me." Paul used this phrase in a good sense. In all of Paul's Epistles he used this phrase to describe the toil that was characteristic of and inseparable from the life of a true pastor. Paul never asked to be freed from hard work. He endured it gladly for the Galatian church. His one fear was that it might have been all in vain. Paul wanted to avoid the endless harassment of the Judaizers and their endless insistence on stigmata, which were signs that were borne externally upon their flesh. To end this persecution, he would show them that he too bore a distinguishing mark, showing that he belonged to Christ.

There was a time that Paul was proud of his mark of circumcision: "Though I might also have confidence in the flesh. If any other man thinketh that he hath whereof he might trust in the flesh, I more: Circumcised the eighth day, of the stock of Israel, of the tribe of Benjamin, an Hebrew of the Hebrews; as touching the law, a Pharisee; Concerning zeal, persecuting the church; touching the righteousness which is in the law, blameless" (Phil. 3:4–6). He was born into a pure Hebrew family and entered into a covenant relationship when he was circumcised. He was of the tribe of Benjamin. Benjamin and Joseph were two of Jacob's favorite sons. Israel's first king was of the tribe of Benjamin. He was a Pharisee of the Pharisees and possibly a member of the Sanhedrin. Paul had every advantage given to him to go somewhere in the Jewish community.

Paul was circumcised on the eighth day. Perry Stone, in his book entitled *"Breaking the Jewish Code,"* stated that circumcision was done for several reasons: First, according to Jewish tradition, the first seven days of a child's life represented the finished creation of the physical world. We must remember that God worked six days to create the heavens and the earth, and on the seventh day He rested. Second, the number eight in biblical numerology represented new beginnings. When a child became circumcised, he became initiated into the Abrahamic covenant. Third, the child, by waiting until the eighth day, will experience one Sabbath day. Fourth, on the eighth day an infant baby had more prothrombin than on any other day. God knew the medical and physical significance of being circumcised on the eighth day.[2]

After Paul became a believer, he was marked in a different way. He now gloried in the scars he received and in the sufferings he endured in the service of Jesus Christ. Dr. H. L. Willmington, in his book *Willmington's Guide to the Bible,* gives unto us the duties of a believer: 1) He is to love his neighbor as himself (5:14–15). 2) He is to be led by the Spirit (5:18, 25). 3) He is to be crucified with Christ (5:24). 4) He is to avoid boasting or being full of envy (5:26). 5) A believer is to be in the ministry of restoration toward those who have fallen in sin (6:1). 6) Bear one another's burdens (6:2). 7) Avoid deception (6:13.) 8) Bear his own burden (6:5). 9) He is to prove himself (6:4.) 10) He is to financially support those who have deposited the Word of God into their lives (6:6). 11) He is to sow the right habits in his life (6:8). 12) He is not to be weary in well doing (6:9). 13) He is to do good to all (6:10).[3]

Many of the people that Paul was writing to in the Book of Galatians were involved in agriculture. Paul used many metaphors that they would understand because of their background. These metaphors included fruit bearing, burden bearing, seed bearing and brand bearing. Many who were involved in agricultural labor were slaves. They were branded to indicate whose property they were.

The legalists were plain to see. The Judaizers wanted to mark their flesh and brag about them being their trophies. Paul was saying, "I bear in my body the brands of the Lord Jesus Christ for His glory." While others may glory in circumcision, rituals, and a great show of converts to an easy religion, Paul was saying, "I will glory in the cross of Jesus Christ" (Gal. 6:14). Those other things are empty, worthless, and crucified by the cross. It is all about being a new creation in Christ Jesus. The cross had the power to make a believing Jew and a believing Gentile a new creation that resulted in a radical transformation of character.

"I bear in my body the marks of the Lord Jesus" (v. 17). Paul used the Greek word *bastazo* in this Epistle, which means to "shoulder or to carry an object that is bulky and heavy; to bear what is burdensome." Whatever the marks of Christ, they are not borne easily. Paul bore them bodily and outwardly. Those marks involved the following:

Fruit Bearing: "The fruit of the Spirit is love, joy, peace, longsuffering" (5:22). Fruit does not grow on the inside of the tree but on the outside for all to see. This is a good lesson for those who only believe that holiness is internal instead of being external. Fruit is to be produced from the inside out.

Burden Bearing: "Bear ye one another's burdens" (6:2). We are to bear the burdens of a people before the presence of God. We are here reminded of the high priest who bore the names of the tribes of Israel on his shoulders, as he bore their burdens before the presence of God.

Seed Bearing: "Whatsoever man soweth, that shall he also reap" (6:7). We determine our harvest. The only influence we have over our tomorrows are the seeds that we sow today. If you don't like your harvest, you are the only one that is to blame, because you are the one that sowed. Too many want a righteous harvest without sowing righteous seed.

Brand Bearing: "I bear in my body the marks of the Lord Jesus" (6:17). The word *marks* comes from the Greek *stigmata*, which signified the marks or brands that distinguished a slave as belonging to a master. Many times these brands announced runaway slaves. The Jews had a practice of earmarking willing slaves who bore the names of their master. Slaves in pagan temples were attached for life to the service of that temple and were branded with the name of their deity, which they were pledged to serve.

The marks that appeared on Christ's hands, feet, and side corresponded to the wounds of Christ. So close was his identification with the Lord, Paul claimed that he bore five wounds of Calvary on His body. He was affirming that he had suffered for Christ's sake. Paul's body was marked by assaults he endured for the cause of Christ. This was something the legalist never did. Paul had on his body the scars to prove it.

Those brands were on the outside, visible, and came as a result of suffering for the cause of Christ. Through him being stoned, flogged, beaten in the synagogue and by Roman throngs, these would leave unmistakable scars of suffering that he gladly endured for the cause of Christ. He was marked as Christ's man. Let us not forget when he said:

> Are they ministers of Christ? (I speak as a fool) I am more; in labours more abundant, in stripes above measure, in prisons more frequent, in deaths oft. Of the Jews five times received I forty stripes save one. Thrice was I beaten with rods, once was I stoned.
> —2 CORINTHIANS 11:23–25

Let us not forget that Paul was a Roman citizen and under Roman law, yet five times He received forty stripes save one. Each time he was beaten, thirty-nine stripes were placed on his body. Three different times the Roman soldiers broke the balls of his feet, and Luke the physician had to put his feet back together so Paul could learn how to walk again.[4] We know that he was stoned in Lystra and left for dead. He had an out-of-body experience and went up into the third heaven and walked with God in His walled garden in intimacy and fellowship, came back to His body, and got up and went right back into the city that stoned him and continued proclaiming the gospel of God

In Paul's day it was not uncommon for a follower of some heathen god or goddess to be branded with a mark of an idol. He was proud of his god and wanted others to know it. It was a practice in that day to brand slaves so they would know who their owner was. Paul was a bond slave to Jesus Christ and he wore the marks to prove it. A bond slave is one whose will is lost in another.

Sin can brand an individual. Sin can mark your mind, personality, and even your body. Very few people are proud of their sin and the marks they bear. Not even conversion can change those marks. The Christian leader who has suffered for the cause of Christ has something to offer—the greater the suffering the greater the ministry. The Judaizers in Paul's day knew nothing of suffering.

Galatians contains a character sketch of the Jewish believers who opposed

Paul in Galatia, Antioch, Jerusalem, and throughout most of the places he ministered.

Paul characterized the Judaizers as troublers and distorters (Gal. 1:7). The word *trouble* comes from the Greek *tarasso* which means "to disturb mentally with excitement, perplexity, and fear." The present tense was used here, which indicates they were still in Galatia at the time of Paul's writing.[4] Paul wrote to them to combat their efforts to bewitch the Galatian believers. Paul treated them with great contempt.

The word *trouble* describes the feelings of the disciples in a ship tossed at sea during a storm (Matt. 14:26). It also describes the feelings of King Herod when he heard that a new king had been born (2:3).

"A perverted gospel works the greatest havoc among young converts. They are assailed before they reach the stage of matured stability. Their half-formed conceptions of truth are confused. The spirit that aims at polluting a young beginner in the way of righteousness is worse than reckless; it is diabolical."[5]

Paul saw the Judaizers as a group that would hinder people in their spiritual growth. He said, "Ye did run well; who did hinder you that ye should not obey the truth?" (Gal. 5:7). The Galatians embraced the truth that came from Paul's lips. They eagerly embraced it, and it changed their lives. Paul was delighted with the results, and he commended their Christian enthusiasm. They were doing fine and making progress in their Christian walk and maturity. Their progress became arrested and their faith was disturbed. They wavered in their allegiance. They were in danger of losing all of the advantages they had gained.

The word *hinder* comes from the Greek *enkopta*, which means "to cut in, make an incision."[6] Paul is using the metaphor of an athlete running the race. The word suggests breaking into to the racecourse, cutting in to another runner's lane, and attempting to slow up his progress. They were trying to trip them up and turn them around.

The Galatian Christians had been running the race well, and the Judaizers were cutting in on their lane and were slowing up their progress in growth and maturity in the Christian life. They were depriving the Galatians of the ministry of the Holy Spirit. They were returning to a flesh attempt to obey the law. They had lost the fragrance of the Lord Jesus Christ and the enabling grace that had formerly enabled them to serve God.

The Judaizers were also individuals who sought to make a good impression outwardly to avoid persecution because of the offense of the cross of Christ (6:12). Many of the Jewish brethren had rejected Jesus as the Messiah and the Lamb of God who took away the sins of the world. They did not believe in grace but works as a means of salvation. To keep from experiencing persecution they embraced salvation through faith in the cross of Christ, while imposing circumcision and the Law of Moses on the Church.[7]

The cross had put an end to the Mosaic Law. Anyone who accepted the law rejected the cross. The Judaizers wished to remain in the good graces of the Jewish community, while attempting to escape persecution. Paul knew that they could not straddle the fence.

Paul described the Judaizers as people pleasers. "For do I now persuade men, or God? or do I seek to please men? for if I yet pleased men, I should not be the servant of Christ" (1:10).

The word *persuade* means to "win over, to render friendly to one's self." His enemies had accused him of sacrificing the truth of God for the sake of winning men's favor. Paul's enemies were accusing him of being a compromiser and adjusting the gospel to fit the Gentiles. They placed a twist on Paul's statement when he said, "I am made all things to all men, that I might by all means save some" (1 Cor. 9:22). They said when Paul was with the Jews, he lived like the Jews, but when he was with the Gentiles, he lived like the Gentiles. They said he was a man pleaser and could not be trusted. They said Paul observed the law among the Jews, and yet he persuaded the Gentiles to renounce it. They said Paul became all things to all men that he might form a party of his own.

It seemed as though the Judaizers had just as much influence over them as someone who offered candy to children. The Judaizers were paying the Galatian believers special attention, but they were not sincere (Gal. 4:17). They were attempting to cut the Galatian believers allegiance away from Paul, so they would continue to give them an open ear into their lives. The Judaizers were great persuaders. They had a sales talk that convinced the Galatians that they needed to step out of the light and go back to the shadows of the law. The Judaizers campaigned for the devotion of the Galatian Christians.

Paul preached a gospel that humbled men; it was one that demanded repentance and reform.

In three other passages Paul used "men pleasers":

"But as we were allowed of God to be put in trust with the gospel, even so we speak; not as pleasing men, but God, which trieth our hearts" (1 Thess. 2:4).

"Servants, obey in all things your masters according to the flesh; not with eyeservice, as menpleasers; but in singleness of heart, fearing God" (Col. 3:22).

"Not with eyeservice, as menpleasers; but as the servants of Christ, doing the will of God from the heart" (Eph. 6:6).

Paul called the Judaizers false brethren. "And that because of false brethren unawares brought in, who came in privily to spy out our liberty which we have in Christ Jesus, that they might bring us into bondage" (Gal. 2:4). Paul and Barnabas had maintained that the Gentile converts were not to be circumcised. The false brethren demanded that they should be circumcised. The false brethren were Judaizers who were secretly brought into the Jerusalem council. They slipped in unwanted. Their purpose was to bring both Jew and Gentile under the law. Why could they not come in the front door? They were sneaked into the back door.[8] Jude spoke of those who "crept in unawares." (Jude 4). Literally they wormed their way in. The Galatian Christians knew who they were.

They were hypocrites in the fact that they wanted them to submit to the law, but they themselves did not obey the law. Jesus said, "They say, and do not" (Matt. 23:3). Their reverence and respect for the law was only a mask to cover up their real goal and intention. In their attempt to win more converts to their cause, they wanted to report more statistics so they could get more glory.

The Judaizers were a party of the circumcised (Gal. 2:12).

Judaizers were manipulators (3:1). The false teachers had bewitched them and turned them into fools.

Judaizers were braggarts (6:12–13). Their main purpose was not to win people to Christ. Neither did they desire to help people grow in grace. They desired to steal other people's converts and then brag over their statistics. Their work was not done for the good of the church nor for the glory of God; it was done for their own glory.

Judaism had been the cradle of Christianity, but it almost became its grave as well. The Judaizers came along and said that it was not enough for them to be saved by grace through faith; they still had to conform to the Law of

Moses. The Judaizers used every possible means to capture the church into legalistic bondage.

The Judaizers were legalistic teachers who came to Antioch and taught the Gentiles had to be circumcised and obey the Law of Moses. They were associated with the Jerusalem congregation but not authorized by it (Acts 15:24). They were identified with the Pharisees (v. 5). These teachers were false brethren who wanted to rob both Jewish and Gentile believers of their liberty in Christ (Gal. 2:1–10; 5:1).

The Judaizers had bewitched the Galatians and caused them to abandon the Holy Spirit and the grace of God and place themselves back under the sphere of the law. There is no provision in the Mosaic economy for the indwelling Spirit to sanctify the believer as the believer trusts Him for that work.

The Judaizers said that it was not enough to be saved by grace through faith, that in order for us to be saved and mature in the Christian life, we had to conform to the Law of Moses.

Note what these legalists were trying to do:

- Attempting to mix law and grace and to pour new wine into ancient, brittle wineskins (Luke 5:36–39). When wineskins won't stretch, they resist change and cannot handle the process of fermentation.
- Attempting to stitch up the veil (23:45) and block the new and living way to God that Jesus opened up through His death on the cross (Heb. 10:10–25). When Jesus died at the cross, the veil in the temple was rent from top to bottom, making access for the common man to come into the presence of God.
- Attempting to rebuild the wall between the Jew and Gentile that Jesus tore down on the cross (Eph. 2:14–16).
- Attempting to put the Jewish yoke on Gentile shoulders, one that the Jews themselves were not willing to bear (Gal. 5:1; Acts 15:10).
- Asking the church to move out of the sunlight back into the shadows (Heb. 10:1; Col. 2:16–17).
- Asking that a Gentile must first become a Jew in order to become a Christian. It was not sufficient for them simply to trust Christ; they must obey Moses.[9]

Every system of religion (occult, cults) except the Bible bases salvation on works of the worshiper. In a pagan culture, acceptance from a deity is by the good works of an individual. Judaizers were part of this present evil age. They were not content to drag themselves down, but they wanted to pull down the Christian church with them. Paul says the substitutionary death of the Lord Jesus is what would rescue poor sinners from the clutches and teaching of the Judaizers. Their system was not content just to bring themselves down but to pull the Galatian believers down right along with them.

Chapter 7

Foolishness of the Galatians

*Are ye so foolish? having begun in the Spirit,
are ye now made perfect by the flesh?*
—GALATIANS 3:3

HAPTERS 3 AND 4 are made up of fifty verses and are some of the strongest verses that Paul ever penned with his own hand. Paul, being a freedom fighter, was in a battle for the freedom of the church. God had once again raised up a Moses by the name of Paul to deliver the church from the bondage of legalism. As God raise up Moses in the house of Pharaoh to deliver Israel from 438 years of Egyptian bondage (remember Pharaoh paid for Moses' education), He raised up the Apostle Paul in the church at Galatia to break the back of legalistic bondage.

Paul accused the Galatians of being foolish when he said, "O foolish Galatians" (3:1). What he was actually saying to them was, "You foolish country bumpkins." It was a spirit of stupidity and spiritual dullness that arises from the deadness and impotence of one's intellect. They lacked the power of perception and failed to use it.[1] Paul was telling the Galatians, "You guys are not using your heads." When Christians embrace false doctrine, it is due to sin in their lives. Paul was saying, "You stupid Galatians, who has hoodwinked you?" They had become blockheads because they did not look at their own experience and they did not examine their own Scriptures. Jesus said, "Ye do err, not knowing the Scriptures nor the power of God" (Matt. 22:29). That is why men and women are going astray and wandering off. It is because they don't know the Scriptures or the power of God.

The word that Paul used for foolish describes a person who acts without thinking or reasoning, and one that does not use his mind. It does not mean that he doesn't have a mind; he just refuses to use it. It speaks of a people that are mentally impotent by choice. Paul is saying, "How foolish to think that you can bring yourselves into a state of spiritual maturity in your Christian life through self-effort alone." This is the work of the Spirit and only He can do that. There was a false sense of spirituality that told them that it was carnal and unspiritual for them to use their minds. They fell into legalism because they divorced their brains from their spirituality. Paul is going to take two chapters and use his brain to rethink for them. Many follow their emotions instead of their intellect.

It needs to be understood that the Christian life is not a feeling. It is an intellectual decision to understand the person and work of Jesus Christ. Yes, the feelings will come. So many people who have made a profession of faith in Christ as Lord and Savior have gotten sidetracked into legalism because they fail to use their brains to examine the Scripture, to think things through. As a boat needs an anchor, the Christian needs the Word of God. If we are allowed to drift with the current we will never make it back to the stream. They will listen to people who are being used by Satan, the archrival of our souls, to play on our emotions.

Because they had experienced the Trinity, their experience should tell them some things: 1) look at your experience with Christ (v. 1), 2) look at your experience with the Holy Spirit (vv. 2–4), 3) look at your experience with God (v. 5). All the experiences they had with the members of the God head should tell them once and for all that they did not need legalism.

Why did Paul call for a biblically renewed mind when he said, "Be renewed in the Spirit of your mind" (Eph. 4:23)? The word *renewed* comes from the word *kainos,* which speaks of new in reference to quality, the fresh, the unworn.[2] The minds of men are made blind because they reject God (Rom. 1:21). When a man believes, God gives back his moral vision. When one experiences progressive sanctification he is given fresh insight. This is a restoration of vision that gradually changes the whole man. You are renewed by what you know. You are transformed by what you know (Rom. 12:2). When you put on the new man that is after God, in righteousness and true holiness, you are renewed in knowledge (Col. 3:10). If there is no renewing of the mind by the Spirit and by the Word, then there will be no discernment. We will not know what is right from wrong or what is good from evil. Then he called for a transformed mind when he said to the church at Rome, "Be transformed by the renewing of your mind, that you might prove what is that good and perfect and acceptable will of God" (Rom. 12:2–3). The word *prove* involves an intellectual process. If you want to be transformed through the renewing of your mind, it is not going to be an emotional thing; it is going to be intellectual. Your faith should not be established in your emotions but in your heads. The emotions will follow. There ought to be change on the outside because something is taking place on the inside. There will never come a change in the way we live until there is change in what we think and believe. There needs to be a steady flow of the Word of God and the Holy Spirit going throughout thought processes on a daily basis. If this does not take place we will soon fall into spiritual boredom. In light of this, how can we divorce our minds from our spiritual walk?

We need to understand that God gave us our brains and intended for us to use it. Before we were saved our minds were at enmity with God (Rom. 8:7), which means that our minds were hostile toward the things of God. Our minds refused to be marshaled by God's law. We had adopted a mentality that was at war with God. Any time a minister can convince a crowd to shelve their minds, they can easily get them to believe almost anything they want them to.

Jesus had given them a warning in His Sermon on the Mount, "But whosoever shall say, Thou fool, shall be in danger of hell fire" (Matt. 5:22). The word for fool that Jesus used was *moros*, from which we get the word *moron*. He was referring to a wicked reprobate, one who was destitute of all spirituality. Jesus was making reference to a godless person. He was giving warning against verbal abuse. It needs to be noted that two different Greek words are being used here.[3]

Jesus again in the Gospel of Luke said, "O fools, and slow of heart to believe all that the prophets had spoken" (Luke 24:25). Jesus used the same word that Paul used in addressing the Galatians, which means spiritually dull, slow, and sluggish in their apprehension of New Testament truth. The Jews were good about believing in the graces and greatness of the kingdom and liked how great it made them feel in the eyes of the Gentiles. But, they were slow in heart and ears to believe all that the prophets had said concerning Christ, their own Messiah.

They were looking for a military leader to come and deliver them from the iron heel of Rome, not from the bondage, lordship, control, and tyranny of sin. Jesus was crucified because He did not fit their image of the Messiah. For Him to die on the cross was a sign of weakness to them. But, in truth

His death accomplished what no other power was able to do and that was to destroy the power of sin.

Paul is saying that the real evidence of conversion is the presence of the Holy Spirit in the heart and life of the believer. Paul speaks of the sanctifying work of the Spirit in the lives of the Galatian believers. He is asking them, "Are you so irrational? Have you begun your Christian life in dependence upon the Holy Spirit, and are you now being brought to a state of spiritual maturity by means of self-effort alone?"[4] The Galatians would have confessed that they received the Holy Spirit by receiving Christ by faith. This is no time to be making the flesh your arm. "Cursed be the man that trusteth in man, and maketh the flesh his arm" (Jer. 17:5). Prayerlessness in the church is a sign that the church is relying more on the flesh than they are the arm of the Spirit.

"Are you now made perfect by the flesh?" (Gal. 1:3). Paul is telling them by using the word *perfect*, to bring something to the place where it is complete or the state of someone who is a spiritually mature Christian. It speaks of someone who is living a well-rounded, well-balanced, mature life.[5] He is asking, "Can your flesh bring you to a state where you are complete?" Can your flesh make you a well-rounded, growing, developing, spiritually mature, enthusiastic Christian? Have you become a product of your own self-effort? Are you apart from the transforming power of the Holy Spirit in regeneration?" Your flesh cannot produce or maintain what the Holy Spirit has produced. It has been birthed in the believer by the Holy Spirit and must be maintained by the Holy Spirit.

Not only was their beginning a gift, but their progress was also a gift. They began in the Spirit and were trying to attain their goal by human efforts. The Galatians' alternative is between living by the Spirit, whom they received when they believed the message of Christ crucified, and seeking perfection by circumcision (food laws, Sabbath observance), which would only identify them as proselyte Jews. Trying to attain perfection by the flesh, in that context, means to attempt to attain spiritual status by conforming to Jewish customs in order to become Jews.

Paul is reminding us all that our beginning in the Christian life is based on our response of faith to the message of Christ crucified and the experience of the Spirit, and our progress in the Christian life must be on the same basis.

Paul cannot accept that God's gracious provision of the Spirit and His miraculous work will be in vain. "Have you suffered so many things in vain?" (3:4). Such a great experience of God's work cannot be for nothing. Paul is now referring to the persecution the Galatians had suffered from their fellow countrymen. They had received such wonderful spiritual experiences with no purpose at all. Will the Galatians slip back into the twilight of a half-Jewish faith? This means the ending of all such manifestations of the Spirit in their midst. They might as well have never experienced the Holy Spirit for all the good that it had done them. Christ would have died and the Spirit would have been given with no purpose at all. The Galatians needed to be shaken out of their stupor. They needed to think deeply again of the wonderful experience of God's activity in their lives.

The Jewish path had become solely dependent upon the efforts of the flesh. Judaism had become a bankrupt religious system going down a dead-end road going nowhere. Jesus had taken the merits of His own blood and from the mercy seat in the holy of holies to the brazen altar in the outer court. He opened up a new and a living way to bring us into the presence of God. From the inside out He opened up a road.

A more literal translation says, "That you have begun in the Spirit, so walk in the Spirit and you will grow in the Lord."[6]

Paul often spoke of the initial entrance of the Holy Spirit into the heart of the Galatian Christians when they put their trust in the Lord Jesus Christ. The reception of the Holy Spirit was the starting point of their Christian life. Paul is saying the whole Christian life from beginning to the end is all supernatural. Is Christianity really Christianity without the supernatural? We are living in a day when a powerless Christianity has become the norm. Paul often contrasted the beginning and ending of a process. He is contrasting the spirit and the flesh. The New English Bible translation says, "spiritual" and the "material."

The Christian life is rooted and grounded in the Holy Spirit. The faith and the life of the Christian are bound up in the Holy Spirit. No true believer is without God's Holy Spirit. Paul said to the church at Rome, "If a man has not the spirit of Christ he is none of his" (Romans 8:9) No one can be a Christian without His indwelling presence. Every believer from the moment of accepting Jesus Christ as Savior and Lord has the Holy Spirit dwelling on the inside of them. From the moment of the Christian's conversion, the Holy Spirit takes up His abode and residence within that heart and life. The Spirit is actively at home within the heart and life of the believer. He has a ministry that He desires to perform in and through the Christian. As Christians yield to the Holy Spirit of God, they come under the Holy Spirit's control.

Through the presence of the Spirit, the believer experiences transformation and empowerment. This transformation results in a change of lifestyle. A new life of obedience is made possible through His indwelling. The Spirit motivates and empowers the man who is not under the law but under grace. The Christian's life is in the Spirit and is lived according to the Spirit. The Christian is in the Spirit and the Spirit is in the Christian. The Spirit governs the Christian's entire existence.

It was the Holy Spirit who convicted the sinner of His sin and revealed Christ to Him (John 16:7–11). It was the Holy Spirit who came as the high sheriff of heaven with a warrant for our arrest and slapped the handcuffs on us and drew us to the foot of the cross. The Holy Spirit was present when we were born again (3:1–8). It was through the Holy Spirit that we were baptized into Christ's body (1 Cor. 12:12–14). We have been sealed by the Holy Spirit (Eph. 1:13–14). The Holy Spirit's presence in our lives is the guarantee that one day we will share in His glory. It is the down payment of the glory that one day will be revealed. The believer has a responsibility to the Spirit.

Paul said in writing to the church at Corinth, "What? know ye not that your body is the temple of the Holy Ghost which is in you, which ye have of God, and ye are not your own? For ye are bought with a price: therefore glorify God in your body, and in your spirit, which are God's" (1 Cor. 6:19–20). The Corinthians were guilty of loose living. They had not taken it seriously that the Holy Ghost had taken up residence on the inside of them. Their lack of love and purity was grieving the Holy Ghost. The Holy Spirit seeks to bring our bodies, souls, and spirits into conformity with Christ. Paul was appealing to the Corinthians to be clean as members of Christ's body. Their bodies belong to Christ (vv. 13–15). Their bodies were temples (v. 19). The body was to glorify God (v. 20).

Inward transformation and a change of lifestyle are the results of the new birth. A new life of obedience is made possible only through the indwelling of the Holy Spirit. The faith and life of the Christian is bound up in the Holy Spirit. No one is a true believer who is without God's Holy Spirit. The day you were born again the Holy Spirit laid His mark upon you.

I believe that the believer individually (3:16) and the church corporately is the temple of God. That same presence dwelt between the cherubim, who were guardians of the holiness of God as they stretched their wings on high, guarding the revelation of God in the Old Testament. The high priest of Israel only had access to the holy of holies once a year, on the Day of Atonement. That same God now lives and abides in us through and by the Holy Spirit. Paul refers to the whole congregation as the temple of God. The temple was regarded by the Jews as a special residence of God. So our bodies become the residence that Jehovah God abides in through the Holy Spirit. As God dwelt in the tabernacle in His Shekinah glory, so He dwells in His people through the Holy Spirit.

The temple at Jerusalem was known as the dwelling place of the God of Israel. In Corinth, the temple of Aphrodite was there, in which fornication was regarded as consecration instead of desecration. Prostitutes were priestesses of Aphrodite to help men worship the goddess of fornication.

Each local assembly is a body of believers united to Christ. The conduct of each individual member affects the spiritual life of the entire community. Unholy alliances with harlots will destroy their union with Christ. Fornication cuts us off from Christ. The sexual union constitutes a permanent bond between two parties. If a man is joined to a harlot he is reduced to her level. The fornicator becomes one with the harlot he uses. When he has committed fornication, he has sinned against his own body (1 Cor. 6:18).

"Which ye have of God, and ye are not your own" (v. 19). When the Holy Spirit dwells in the temple, it belongs to God. The Christian has entered into a transaction, signed a deed, and turned over the possession of our lives to God. The dwelling of the Holy Spirit is a gift of God's grace. He cannot dwell in a polluted sanctuary.

Paul said, "You are bought with a price" (v. 20). The word *bought* comes from the Greek *agorazo* which means that Jesus entered into the slave market of our sins. We were on the auction block and the devil was the auctioneer. The devil said, "Who will make the first bid for this man?" Then when men were laying down their gold and silver to purchase the man, in walked the Light of the World. He said, "I will make the first bid for this man." The devil asked, "What are your credentials?" He said, "I am the buyer and the price, the Shepherd and the Lamb, the High Priest, and the altar as well as the offering. I am willing to go to a place called Calvary and bleed and die that this man might go free. So Jesus purchased us from the slave market of our sin.

The greatness of the price tells me of man's dignity and worth. His real worth is seen at Calvary. Christ died for us to redeem us from bondage. Jesus talked about giving His life as a ransom (Matt. 20:28). Each person is bought with a price. This speaks of payment in exchange for ownership. The sacrifice of Jesus on the cross was the purchase price for man's redemption. The blood of Jesus has purchased our bodies and our spirits.

Therefore, we are to glorify God in our bodies and in our spirits, which are God's. We must keep the body from immorality. Glorifying God in our body is both an obligation and a sign of gratitude and devotion. I am to treat my body as a sanctuary of the Holy Spirit that is united to the Lord Jesus. We glorify God by chastity and holy living and by devotion and sacrifice. We yield our bodies to Him as a living sacrifice. (Rom. 12:1).

The Holy Spirit is for the glorification of Jesus Christ (John 16:14). The Spirit of the Lord can use our bodies to glorify and magnify Him. God the Father, Son, and Holy Ghost are involved with what we do with our bodies. God the Father created our bodies. God the Son redeemed us from the prison house of sin. God the Holy Spirit indwells in our bodies and makes them the temple of God. When we use our bodies for immorality, we defile the temple of God. When we go outside the church and practice a lifestyle of sin, we weaken the testimony of the church before a world that is lost. If we do not repent, we will infect every one in the house or in the community.

The proper response of the Christian is to glorify God, who is our Maker and Redeemer, in our actions, our motives, and in our conduct. If the Christian is dedicated to the glory of God, shameful lawsuits and fornication will disappear from the church. A newfound faith produces new fellowship, which swallows up petty differences. Fellowship in Christ brings unity and peace to the believer.

We must keep the temple pure lest the divine guest departs. All that is unworthy of the heavenly guest—drinking, immorality, and other unclean habits—have no place in the life of a child of God. Such sins grieve the Holy Spirit and defile His dwelling place. Every precaution must be taken to ensure that He enjoys a clean temple.

The Christian should be walking in the Spirit. Paul said to the church at Galatia, "This I say then, Walk in the Spirit, and ye shall not fulfill the lust of the flesh" (Gal. 5:16). Then he said, "If we live in the Spirit, let us also walk in the Spirit" (v. 25).

The Christian should not grieve the Holy Spirit. The apostle Paul, in writing to the church at Ephesus, said, "And grieve not the holy Spirit of God, whereby ye are sealed unto the day of redemption" (Eph. 4:30). We need to realize that we cause the Spirit pain when we ignore His presence, voice, and leadership. Paul wrote to young Timothy to "neglect not the gift that is in thee, which was given thee by prophecy, with the laying on of the hands of the presbytery" (1 Tim. 4:14).

We as Christians have been commanded to stay full of the Holy Ghost. "Be not drunk with wine, wherein is excess; but be filled with the Spirit" (Eph. 5:18). We are commanded, not given the option, to stay under the Spirit's control and stay richly furnished with the gifts and power of the Holy Spirit. The spiritual life of a child of God must experience continual renewal by repeatedly being filled with the Spirit. When Luke, the first century historian, said, "And they were all filled with the Holy Ghost, and began to speak with other tongues, as the Spirit gave them utterance" (Acts 2:4). Luke was saying, "They continued to be filled." It was not a single, unrepeated act that happened one time and never again. In these last days we need to be refilled afresh and a new with the Holy Ghost. The times demand it.

By and through the Spirit, Christ dwells in the believer. The Spirit brings the believer into conformity to the image of His Son, and Christ expresses His authority through the agency of the Holy Spirit. Our Spirit has been made alive to worship God. The Spirit gives life to the body so that we can serve God.

The apostle Paul said in 2 Timothy, "That good thing which was committed unto thee keep by the Holy Ghost which dwelleth in us" (1:14). Guarding that deposit of faith must be done by the help of the Holy Spirit. He is the One that inspired the infallible truths of Scripture. He leads and guides the believer into all truth (John 16:13). If we are going to defend the faith that was once delivered to the saints we are going to have to stay with the Holy Spirit (14:7; 15:26–27; 16:13).

Galatians teaches us that there are two ways in which the Christian life is to be lived. The Christian life is to be lived through a dependency on the Holy Spirit and the grace of God. Wiersbe states, "When the Holy Spirit takes over, there will be liberty not bondage, there will be cooperation, not competition, and there will be glory to God, not the praise of men. Then the world will see what true Christianity is all about, and sinners will come to know Jesus Christ as their Lord and Savior. It is then that we will experience genuine revival and it will be a lifestyle, not one week out of the year."[6]

Grace is more than that which justifies us, forgives us, and makes us righteous in His sight. Grace is God's power working in and through us giving us the power and the ability to overcome sin. Grace is not a license to sin, but it is that which gives us the ability to serve God and our fellow man. "God is able to make all grace abound toward you" (2 Cor. 9:8). That means that the day He saved us, grace was on hand in abundance. As we walk through this life, it is on hand in abundance. The day we cross the finish line, it will be on hand in abundance. As a matter of fact, it superabounds. James portrays God as the giver of grace (James 4:6), which means the greater the need, the greater the supply. The Lord told the apostle Paul when he had a thorn in his flesh, "My grace is sufficient for thee: for my strength is made perfect in weakness" (2 Cor. 12:9).

Many people have adopted the mentality that says, "We are not under the law, but under grace; therefore, rules do not apply." According to the apostle Paul in the Book of Romans, it is the Holy Spirit that takes the righteousness of the law and fulfills it in us, as we walk not after the flesh but after the Spirit (Rom. 8:4). So even in the Christian life, rules still apply. It is the Holy Spirit that enables us to obey God. It is the Holy Spirit that creates within us a desire to serve God. Paul is saying, "How foolish to think that you can bring yourselves into a state of spiritual maturity in your Christian lives. This is a work of the Spirit. Only He can do that."

At the Galatians' conversion, it was the Holy Spirit that came as the high sheriff of heaven with a warrant for their arrest, slapped handcuffs on them, and drew them to the foot of the cross. We realize that no man can come to the Father unless the Father first draws him (John 6:44). The pull of God was on that generation, and they resisted. Stephen's generation was known as the generation that resisted the drawings of God. "Ye stiffnecked and uncircumcised in heart and ears, ye do always resist the Holy Ghost: as your fathers did, so do ye" (Acts 7:51). Israel had become like a backslidden heifer according to the Book of Hosea (4:16). They were arching up their backs and pulling their necks out from under the yoke of truth. They were uncircumcised in heart and ears.

Circumcision is a mark of covenant, the cutting away and the removal of that which is unclean. Their hearts had become calloused, and their ears had become clogged with the mud of this world. They resisted the drawings of God. They were acting just like their fathers in the wilderness. When the Father sent John the Baptist and Herod had him beheaded, they sinned against the Father. When the Jews crucified Jesus, they sinned against the Son by crucifying their Messiah. When they stoned Stephen, they sinned against the Holy Spirit. They silenced the voice of God in their generation. Shortly after that Rome came in and destroyed their temple. The Jews defiled it, God abandoned it, and Rome came in and destroyed it.

It was the Holy Spirit that convicted us of our sin and revealed Christ to us. Jesus said, concerning the operation of the Holy Spirit when He came:

> And when he is come, he will reprove the world of sin, and of righteousness, and of judgment: Of sin, because they believe not on me; Of righteousness, because I go to my Father, and you see me no more; Of judgment, because the prince of this world is judged.
> —John 16:8–11

Jesus said, "He will reprove the world of sin…because they believe not on me" (vv. 8–9). The word *reprove* comes from the Greek *elencho*, which means "to convict, to expose, and to cross examine"—just like convicting a law breaker in a court of law, or like a prosecuting attorney going after a criminal on a witness stand to reach a verdict.[7] It is a legal term to bring to light, to refute, to convince, to pronounce a verdict. He comes to so that we might acknowledge the truth that we are in a lost condition in need of a Savior. It is a Latin derivative, which means "to cause one to see." When one is convicted of his sin, he will see his sin. When the Holy Spirit touches the human soul, He reveals its sinful condition. The soul of a man will feel exposed, naked, embarrassed, ashamed, and confronted.

When is the last time you heard someone say, "I was confronted by God this morning through the message, and I am going to have to change"? When is the last time the Holy Spirit exposed some area in your life, convicted you, and brought you to a place of decision? Have you ever felt cross-examined? Has the Holy Spirit ever gone after you like a prosecuting attorney would go after a criminal on a witness stand? He will not only convict you of your sin, He will give the grace to judge it, overcome it, and put it away. This is a language that is almost forgotten in the life of the church.

The principle work in reproving will be found in our relationship to witnessing and proclaiming the gospel to sinners. As witnesses, believers tell what they have seen and heard in the court of law. The Holy Spirit is the prosecuting attorney. The unsaved are the guilty prisoners. The purpose of the indictment is not to condemn but to bring to salvation. Jesus said, "For God sent not his Son into the world to condemn the world; but that the world through him might be saved" (John 3:17).

The Holy Spirit came to reprove the world. The word *world* comes from the word *kosmos.* Four times John referred to the *kosmos.* The world may have been the object of God's love. "For God so loved the world, that he gave his only begotten Son, that whosoever believeth in him should not perish, but have everlasting life" (3:16). Christ did not come to condemn, but to save. The world rejected Christ (9:39). The world is under judgment and under the control of Satan who is the prince of this world (12:31). The world had to be overcome by Christ Himself. Jesus said, "In the world ye shall have tribulation, but be of good cheer; I have overcome the world" (16:33).

The word *sin* comes from the word *hamartia,* which means "to miss the mark." Sin can make you hard-hearted, spiritually blind, and past feeling. The Bible said that a lost person is "dead in trespasses and sins" (Eph. 2:1). Dead people cannot feel, see, hear, or respond. The spirit of man is dead and dormant until the Holy Spirit wakes it up. How can you convince a dead man that he needs to change?

Why does the Holy Spirit reprove the world of sin? "Because they believe not on me" (John 16:9). It is unbelief that condemns the lost sinner, not the individual sin. In light of this passage, the sin is not the problem; it is the unbelief in the hearts of men. If they believed they would not be living the way they were living. A person can clean up his act, quit bad habits, and still be lost and go to hell. The Holy Spirit will cause us to see and convict us of our unbelief. It is the work of the Holy Spirit, through the witness of believers, to expose the unbelief of this world. The law of God and the conscience of men will convict the sinner of his sins.

Jesus said:

> He that believeth on him is not condemned: but he that believeth not is condemned already, because he hath not believed in the name of the only begotten Son of God. And this is the condem-

nation, that light is come into the world, and men loved darkness rather than light, because their deeds were evil. For every one that doeth evil hateth the light, neither cometh to the light, lest his deeds should be reproved. But he that doeth truth cometh to the light, that his deeds may be made manifest, that they are wrought in God.

—John 3:18–21

Jesus said, "Of righteousness, because I go to my Father, and ye see me no more" (16:10). The Holy Spirit makes us realize that all of our righteousness is nothing more than filthy rags in the sight of God (Isa. 64:6). "Filthy rags" is a reference to the menstrual rags worn by women at their time of the month. That is how God feels about us existing in our own righteousness instead of us being clothed with His. Paul said to the church at Corinth, "For he hath made him to be sin for us, who knew no sin; that we might be made the righteousness of God in him" (2 Cor. 5:21). Our sin was placed on His account, and His righteousness was placed on ours. We are not *going to be* but we *are* the righteousness of God in Christ Jesus. Jesus came to convince us that we had no righteousness of our own.

Then Jesus said, "Of judgment, because the prince of this world is judged" (John 16:11). Satan has already been judged and sentenced, and we are waiting on the execution of that sentence. This is no time for us to get wrapped up in a world where Satan is the god. If we get wrapped up in this world, we will be cast out with him. The world itself is already under judgment.

So when a lost person is under the conviction of the Spirit, the following things will occur: First, having been brought to a place of undeniable conviction, they are awakened from their sinfulness and see the folly of their unbelief. They will realize that they are in a lost condition, bound for a devil's hell. Second, they will realize that they do not measure up to the righteousness of Jesus Christ, and the Spirit will beckon them to Christ. Remember, we cannot come lest the Spirit draws us. Third, they will realize that they are under condemnation because they belong to a world system that is under judgment and under the grip of Satan. Then God will raise their spirit from spiritual death to spiritual life. Paul said to the church at Ephesus, "Awake thou that sleepest, and arise from the dead, and Christ shall give thee light" (Eph. 5:14).

The Holy Spirit will awaken the conscience of guilt and the need for forgiveness. Conviction will make known the fearful results if the guilty persist in wrongdoing. After conviction a choice must be made. This will result in true repentance and a turning to Jesus Christ as Lord and Savior (Acts 2:38–39).

If one is truly baptized in the Holy Ghost and if he is truly a Spirit-filled believer, there will be conviction of sin, a new awareness of God's righteousness, and judgment. The convicting work of the Holy Spirit is not optional for those who want to progress into a mature Christian. It is obvious from this passage that any preacher or church that does not publicly reprove sin, call for biblical righteousness, and call for repentance, is not of the Holy Spirit.

While condemnation is for the sinner, conviction is for the child of God. I thank God that the Holy Spirit still convicts us and does not turn us over to our own ways. Many have the idea that we ought to leave church feeling good about ourselves, but I think it is more important that we leave church living good. We need to remember that real Pentecost is God in your face.

On the day of Pentecost Peter made the statement, "For David speaketh concerning him, I foresaw the Lord always before my face, for he is on my right hand, that I should not be moved: Therefore did my heart rejoice, and my tongue was glad; moreover also my flesh shall rest in hope" (vv. 25–26).

There is no conversion without conviction. I remember my father telling me many times when he grew up in the church how his knuckles would turn white as he grabbed the pew in an attempt to fight off Holy Ghost conviction. Charles Finney, one of the greatest revivalists of all times, made the statement, "If sinners can look you in the eye when you preach then it is a sure sign there is no conviction of the Spirit."[8] Charles Finney was a man who got up at 4:00 a.m. and prayed until 8:00 a.m. every morning. He stood on top of tombstones and preached the gospel and sinners fell out under the power. He walked into businesses, and women would look him in the eyes and fall to their knees in conviction. The president of the company would say, "Shut down the mill, it is not time to work, it is time to have revival."[9] The Holy Spirit's presence is the evidence of conversion. Where are the Charles Finneys today?

The work of the Holy Spirit is to convict sinners of their lost condition. Paul tells us in Romans that the whole world stands guilty before God (3:19). Without the work of the Holy Spirit to expose our sinful condition, we would still be in darkness today, eternally lost, and without God. The Spirit brings us to a deeper understanding of our sinful condition. He deepens and intensifies our awareness of the burden of not obeying God's laws and not following His will for our lives. Salvation is more than fire insurance. It is more than you and I taking a course in self-improvement. Salvation is not a work of human effort; it is a work of sovereign God. We did not crawl from the casket; we were made alive by Christ Jesus. We were spiritually raised from the dead.

Christ was filled with the Holy Spirit, and He testified to the world that its works were evil. Jesus said that the world "hateth [me], because I testify of it, that the works thereof are evil" (John 7:7). Christ condemned its injustice, pride, ambition, and its way of life. Jesus exposed the sin of His generation, and they resented the exposure. Jesus also said, "If the world hate you, ye know that it hated me before it hated you" (15:18). Jesus' first and last message to the church was repentance. Jesus called people to repent. "From that time Jesus began to preach, and to say, Repent, for the kingdom of heaven is at hand" (Matt. 4:17).

John the Baptist, who was filled with the Holy Ghost from his mother's womb, exposed the sin of the Jewish people and commanded them to change their ways. Peter at Pentecost proclaimed a message to the Jewish people, convicted the hearts of 3,000, and called them to repent and receive forgiveness (Acts 2:37–41).

When the apostle Paul wrote his letter to the Corinthian church, he stated that God's presence in the life of the church would expose the sin of the unbeliever. "He is convinced of all, he is judged of all: And thus are the secrets of his heart made manifest; and so falling down on his face he will worship God, and report that God is in you of a truth" (1 Cor. 14:24–25).

We need to understand that the real evidence of conversion is the presence of the Holy Spirit in the heart and life of the believer. Paul said to the church at Rome, "Ye are not in the flesh, but in the Spirit, if so be that the Spirit of God dwell in you. Now if any man have not the Spirit of Christ, he is none of his" (Rom. 8:9). The Spirit of God is actively at home in the heart and life of the believer. He has a ministry to perform in him. The Holy Spirit gives him victory over sin and produces the fruit of the Spirit. God has broken the power of the sin nature. The saved person is in the grip and under the control of the Holy Spirit. The moment one believes in the person of Christ, the Spirit takes up residence on the inside of him.

Paul said in the Book of Romans, "The Spirit is life because of righteousness" (8:10). Your spirit has been made alive by the Holy Spirit, to enable you to worship God and live right. Your spirit is alive because it is energized by the Holy Spirit. The Spirit is not won by striving to obey the law's demands. The Spirit is God's free gift. The Spirit is received by simple faith by hearing and believing. As the gospel is preached in the power of the Spirit, the Spirit creates faith. The Spirit came because we believed the gospel message.

The believer has two parents when it comes to spiritual birth. Two spiritual parents are required for a child to be born into God's family: the Holy Spirit and the Word. You have begun in the Spirit, now walk in the Spirit, and you will grow in the Lord. When a child of God has been born again into the family of God, he has all he needs for spirituality. Jesus told Nicodemus, "Verily, Verily, I say unto thee, Except a man be born again, he cannot see the kingdom of God" (John 3:3). Spirituality is living in the world with God. True spirituality is walking with God, talking with God, and breaking bread with God.

It was the Holy Spirit that baptized us into Christ's body (1 Cor. 12:12–14). It is the Holy Spirit that seals us to the day of redemption (Eph. 1:13–14; 4:30). The Holy Spirit's presence in our lives is the down payment of the glory that will one day be revealed. His presence in the life of the believer is the guarantee that one day he will share the glory of Christ. He is the firstfruits of the Spirit in our lives. The believer has a responsibility to the Spirit. (See 1 Corinthians 6:19–20.)

The Christian should be in pursuit of the Holy Spirit of God—not lagging far behind Him, but staying in step with Him (Gal. 5:16, 25). We are to keep an atmosphere in our lives that is charged with the presence of the Holy Spirit and the Word of God so heaven's fruit can grow on the branches of our lives. Christians are not to grieve the Holy Spirit of God lest they forfeit eternal salvation (Eph. 4:30). The believer has been given the command to stay full of the Holy Ghost (5:18). In Christ we are blessed with all spiritual blessings in heavenly places (1:3). It is the Holy Spirit that lays His hands on all that Christ purchased for us at the tree and manifests and demonstrates it in our lives. I refuse to settle for less than what Jesus died for me to have.

Jesus came from heaven to earth to show me how the Christian life is to be lived so that one day I could go from earth to heaven. Jesus lived His life in the power of the Holy Spirit. It was the operation of the Holy Spirit in Jesus' life that set Him apart from the nominal religion of His day. Repeatedly it was said in the Gospels that Jesus was full of the Holy Ghost. There was no provision in the Mosaic economy for the indwelling Spirit to sanctify the believer as the believer trusted Him for that work.

Through the presence of the Holy Spirit, we are changed, we see miracles occur, and we are continually filled with the Holy Spirit. "They were all filled with the Holy Ghost, and began to speak with other tongues as the Spirit gave them utterance" (Acts 2:4). The baptism in the Holy Spirit is not supposed to be a single, unrepeated act that happens one time and never again. The more literal translation would be: "They continued to be filled." It happened in Jerusalem, Judea, Samaria, and Ephesus. There is one baptism, but there are many fillings.

Paul is saying that we begin our Christian life in dependence upon the indwelling Holy Spirit, and will not be brought into a state of spiritual maturity by means of self-effort alone. The reception of the Holy Spirit into our lives is the starting point of the Christian life. Paul often contrasts the beginning and ending of a process. If your Christian life begins with the Spirit, you cannot go on to spiritual maturity without Him. You cannot be brought to a level of spiritual maturity in the Christian life by your self-effort.

The word *flesh* speaks of a person who is a product of self-effort. A person in the flesh is someone who is apart from the transforming power of the Holy Spirit in regeneration (which is the recreation of the new nature). A person in the flesh is one who is controlled by the depraved nature. In fact the New Testament has nothing good to say about the flesh. Paul said, "In my flesh... dwelleth no good thing" (Rom. 7:18). He said to the Philippians that they were to "have no confidence in the flesh" (Phil. 3:3). Jesus said in John's Gospel, "It is the spirit that quickeneth; the flesh profiteth nothing" (John 6:63). Paul said to the church at Rome that, "So then they that are in the flesh cannot please God" (Rom. 8:8). So the flesh cannot produce what the Holy Spirit has produced in our lives. The flesh cannot make us into mature Christians, well-rounded, well-balanced, and mature. It cannot bring the Christian life to a point where it is complete.

The Christian life is not a flesh attempt to serve God, but a Spirit-led relationship. It is not about a struggle but being borne along by the Spirit. We know that what separated Jesus Christ from the nominal religion of that day was the operation of the Holy Spirit in His life. Let us stay the course in order to maintain the walk of the Spirit with a deep dependency on the sanctifying, enabling grace of God. Let us never forget that all perfection comes through and by the Spirit, not through the efforts of the flesh.

There are many who feel embarrassed and attempt to lock the Holy Spirit in a back room somewhere to keep from offending a visitor who attends the house of God. I thank God for those who refuse to apologize for the operation, demonstration, and manifestation of the Holy Ghost in our midst.

We need to refuse to be torn away from the operation of the Holy Spirit and the sanctifying, enabling grace of God in order to make a flesh attempt to serve God. There needs to be a heartfelt appreciation for those who know and realize that the flesh cannot produce the same results that the Holy Ghost can produce. What has started in the Spirit has got to be maintained by the Spirit. We are not made perfect through the flesh.

Paul said to the Galatians, "Have ye suffered so many things in vain?" (Gal. 3:4). Many of the Galatians had suffered persecution from their fellow countrymen. For them to abandon the Holy Spirit after receiving such wonderful spiritual experiences would have been of no purpose at all. Was all this done in vain? Would the Galatians slip back into the twilight of a half Jewish faith? This would have meant the end of all such manifestations of the Spirit in their midst. They might as well have never experienced these wonderful experiences for all the good that it had done them. Christ would have died for no purpose.

Chapter 8

Bewitched and Bothered

O foolish Galatians, who hath bewitched you, that ye
should not obey the truth, before whose eyes Jesus Christ
hath been evidently set forth, crucified among you?

—Galatians 3:1

DEFECTION AND DESERTER are two words that are not pleasant to hear. There is nothing that is sadder than to see a Christian defect and desert from the Christian life after he has been born again and nurtured in the faith. To see him settle for something less is disheartening. The truth of the matter is that many Christians do this. Many of them began well after they have been saved by grace through faith. Right after their Christian journey begins they fall into the clutches of legalism. How many come into the saving knowledge of Christ, fall into the ritual of what we call church, and begin to make their substitutes of ritual for power and form for force?

Why has God's church become feeble and many of us who profess the name of Christ are not living up to our potential in Christ? Nowhere in Scripture am I called to be content to be average. I am called by Christ to live the highest kind of Christian life possible. It is Christ who is able to keep us from falling. Jude said, "Now unto Him who is able to keep you from falling and to present you faultless before the presence of his glory with exceeding joy" (Jude 24). He wants me to become surefooted like a horse so I will not lose my footing and stumble. As the Head, He is the source and origin of the life of His church. If it is real in the Head it ought to be real in each member of the body. It is the work of the Holy Spirit to make the presence of Christ real in the believer individually and the church corporately. As the Head, He is imparting and communicating to His church all that we need. Then why are we not living up to our potential and privileges in the kingdom?

God has called the church of the living God to live in the power of the Spirit. The church is trying to accomplish in the flesh instead of the energy of the Holy Spirit. The church needs to return and acknowledge that the Holy Spirit is her strength and her help. If we will one more time be indwelt by God's Holy Spirit, then our days of beauty and gladness will return.

When Paul went to Galatia he had a great revival. The Galatian believers heard this truth, believed it, and obeyed it. They were born into the family of God. Souls were saved, sanctified, and filled with the Holy Spirit. There was a glow on their countenance, and the beauty of Christ was seen in their experience. So the Galatians began to abandon the Holy Spirit and the grace of God and made a flesh attempt to serve God. The present tense indicates that the Galatians had already begun this departure. The Galatians were turning away from the teaching ministry of the Holy Spirit. They were starting to depend on self-effort in an attempt to obey a legalistic system of works. As Paul said to the church at Rome, "They went about trying to establish their own righteousness" (Rom. 10:3). They had begun their Christian life in dependency upon the Holy Spirit. Now they were depending on self-effort alone to continue the work of sanctification in them, which the Holy Spirit had begun.

Paul had been used as a mouthpiece for God to introduce to the Galatians the truth of the gospel. He preached salvation by grace. He watched the Holy Spirit take up His abode on the inside of them. He watched a transformation in their lives occur as they entered into the finished work of Christ at Calvary. Then he watched them defect and deserted the gospel of grace for a form of religion that inferior. They substituted the fullness of their life in Christ for a form of religion that had no power and no joy. The Galatians were robbing themselves of the fullness of the blessing. They were robbing the world of the right doctrine of salvation. No one is saved in any other way lest it be though faith in the crucifixion and resurrection of Christ.

It is through justification by faith in Christ that we are declared righteous. How can a man stand in right relationship with God and enter into His presence? How is it that a man can be acceptable to God? The New Testament says, "It is by faith alone." It is by a man's faith in the work of Christ at the cross. There is no other way. There is nothing that man can attempt to do in his own righteousness. It is by believing in Jesus Christ that a man is justified.

The idea of being a Christian cannot be separated from being baptized in the Holy Spirit. Pentecost is about rekindling a passionate desire in us to know more and more about Jesus. At Sinai God took His finger and wrote His laws on tables of stone; today He writes them on fleshly tables of the human heart, written with the Spirit of the living God (2 Cor. 3:3).

Paul in Galatians 3:1–5 placed his focus on the Galatians' reception of the Holy Spirit (vv. 1–2). He dealt with their progress in the area of their spiritual maturity (v. 3). Then Paul dealt with the Spirit's continual bestowal of miracles in their midst (vv. 4–5). Many of the same issues that had been going on in Galatia had already been debated by the Jerusalem Council in Acts 15. There were two questions that were debated: 1) Is faith in the Lord Jesus Christ the only requirement for salvation? 2) Are there Old Testament laws required to obtain salvation? It was believed that Paul wrote the Book of Galatians before the debate by the Jerusalem Council. Galatians was actually the first epistle written by Paul.

The false teachers had bewitched them and turned them into fools. By Paul using the word *foolish,* he was referring to them as being spiritually dull. Kenneth Wuest in his book *Word Studies in the Greek New Testament* says that Paul used the word *anoetos,* meaning "the stupidity that arises from deadness and impotence of intellect." It means "lacking the powers of perception in an unwise manner." It refers to one who does not reflect. It implied the failure of using one's powers of perception. Paul said that they were not using their heads. They had truly experienced a meeting with God: They saw the Son of God (3:1), they had received the Holy Spirit (3:2–3), and they had experienced miracles from God the Father (3:5).

Every heathen in every religion is trying to earn his own salvation—just like many of the Jews today who are seeking to be justified by the works of the law. "The law was our schoolmaster to bring us unto Christ" (3:24). Paul used an illustration that was familiar to all his readers and that was a child's guardian.[1] In many Roman and Greek households, well-educated slaves took children to and from school and watched over them through the day. Sometimes they would teach, protect, prohibit, and at times even discipline. This is what Paul meant by schoolmaster. God had given the Jews over 4,000 years of history under the law. Paul was hoping that the Jews would give up seeking justification before God by the works of the law. When the bus pulled up the dock of grace, the Jews refused to get off the bus and went on with the law.

What then is the purpose of the law? (Gal. 3:19). If the inheritance of the promised blessing does not depend on the law, then why was the law given by God? (vv. 19–20). According to Paul the law had a negative purpose: "It was added because of transgressions" (v. 19). Paul has already told us that the law does not make us righteous before God (v. 11), it is not based on faith (v. 12), and it is not the basis of inheritance (v. 18). So if the law is divorced from these things, why was it given?

Paul said it was related to transgressions. A transgression is a violation of a standard. The law provided a standard by which violations are measured. In order for sinners to know how sinful they are or how far they have deviated from God's standards, God gave them the law. Sin was not imputed where there was no law (Rom. 5:13). But after the law was given, sin could be clearly measured (3:20; 4:15; 7:7). Each act or attitude could be labeled as a transgression by the commandment of God found in the law.

The law itself made no provision for mercy, pardon, and forgiveness, but "By the law is the knowledge of sin" (Rom. 3:20). The law was there to remind the Jews of how bad they had blown it. There were over 613 Jewish Laws, each one saying "thou shalt" and "thou shalt not." None gave the Jews any ability to live up to the law through their flesh. It could identify sin but left the Jew powerless to do anything about it.

The Jews were brought up by the law. The law had been a child's guardian and disciplinarian. The law regulated the life of Israel. It governed every aspect of their lives. It separated Israel from the Gentile nations (Eph. 2:12–18). The Judaizers taught that the law was necessary for life and righteousness. The work of a guardian was preparation for the child's maturity. Once the child became of age, he no longer needed the guardian. The law was preparation for Israel until the coming of the promised seed, Jesus Christ. Before faith came, the nation was imprisoned by the law.

When the Savior came, the guardian was no longer needed. It was a sad day when the nation of Israel did not recognize their Messiah when He appeared. God destroyed their temple and scattered their nation, so today it is impossible for a devout Jew to practice the faith of their fathers. He has no altar, no priesthood, no sacrifice, no temple, no king (Hosea 3:4).

Paul asked them, "Who hath bewitched you, that ye should not obey the truth" (Gal. 3:1). The Greek word translated *bewitched* is *ebaskanen*, which means "the popular superstition and the fascination of an evil eye." It meant "to mislead by hypnotizing or fascination"[2]—like a snake hypnotizing a bird and drawing it helplessly into its mouth. It means to cast a spell upon someone. Here Paul speaks of the evil eye. The Greeks had a great fear of a spell cast by an evil eye. This belief in the evil eye is old and persistent (Deut. 28:54). The

Judaizers had the Galatians under their spell. The Galatians had been poisoned by a perversion of the gospel. They had come under the control of an evil magician and his demonic spells. "Who tickled your fancy and drew you off course?" The Galatians were being drawn under the spell of persuasive teachers telling them that through the law they might attain spiritual perfection; and they did not even realize they were being enslaved by demonic power (Gal. 4:8–9). They were saying that their faith was not enough, if you want to go further than that you have to have works to gain the fullness of God's blessings. Paul knew that you could not be dragged away if you were rooted, grounded and settled in the faith of the gospel. Being a student of the Word is a great protection against false doctrine. The quest for perfection under the law is an illusion from which we must be awakened. How will this spell be broken?

There are many who will not allow themselves to come under this demonic spell. It is like a snake hypnotizing a bird to walk up into its mouth. I refuse to come under this spell. Any attempt to seek to tear us away from the Holy Spirit and the sanctifying, enabling grace of God is demonic. I believe that Calvary was enough to break the dominion, lordship, and control of sin in our lives. There is no Pentecost without Calvary. Salvation has been turned into nothing more than a course in self-improvement by this false teaching.

Paul was saying that "Jesus Christ was openly set forth crucified among you." Paul is recalling their conversion. The Galatians had openly seen the Gospel of a crucified Christ presented among them. The gospel had come to them in clarity and power. The Galatians had received it, believed it, and were transformed by it. Jesus had been presented to them as the source of salvation. It was inexcusable for the Galatians to yield to these false teachers

There are many within the life of the church who have become embarrassed and have attempted to lock the Holy Ghost in a back room some where in order to keep from offending a visitor who has attended the house of God. There is much to be said concerning those who refuse to apologize for the operation, demonstration, and manifestation of the Holy Ghost in our midst. These believers realize that their flesh cannot produce the same results through self-effort that the Holy Spirit can produce. What has started in the Spirit has got to be maintained by the Spirit. There is no perfection through the flesh.

Paul pressed hard with questions to put the Galatians back in touch with their own experience with God. These questions are the way to start breaking the grip of illusion. What kind of spell has the house of God fallen under when we hear from our pulpits that the baptism of the Holy Ghost is not for our day? Who has misled us into believing that what started in the Spirit could be maintained through the efforts of our flesh? If it was not for the baptism of the Holy Ghost, the early New Testament church would have fallen back into Judaism. We must beware of this demonic spell and influence lest we drift off into nothing more than a religious experience, without having the life of the Spirit of God in our midst. If you have fallen under this demonic spell are you ready to do the following:

1. Fall from grace?
2. Become a runner on a detour and lose your spiritual direction?
3. Return to the graveyard (spiritually)?
4. Return to the weak and beggarly elements?
5. Lose your spiritual inheritance and become a spiritual pauper?
6. Undo everything that Calvary has ever accomplished?
7. Christ to become of no effect to you?
8. Become a slave to sin again and lose your liberty?
10. Become a debtor and lose your spiritual wealth?
11. Leave spiritual adulthood and return to the cradle?
12. Leave the school of grace for the kindergarten of the law?
13. Return to religious bondage, spiritual infancy, and immaturity?

Paul takes the Galatians back to their first exposure to the message of Christ crucified. Paul had preached Christ and Him crucified with such effectiveness that the people could almost see Jesus being crucified for them on the cross. It had been done in such an intense manner that it was like Christ was crucified in their presence. Paul said, "Before whose eyes Jesus Christ hath been evidently set forth, crucified among you" (Gal. 3:1). The phrase "set forth" means "publicly portrayed, announced on a poster." His preaching was like painting a picture with words or putting up a public poster for all to see,[3] just as we put information on a poster and display it in a public place, like a billboard by the roadside. It could be used by a father for putting up a notice that he is no longer responsible for his son's debts. It could be used for putting up an announcement for an auction sale. Today, we get our announcements from the newspaper. Paul is saying, "Christ has been placarded in front of you!" Paul is saying you have seen that He has been crucified. You could not have missed the announcement. Paul had openly presented Christ, with great emphasis on His death for sinners.

With their very ears they could have heard the hammer drive the nails in His hands and feet. They could hear His cries, sense His tears, feel His pain, and through their eyes of faith visualize the blood that poured from His body. He was so vividly portrayed to them that they could see Him being crucified. They were convicted of their sins, arrested by the Holy Spirit, and drawn to the foot of the cross. As the Galatians repented of their sins, they accepted His perfect sacrifice. They forsook their sin, came out of their paganism, and entered into the kingdom of God. Paul said, "It was all open, public, and you responded to it." The Galatians walked into newness of life. If they had seen Christ crucified, how could they ever believe that legalism could save a man? They knew that there was only one thing that could redeem a man and that was the death of the Son of God. God had to prepare a perfect sacrifice and pay the penalty for sin and satisfy the justice of God.

Paul was God's herald and town crier. The message of the cross was no accident; it was deliberate. Paul had a set purpose in mind. The message of Jesus Christ as the Messiah who died on the cross was plastered on the billboards before their very eyes. Paul said, Christ was "crucified among you" (v. 3). The word *crucified* comes from the perfect passive participle, which was an action completed in past time with continued results in the future. This means that it was not only an historical event but also in the present.[4] It is the saving power of the cross of Christ for all who believe. It should have been enough to keep the Galatians from wandering off to the enticements of the Judaizers. It was a reminder to the Galatians of their vision of Christ crucified that is set against their foolish submission to a bewitching influence. Paul is asking them how they could have succumbed to any other influence, no matter how charming or intoxicating, after they had seen Christ portrayed as crucified.

Paul's first question drives us along with the readers back to the foot of the cross of Christ. This is the place to find release from any enchantment that draws us away from Christ. We need a renewed vision of Christ crucified if we are to gain freedom from illusions of perfection through law observance. Such a vision is a vivid reminder of the cross, not human achievement, as the basis for God's blessing. Paul's question moves from the experience of the preaching of the cross of Christ (v. 1) to the experience of the Spirit (vv. 2–5). The two are linked: the cross opens the door for the Holy Spirit, and the experience of the Spirit is the result of faith in the message of the cross of Christ. You can't have a Pentecost without a Calvary.

This should have cut the ground out from under the Judaizers. Paul is not speaking of a dead Christ on a crucifix. He is speaking of a risen, ascended Lord, who has been crucified, who is alive, and whose glorified body bears the marks of the nail prints in His hands and feet and scars of a crown of thorns on His head. He is the living Savior by virtue of His atoning work on the cross. We have no right to wear a cross unless we are willing to carry one. If we desire not to be bewitched and fooled, then we need to follow the One who was crucified for our sins. Listen to Him and His apostles with the hearing of faith. We need to remember what has been clearly portrayed: Jesus and Him crucified (3:1). We need to remember that He was crucified for our sins. The Law of Moses can't save us, nor can any doctrine that denies the atoning death of Christ. There is no other gospel that can save us.

The Galatian believers were taken back to the beginning, when they first received the Spirit by believing in the message of the cross of Christ. The evidence of the entrance of the Spirit into their lives at conversion was so clear to Paul that he used it as a reference point in his argument. Their baptism (3:27) and the full assurance of the Father's love, which was given by the Spirit (Gal. 4:6; Rom. 5:5; 8:15–16), left a mark on their lives. The reference to miracles in Galatians 3:5 is the evidence that they also experienced outward manifestations of the Spirit's presence.

Paul has taken them back to the roots of their spiritual experience to remind them that the beginning was a gift of God's Spirit. This destroys the delusion that God's blessings depend on joining the Jewish people or attaining certain levels of moral excellence by observing the Law of Moses. The Galatian converts were excluded from the Jewish nation; they had not observed the law, but there was no denying that they had experienced the gift of the Spirit.

In verse two it was Paul's desire to break the spell of the Judaizers by showing the contradiction between the Galatians' recent interest in observing the law and their initial experience of believing what they heard. Paul was reminding the converts that they did not have to become Jewish proselytes in order to receive the Spirit or to experience the continuous outpouring of the Spirit and miracles in their lives.

Chapter 9

What Has Happened to the Fire of the Holy Ghost?

WILLIAM BARCLAY STATED: "If life is drab, inadequate, futile, earthbound, it is because the believer has neglected the Holy Spirit and has failed to enter into the sphere that is dominated by the Spirit through the baptism that Christ alone has the power to give."[1]

On the banks of the Jordan River, John the Baptist declared, "I indeed baptize you with water unto repentance: but he that cometh after me is mightier than I, whose shoes I am not worthy to bear: he shall baptize you with the Holy Ghost, and with fire" (Matt. 3:11).

John's baptism was in water. He baptized those who came out to the river Jordan repenting of their sins. Under John's ministry a fresh move of God hit the land. People began to forsake the dead rituals in the temple to go hear a man sent from God whose name was John. Even the Pharisees and Sadducees, who could never get along, dropped their petty differences to go out to hear this man sent from God.

John looked forward to the coming of the Messiah. His baptism had two purposes: 1) It prepared a nation for Christ. 2) It presented Christ to the nation. John came to prepare the way of the Lord. If he came to a river, he built a bridge over it. If he came to a rough place, he made it smooth. If he came to a crooked place, he made it straight. If he came to a valley, he filled it up. If he came to a mountain, he brought it down. John through his baptism prepared a highway for the King to come and reign in the hearts of men. His baptism was authorized from heaven (21:23–27).

John had proclaimed himself to be the forerunner of the Savior. A mighty revival had shaken the whole nation. If John's ministry was from heaven, then Jesus was the Son of God. The evidence was overwhelming: His birth, His ministry, the voice from heaven at His baptism. If the Pharisees would have said that John's ministry was from heaven, then they should have followed the preaching of John and repented. The entire nation held John to be a prophet, so their mouths were closed and they dared not answer.

John refused to wear the garments of those who were in the temple. He had a different look. He was dressed with camel's hair. He had a different appetite. He was not feeding on the stately lamb at the temple. His diet was one of locust and wild honey. He was also attended with a different glory. He was filled with the Holy Ghost from his mother's womb. The Pharisees did not like his message. They did not like the attention he was getting.

John the Baptist came to the very place that was prophesied by Isaiah (40:3). He came to the lower Jordan Dead Sea valley. He baptized those who came to him confessing their sins. He refused to baptize anyone who gave no evidence of repentance. He referred to the Pharisees and Sadducees as a "generation of vipers" (Matt. 3:7). John said their behavior had never changed. There was no change in their attitude. They had the nature of a serpent that was filled with deadly poison. He demanded "that they bring forth fruit evidence of repentance" (v. 8). Talk was cheap; they were to bring forth fruit that gives evidence of their repentance. They may have been the physical descendants of Abraham, but they were not His spiritual offspring. They were self-satisfied and secure that they were the children of Abraham.

Abraham prayed, built altars, and was strong in faith. He did not stagger at the promises of God through unbelief, but was fully persuaded that what God had promised He was able to perform (Rom. 4:20). Abraham tithed. He was a friend of God, yet the Jews were trying to kill Jesus. When we are the spiritual descendants of Abraham, we will take on his nature.

There is coming One after me who is "mightier than I, whose shoes I am not worthy to bear" (Matt. 3:11). In a Jewish household, it was the least of the servants whose job was to stoop down and remove the sandals from someone's feet. John felt unworthy to stoop down and remove the sandals from the feet of the Messiah. John had declared" "I have need to be baptized of thee, and comest thou to me" (v. 14).

There are many that have been baptized by the Holy Spirit into Christ's body. When Paul wrote to the church at Corinth, he said, "For by one Spirit are we all baptized into one body, whether we be Jews or Gentiles, whether we be bond or free; and have been all made to drink into one Spirit" (1 Cor. 12:13). This baptism took place at salvation. It has to do with the indwelling of the Holy Spirit.

Yet there are many who have not been baptized by Christ into Holy Ghost and fire. All four Gospel writers record John's prophecy that the coming One will baptize with the Holy Spirit. Matthew and Luke add that He will baptize with the Holy Ghost and fire.

What does it mean to be baptized in the Holy Ghost? The word *baptized* means "to immerse or to dip: like clothes being dipped in dye; like a ship submerged beneath the waters; like a drunk who is soaked in his own alcohol;"[2] like a dill pickle. You have got to get the pickle into the dill and the dill into the pickle. Unlike the pickle, we don't spend enough time in the dill.

John has identified Jesus as the Holy Ghost baptizer. John expected the Messiah to baptize the people he was preaching to with the Holy Ghost and fire. John said that it would be the work of the Messiah. It was promised by Joel (Joel 2:28) and reaffirmed after Christ's resurrection (Luke 24:49; Acts 1:4–8). The Spirit is not only poured out upon them, they are immersed into Him, saturated with Him. Jesus would bring the Spirit, and we have become flooded with the Holy Spirit.

When the word *with* is used with the word *immersed,* it suggests that something is being done in the presence of the Spirit. When the Holy Spirit is mentioned in conjunction with the word *with*, the Holy Spirit is the element and Jesus is the doer of the action. We are not just baptized with the Holy Spirit, we are actually immersed into the Spirit.[3]

Christ's ministry of baptizing in the Holy Ghost and fire is a continual ministry throughout this present age. While John was on the banks of the Jordan River, he had declared that Jesus was the "Lamb of God, which taketh away the sin of the world" (John 1:29).

> And John bare record, saying, I saw the Spirit descending from heaven like a dove, and it abode upon him. And I knew him not: but he that sent me to baptize with water, the same said unto me, Upon whom thou shalt see the Spirit descending, and remaining on him, the same is he which baptizeth with the Holy Ghost.
> —JOHN 1:32–33

When John said, "The same is he which baptizeth with the Holy Ghost" (v. 33), he used a present tense participle of the word *baptize*, which means He will continue to baptize with the Holy Ghost. So the references in Luke and John are not just for the first century outpourings at Pentecost. John is speaking of the primary role and ministry of Jesus as baptizer in the Holy Ghost throughout the age of the Spirit. Peter at Pentecost said, "The promise [of the Holy Spirit] is unto you, and to your children…even as many as the LORD our God shall call" (Acts 2:39). Peter makes reference to the fact that the promise of the Holy Spirit was not confined to one generation or to the age of the apostles.

The Messiah had to suffer and die before He could enter into His glory. He first had to make his soul an offering for sin before the "pleasure of the LORD [could] prosper in his hand" (Isa. 53:10). Jesus had to be glorified before the Holy Ghost was given. He had to do His High Priestly work before He could reign on His throne.

The Hebrew or Old Testament word for *Spirit* is *ruach*. It means three things: the Spirit is power, the Spirit is life, and the Spirit is God. The Holy Spirit is the dynamic in the human existence.[4]

"He shall baptize you with the Holy Ghost, and with fire" (Matt. 3:11). Spirit and fire are coupled with one preposition. It is a double baptism of Holy Ghost and fire. Many have a Burger King Holy Ghost. Hold the pickles, hold the lettuce—aren't you glad we let you have it your way?

I want to know why it is when it comes to everything else (secular or material) that we are all so gung ho. There are no limits to how far we will go. When it comes to the baptism of the Holy Ghost and getting on fire for God, we are ready to put the brakes on. We need to remember that gold does not fear the fire. It is the impurities in gold that fear the fire. Many are too afraid to get close to the fire because the worldliness and carnality in us will get burned up. We won't be able to do cute church anymore. We might even get changed. Our flesh might even come under subjection to the Holy Ghost, and our carnal desire may begin to die. Everything in us that is unlike Jesus Christ might get burned up. For this reason many are afraid to get too close to the fire of the Holy Ghost.

Jesus came "to send fire on the earth" (Luke 12:49). It was the dawn of the kingdom of God through the outpouring of the Holy Spirit upon all flesh. The very images that Jesus used (fire, baptism, division) speak of opposition and conflict. No wonder people are looking for a comfortable place to go to church. To many of the Jewish people, fire was a symbol of judgment. Our Lord's coming into the world did bring judgment (John 9:39).

A. T. Robertson describes the fire in Luke 12:49 as Jesus suddenly letting the volcano in his heart burst forth.[5] The fire was already burning. Christ came to set a world on fire. And this igniting of fire had already begun. The very passion in Christ's heart would set his friends on fire and his foes in opposition, "laying wait for him, and seeking to catch something out of his mouth, that they might accuse him" (Luke 11:54). Jesus did not come to bring peace, but a sword, to bring a division among men (Matt.10:34–35).

The Message translation brings great clarity to Luke 12:49–51. Jesus said, "I've come to start a fire on this earth—how I wish it were blazing right now! I've come to change everything, turn everything right side up—how I long for it to be finished! Do you think I came to smooth things over and make everything nice? Not so. I've come to disrupt and confront!"

Jesus was saying that His first coming would either burn up or purify the lives of men. He said it would cause division. History has proven this to be true over and over again. He will bring division right inside of your own family, and a man's enemies will become those of his own house (Matt.10:36). Many times our confession of faith in Christ becomes a declaration of war among families and friends. Jesus becomes a cause of division. When we were in sin we were downstream swimmers in a downstream world. We went right along with the tide. Now that we are born again, hell has declared war on us. We are now upstream swimmers in a downstream world. We don't go along with the tide; we go against it.

"What will I, if it be already kindled?" (Luke 12:49). Christ was saying how He wished it was already kindled. The Greek word He used for *kindled* was *anephthe*, first aorist passive of *anapto*, which means to "kindle, to set fire to, to make a blaze."[6]

Fire is a symbol of the Holy Spirit. It is the sign of His presence and approval. When fire went out in a Roman Senate, it meant business was over. When the fire of the Holy Ghost goes out in the church, we are not open for business. The fire that burned upon the brazen altar was lit by God Himself. He put it in the hands of the priest and told him to keep it burning. You do not find God coming again and again to light that fire. If the priest neglected it, the fire of God that was placed on that altar went out.

At salvation the Holy Spirit lit a fire on the altar of our hearts. He placed it in our hands to be taken care of. It was not to be neglected or smothered by this world. We as God's priests have been given the charge to keep it burning.

We are never to allow it to go out. If a fire burns low in the fireplace, we have enough sense to poke around that fire giving it room to breathe. We know that we have got to lay another log on that fire. The fire must be fed. We as God's priest are keepers of the flame. So many wonder why they cannot keep their spiritual excitement going, while they continue to neglect the fire that God has placed within them.

This baptism of fire identifies Christ's followers on the earth. Where you find the Spirit, you find the church; where you find the church, you find the Spirit. It is the Spirit that identifies us before a lost and dying world.

Others have identified fire as zeal and enthusiasm. What has happened to the zeal and enthusiasm of our people? Many show up at church showing no signs of enthusiasm about being at the house of the Lord and revealing no zeal in their worship. When we lose our zeal for the things of God, we have backslidden, and I am not sure we realize just how far. Jesus said, "The zeal of thine house hath eaten me up" (John 2:17). When is the last time your zeal for the house of the Lord got you in trouble with religious folks who did not know a thing about biblical spirituality?

The gifts of the Spirit are to be a balanced ministry of fruit and fire. Paul saw it as the more excellent way to edify the church. The fire comes out of our fruit. If we are having fruit trouble, it is going to have to be corrected before we see the gifts of the Spirit in operation.

Paul told the church at Rome to be "not slothful in business; fervent in spirit; serving the Lord" (Rom. 12:11). Here the fire speaks of fervency: a boiling, burning zeal of the Spirit. You are to become heated to a boil in the pursuit of doing good. What is boiling point in your local church?

The fire is the fire of purification. Fire purges and it purifies. It is the image of the new creation. Malachi said:

> But who may abide the day of his coming? and who shall stand when he appeareth? for he is like a refiner's fire, and like fullers' soap: And he shall sit as a refiner and purifier of silver: and he shall purify the sons of Levi, and purge them as gold and silver, that they may offer unto the Lord an offering in righteousness.
>
> —Malachi 3:2–3

The Lord's coming will be very different from what carnal Jews expect. He will not come to flatter national pride. Nor will He come to gratify national wishes. He will come to test them by fire.

He will come to His temple to beautify and adorn it with His glory. He will come to purify it from those who have profaned His worship (Matt. 21:12–13). He will judge the wicked and purify the godly.

The purest church and the holiest among saints need refining. Gold, the thing that is valued the most, is tried and proven by fire. He will set the right temperature. He will keep the metal (Levi) in the fire the right time. Either we submit to God's refinement or we will have to deal with the wilderness. Right services spring from the purest among men.

Whereas gold never fears the fire, the dross of evil things and the alloy of lower things surface to the top. Our purity will precede our power. Fire speaks of purification, progressive sanctification. When Paul addressed the church at Rome as having presence of the Spirit, He told them to "count [themselves] dead to sin but alive to God" (Rom. 6:11, NIV). He told them to "mortify the deeds of the body" (Rom. 8:13). Paul is telling them to keep on putting to death the evil desires of the body, and then they would keep on living.

Fire speaks of warmth, light, burning in the bosom. God is not trying to give hot heads, but hot hearts. The fire is also the awareness of enlightenment. The Spirit not only gives us the knowledge to know what is right, but also the strength and power to do it. The Spirit gives us the triumphal adequacy to cope with life.

"Whose fan is in his hand" (Matt. 3:12) takes us to the threshing floor, which was an open place in the field. Usually it was an elevated part of the land. It had no covering and no walls. It was thirty to forty spaces in diameter. It was made smooth by treading it hard. It was selected for the purpose of keeping the harvest dry.

The harvesters of grain would take a winnowing shovel that was used for throwing grain. The grain was usually trodden down by the oxen. Sometimes it was beaten. Sometimes a sharp instrument was used to roll over the grain to separate the wheat from the straw. After it was threshed into the air, the chaff was driven away by the wind while the grain would fall back down to the threshing floor.

"He will thoroughly purge his floor" (v. 12). The Messiah will thoroughly clean. He will take His broom and sweep from side to side to make it clean.

"He will gather his wheat into the garner" (v. 12), which means the granary, the place to deposit the wheat.

"He will burn up the chaff with unquenchable fire" (v. 12). The fire here can mean eternal punishment for the wicked. Those who turn from sin and receive Christ and His Word will be baptized with the Holy Spirit and fire. Those who cling to their sins will be punished with unquenchable fire.

The rebuilding of Zion (the church) is the renewal of the people, where sin is laid bare and sinners are cleansed. This is a special work of the Holy Spirit.

"When the Lord shall have washed away the filth of the daughters of Zion, and shall have purged the blood of Jerusalem from the midst thereof by the spirit of judgment, and by the spirit of burning" (Isa. 4:4)

Paul told the church at Thessalonica to "quench not the Spirit" (1 Thess. 5:19). The church at Thessalonica was founded during Paul's second missionary journey. The church there was established through a mighty move of the Holy Spirit. Because of violent opposition, Paul was forced to leave. He wrote a letter to encourage them. They had forgotten how the gospel first came to them. It "came not unto you in word only, but also in power, and in the Holy Ghost, and in much assurance" (1:5). The preaching of the gospel was accompanied by conviction of sin and deliverance from satanic bondage. They believed in the message, obeyed the Word, and lived it out in their lives before a world that was lost.

Many of those who believed became followers (imitators) of Paul and the Lord Himself. They had "received the word in much affliction, with joy of the Holy Ghost" (1:6). It was said of Paul and his companions that these men "have turned the world upside down are come hither also" (Acts. 17:6) to our town. Believers were filled with joy.

Paul had urged the Gentiles to abstain from sexual sins. "For this is the will of God, even your sanctification, that ye should abstain from fornication" (1 Thess. 4:3). Many of them had come out of a Greek culture; they had no idea about moral purity or what the Bible teaches about marriage. Paul emphasized the necessity of holiness and the power to live the Christian life. He stressed to them that believers must be holy. "For God hath not called us unto uncleanness, but unto holiness. He therefore that despiseth, despiseth not man, but God, who hath also given unto us his holy Spirit" (vv. 7–8). Paul was issuing a call to live a holy life. Being dedicated to God's will is in line with the nature of God and the holy nature of the Spirit. We claim to be a people of the Spirit, but do we have the nature of the Spirit?

Paul is holding up the new man and the kind of life that is only possible for those who draw upon the supernatural power of the Holy Spirit. Here in chapter five of 1 Thessalonians, in verses 12–22 Paul is giving us a series of exhortations. These commands are spiritual in regard to our relationship with the Lord.

When Paul says, "Quench not the Spirit" (v. 19), he is using the present imperative of the Greek word *subbenomai*. Here Paul issued a command to stop trying to put out the fire of the Holy Ghost in the life of the church. It is a command to cease from doing something that was already in process in the life of the church. Paul said, "Stop it!" He is saying, "Stop doing it, and don't get in the habit of doing it."[7] He is saying, "Stop trying to put out the fire of the Holy Ghost in your hearts." The word *quench* means stop stifling and suppressing divine influence, trying to extinguish His light and heat. There were those in the church who were throwing their wet blankets on the fire. Many today are also trying to pour their water buckets of doubt and unbelief on the fire of the Holy Ghost in the life of the church.

It is not simply a warning to avoid this kind of thing in the future. There is always someone who desires to throw a wet blanket on your fire. You can kill a fire in two ways: neglect it and smother it and not let it breath.

When Paul wrote to the church at Thessalonica, he warned them about quenching the Spirit. The Christian is not to quench the Holy Spirit. There are too many in the church who are trying to blame their pastor when they cannot maintain their excitement. In the Old Testament we find God coming to the brazen altar one time and lighting the fire upon it. Then He put the responsibility in the hands of the priests and told them to keep it burning. When God saved us He lit a fire on the altar of our hearts and told us to keep it burning. The writer in the Book of Proverbs said, "Where no wood is, there the fire goeth out" (Prov. 26:20).

Putting out the fire is a reference made to the fire of Gehenna, the lake of fire that cannot be quenched (Mark 9:44, 46, 48). We need to remember the five wise and five foolish virgins. The five who were foolish took no oil for their lamps. When their lamps went out they were disqualified from being a part of the wedding party. Jesus made reference to John the Baptist when He said, "Smoking flax shall he not quench" (Matt. 12:20). The writer of the

Book of Hebrews said the heroes of faith "quenched the violence of fire" (Heb. 11:34).

When the fire of the Holy Ghost is put out in the life of the church, the witness of the local church and that of the believer becomes ineffective. The Spirit brings warmth to the heart, light to the mind, and power to kindle the human spirit. That is why the apostle Paul told Timothy to stir up the gift that was in him (2 Tim. 1:7). The discouragement of Timothy was the church declining and knowing that at any moment he could become a martyr for the faith that had weakened his fervency in the Spirit.

The church today must be very hesitant about dampening down real spiritual fervor. We must always recognize the work of the Holy Spirit. We need quit apologizing for His operation in our midst. We need to remember what it cost us to have this kind of move of God. When we don't appreciate Him and reject the manifestations of the Spirit, it can result in the loss of the moving of the Spirit in and through the life of the church.

Here is a note of caution: with only the Holy Spirit you will blow up. With only the Word you dry up. When the Spirit and the Word come together you can conquer the world and everything that is around you.

WAYS TO QUENCH THE HOLY SPIRIT OF GOD

- When we stifle and suppress the Holy Spirit.
- When we despise prophesying and count it as nothing, treating it as though it is worthless, and having an arrogant disdain for it. There are too many that are looking down their noses at those who are thrilled over the prospect of the Holy Spirit using them.
- Prophecies should be put to the test. We are to reject the bad and hold fast to that which is good. Many had brought their reports and forged letters from Paul, while claiming support from the Holy Spirit.
- When we frown on those who are enthusiastic about the operation of the Holy Spirit and who are in eager pursuit of the gifts of the Spirit.
- When we refuse to hear prophetic words of a Spirit-inspired member of the church.

- When we profess the gifts of the Holy Spirit and our lifestyle does not measure up to biblical holiness.
- When we extinguish the sanctifying power and work of the Holy Spirit. Remember it is the Holy Spirit who protects us from the sin nature.
- When there is despondency of life, immorality, and idleness.
- When we become disobedient through fear.
- When we take on evil desires and compromise with the world.
- When we desire honor, praise of men, fame, and popularity instead of totally surrendering to the Holy Spirit.

Paul made reference to the joy the Thessalonians had in their spirit as they served God and waited for Christ's return (1 Thess. 1:6, 9–10). If we stifle the Spirit, we will lose the joy in the Holy Ghost as we wait for Christ's return.

What has happened to our spiritual fervor? When Paul wrote the church at Rome, he said, "Be not slothful in business; fervent in spirit, serving the Lord" (Rom. 12:11). The Message translation says it this way: "Don't burn out; keep yourselves fueled and aflame." The word *slothful* comes from the Greek word *okneros* which means "to delay, to feel lazy and lethargic, to be slow and hesitant."[8] Our zeal is not to be flagging. We are not to be slow and goofing off in the work of the Lord.

In the parable of the talents, there was a servant that took what the master of the house had given to him and went out and dug and hole and buried it. He did not take it and invest it in the work of the kingdom. "His lord answered and said unto him, Thou wicked and slothful servant, thou knewest that I reap where I sowed not, and gather where I have not strawed" (Matt. 25:26). "Cast ye the unprofitable servant into outer darkness: there shall be weeping and gnashing of teeth" (v. 30). What have we done with what the Master of our house has given to us?

When Paul said that we were to be "fervent in spirit" (Rom. 12:11), he used the Greek word *zeo,* meaning "to boil with heat, be hot."[9] We are never to be lagging in our zeal. We are to be aglow with the Spirit. Fervency in the Christian life is energized by the Holy Ghost. It is not something produced through efforts of the flesh. Its origin lies in the Holy Ghost. The Christian should be a man or woman on fire for God. When we walk into a room there should be a glow upon our countenance that radiates the circle we fill.

When one is fervent in the Spirit about the accomplishment of any work, we will become a person of one idea. Paul said, "This one thing I do, forgetting those things which are behind, and reaching forth unto those things which are before" (Phil. 3:13). If we are trying to do forty things around the church, we will not be good at any one thing we do. If we can learn to do one thing and do it well, we will be better for it. Are we souls that are possessed with one idea? We need to realize that if we are going to serve God effectively, it will require everything within us.

For us to be fervent in the Spirit will require the active, energetic exercise of all our powers. We should not be half-hearted in our service. We need unity of heart. The psalmist said, "Unite my heart to fear thy name" (Ps. 86:11). We cannot serve God with a divided heart.

It was said concerning Apollos that he was "fervent in the spirit" (Acts 18:25). He was aglow with the Spirit, boiling in the pursuit of doing good. Martin Luther said "In regard to zeal be not lazy."[10] Zeal describes the moral earnestness in which one should give themselves to their vocation. When it comes to zeal, we are not to be backwards. What good is a Christian who has no zeal for the cause of Christ?

Paul said that Christ gave Himself to purify for himself a "peculiar people, zealous of good works" (Titus 2:14). We are a peculiar people because of who we belong to. It does not mean that we are oddballs. It means that we are unique because of who owns us. We are to be heated to boiling in the pursuit of doing good.

A zealous man is fervent in the Spirit. He is ardent about his pursuit of an object. How ardent should we be in pressing forward to apprehend that for which Christ has apprehended us? (Phil. 3:12). It takes a vigorous plant to survive vigorous winters. Fervency in the Spirit will protect us against the blast of earth's winters. Vigorous Christians, who are fervent in the Spirit, will be the ones who will survive vigorous times.

When it comes to serving the Lord, we must remember that there is a work to be done. The man or woman who serves the Lord faithfully is the one who takes a wise and holy advantage of every opportunity. We are to serve the Lord in every department of life. It is the best way to serve the time. In fact, serving the Lord will never lose its attractiveness to the spiritual man.

Serving Christ can mean satanic opposition and can bring on days of discouragement. We need to maintain our spiritual zeal because we are serving the Lord. When life becomes difficult, the Christian cannot permit his zeal to grow cold. "Because iniquity shall abound, the love of many shall wax cold" (Matt. 24:12). Because sin and transgression are multiplying and increasing, people's love and zeal for God does grow cold. What is the key? "Be joyful in hope, patient in affliction, faithful in prayer" (Rom. 12:12, NIV).

The spiritual man will show new graces, expand fresh powers, and introduce varied pleasures to the soul. The command is still to all: "Go and work in my vineyard" (Matt. 20:4, NIV).

Jesus said, "The zeal of thine house hath eaten me up" (John 2:17). Jesus revealed His zeal for His Father's house by cleansing the temple. The religious leaders of Israel tried to turn the house of the Lord into a business, not a ministry. Jesus had intense zeal in the pursuit of God's glory that became a consuming fire within Him. The strong nature of Jesus was eaten up by His zeal. There were times it was so strong that He forgot to eat His necessary food. When the disciples returned with food, they were concerned that Jesus had not eaten. "My meat is to do the will of him that sent me, and to finish his work" (4:34). Jesus' zeal got Him in trouble with the religious leaders of the nation.

Zeal in our Christian duty is the natural consequence of agape love filling our hearts. In chapter 12 of Romans, love and holiness dominate Paul's presentation of spiritual living. Love is holiness and is bound by the ethics of holiness. "He that loveth not knoweth not God; for God is love" (1 John 4:8). Love is the circulatory system of the body of Christ and spiritual gifts.

Love must be sincere, Paul exorts, "Let love be without dissimulation" (Rom. 12:9). Love will be honest, not hypocritical. You won't tell people you love them to their face and cut them behind their back. James made it clear that if we are going to have pure, undefiled religion, we can't curse our brother and then come into the house and bless God. Love will dominate the personal relationships of believers. It will bind them together. When we are "knit" together in love, there is no way the enemy can tear us apart. The greater the attempt to pull us apart, the more fabric that is knit together will grow tighter and stronger. Lord, bind us together with cords that cannot be broken.

"Abhor that which is evil: cleave to that which is good" (v. 9). The word *cleave* speaks of one being bound to a master. It speaks of our spiritual union with the Lord. As Christ loved righteousness and hated iniquity, it was then that He was anointed with the oil of gladness above his fellows (Heb. 1:9).

"Be kindly affectioned one to another with brotherly love" (Rom. 12:10). Our love for one another should be warm, spontaneous, and constant. There should be a family affection that characterizes our relationships. We have been birthed from the same womb and washed in the same blood; we are fighting for the same cause and heading for the same destination.

"In honour preferring one another; Not slothful in business; fervent in spirit; serving the Lord; Rejoicing in hope; patient in tribulation; continuing instant in prayer" (vv. 10–12). Love will manifest itself in joy, patience, and prayerfulness.

We "rejoice in hope of the glory of God" (5:2). Here it is not only our pardon and acquittal from the guilt of sin, but also our sanctification as well. We need to rejoice in our participation of Christ's kingdom. We need to treat the promises of the kingdom as if they have already been fulfilled. We need to be living on the tiptoes of expectancy.

Jesus had made it clear that "in the world ye shall have tribulation: but be of good cheer; I have overcome the world" (John 16:33).

Our tribulations need to be turned into patience. The word *patience* comes from the Greek *upo-meno*, which means "to remain under a test in a God-honoring manner."[11] We are not to look for a way out, but to have an eagerness to learn the lessons the test was sent to teach—to remain, to abide, not to recede, to flee, to bear bravely and calmly. Through prayer we need to keep the renewal of the Holy Spirit alive within our hearts.

Paul continues to describe love in action: "Distributing to the necessity of the saints; given to hospitality" (Rom. 12:13). There are three Greek words translated *love* in the New Testament:

1. *Agape*: is essentially the nature of God. It is sacrificial love where an individual will sacrifice himself for the good and welfare of his fellow man. Agape love enables us to love the unlovable. When it comes to agape, something of God's nature has been imparted to us. It is the love by which God loves us and demands in return. "And hope maketh not ashamed; because the love of God is shed abroad in our hearts by the Holy Ghost which is given unto us" (5:5). "The fruit of the Spirit is love" (Gal. 5:22).

2. *Phileo*: means friendship love or affection.

3. *Eros*: is sensual love between a man and a wife.

Paul has made it abundantly clear that our spiritual fervor is the result of agape love taking its rightful place in our hearts. Remember when "Jesus went forth, and saw a great multitude, and was moved with compassion toward them, and he healed their sick" (Matt. 14:14). It has been said that the day we lose our compassion our ministry is over.

When the love that dwelt in Jesus and moved Him lives in and moves the church, we will be fervent in Spirit. The more I love God, the more I will love my fellow man. Love is diligent, eager to manifest itself, and is never reluctant.

When my love for God is what it should be, so will be my service in His kingdom. In the Book of Malachi, the priest looked upon serving God as a wearisome thing (1:13). Faith had turned into cynicism, and optimism had turned into pessimism. They had forgotten what it meant to be called by God to serve as priest in His house. The tablecloths were supposed to be clean and white and were allowed to become dirty. The bread had become molded instead of being fresh bread hot out of heaven's ovens. When love for God is not what it should be, things become neglected in His service. The opposite of love is not hatred; it is indifference. If I am not in love with God, I will be indifferent to Him. There will be no fervency in my service to Him.

Remember when Peter bragged that He was not only willing to go to Jerusalem, but was ready to die with Christ if he had to? Jesus told him, "Verily I say unto thee, That this night, before the cock crow, thou shalt deny me thrice" (Matt. 26:34). Three times in the courtyards of the house of Caiaphas, Peter denied that he even knew Christ. He warmed up beside somebody else's fire instead of having a fire of his own. In one of those instances his speech betrayed him.

Do I ever give the Lord a reason to question my love for Him? Peter had boasted that He would stand by Christ though all forsook Him (Mark 14:29). Then in the Book of John, Jesus asked Peter if he loved Him three different times, "Simon, son of Jonas, lovest thou me more than these?" (John 21:15). The word *these* was in the neuter form. Jesus was saying, "Do you love me more than your fishing boat, nets, and your material possessions? Keep in mind that twice Jesus asked for agape love. Peter could only reply that he was *phileo*, meaning he had affection for Him. Peter made no claim of superior love. The third time Jesus asked if he had affection, or *phileo,* and Peter answered affirmatively. Peter loved Him as a friend. Peter was cut to the heart.

The third time reminded Peter of the three denials when he had betrayed Him. He repeats his love for Jesus with the plea, "Lord, thou knowest all things" (v. 17).

Jesus always responded to Peter, telling him that He loved him. First it was to "Feed my lambs" (v. 15). There are two different Greek words translated *feed* in this text: *Basko,* present active imperative, meant to lead them to pastures where they could find proper nutrition. *Poimen* meant "to govern, counsel, and advise the flock." Jesus was saying, "Peter, if you love me, you will lead my lambs to pastures where they can find nutrition. You will govern, council, and advise my flock."

Chapter 10

Under a Curse

For as many as are of the works of the law are under a curse: for it is written, Cursed is everyone that continueth not in all things which are written in the Book of the law to do them.

—GALATIANS 3:10

PAUL IS SEEKING to drive his opponents into a corner where there seems to be no escape. They were attempting to try to win God's approval by accepting and obeying the Law. The Law was the greatest thing in their national life. God gave it to Moses, and the Jews depended on it. Man will choose to stand and fall by his decision. If they decide to live under the Law they will not be able to live in the sphere of God's grace. If they choose the Law they are going to have to live by it. No one has ever succeeded trying to live by the Law as if by their works it will cause them to stand in a right relationship with God. The Judaizers were ignoring the substitutionary death of Jesus and were falling back on works as a ground of acceptance. If they did so, they would be placing themselves under a curse.

The Judaizers wanted to seduce the Galatian Christians to enjoy a religion of works based on the Law. Paul wanted them to enjoy a relationship of love and a life of faith in Christ. For the Christian to abandon salvation by grace through faith for works was to lose everything he could experience in his daily fellowship with the Lord.

The Law *cannot* do the following:

- Justify the sinner (Gal. 2:16)
- Impute righteousness (2:21)
- Give the gift of the Spirit (3:2)
- Guarantee a spiritual inheritance (3:18)
- Give life (3:21)
- Bring liberty (4:8–10)

So why go back to the Law?

The Judaizers wanted to lead Christians into slavery. Christ died to set them free. Salvation is being set free from the bondage of sin and the Law and being brought into the liberty of God's grace through Christ. How could the Judaizers ever convince the Galatian Christians that the letter of the Law was better than grace? Why would any believer want to choose bondage instead of liberty?

Why? Because legalism appeals to the flesh. The flesh loves to boast of its religious achievements. A person who depends on his religion will measure and compare himself with others. The true believer will compare himself with Christ. There is no room for pride in the spiritual walk of the Christian who lives by grace.

The Galatians had come to a fork in the road. Jewish Christians were deeply rooted in Jewish tradition and were still pointing Gentile converts to a well-traveled road that had been taken by the Jewish people for centuries. They felt that the only way the Gentiles could find the path of blessing was for them to identify with the Jews. Paul said this was not the path that leads to blessing. The path of blessing was not going to come by them identifying themselves with the Jews. The pathway to blessing would come by them identifying themselves with Christ. Who would have ever believed that when the Galatians backed off the operation of the Spirit and a dependency on the grace of God, they placed themselves back under the curse?

According to Deuteronomy 28 and Leviticus 26, the curse fell under three categories: sickness, disease, and poverty. There were curses pronounced upon the disobedient.[1] These curses have been fulfilled in the life and history of Israel for many centuries.

THE CURSES

1. Cleaving pestilence (Deut. 28:21–22)
2. Death (v. 22)
3. Consumption (Lev. 26:16).
4. Fever (v. 16)
5. Inflammation (Deut. 28:22)
6. Extreme burning (v. 22)

7. Sword (Lev. 26:17)
8. Blasting (Deut. 28:22)
9. Mildew (v. 22)
10. Heavens as iron (Lev. 26:19)
11. Earth as brass (v. 19–20)
12. Drought, dust, and no rain (Deut. 28:24)
13. Destruction because of long drought (v. 24)
14. Smitten before enemies (v. 25)
15. Going out one way, fleeing seven ways before their enemies (v. 25)
16. Scattered into the kingdoms of the earth (v. 25 and many more)
17. Bodies eaten by fowls and beasts (v. 26)
18. No help in driving them off (v. 26)
19. Botch of Egypt (v. 27)
20. Emerods (v. 27)
21. Scab (v. 27)
22. Itch (v. 27)
23. No healing or relief (v. 27)
24. Madness from helplessness (v. 28, 34)
25. Blindness (v. 28)
26. Astonishment of heart (v. 28)
27. Groping at noon day (v. 29)
28. No prosperity (v. 29)
29. Oppressed, spoiled, and crushed forever (v. 29)
30. No man to save (v. 29)
31. Enemies capturing and ravishing betrothed wives (v. 30)
32. Enemies taking over newly built houses (v. 30)
33. Enemies taking over freshly planted vineyards (v. 30)
34. Livestock slain and eaten before their eyes (v. 31)
35. Work animals taken and not restored (v. 31)

36. Sons and daughters sold into slavery, given to other people (v. 32, 41)

37. Longing for deliverance and it didn't come (v. 32)

38. Powerless to help (v. 32)

39. Enemies eating crops and enjoying the labors of their hands (v. 33)

40. Serving idol gods (v. 36)

41. Crops destroyed by locust (v. 38)

42. Vineyards eaten by worms (v. 39)

43. Loss of olive crops (v. 40)

44. Strangers exalted while they were humbled (v. 43)

45. Strangers the head and them the tail (v. 44)

FOUR THINGS THESE CURSES WILL DO (DEUT. 28:45)

1. They will come upon you.

2. They will pursue you.

3. They will overtake you.

4. They will destroy you.

SIX REASONS FOR CURSES

1. Because of wickedness and backslidings (v. 20)

2. Because they did not hearken to the voice of the Lord their God (v. 45)

3. Because they would not keep His commandments and statutes (v. 45)

4. To be a sign and wonder to teach them and their children lessons forever (v. 46)

5. Because they did not serve the Lord with joyfulness and gladness of heart (v. 47)

6. Because they would not obey the voice of the LORD their God (v. 62)

There are many examples found in God's Word where God punished His people when they persisted in sin and rebellion lest they die in their sins. He has been just and good to all in every age. He blesses men when they obey and curses men when they are in disobedience. He is no respecter of persons. He has given us many examples of angels, demons, and kings, and we have the entire history of Israel and men from all walks of life who have actually suffered such a destiny.

There are four scriptures in Galatians chapter 3 that can used as signposts at this fork in the road to indicate which way leads to the curse and which way leads to blessing. These four signposts are labeled with four words: curse (v. 10), faith (v. 11), law (v. 12), and cross (vv. 13–14). We need to beware of those who map out roads based on cultural customs.

The first signpost is the curse. Paul placed this as the fork in the road for the Galatian believers. This is a harsh warning to all who rely on observance of the law. They are under a curse. Anyone is cursed who does not do everything written in the Book of the law" (Deut. 27:26). In Deuteronomy there are several lists of curses which conclude with severe warnings of complete destruction. The curses were the result of failure to do the law. It was the assumption of the apostle Paul that all who rely on observing the law for blessing fail to keep the law. Paul said at the end of his Galatian letter that "not even those who [were] circumcised obey the law" (6:13).

Paul was trying to discourage the Galatians from seeking membership among those who rely on observing the law and wind up placing themselves under the curse of the law. When the Judaizers were trying to persuade the Galatian believers to enter into their circle by keeping the Law, Paul was very careful in his attempt to prove to the Galatians that the very ones who were inviting them to join the group of lawbreakers were under a curse themselves. If the lawbreakers themselves are under a curse for having failed to keep all the law, then the risk for the Gentiles taking on a curse was greater. The acceptance of requirements such as circumcision and Sabbath keeping obligates them to keep the whole law (5:3). If all who rely on observing the Law cannot keep the whole Law (2:14 and 6:13), then surely the Galatian believers would not be able to do it either. They would come under a terrible curse for their failure to keep the whole Law.

The Law placed sinners under a curse. Christ has redeemed us from the curse. Do you want the blessing of Abraham? It comes through Christ. Do you want the gift of the Spirit? It comes through Christ by the cross. It was the cross that opened the door for the Holy Spirit. All you need is Jesus. There is no reason to go back to Moses.

The second signpost is faith. Habakkuk said, "The just shall live by his faith" (Hab. 2:4). Since faith is the way to righteousness, the law cannot be the way. No one is justified by the law. The signpost tells us that faith and law are two different ways. The Judaizers were trying to get the Galatians to believe that if they kept the requirements of the law, they would gain entrance into the Jewish nation and be assured of acceptance as God's people. Acceptance with God and justification before God cannot be possibly found through the law. According to the Scripture, righteousness comes by faith.

It is the man who is justified by faith in Christ that will really live (Rom. 5:1). The only way to get right with God and to know His peace is through faith. You cannot direct your life by works and grace at the same time. We need to abandon the way of legalism and come the way of faith. We need to learn to take God at His Word and trust in Him.

The third signpost is the law. The nature of the law is that it requires doing. There were specific requirements given to the Jewish people by the law. These decrees and laws were given by God to Israel at Mount Sinai. It distinguished Israel from the Egyptians and Canaanites (Lev. 18:1–4). In the Galatians dispute, the law refers to a set of requirements (circumcision, food, other rituals, and Sabbath laws) imposed on Gentile believers which would identify them with the Jewish nation and set them apart from Greeks and Romans.

Paul rebukes the Galatians for their assumption that doing the works of the law would cause them to participate in the life and blessing of the covenant people of God. The law was not of faith, because it demands doing the works of the law as the way of life. The law demanded perfect obedience (Gal. 3:12), even though it could not impart life and righteousness before God (v. 21). So Paul is putting a stop sign in front of those who want to follow the law as a way of life. You cannot get to life by going through the observance of the law. Life is found only through faith in Christ. John declared, "In Him was life, and that life was the light of men" (John 1:4). Jesus is the source and origin of life. If we have not come to know Him we are existing, not living.

The fourth signpost is the cross of Christ. The only way to be delivered from the curse of the law is to turn in faith to the cross of Christ. The cross put an end to the Mosaic Law. If you accept the law you reject the cross. "Christ redeemed us from the curse of the law by becoming a curse for us" (v. 13, NIV). He was rejected that we might be accepted. He was cursed that we might be blessed. He was broken that we might be made whole. He was hung up for our hang-ups. He was hung in naked shame that we might be clothed with His righteousness. He went to hell so that one day we can go to heaven. He became sin for us that we might be made the righteousness of God in Him. In fact the scripture says, "Cursed is everyone who is hung on a tree" (Gal.3: 13; Deut. 21:23).

The Jews did not crucify criminals. They stoned them to death. In the cases where the law was shamefully violated, the body was hung on the tree. It was exposed for all to see which was the greatest kind of humiliation. The Jews were very careful how they treated a dead body. They put to death malefactors by hanging. Then they hung their bodies on a tree. The Jews in contempt called him that hanged on a tree a cure. They were hung between heaven and earth not being worthy of either. Then the body was taken down and buried. Christ was made a curse for us. The allusion was to expose a dead body on a stake and cross (Josh. 10:26). The one who hung there was willingly enduring the curse for us.

Jesus hung on a cross from 9:00 a.m. to 3:00 p.m. He was nailed alive to a tree and left there to die. Because He bore the curse for us now we are no longer under the law and it's awful curse. Justification by faith and the gift of the Spirit is now ours through faith in Jesus Christ. Now all the terrors and penalties of the law would disappear. It was absorbed din the cross of Christ. The time of release had come for all men.

Thank God, we are blessed beyond the curse! And that blessing is by the proclamation of redemption by the One who hung on a tree. By hanging on a cross, Jesus came under the burden of the curse for those who failed to keep the law. By bearing the total burden of the curse Himself, Jesus set us free from the terrible weight of the curse. The penalty that was brought on us by our violation of the law, Jesus bore it. He removed it and took it away and made a way for forgiveness.

The word *redeemed* comes from the word *exegorasen*. It is the first aorist active, which means "to buy back from, to buy back, to ransom." This word opens up a metaphor of a whole new understanding of the atonement. It had to do with the purchase of slaves in a will for the purpose of setting them free. Jesus shed His blood on the cross that we might be set free. To bring for this truth Jesus had to die on the cross to free us from sin's curse. Christ purchased us out from under the curse of the law. Jesus Himself had to become a curse for us. We were under a curse. Christ became a curse over us. The curse that should have fell on us fell on Him. Christ brought us out from the curse that was brought upon us by our failure to keep the law. "He became sin for us who knew no sin that we might be made the righteousness of God in Christ Jesus" (2 Cor. 5:21).

This word was used elsewhere in the New Testament. "Forasmuch as ye know that ye were not redeemed with corruptible things, as silver and gold, from your vain conversation received by tradition of your fathers; but with the precious blood of Christ, as a lamb without blemish and without spot" (1 Pet. 1:18–19). Again it was used in the Book of Acts: "Take heed therefore unto yourselves, and to all the flock, over the which the Holy Ghost hath made you overseers, to feed the church of God, which he hath purchased with His own blood" (Acts 20:28.)

Have you ever stopped to wonder the cost of the Christian gospel? We should never forget the peace, liberty, and right relationship with God that we now possess. It cost Jesus Christ His very life. We would have never known what God was like if Jesus Christ had not come to live among us and die to tell us of His great love.

Our redemption was effected by Christ when He endured the penalty of the Law. It brought blessings to all nations. "The blessing of Abraham might come on the Gentiles through Jesus Christ" (v. 14). Abraham's blessing that had long been withheld is now being imparted. The spiritual results of redemption are only realized through faith. "That we might receive the promise of the Spirit through faith" (v. 14). In Christ Jesus, crucified, buried, risen, reigning, a new world comes into being that restores and surpasses the old.

The Judaizers who pestered the Galatian believers had drawn two circles: the circle of blessing for the Jews and the circle of the cursing for the Gentiles. The Galatian believers were moving from the circle of Gentiles to the circle of the Jews so they could be free from the curse and obtain the blessing. Paul had already demonstrated that the circle of the Jews is also under a curse for failure to keep all the law. Transferring from the Gentile circle to the Jewish circle was no way to escape the curse of the law. Always, the only way to escape the curse is to turn to Christ.

The fourth signpost points toward the blessing of Abraham and the promise of the Spirit. In verse 14 Paul tells us that the reason Christ set us free from the curse of the law was to open the way for us to participate in the promised blessings of Abraham. The blessings given to Abraham are equivalent to the promise of the Spirit. When the Galatian believers received the Spirit by faith in Christ crucified (vv. 1–2), they were recipients of the blessings promised to Abraham. The Galatian believers were already recipients of the promised blessings to Abraham but were now trying to keep the law in order to obtain the blessings they already possessed; they deserved to be called foolish. Why would anyone be so foolish as to take the road toward a curse when they were already on the road to blessing?

Salvation is by faith not by the law. Salvation could never come by obedience to the law because the law brought a curse, not a blessing (Deut. 27:26). The law demanded obedience. It was no religious cafeteria where people were allowed to pick or choose.

It was impossible to keep all the commandments of the law. It brought all men under a curse. There were over 613 Jewish Laws, each one said "thou shalt" or "thou shalt not!" If you broke one you were guilty of breaking the whole law. The rabbis of Paul's day knew this, and Paul knew it from his own experience. Many of the Jewish people simply clung to the merits of their fathers.

Many of the rabbis have tried to prove that the patriarchs kept the law even though it had not yet been revealed. They felt strongly that if God in His mercy had used some other system with Abraham, it was because there was no law to keep. The Judaizers were preaching to the Galatians the utter necessity of keeping the law. To them the talk of Abraham was irrelevant to the main issue. The common opinion of Jewish scholars was that the common people who had no knowledge or interest in the law were under a curse.

It was the view of the Pharisees in the Gospel of John that "this people who knoweth not the law are cursed" (John 7:49). Neither knowing the law nor keeping it saves the soul. The law only condemned them and made them guilty. (Rom. 3:9–23; 7:7–25; 1 John 3:4). Here Paul turns the tables on them; it is those who keep the law, not the Gentile sinners who are under a curse.

Everyone who hunts for acceptance with God on the grounds of doing what the law commands are under the curse of God. Everyone who fails to stand fast by everything written in the law, and do it, is under the curse of

God. It is perfectly clear that no one obtains right standing with God by the law. Those who obtain right standing through faith will win life.

Paul is contrasting men of faith with those who rely on obedience to the law. The first one applies to the Christian the second one applies to the Jews. They speak of the two ways we approach God. Either we approach Him completely without merit, on the grounds of His grace alone; or we approach Him on the grounds of our own merit. Abraham was in the first group, while the Judaizers were in the second.

When Paul talked about being "under a curse" (Gal. 3:10), he used the phrase *hupo kataran*, which was a Jewish form of expression. The curse is related to the reaction of God to sin. If you will recall in Genesis 3:14–19 God cursed the woman, man, and serpent and then He cursed the earth.

> If ye will not hear, and if ye will not lay it to the heart, to give glory unto my name, saith the LORD of Host, I will even send a curse upon you, and I will curse your blessings: yea, I have cursed them already, because you do not lay it to heart.
> —MALACHI 2:2

Chapter II

Spiritual Descendants of Abraham

And the scripture, forseeing that God would justify the heathen
through faith, preached before the gospel unto Abraham,
saying, In thee shall all nations be blessed. So then they
which be of faith are blessed with faithful Abraham.

—GALATIANS 3:8–9

ODAY IN THE life of the church we have an identity crisis. Christians are going to have to discern between their identity as God's children and the identity offered to them by surrounding cultures. How does one's faith in Christ affect one's identity before a lost and dying world? If we were of the world system that was alienated from Christ would not the world recognize us? Because we are of God the world does not recognize us. Because of our profession in a crucified, buried, and resurrected Savior hell has declared war on us. When we were in sin we were downstream swimmers in a downstream world. We went along with the tide, not against it. Now that we are saved we are upstream swimmers in a downstream world. We don't go along with the tide; we go against it. Questions have been raised in every generation and culture by Christians who are seeking to find their true identify in Christ. The Galatian believers were living between Jewish synagogues and pagan temples and were not welcome in either, even though they read the Jewish Scriptures and believed in a Jewish Messiah. They were new to the Christian faith and did not have a clear sense of true identity. They were being told that if they wanted to become the true church they would have to identify themselves with the Jewish community. They knew the church at Jerusalem was a law-observing church, and if they were going to become truly Christian they would have to identify with the Jewish people.

Their true identity as members of the family of God was based on their faith in Christ. It not based on them becoming identified with an ethnic group. So whether you are New Testament Israel, spiritual descendants of Abraham or the church, you belong to the people of God. This has been confirmed through the Scriptures (v. 8).

Jesus Himself had to find His identity in a world that was held captive by sin. John said, "He was in the world and the world was made by Him, and yet the world knew Him not" (John 1:10). The world had become so marred because of sin that it did not recognize its Creator when He came. The story of Jesus is one of rejection. Although He was in the world, and He was the Creator of it all, the world failed to recognize Him for who He was. Throughout the gospel of John, there were many who speculated who Jesus was but fell short when it came to recognizing Him as the Christ, the Son of the Living God.

He also stated, "He came to His own, and His own received Him not. But as many as received Him, to them gave He power to become the sons of God, even as many as them that believe on His name" (John 1:11–12). If anyone should have been able to identify Jesus and should have been ready to receive Him when He came, it should have been the Jews. They had the Law, prophets, and the Scriptures, yet they gave Him no hearty reception when He came. Devils knew Him while the religious leaders of Israel tried to ignore Him. If anyone professed faith in Christ they were cast out of the Synagogues (John 9). Even nature knew more about who was hanging on the cross than the religious leaders who stood at the foot of it. Hell could not stop Him; water could not drown Him. Storms could not kill Him. Death could not hold Him. Grave could not keep Him.

Do the Galatians have to take on Jewish identity in order to become Christians? Absolutely not! Their identity as members of the family of God rests on their faith in Christ. It is not based on whether or not they are willing to become Jewish. Believers in every generation need to find their true identity in Christ. So we find that the church has a clear identity. We belong to the people of God. It began with Abraham and is confirmed through Scripture (v. 8.)

In Galatians 3:6–9, Paul tells us that there are some steps by which they can regain and strengthen their sense of identity. Paul identifies of the Galatian believers: First of all, Paul compares them with Abraham (v. 6); Secondly, he identifies them as children of Abraham on the basis of faith (v. 7); Third, he confirms their identity by quoting Scripture (v. 8), fourthly, he includes them in the family blessing, "In you shall all the nations be blessed" (v. 9).

Paul points to the story of Abraham's faith: "Consider Abraham" (v. 6, NIV). He is the father of God's people. His experience with God establishes a guide and a pattern to find the will of God. If the experience of the Galatians can be shown to parallel with the experience of Abraham, then it proves their identity as the people of God.

God made Abraham's name great. He is revered not only by the Jewish people, but also by Christians and Muslims. God multiplied his descendants and blessed those who blessed Abraham. He also judged those who cursed his descendants.

Abraham was an incredible man that was *unshakable in his faith*. Romans said that "He staggered not at the promises of God through unbelief; but was strong in faith, giving glory to God. Being fully persuaded that what God had promised He was able to perform." (Romans 4:20-21) When God called him at the age of 75, he went out not knowing where he was going (Heb. 11:8). Abraham continued to believe when all hope was lost. When Sarah was 90 and her biological clock had stopped, "And he being not weak in faith, he considered his own body now dead, when he was about a hundred years old, neither the deadness of Sarah's womb:" (Rom. 4:19). "Who against hope believed in hope, that he might become the father of many nations, according to that which was spoken, So shall thy seed be" (Romans 14:18).

Abraham was not just a man of unshakeable faith. He was a man of unquestionable obedience. Whether it was to get out of His father's house unto a land that God would show him (Gen. 12). Whether it was to sacrifice his only son Isaac, or to fight the Babylonian Army (4 kings of the East), his response was always, "yes Sir!" For this reason he was known in Scripture as being the friend of God (James 2:23).

Abraham was *a man of unbroken communion with God*. When Abraham was under the tent of Mamre God said to Abraham, "Shall I hide from Abraham the thing that I am about to do" (Gen. 18:7) The Scripture declares, "The Lord confides in those who fear him; he makes his covenant known to them." (Psalms 25:14).

Paul has pointed the Galatians to Abraham as a man who has embodied faith. Abraham pleased God not by the works of the law, because at that time the law did not exist. He pleased God by taking God at His word in a great act of faith. He was seventy-five years old when he left his father's house. He was raised up in an idolatrous background where they worshiped Sin, the moon god. He was also called Nanna by he early Samaritans. Abraham before his call lived in an idolatrous, materialistic culture. The name "Ur" was derived from the meaning of "light."[1] Abraham's lineage was traced all the way back to Seth. Under Seth, the fires of true worship began to burn again. It may be the Abraham's faith was the full bloom's flower of Seth's faith. When people "began to call on the name of the Lord." (Gen. 4:26). God speaks to him and tells him, "Get thee out of thy country, and from thy kindred, and from thy father's house, unto a land that I will shew thee" (Gen. 12:1). He left and did not know where He was going.

Paul seeks to prove that Abraham was saved by faith and not by the works of the law. Paul points out that salvation is by faith in response to faith, not by works. If sinners earned salvation by works, then salvation would not be the result of grace. If salvation was given only on the basis of works, then only the Jew then could be saved. The Gentile was never given the law. Paul's message of salvation by faith through grace was divine in its origin and the Judaizers opposed it.

Abraham was a spiritual man. Everywhere he went he was building altars. He sanctified the earth that around him. He sought after spiritual things. Abraham visited Salem on many occasions and paid homage to its king. Abraham was not looking for a natural Jerusalem. The Bible said, "He was looking for a city which had foundations, whose builder and maker is God." (Heb. 11:10) For this reason God was not ashamed to be called their God for he had prepared for them a city" (Heb. 11:16).

Is God ashamed of us today? Are we looking for the spiritual or are we clinging to the natural? Abraham sought and received a spiritual heritage, a spiritual family. God promised that in his seed (singular in the Hebrew) all nations of the earth would be blessed. That singular seed would be the Messiah that would come through the Jewish line. In the Messiah (Jesus) all nations of the earth would be blessed. Through the Messiah there would arise a family of faith on earth that would be as numerous as the heavens and the sands of the seashores. The blessing of God's spirit would rest on men (Gen. 3:14).

The Jews were proud of their relationship with Abraham. They thought their relationship with him guaranteed them salvation. John the Baptist warned them that their physical descent of Abraham did not guarantee them spiritual life. They said "We have Abraham to our father" (Matt. 3:9), as if their nationality guaranteed them a place in the kingdom. Like many of us they felt that repentance was something everybody else needed to be doing. There is a difference between being the physical descendant of Abraham and being his spiritual descendant. Nature is determined by birth. The Jews in Christ's day did not have Abraham's nature. The spiritual children of Abraham bear family resemblance. They build altars, pray, and are strong in faith. They do not stagger at the promises of God through unbelief; they are fully persuaded that what God has promised, He is able to perform (Rom 4:20–21). They tithe and they are friends of God.

The Jews felt because they were Abraham's seed that their nationality guaranteed them a place in the kingdom. This is why the Jews clung so insistently to the fact that they were the physical descendants of Abraham. They were his physical descendants but not his spiritual children. Their birth should have determined their nature. The Jews were his descendents but they did not bare his nature. They did not pray, they did not build altars, and they were not strong in faith. Two things were missing from the Jewish people at the time of Christ: faith and prayer. Many of the Jewish people, unlike Abraham, staggered at the promises of God through unbelief and were not fully persuaded that what God had promised, He was able to perform. Abraham had showed hospitality to the Lord Himself when He and two angels came to his tent at Mamre (Gen. 18:1); the Jews tried to kill Jesus. We know from the scripture that Abraham tithed to the Melchizedek, king of Salem (Heb. 7:2); the Jews were robbing God through their tithes and offerings (Mal. 3:8).

Paul was saying that Abraham was justified by faith, not by circumcision. Abraham was declared to be righteous several years before he was circumcised. Abraham was declared to be righteous before the ordinance of circumcision was given and before the law was instituted under Moses 400 years later, which proved that circumcision had nothing to do with Abraham being declared righteous. "Abraham believed God, and it was accounted to him for righteousness" (Gal. 3:6).

The word *accounted* comes from the Greek *logizomai*, which was a business term meaning "to put to one's account." Abraham's act of faith was placed as a deposit for him. It was credited to him for righteousness. He could never have merited it through human efforts. His faith resulted in righteousness. Abraham laid aside all his dependence upon good works as a means of finding acceptance with God. He entered into acceptance with God by believing and realizing he could not merit it in himself. He confessed it to God and threw himself at God's feet. He looked to God to do what he could not do himself. This alone is right standing with God. Any other attitude is stubborn pride and self-righteousness. His faith was answered by God declaring him to be righteous.

Paul is showing a very strong similarity between the experience of the Galatian Christians, who believed when they heard the preaching of the cross and received the blessing of the Spirit, and the experience of that great patriarch of God's people, who believed God's promise and received the credit of righteousness.

The circumcision of Abraham is mentioned thirteen times in the Torah. Circumcision was a token and a sign of a Jewish son becoming a part of the covenant with God. It was commanded by the law, and any Hebrew male child that was not circumcised was cut off from the people. "And the uncircumcised man child whose flesh of his foreskin is not circumcised, that soul shall be cut off from his people; he hath broken my covenant" (Gen. 17:14).

Paul draws upon two significant parallels between the Galatians' experience (human response of faith) and Abraham's experience (divine blessing). In the human response of faith, the Galatian believers were being excluded from the family of Abraham because they did not have the required membership badge: circumcision and the works of the law. Circumcision was the sign of the Abrahamic covenant, and Genesis 17 declared that anyone without this sign was to be cut off from the covenant family. So these Gentiles who were not circumcised could not be included in the Abrahamic family and blessing. Basically they were saying, "You do not belong!" This must have been very upsetting, to be excluded from the blessing of God and the fellowship of the people of God on the basis of racial, social, and religious entry requirements.

Circumcision identified the Jews as the spiritual descendants of Abraham. Circumcision spoke of covenant, obedience, purification, cutting away, and the removal of that which is unclean. In the time of Joshua, if Israel wanted the Lord to fight for them, they had to have the mark of the covenant on their flesh. Even in the days of the Galatians, though many may have borne the physical mark, they had totally lost sight of the meaning of circumcision. To be uncircumcised was a term of reproach; it meant to be as the heathen.

Circumcision meant separation from the prevalent sins of that time. "Circumcise your hearts, therefore, and do not be stiff-necked any longer" (Deut. 10:16, NIV). (See also Deuteronomy 30:6 and Jeremiah 4:4.) When we stiffen our necks, we become like a backsliding heifer, arching our backs and pulling our necks out from under the yoke of truth (Hosea 4:16). It is then that we are not useful to God, our farmer. That is why Stephen referred to Israel as "stiff-necked and uncircumcised in heart and ears, ye do always resist the Holy Ghost: as your fathers did, so do ye" (Acts 7:51). They became a generation that resisted the pull of God.

Circumcision referred to the casting away of corrupt affections that hinder from fearing and loving God with the whole heart (Deut. 30:6). We are going to have to yield our hearts totally to God if we are going to meet God's requirements. Circumcision was not a matter of the letter of the law; it was a matter of the heart as well.

Circumcision was the cutting away of carnal lust. It is not just a mark on the flesh; there must be holiness in our lives as well. Our carnal nature has been judged. We have to treat it as a condemned enemy that deserves no favors.

Anything that hindered obedience or kept from being in love with God had to be circumcised. When the Israelites were circumcised, they had to be ready to obey God. It is time for a new generation to arise that is marked by obedience. Paul said we have been circumcised in Christ.

In the time of Christ, the Jews may have been the physical descendants of Abraham, but they were not his spiritual descendants. In the time of Christ, the Jews were not about prayer, faith, and worship. The Jewish people did not build altars; they staggered at the promises of God through unbelief. They did not tithe, and they did not show hospitality to Jesus. Nature is determined by birth, and they did not have the nature of their father Abraham. Jesus told them, "Ye are of your father the devil" (John 8:44).

Circumcision was an act performed by the father of the house or a priest. It was performed when a child was eight days old. Abraham was circumcised when he was ninety-nine. Any foreigner who wanted to become a member of the commonwealth of Israel was required to submit to circumcision. No one could partake of Passover until they were circumcised.

Many of the Jewish people at this time bore in their bodies the mark of circumcision, and it reminded them of God's covenant with them. The Jews believed that no son of Abraham that was circumcised would go to Gehenna. This sounds like those who participate in church membership and who have experienced water baptism.

Circumcision was a mark of separating the Jew and isolating him in the

163

midst of Gentile nations so that God would use Israel for His purposes. It had nothing to do with the Jew receiving salvation. By the time the Book of Galatians was written, circumcision had lost its meaning. The Jews carried the external physical mark, but did not have the mark of the Spirit.

Paul said in the Book of Romans, "Cometh this blessedness then upon the circumcision only, or upon the uncircumcision also? for we say that faith was reckoned to Abraham for righteousness. How was it then reckoned? when he was in circumcision, or in uncircumcision? Not in circumcision, but in uncircumcision" (Rom. 4:9–10). Here Paul pronounces spiritual prosperity upon the righteous, those whose sins are put away and those who sins are covered.

Paul quotes from Genesis 15:6 to prove that faith is the only entrance requirement for full membership in the family of God. Galatians 3:5–6 sets Abraham's faith in contrast to the works of the law. Keeping the requirements of the law is not the way to belong to the covenant family of God. Faith in Christ is the way to enter into a new relationship with God.

Abraham trusted God and took God at His word. He accepted it by faith. Here Paul was linking the experience of the Galatians with the experience of Abraham. The Galatians' faith was essentially the same. Their faith was in believing what they heard (Gal. 3: 2, 5). What they heard was the gospel of blessing for Gentiles through the cross of Christ. The similarity in their faith cannot be denied. So Paul concludes this comparison with Abraham by telling them that they belong to the Abrahamic family.

There is a divine blessing in believing what was heard. That is the basic parallel between the experience of the Galatians and the experience of Abraham. Paul sets up a parallel between the bestowal of the Spirit upon the Galatians and the crediting of righteousness to Abraham. To Paul the bestowal of the Spirit is the evidence of God's acquittal that brings the believer into covenant relationship. Miracles (3:5), the heart cry of Abba (4:6) and the fruit of the Spirit (5:22–26) provide solid evidence of the bestowal of the Spirit. It indicates that the crediting of righteousness has taken place.

Paul quoted Moses in Genesis 15:6 to show to us that God's righteousness was placed on Abraham's account because He believed God's promise. When the sinner trusts Christ, God's righteousness is placed on his account. The believer's sins are no longer put to his account. So Paul takes his readers back to the beginning of the story of God's family. Abraham believed God: that was how the covenant relationship with God began. The terms of our relationship with God have not changed. Receiving the blessing of God by faith is the central theme of the entire story of God's people, from the first page until the last.

"Know ye therefore that they which are of faith, the same are the children of Abraham" (Gal. 3:7). Those who exercise faith are the children of Abraham and are his spiritual descendants. Their standing and true identity are dependent on them possessing the family trait which is faith. If the Galatians were going to be members of Abraham's family they were going to have to act as Abraham did. Abraham heard the word and acted on it. Faith in Christ is the true sign of the covenant, not our identification with the Jewish nation through circumcision and the works of the law.

God credits righteousness to the account of every believer who acts in faith. The troublemakers insisted that circumcision was the sign of the covenant family. Paul uses Genesis 15:6 to prove that everyone who believes can make the claim that they belong to the covenant family or the people of God as children of Abraham.

In the beginning, the Old Testament was the only Bible for the New Testament church. Those who have faith and believe God are Abraham's spiritual descendants. They have his nature. God's told Abraham that all the Gentiles would be blessed through him (Gal. 3:8). So those who believe will enjoy the blessings along with Abraham. It was a gospel of blessing for the Gentiles. Paul sees in Abraham's faith as a response to this gospel of blessing for Gentiles. In Genesis 15:6 we find the action of Abraham's faith believed God's promise of innumerable offspring. One clear night God challenged Abraham to count the stars. Then God gave Abraham His promise: "So shall your offspring be" (Gen. 15:5, NIV). When Abraham heard God's promise, he believed. His faith was a response to God's promise.

Righteousness ought to be the goal of every human desire—being in right standing with God and doing those things that are pleasing in His sight. We are disillusioned if we think we can walk in God's power without practicing a lifestyle of righteousness.

While physical descent was being stressed by the Jews, spiritual descent was being stressed by Paul. The Judaizers taught that the natural descendants of Abraham were God's children and were accepted by God. This means that only the circumcised could be saved. They taught that circumcision was a prerequisite for salvation. They taught that no one else could participate in the blessings of God's covenant with Abraham or Messianic salvation unless they were circumcised. So the Jews believed that their physical descent from Abraham put them on a different footing than the Gentiles. Paul told them that to be a true son of Abraham was not a matter of physical descent or one of flesh and blood. The spiritual descendant of Abraham is the man who makes the adventure of faith.

Paul is telling the Galatians, "Don't seek to merit the promises God made to Abraham by conforming to the law; but repeat his acts of faith." Walk in the footsteps of Abraham. It was through their acts of faith that the Gentile Christian life began. Surely, they would not slip back to Judaism. It would be like an adult going back to the cradle.

The Jews did not understand God's covenant with Abraham—that Israel would become a channel to bring God's salvation to the earth. Salvation would come through a descendant of Abraham, the Messiah.

Paul defines a New Testament circumcision in Colossians. Paul said, "In whom also ye are circumcised with the circumcision made without hands, in putting off the body of the sins of the flesh by the circumcision of Christ" (Col. 2:11). It is where we worship God in the Spirit. We make our boast in Jesus Christ, and we have no confidence in the flesh. No longer was it a mark upon Paul's flesh, but the imprint of the Spirit upon his life.

Paul said, "The just shall live by faith" (Rom. 1:17). This statement was so important that the Holy Spirit inspired three New Testament books to explain it. The Book of Romans beautifully explains how a believing sinner can stand justified before God. Galatians gives to us the lifestyle of the justified. Hebrews tells us that it is truly by faith that we please God. No one can live by the law because the law kills and shows the sinner how guilty before God he really is (3:20; 7:7–11).

Leviticus tells us that it is the doing of the law, not just merely believing it, that God requires (Lev. 18:5). The law says to do and live. This was Paul's experience (Phil. 3:1–10), and it was the history of Israel. Paul knew the law before he ever met Christ on the Damascus Road. It was then that religion died in his life, and Christ was made alive. Paul shows us that the works of righteousness can never save the sinner; only faith in God's righteousness can do that (Rom. 10:10).

The Judaizers were attempting to seduce the Galatians into a religion of legal works, while Paul wanted them to enjoy a relationship of love and a life of faith in Jesus Christ. For the Christian to abandon faith and grace for the works of the law is to lose everything that the Christian can experience in his daily fellowship with the Lord. The law cannot justify the sinner (Gal. 2:16). Neither can it give him righteousness (v. 21). The law cannot give him the gift of the Spirit (3:2). Neither can it guarantee the spiritual inheritance that belonged to God's children (v. 18). The law cannot give life (v. 21). It cannot impart liberty (4:8–10). The law cannot change us, work miracles, or bring us into the presence of God. So why go back to the law?

Paul had to swing one more time to meet the attack of the Judaizers. The Judaizers being filled with impatience about this time would say, "Why talk about Abraham when the real issue is the law?" Abraham represented the beginning of God's revelation process. Centuries later God crowned that process by giving the Law to Moses. It was by the Jews observing the Law that Israel looked for salvation, even though the law pointed them to Christ.

When Paul says, "The Scripture saith," it was defined as a normal form of Jewish speech. It is equivalent to saying, "The Lord of the Scripture says." This is no accident with Paul. Paul believed that God was in control when it comes to the content of Scripture. In the Scripture we see and hear God's ability to see into the distant future. The Jews had a saying: "What does the Scripture foresee?" Paul believed that Scripture was a written text that sees and speaks. It was a written text that expressed the very voice of God. Whatever is stated by Scripture is what God is actually saying. God never acts independent of His Word. The Scripture foresaw what happened to the believers in Galatia, that God would justify Gentiles who placed their faith in the gospel message. The Scripture announced long ago to Abraham the gospel would be preached to the Gentiles, and the blessing of Abraham would rest upon them.

The Scripture foresaw that God would justify the Gentiles by faith and announce the gospel in advance to Abraham: "Preached before the gospel unto Abraham" (3:8). He did it centuries ago. Paul preached the same gospel to the Galatians that was preached to Abraham. The message was received by faith. God is the Justifier who justifies on the grounds of faith. As the Galatians commit their lives to Him in total surrender, they would stand justified in His sight. This is the same thing that happened in the case of Abraham.

A Savior would arise out of the nation of Israel. The Gentiles would be saved through Him as Abraham was saved. Abraham rejoiced to see the coming of that day. Jesus said, "Abraham rejoiced to see my day: and he saw it, and was glad" (John 8:56). Abraham saw three things clearly: 1) he saw the plan of God to send the Messiah for His people to redeem them, 2) he saw that the Messiah would come through his seed and rejoice in faith, and 3) he saw the Lord in visible form. One of the three angels that came to him in the tent of Mamre was the Lord Himself (Gen. 18:1–8).

Abraham would become a pattern and an example to us, and for all those who would come by faith, how a sinner, whether Jew or Gentile, might receive salvation. He is a beautiful illustration of how a person is justified by faith. Abraham was declared to be righteous fourteen years before he was circumcised. He was not declared to be righteous the day he was circumcised. This was a strong argument against the teachings of the Judaizers.

Gentiles were all those who were not the descendants of Abraham, Isaac, and Jacob. In Galatians Paul was quoting Moses' record of when the Lord spoke to Abraham, "I will bless those who bless you, and whoever curses you I will curse; and all peoples on earth will be blessed through you" (Gen. 12:3). It proved that from the very beginning of Abraham's relationship with God, the blessings of salvation were promised to all the nations of the world.

Abraham was an educated, wealthy, sophisticated citizen of the world. Those who exercise faith share the same salvation he received from God. In the covenant that God made with Abraham in Genesis 12:1–3, you will discover multiple blessings that were promised to him by God: personal, national, political, universal, and spiritual. God made his name great. He is revered not only by Jews, but also by Christians and Muslims. Many of the Jews regarded Abraham as a prophet. He went down to Egypt and lied about Sarah being his sister. God told Abimelech to "restore [Abraham's] wife, for he is a prophet" (20:7). God did multiply his descendants, and God blessed those who blessed Abraham. God also judged the nations that had oppressed them and cursed their descendants (e.g., Egypt, Babylon, and Rome). The greatest blessing was Jesus Christ, the promised seed (3:15). Through the Messiah we will be blessed eternally: "In thee shall all nations be blessed" (Gal. 3:8).

Sinners are justified by faith not by observing the law. If God promised to justify Gentiles who came to believe on Christ, then the Judaizers who were attempting to put Gentile believers back under the law were wrong. The true children of Abraham are not his spiritual offspring by physical descent, but Jews and Gentiles are his spiritual offspring by believing in Jesus Christ, that He is the only way to salvation. Through faith Gentiles would become his spiritual children, not by them submitting to circumcision. When Gentiles wanted to invoke blessing on one another, they would say, "May the God of Abraham bless you." They could not conceive any higher blessing to use.

The blessing promised to Abraham for all nations is received by those who have faith. What is the blessing? 1) It is innumerable offspring in the land in which they would dwell. Why are many of our Gentle churches not going from addition to multiplication as the early church did in the Book of Acts? 2) It is also justification by faith and 3) the presence of the Spirit (vv. 2, 5, 14) The Galatian believers were by faith enjoying the blessing of Abraham and their Churches the presence of the Spirit.

We find the word *faith* appearing seven times in vv. 1–9, and the word appears in not only as a noun but also a verb. Faith is *pisto*, active in the sense of believing rather than passive for trusted. No one will be excluded from the blessing because of race. Men from every tribe, tongue, kindred and nation through faith can enjoy the blessing. You do not have to belong to the Jewish race to participate in the blessing of Abraham. All you have to do is have faith in Christ.

"So then they which be of faith are blessed with faithful Abraham" (v. 9). The Jews have relied on the promises of blessings made to Abraham's descendants for centuries. They believed that their physical descent put on them on a different footing with God from other men, especially when it came to the Gentiles.

So people of faith are right now enjoying the blessings of God. They are blessed with salvation, rather than on those who depend on good works as the Judaizers did. Abraham chose faith as the way of salvation rather than to depend on personal merit or good works.

Chapter 12

What Happened to the Miracles?

He therefore that ministereth to you the Spirit, and
worketh miracles among you, doeth he it by the
works of the law, or by the hearing of faith?

—Galatians 3:5

I N F. J. May's book on *The Book of Acts & Church Growth,* he quotes
from Carl Bates who states: "If God were to take His Holy Spirit out of
the midst of the church today, about 95% of what was going on in our
churches would go on and no one would know the difference. If God were
to have taken the Holy Spirit from the life of that first century church in the
Book of Acts, 95% of what they were doing would have come to an automatic
stop and everyone would have known the difference."[1] This tells us just how
much activity of the Holy Spirit was going on in the life of the church of the
Book of Acts compared to how much is going on today in modern-day Christianity. It describes their dependency upon the Holy Spirit. What was taking
place was not due to the efforts of the flesh.

The moment the Galatians placed their faith in Jesus Christ as Lord and
Savior the Holy Spirit entered into their hearts and lives. Nowhere in the Jews'
legalistic mind-sets was their room for the sanctifying work of the Holy Spirit
in the lives of men and women. Paul said to the church at Corinth that "The
manifestation of the Spirit is given to every man to profit withal" (1 Cor.
12:7). These gifts operate in the life of the church for the edification of the
body and for the glory of God. There were certain members of the church at
Galatia who were endowed with these special gifts. The Holy Spirit who came
into their hearts and lives at conversion continued to work miracles in and
through them. This resulted in the body of believers being built up and edified
in the faith. Here salvation by grace through faith, which was the indwelling
of God, was being accompanied by supernatural ministry of the Holy Spirit.

In the NIV it is translated this way: "Does God give you his Spirit and work miracles among you because you observe the law, or because you believe what you heard?" We need to take note of the present tense of the participles in the Greek text, realizing that it is not only God who *gives* but it is also God who *works*. He always works and gives in this way. The word translated "give" was used in marriage contracts for a groom to provide faithful and generous support for his wife. God is a faithful husband caring for His bride.

The KJV uses the phrase "ministereth to you the Spirit." The word *ministereth* comes from the word *epichoregeo*, which means "to supply abundantly or bountifully."[1] It is a compound word. It is a great word for the activities of God. The present tense was used, which spoke of continuous manifestations of the Spirit's gifts. The Holy Spirit was bestowed on them abundantly and bountifully. God, who is a faithful Husband to His Bride the Church, has supplied in an abundant and bountiful fashion the Spirit. There was a continual and generous supply of the Spirit to the Galatian believers that is linked with His work of miracles in their midst. The Galatians still had the miracles among them, proving that grace and not works are the way of salvation. Though Paul anticipated that the Spirit would produce fruit in those who are led by the Spirit (5:22–23), his focus is primarily on outward manifestations of the Spirit's presence in miracles. So here Paul is reminding them of the overwhelming evidence of God's gracious work in order to draw his readers away from the fixations of the requirements of the teachers of the law. This would release a demand for God's continual work in them and through them. It is God's performance not ours. The undeniable presence of the Spirit in the Galatian church is presented as irrefutable evidence that these Gentile believers who call God, Abba, Father, are true children of God.

The undeniable presence of the Spirit among Gentile believers who were not observing the Law of Moses must have come as a shock to the Jewish Christian teachers, even at the house of Cornelius, when an angel of the Lord kicked the door wide open to bring Gentiles into the gospel realm. Many of the Jews had lost the excitement of a Pentecostal experience. The same feeling prevails today in many Pentecostal circles. We would rather do anything than fast and pray and get the Holy Spirit stirred up in the life of the church. Many of them wanted to hang around the temple at Jerusalem and not go from Jerusalem, Judea, Samaria and to the uttermost parts of the earth (Acts 1:8). Jesus in this verse of Scripture was prophesying the missionary strategy of the early New Testament church. Are we a Spirit-filled community if we are not interested in sharing Christ with others? Can we be filled with the Spirit and not be mission minded? Many believers in Christ will rather hide behind church walls and never share the saving message of Jesus Christ with those who are perishing in sin outside our church walls. Evangelism will never occur within the walls of a church house. Every time the early church was filled with the Holy Spirit the result was always evangelism. "They spake the Word of God with boldness" (Acts 4:31). In the Book of Acts, when the Sanhedrian could not deny the presence of the miracle of the healing of the lame man by the gate (Acts 3), they threatened Peter and John that they speak no more in the name of Jesus Christ (Acts 4:17). You see religious people get upset when the focus gets off them and it is placed on Jesus Christ.

God allowed persecution to come and scatter the church. By the word of an angel, Cornelius was instructed to send for Peter who would bring them word by which they as well as their household would be saved. This was a strange thing for Peter because Peter being an orthodox Jew knew that no Jew could enter into the home of a Gentile without being ceremonial defiled.

Peter walked into the home of Cornelius and Cornelius "met him, fell down at his feet and worshipped him" (Acts 10:25). Peter knew that "of a truth that God was not a respecter of persons: but in every nation he that feareth him, and worketh righteous, is accepted of him" (Acts 10:34–35). He preached peace to them that were afar off (v. 36). He declared Jesus Christ to be the Lord of all (v. 36). He preached about the anointing that accompanied the ministry of Jesus (v. 38). The Romans slew him and hanged him on a tree (v. 39). God raised Him up on the third day (v. 40). He discussed how after his resurrection he was seen, and some even ate and drank with him (v. 41). Peter said that those believed received forgiveness of sins. The Holy Spirit fell upon those who heard the message. The outpouring is tied to the message. Again, this is a prime example in the fact that Cornelius' house was not circumcised; they did not conform to the Law of Moses, and yet when they placed their faith in the message they encountered the Holy Spirit.

As Peter preached the word, the Holy Ghost fell on all those who heard the Word (Acts 10:44). "They heard them speak with tongues and magnify God" (Acts 10:46). The circumcision was astonished as they took note that upon the Gentiles, the uncircumcision, had been poured out the gift of the Holy Ghost (Acts 10:45). Here God was pouring out the blessing of Abraham on the congregation of the Lord. Many of the Jews discovered that they did not have a monopoly on the Pentecostal blessing. They actually believed that the Holy Spirit would only be poured out upon righteous Jews who faithfully kept the Law of Moses. In the experience of the Galatian Christians, the demonstration of the Spirit's presence came before they were even taught the law or tried to live by its requirements. God delights in doing miracles for new Christians who believe His promises. They may have much to learn before they can live saintly lives, but at least they know that the Spirit of God is with them.

Paul's questions call for a reaffirmation of their faith. Paul reminded them so that their faith would be renewed. Not by observing the law, but by believing what they heard about Christ crucified! Not by flesh, but by the Spirit! This clear choice will break the spell of any bewitching influence. It is a choice that needs to be made today.

By the Galatians being bewitched by the Judaizers, they were forsaking their stance of grace to take their stand under the law. Just like the Hebrews, they were stepping out of the light back into the shadows. The Judaizers had no evidence that their ministry was from God. Their teachings and works were certainly not endorsed by the Holy Spirit.

Works do not produce salvation, but they are the result of salvation. We are to be "a peculiar people, zealous of good works" (Titus 2:14). We are peculiar in the fact that we are unique because of who we belong to. It means that we are a special people and God regards us as His very own. We are God's own special possession. The word *zealous* means that we are to be heated to a boil, hot or fervent in the pursuit of doing good. It is rare that we find this kind of spiritual temperature even in the House of the Lord. When is the last time your spirituality went to the boiling point? So works are the evidence of salvation.

God the Father who ministered the Spirit to the Galatians in salvation is the God the Father who wrought miracles among them. The Holy Ghost operates the gifts of the Spirit through the believer as He wills. Where there is a decline in the operation of spiritual gifts, it could mean that we have gone back to a fleshly attempt to conform to God's law instead of staying in step with the Spirit. It is only as the church stays in step with the Holy Spirit that we will see the supernatural power of God in our midst.

Paul said, "[He that] worketh miracles among you" (v. 5). The word translated *worketh* is a present tense participle, which gave reference to the continuance of miracles in their midst. The One who ministers to you by the

Spirit is the One that worketh miracles among you. If the church leaves the Spirit and goes back to trying to do it themselves, in the strength of their own flesh, there will be a decline of the miraculous, and the work of the Holy Spirit will become hindered. By the Galatians being bewitched they were cutting themselves off from the miracles. The power of God was going to die in their experiences.

The word *miracles* comes from the Greek word *dunamis* which speaks of charismatic manifestations of the Spirit, and the Spirit coming with power. God confirmed the truth of the Gospel through miracles. These gifts can be summed up in three categories: 1) *power to know*—word of wisdom, word of knowledge, and discerning of spirits; 2) *power to speak*—tongues, interpretation of tongues, and prophecy; and 3) *power to act*—gifts of healing, gift of faith, and the working of miracles. (See 1 Corinthians 12:8–10.)

Paul said, "Truly the signs of an apostle were wrought among you in all patience, in signs, and wonders, and mighty deeds" (2 Cor. 12:12). The same Spirit who performed His work of progressive sanctification also bestowed miracles among them. It is hard to understand people who profess to be sanctified and yet they have no life in the Holy Ghost. It is sad that we have become like Corinth; we boast of our knowledge and our gifts but we do not blush at sin.

Chapter 13

Receiving the Holy Ghost Through Faith

*This only would I learn of you, Received ye the Spirit
by the works of the law, or by the hearing of faith?*
—GALATIANS 3:2

PAUL USED ANOTHER argument to prove that it is through faith and not the works of the law that a man is put right with God. The converts in the Book of Acts always received the Holy Spirit in a visible way. The early chapters of Acts show this happening again and again. There came to them a new surge of life and power that anyone could see. At Pentecost they could fill the rushing mighty wind as it filled all the house where they were sitting. They saw cloven tongues like as fire sitting on the heads of those who were in the upper room. "They heard them speak with other tongues as the Spirit gave them utterance" (Acts 2:1). In Acts 4, "When they had prayed, the house was shaken where they were assembled together, and they were all filled with the Holy Ghost and spake the word of God with boldness" (Acts 4: 31). In Acts chapter 8, "When Peter and John laid their hands on the Samaritans, they received the Holy Ghost" (Acts 8:17). A visible manifestation took place that caused Simon the sorcerer to want to buy the power of God with money (Acts 8:18). At the house of Cornelius, when the Holy Ghost fell on those who heard the Word, "They heard them with speak with tongues and magnify God" (Acts 10:46). When Paul was in Ephesus, he laid his hands on twelve disciples of John's baptism: "The Holy Ghost came upon them, and they spake with tongues and prophesied" (Acts 19:6). So in each instance in the Book of Acts there was a literal manifestation of the Spirit's power each time someone received the Holy Spirit.

So the believers in Galatia had received the Spirit by faith and not by observance of the law. If we have been saved by the Spirit, not through the flesh or by the law, then why change our course?

Paul is reminding his converts that they did not need to become Jewish proselytes to receive the Spirit in the first place or to experience the continuous outpouring of the Spirit and miracles in their lives (v. 5). Paul is attempting to break the bewitching spell by showing them that they received the Spirit by believing what they heard through the gospel and not by observing the law.

The Spirit is not received by striving to obey the demands of the law. The Holy Spirit is God's free gift. The Holy Spirit is received by simple faith. As the gospel is preached in the power of the Spirit, the Spirit creates faith. "So then faith cometh by hearing, and hearing by the word of God" (Rom. 10:17). This was just as true for the Galatian believers as it was for Paul. You can receive the Holy Spirit by believing the gospel message, the good news of the love of God, and by responding to it in an act of trust. The Galatians received the Holy Ghost through faith in Paul's message of salvation by grace through faith.

Two human parents are required for a child to be born into a family. The Holy Spirit and the Word are the two parents of my spiritual birth when I was born into the family of God. Those who have begun their walk in the Spirit need to continue to walk in the Spirit in order to grow. If we begin with the Spirit we cannot go on to spiritual maturity without the Spirit. Why are we depending on the strength of our flesh for perfection? Paul is speaking of the sanctifying work of the Holy Spirit in the life of the Galatian believers. We cannot be brought to a level of spiritual maturity by and through our own self-effort.

The Holy Spirit is mentioned eighteen times in this Epistle. The Holy Spirit plays an important role in Paul's defense of the gospel of the grace of God. The evidence of conversion is the presence of the Holy Spirit. Where you find the church, you find the Holy Spirit, and where you find the Holy Spirit, you find the church.

If we have begun in the Spirit, then we cannot go on to maturity without the Spirit. We are not supposed to depend on our flesh for perfection. Paul is speaking about the sanctifying work of the Spirit in the lives of these saints. We cannot be brought to a level of maturity through self-effort.

Paul, in writing to the church at Rome, said, "But ye are not in the flesh, but in the Spirit, if so be that the Spirit of God dwell in you. Now if any man have not the Spirit of Christ, he is none of his" (Rom. 8:9). The moment we believe on the Lord Jesus Christ, the Holy Spirit takes up His abode on the inside of us. He resides in the heart and life of the believer. The Holy Spirit has a ministry to perform in the believer. He gives the believer victory over sin and produces the fruit of the Spirit. God, through the Holy Spirit, has broken the power of the sin nature and placed the believer in the grip and control of the Holy Spirit. We are now in a world where the Spirit rules.

Paul said to the church at Rome, "The Spirit is life because of righteousness" (Rom. 8:10). Your spirit has been made alive because it is energized by the Holy Spirit, and the Holy Spirit has enabled you to worship God and to live right. It is the Holy Spirit and the grace of God that enables you to live this Christian life.

Paul asked the Galatians, "Did you receive the Spirit by observing the law, or by believing what you heard?" (Gal. 3:2, NIV). The Galatians tried to live their Christian lives through the efforts of the flesh, which was not the same process that they entered into when they began their Christian journey. The Spirit is received by simple faith and by believing and hearing the gospel message. As the gospel message is preached in the power of the Spirit, the Spirit creates faith. God is still providing us with the Spirit as a free gift and continually doing deeds of power among us.

"By the works of the law" (v. 2). They received the Holy Ghost—not because they obeyed the regulations of the law but because they heard the good news of the love of God and responded to it. It is the message that announces faith whereby anyone receives salvation. Paul's message of salvation was by grace through faith. The Spirit came into their lives at salvation because they trusted Jesus Christ as Lord and Savior.

The Holy Spirit can convict the lost sinner and reveal Christ to him. The sinner can resist the Holy Ghost (Acts 7:51), or he can yield to the Spirit and trust Jesus Christ as his Lord and Savior. He becomes baptized by the Spirit into Christ's body (1 Cor. 12:12–14). The believer is then sealed by the Holy Spirit (Eph. 1:13–14), and given the guarantee that one day he will share in the glory of God.

The believer has a responsibility to the Holy Spirit, who now lives in his heart and life. He should then be embracing the walk of the Spirit (Gal. 5:16, 25). If he is disobeying God he will grieve the Holy Spirit (Eph. 4:30). If he persists in doing so he will quench the Holy Spirit (1 Thess. 5:19). Believers are to be filled with the Spirit (Eph. 5:18), which means they are to be continually under the control of the Holy Spirit. Remember, it is what you spend most your time talking about that controls you. Cooperating with the Holy Spirit is a continual experience.

Chapter 14

Becoming Easily Deceived

HOW DOES APOSTASY take place in a believer's life? How does a committed Christian become so seduced that eventually he or she begins to withdraw, shrink away from, and eventually depart from the faith? Paul says that this type of departure takes place very slowly. Most of the time when someone departs from the faith, he will not even realize that this departure is taking place. Many times what accompanies an apostate is an "I don't care" attitude. He is totally unconcerned about being in right standing with God.

Rick Renner says, "It is not always a blatant, outright rejection of the faith. It is a careful, slow, almost unnoticeable, inch by inch, step by step departing from the faith over a period of time. This is a slow withdrawal. There is a great difference in rejecting the faith is a deliberate act on the part of a man and a departure from the faith is a slow process and may be unintentional."[1]

Jesus told us that "By their fruits ye shall know them" (Matt. 7:20). The word translated *know* is from the Greek *epiginosko*. The word *epi* means "to fully know"; the word *ginosko* means "to know." It describes accurate knowledge or exact knowledge.[2] Jesus was saying that by examining the outward fruit of a ministry, you may determine with exact and accurate knowledge whether a ministry is good or bad. Jesus told us to judge the fruit, not the method, style, personality, or hearts but the fruit. Jesus instructed us to weigh the fruit because you cannot see the hidden motive of the heart. Jesus said, "Beware of false prophets, which come to you in sheep's clothing, but inwardly they are ravening wolves" (Matt. 7:15).

A PROPHETIC FRUIT TEST[3]

- Is the message in agreement with the teaching of Scripture?
- Does it line up with the Word? If it is not scriptural, it is not spiritual.
- Can their new revelation be defended by God's Word?

- How is it impacting the congregation? Does it cause them to become rebellious, arrogant, prideful?
- Is there a resistance to come up under authority?
- Does it produce the fruit of the Spirit? Character of Christ; the Spirit of Holiness in the New Testament; fruit that comes as a result of the life of the Spirit.
- Does it undergird the work of the local church?
- Does it draw people away from the church?
- Does it make people feel that a commitment to the church is not necessary?
- Does the ministry support or undergird the authority of local church leadership?
- Does it tear leadership down?
- Does their new revelation draw attention to themselves or to the Lord?

Both Jesus and John had warned the people of false prophets (Matt. 7:15; 1 John 4:1). In these last days there is going to be a great tolerance for unbiblical doctrine that will increase toward the end of the age (1 Tim. 4:1; 2 Tim. 4:3–4).

Christians are commanded to test anyone who claims their work and message comes from the Holy Spirit. This includes any one who professes to be a teacher, preacher, and especially a prophet. Christians are not to be gullible by assuming that a ministry is spiritual or of God just because it claims to be. All teaching must be put to the test by seeing whether or not it lines up with the Word of God. No teaching or doctrine is to be accepted as true solely on the basis of success, miracles, or apparent anointing. We need to be aware of any teaching that a person claims to have received from an angel or from the Holy Spirit that cannot be supported by the Scriptures. The teacher's life must be tested as to his relationship with an ungodly world and to the lordship of Jesus Christ.

Paul, in writing to young Timothy, said, "Now the Spirit speaketh expressly, that in the latter times some shall depart from the faith, giving heed to seducing spirits, and doctrines of devils" (1 Tim. 4:1). There was opposition to the gospel in Ephesus because error had raised its head. Many in the life of the church began to apostatize from the faith. Sound doctrinal preaching began to be rejected. The Holy Spirit announced that there was coming a time where the spirit of apostasy would grip the lives of men and women within the church. The phrase "speaketh expressly" comes from the Greek word *rhetos*, from which we get the word *rhema*. Paul is saying that the Spirit has spoken in clear, unmistakable, undeniable terms.[4] The future events he is describing are definite and will come to pass.

Paul had made known to the church about the rise of false teachers. He had warned the church at Thessalonica and the elders of the church at Ephesus of the dangers of apostasy. (See 2 Thessalonians 2:1–12; Acts 20:29–30.) The Holy Spirit had made it clear to Paul that in the latter times error would flourish.

The phrase latter times covers the time from Pentecost until the Rapture of the church. It is the time between the first and second coming of Christ. The word *latter* comes from the Greek word *husteros* which emphasizes the extreme end of something; it emphasizes the ultimate end of a thing. The word *times* comes from the Greek word *kairos* which speaks of a season, or specially allotted period of time.[5]

Because church is living in the Saturday evening of time, the Holy Spirit is sounding an alarm. He is also exposing the plan of the enemy and his strategy that he will use against the church in this final hour. This assault of the enemy upon the church the Holy Spirit has not taken lightly. The Holy Spirit was pointing His prophetic finger 2,000 years down the road and telling us what was going to occur in the life of the church in this final hour.

Paul prophesied that "some shall depart from the faith" (1 Tim. 4:1). The word *depart* is translated form the Greek word *aphistemi*, which is a compound word made from two words meaning "away from" and "to stand." It means to stand or step away from, to withdraw from, or to shrink back from.[6] We are watching many people today step away from the landmarks of the faith. There are many that are drawing back instead of going forward. The writer of the Book of Hebrews tells us "that we are not among them that draw back unto perdition, but those that believe to the saving of the soul" (Heb. 10:39). Eventually they will depart from the faith. The Greek indicates that this departure takes place very slowly. Just like the prodigal son while he was at home with the father, a far country had caught the corner of his eye. He may have been present in body, but his heart and spirit were already gone. It is possible for someone to depart from the faith and not even realize it until after the departure has taken place. No, you may not have rejected the faith, but you are gradually making progress in the area of your departure. It is a careful, slow, almost unnoticeable, inch-by-inch, step-by-step departure from the faith over a period of time. It is a slow shrinking back and withdrawal. There is a difference between withdrawing from the faith and rejecting the faith. Rejecting is deliberate, but a departure is slow and unintentional.[7] Their thinking was slowly beginning to change.

Some will depart from the faith because of seducing spirits and doctrines of demons. When I speak of the faith, I am speaking of the basic tenets of Scripture. It is what the prophets foretold, what Jesus taught, and what the apostles proclaimed. I am speaking of the sound teaching of the Word of God. The Holy Ghost is predicting that in the last days there will be those who will step away from the sound teaching of Scripture.

We have come to a day when people are tired of the Word of God. To them the Word is boring. We have reached a point in the life of the church where people have heard so much Word that they are nearly choking on it. Like Corinth, we need to watch out for those who brag about their knowledge and the gifts they operate in and yet cannot handle the meat of the Word.

"Evil men and seducers shall wax worse and worse, deceiving, and being deceived" (2 Tim. 3:13). The word *seducers* refers to sorcerers, those who use incantations, magic, and spells. Paul through the gift of prophecy is prophesying that there will be a revival of sorcery and that these sorcerers will know how to produce the supernatural. They have committed their life to the acts of sorcery. Rest assured, my friend, if we think men are evil now, we are definitely going to be surprised as we draw closer to the end of the age. The spirit of sorcery will reach such a point of acceleration that it will startle the minds of men. It will surpass anything that we ever seen come to the stage of history.

The very world that we live in is becoming impacted by this spirit of sorcery. It is in our educational systems. Our kids are being made to read books in school that dabble in witchcraft and sorcery. It is in our government, homes, families, and in the lives of our children. There are cartoons that on Saturday comes no our T.V. that are filled with New Age symbolism and sorcery. It is amazing how the enemy of our soul has introduced this spirit very slowly into our generation and how we have developed a spirit of tolerance for it.

Arrington, in his book on *Maintaining the Foundations*, maintains that men were already distorting the truth of the gospel.[8] Timothy was in the midst of a storm, and Paul offered not such hope that it would soon pass. As we preach and proclaim this gospel there will be troubles and perils that will befall us as we stand firm for the gospel.

This falling away from sound teaching will come in a two-fold manner: 1) There will be activity of deceiving spirits and doctrines taught by demons. The word *seducing* comes from the Greek word *planos,* which means to take someone by the hand and lead them off track. They don't even realize they are being led from the right track. It looks right, it sounds right. It is being done so seductively and slowly that they don't even realize it until the transition has been made. These deceiving spirits are demons. It is the work of the adversary of our soul to frustrate God's purpose in our lives and lead God's people astray from the faith. The enemy desires to distort the faith that Christ had entrusted to the church for safekeeping. 2) Some have become agents of the demonic spirits, have forsaken the truth, and have become hypocritical liars. They are spreading deceitful doctrines that are inspired by demons. They have abandoned the truth and the purity of the gospel. They see nothing wrong with lying. Paul said their "consciences have been seared as with a hot iron" (1 Tim. 4:2, NIV). The word *seared* is translated from the Greek *kauteriazo* from which we get the word *cauterize.* Their conscience had become calloused. Their sensitivity to the truth was lost. Their lying became habitual.[9]

In 1 Timothy 4:3 Paul mentions two of those doctrines: forbidding marriage and abstaining from meats. They were teaching that in order to please God that one had to become an ascetic. The body and everything connected to it was evil, therefore marriage was evil. But, marriage is a divine institution and was instituted by God. It must be defended against those who exalt celibacy. The teaching of not eating meat was an outgrowth of the assumption that all matter was evil. Food is matter and considered to be evil. But, God said that everything that He had created was good (Gen. 1:31). Asceticism does not result in genuine spirituality.

Paul warned us of a departure from the faith (1 Tim. 4:1). The Holy Spirit has spoken in clear, unmistakable, undeniable terms and has revealed that from the Day of Pentecost until the Rapture of the church, there would be a falling away from personal faith in the Lord Jesus Christ. Ministers will appear in the church who appear to be highly gifted and seem to be highly anointed of God. They will seem to accomplish great things for God and be able to preach the truth with great effectiveness. The Holy Spirit says they will depart from the faith and gradually turn to seducing spirits and false doctrines. As a result, many will be misled into error.

Renner states that Paul is giving us a description of demonic activity that will occur in the lasts days to lure believers away from the faith. No one would automatically get involved with outright deception. Many times their greatest candidates are those who have become bored with their spiritual walk and feel that they are stuck in a spiritual rut. The enemy loves to offer believers who have never grown up in Christ error that comes under a disguise of a new spirituality. [10] Many people have come into the kingdom but they have lost their sense of adventure in the kingdom. They have settled down into spiritual boredom. Now they are looking for the latest fads to keep their excitement going.

Paul told Timothy, "This know also, that in the last days perilous times shall come" (2 Tim. 3:1). Paul is admonishing young Timothy to *know* this. Paul uses the Greek word *ginosko*, which means to "realize these facts, come to recognize what is happening, mark this, make careful notes." Timothy as well as we within the life of the church are going to have to come to grips with this.

Being keenly aware about the times that were coming, Paul is giving to us a sharp and intense warning to Christians and to every spiritual soldier of the cross to be on their guard. It is definitely a time for a call to arms. Paul, speaking by the inspiration of the Holy Ghost, is telling us that as the end draws near, things are going to get worse. It will be a time that wickedness will abound on every hand. There will be a decline in morality. There will false Christians, false righteousness, false churches, and a false gospel. It will be a difficult time for those who are true servants of God.

Then Paul makes reference once again of the last days (v. 1). Here he uses the Greek word *eschatos*, from which we get the word *eschatology*. Eschatology is the study of end-time events. It covers the period from the day of Pentecost until the Rapture of the church. Paul shared with Timothy about the perilous conditions of the church and the world right before Jesus' return.

Paul tells Timothy that "perilous times shall come" (v. 1). The word *perilous* comes from the Greek *chalepos*, which speaks of times that are treacherous, dangerous, difficult, and hard. The word emphasizes that these will be dangerous times and times that are hard to bear. The word *perilous* can be translated *exceeding fierce.* It will be a time when men will become uncivilized. In Matthew's gospel it was used to describe the demoniac of Gadara (Matt. 8:28). It will be a time when Satan will attempt to turn this world that he is the god of into his own personal graveyard. It will be a high-risk period that will be characterized by danger, harm, and hurt. The word *chalepos* tells us something else about this period. It will be a time when the devil will set his sights on the life of the Holy Spirit in the believer individually and the church corporately with the intention of reducing our strength. In these last days the powers of darkness will intensify in their strategy against Christ and His church to make us easy prey. These powers will undermine the very foundations of the Christian's strength.

We know that the church age will end in a Laodicean church age where men will be neither cold nor hot but lukewarm (Rev. 3:14–15). It will be a church where the people rule, where they will be more concerned about being democratic (church where the people rule) than being theocratic (the rule and reign of God). They will have waters that bring no healing or refreshment. Paul saw the mystery of iniquity that was at work in the first century as being in check because of the presence of the Holy Spirit in the life of the believer and of the church. He saw the presence of the Holy Spirit in the life of the church as being the restrainer against the man of sin that was soon to be revealed. He said, "Let no man deceive you by any means: for that day shall not come, except there come a falling away first, and that man of sin be revealed, the son of perdition" (2 Thess. 2:3). Paul is saying that the reason men are falling away is that the devil has targeted the life of the Holy Spirit in the life of the believer and the church and as a result there is no strength to stand or to resist what is coming on the scene. Just how strong are we in the Holy Ghost in these last days?

Paul is saying that the powers of darkness will target the life of the Holy Spirit in the life of the church and that much of our strength will be diminished. It was Paul's prayer for the church that "that he would grant you, according to the riches of his glory, to be strengthened with might by his Spirit in the inner man" (Eph. 3:16). If we make the baptism of the Holy Ghost an optionally lifestyle instead of a command like Jesus and the apostles said, then the devil will succeed in reducing the strength of the church. In these last days the church has to struggle against the forces of deception. It was Timothy's purpose to teach the Christians to watch for the signs of Christ's return. We need to anticipate an onslaught from Satan against the very foundations of the church. The reason why perilous times have come is because of the widespread deception within the church. This warning is repeatedly sounded in the pages of the New Testament.

Paul said there would be perilous times within the church. The word *times* comes from the Greek word *karios,* which speaks of specific allotted periods of time. Here it refers to decades. Each decade will add its own measure of new danger, new risk, new harm, and new hurt. Accompanying each decade will be its own way of thinking; respect for those in leadership within the life of the church will begin to disappear. One's personal faith in God will begin to fade. We have a conglomeration of demonic powers that have characterized each decade. Paul told Timothy two centuries ago what we are now seeing transpire:

> For men shall be lovers of their own selves, covetous, boasters, proud, blasphemers, disobedient to parents, unthankful, unholy, Without natural affection, trucebreakers, false accusers, incontinent, fierce, despisers of those that are good, Traitors, heady, highminded, lovers of pleasures more than lovers of God; Having a form of godliness, but denying the power thereof: from such turn away.
>
> —2 Timothy 3:2–5

A strong part of the strategy of Satan to reduce the strength of the believer and that of the local church is to get us to back off the power of the Holy Spirit.

The writer of the Book of Hebrews said, "Now the just shall live by faith: but if any man drawn back, my soul shall have no pleasure in him. We are not of them that draw back unto perdition; but of them that believe to the saving of the soul" (Heb. 10:38–39). For us to have known more and settle for less is a sin. What are former Pentecostals doing sitting in a house that does not believe in their doctrine or their experience?

Many will fall away because they have no love for the truth. Paul said, "And with all deceivableness of unrighteousness in them that perish; because they received not the love of the truth, that they might be saved" (2 Thess. 2:10). If we love the truth we will not be offended by it. Many will fail to resist the sinful trends in these last days. Compromising ministers and a distorted gospel will meet little resistance within the life of the church.

First Timothy was written by Paul from Macedonia to Timothy, his son in the faith. Paul composed this letter around 62–63 B.C. Luke tells us that Paul spent two years in a Roman prison where he wrote Philippians, Colossians, Ephesians, and Philemon. In his letters he had expressed that his release would come shortly (Phil. 1:23–25; 2:24; Philem. 1:22). In Paul's first Roman imprisonment he was under house arrest, could be visited by friends, and had the hope of release. He was a political prisoner awaiting trial. He was released from Roman imprisonment and continued his missionary journeys (Acts 28). Paul sent Timothy to Philippi. Paul himself went to Ephesus. Timothy joined him, and Paul instructed Him to abide while he journeyed to Macedonia. When Paul was delayed he wrote 1 Timothy.

The conditions were different in his two imprisonments. In 2 Timothy the apostle Paul was a condemned criminal, moments away from going to Nero's chopping block, knowing that shortly He would be standing in the presence of the Lord. He was arrested at Troas, and no one supported him as he gave his defense before the courts (v. 16). He was without his cloak, parchments, or Old Testament scrolls (2 Tim. 4:13). That is amazing that this man of God as much of the power of God as he had known in the closing moments of his life is asking for the Word of God to be brought to him so he could refresh his mind by the study of the Scriptures. This is a great lesson to us who are trying to divorce the Word of God from our spirituality. He was trusting that Timothy would visit him before winter. In his first imprisonment he lived in his own hired house, now he was in cold, dark Roman cell. He was regarded as an evildoer (2:9). He was without hope of being released in spite of his defense (4:6–8). In his second imprisonment he was forsaken by all. It was certainly not the best of times when Paul wrote 2 Timothy. Many of the Asian believers who feared for their own lives failed to support him, which led them to reject him.

Ephesus was the fastest growing church in the first century era. Paul was the pastor. In 2 Timothy the situation is different. Timothy is now the pastor, and the church is rapidly declining. Timothy at this time was greatly discouraged. Paul wrote to Him and told him that he needed to "stir up the gift of God that was on the inside of him" (2 Tim. 1:6). To those who professed Christ, persecution was real. Nero, who was the emperor of Rome (A.D. 54–68), was responsible for the persecution of Christians. He set Rome on fire and blamed it on the Christians (A.D. 64). Christianity then became an illegal religion, and to evangelize or share one's faith was punishable by death. Timothy while combating false doctrine was busy setting things in order.

Look at the different roles that Paul took on when he wrote to the churches:

- In Romans we see Paul the theologian.
- In 1 Corinthians we see Paul the counselor.
- In 2 Corinthians we see Paul the preacher.
- In Galatians we see Paul the defender.
- In 1 Timothy and Titus, we see Paul the statesman.
- In 2 Timothy we see Paul the man.

Paul is telling us that there is coming a time when apostasy and wickedness would abound. It will be a time when people will be fall prey to empty religion and false teaching. Right inside the household of faith and the community of believers we are witnessing Seducing spirits trying to get men and women to lose respect for the operation of God's Holy Spirit. Many within the local church are backing away from the baptism of the Holy Spirit. What Jesus and the apostles said was a command and many believers have made it an optional lifestyle. If it were not for the baptism of the Holy Ghost and fire, the early church would have fallen back into Judaism. In an hour when we need the power of God the most, we seem to believe in it the least.

God has set His power in the church—not the organization but the organism. Believers (the organism) have to have three characteristics. 1) We have to be growing spiritually. 2) We have to become channels of the Holy Ghost. 3) We have to reproduce. One Sunday right before I preached my message, I had one of my ushers bring me a rocking chair from the nursery. I placed it right before my pulpit and used it for an illustration. I shared with my congregation, "Here we have a beautiful chair that we have brought from the nursery. It is white in color and beautifully designed. It has all the appearances of a rocking chair, but you would not want to sit in it because white ants have eaten away its insides. It has the outward shape, but no substance within. It probably would not support a person's weight."

This reminded me of many professing Christians in the house of the Lord.

Many have taken up the rocking chair in their Christian experience. The devil has cocaine and chloroformed them and rocked them to sleep. They are like the chair; they have the hull but no substance. They have the shell but no nut on the inside. They are like synthetic sugar. It looks like sugar and resembles it, but does not produce the affects of sugar. They are like synthetic rubber. It looks like rubber and resembles it, but does not produce the effects of rubber. Many have taken on a synthetic Pentecost. It looks like Pentecost and resembles it, but does not produce the affects of it. Many have taken on a synthetic worship. It looks like worship and resembles it. It creates the allusion of worship, but does not produce the effects of worship. So appearances can be deceiving.

Jesus said the Pharisees appear to be like whited sepulchers that outwardly appear to be beautiful, but they are full of dead men's bones and all uncleanness (Matt. 23:27). So appearances can be deceiving.

You might say you have never experienced God's power. Maybe you're not the church. It is the Holy Spirit's presence that constitutes the church. Where you find the church you find the Holy Spirit, and where you find the Holy Spirit you find the church. I not only believe in the priesthood of all who believe but I also believe in the prophethood of all who believe. It is time for the church to rise up, break new ground, and take the high ground.

There are six words used in the New Testament for power:

Dunamis is dynamite or explosive power. One is enabled by this power and given the ability to accomplish. It is through this power that our lives are transformed so the world can see the change so that a door may be opened up for the gospel.

Exousia is expressing authority given through this power over sickness, disease, and devils.

Kratos is the power of God in demonstration and through that power we take dominion over the works of His hands. It was this power that raised Jesus Christ up from the dead and caused sixteen soldiers outside the tomb to fall like dead men. It was this power that caused 600 soldiers to fall to the ground in the garden of Gethsemane when Jesus said, "I am" (John 18:6). The Jews knew that no one would use that kind of terminology unless they had deity about them. They knew they were standing on holy ground.

Ischus means strength, might, and force. Paul said we are "to be strengthened with might by his spirit in the inner man" (Eph. 3:16). There has been an infusion of supernatural strength poured into the receptacle of our spirit.

Endunamo is where we become infused with this power. The classical Greek writers in Greek mythology spoke of a Zeus an immortal Greek god, who picked out Hercules and infused him with supernatural strength and ability. And Hercules performed the works of the gods. In the Book of Acts, they thought the God's had come down in the likeness of men. "These that have turned the world upside down are come hither also" (Acts 17:6).

Energia is where we get the word *energy* from. One is energized by this power. The Scriptures says, "For it is God which worketh in you both to will and to do of his good pleasure" (Phil. 2:13). This means that it is God who is constantly pouring the energy into us so that we can perform His good pleasure in the earth.

Paul said that men would have "a form of godliness, but denying the power thereof: from such turn away" (2 Tim. 3:5). There would come a time that men would go to church and not hear any thing. There would come a time when ritual would replace power and form would replace force. This was an outward denial of the power of God. They have an outward shape but without reality.[11]

They have the hull without the substance. Religion is not outwardly denied, but it amounts to more than an empty shell. There is an outward *form*, which comes from the Greek word *morphosis* meaning an outline or semblance but with no power. They will have all the resemblance of a walk with God but lack the inward reality.

Paul has envisioned that there will be many church goers who will be content with the mere resemblance of Christianity. He saw a people who would convey the image to those around them that they were walking with the Lord, even though it really was not so. They would be unwilling to allow the Holy Spirit to bring correction into their lives. They would resist the power of God that desired to do a deep, inward work in their lives.

I believe this sin comes when we get so bound to the form and ritual that we fail to give way to the power. Paul is saying that there will be an outward form of religion without reality. We can have an outward form of religion and yet be far away from the power. We can go to church and go through the motions of worship and have a wicked heart; we can say the prayers and sing the songs and carry a Bible under our arm big enough to choke a mule, partake of communion every Sunday, and still be far away from the power. God help us; open our spiritual eyes!

The word translated *denying* is the Greek *arneomai* (perfect, middle, participle) in "denying the power" (v. 5).[12] It means that they know the power exists and they know that it is real, but they are going to stop its operation. Paul is saying that there will come a time in the life of the church where men and women will deliberately refuse the power of God. It is an outright rejection of the power. They have no conception of the gospel as being a generating force. The writer of Hebrews said:

> For the word of God is quick, and powerful, and sharper than any twoedged sword, piercing even to the dividing asunder of soul and spirit, and of the joints and marrow, and is a discerner of the thoughts and intents of the heart.
>
> —HEBREW 4:12

They don't see their faith as a force. Many have lost their sense of adventure in the kingdom of God. Those who take on this spirit are cooperating with the anointing of Satan. It is like what James said: "As the body without a spirit is dead, so faith without works is dead also" (James 2:26). We have come to a day where men have religious observance without a Redeemer. Remember, Israel for many years in the Old Testament had learned to go through the rituals of worship without God being in their midst. The priesthood of Jeremiah's day was eaten up with a spirit of religion but did not have an ounce of God. Why are we content to live in the King's palace without the presence of the King? Why are we content to live in a house that He is not in?

The phrase "from such turn away" (v. 5), is the present, middle, imperative of the Greek word *apotrepo*. Paul tells us we should not associate with these people because deception is the name of their game. The Greek implies that we are to avoid them with horror, run from them, having nothing to do with them, not thinking about what they are saying, and not be involved in what they're doing. Deception is in their message. Is there enough power flowing through the church to confront an unbelieving world? Can a church like ours save a world like ours?[13] Timothy had to exercise discernment to prevent the admission of such people into the membership of the church. Let's not kiss the power of God goodbye.

If you don't believe in the power of the old rugged cross; if you don't believe in the power of the blood; if you don't believe in the power that raised Jesus Christ from the dead; if you don't believe that the Word of God is the power of God unto salvation; if you don't believe that the church can pray and God can answer; if you don't believe that God can sanctify you and fill you with the Holy Ghost; if you don't believe that God can transform and empower your life with promise, purpose, and destiny, then are you denying the power that makes men godly? What about the power that turns men from darkness to light, from the power of Satan to God, and gives them an inheritance among them that are sanctified (Acts 26:18). What are you doing being a member of the church? What back door did you come in? How did you slide through a new convert's class?

There seems to be a longing in the hearts of men and women to experience God's power. They want to see something real from the presence of the Lord. They long to be touched in their hearts by words that have the unction of the Holy Ghost. They want to sense the very energy of God moving, invigorating, and empowering them and kindling a new a love for Jesus Christ.

When Constantine declared Christianity to be the official religion in A.D. 325, people started joining the church who did not have a true relationship with God. They came into the church and got offended over the operation of spiritual gifts and the true church had to go underground. It is time we quit apologizing for the power of God.

Where is that power that turned a Saul of Tarsus into Paul the Apostle? Where is that power that transforms men from sinners into saints? Steve Gallagher, in his article on *"Denying, Resisting, Disdaining the Power of God,"* said, "The greatest need for Christianity today is for the invigorating life of God to flow through their beings, enlighten their minds with truth of the Word, purify their motives, fortify their convictions, mold their personalities, sweeten their natures, renew their hearts and subdue their flesh. The quickening power of the Holy Spirit that revitalizes and renews needs to be experienced by the church today.[14]

Gallagher said that "many are content with their weak form of godliness because it allows them to maintain control over their own lives and worship idols which are abounding in our culture today. He is not the Jehovah of the Bible."

The writer of the Book of Hebrews said something along the lines of us denying the power. "Take heed, brethren, lest there be in any of you an evil heart of unbelief, in departing from the living God" (Heb. 3:12). When the writer said "take heed," he was emphasizing that there are spiritual dangers that exist. He was saying they needed to pay attention to what was being said. It also emphasizes that we need to be encouraged to be faithful to the Lord. What do we need to take heed? Let's visit the sad history of the nation of Israel and the important lessons that it teaches us. God had delivered His people from Egypt and had cared for them. He had revealed His mighty power to them. Israel saw His signs and wonders, but they did not bring them closer to God. They actually hardened their hearts against God. They put God to the test and He did not fail them; yet they failed Him.[15]

When a person has an erring and disbelieving heart, the result will also be a hard heart. This kind of heart is insensitive to the Word and the work of God. The hearts of Israel became so hard that they wanted to return to Egypt. Imagine wanting to exchange their freedom under God for the slavery of Egypt. The word *evil* is translated from the Greek word *poneros*, which speaks of evil, active opposition against the good. It speaks of a heart that is not content to go down by itself but wants to pull the child of God down right along with them. This was the condition of ten of the twelve spies that Joshua sent in to spy out the land. Ten brought back a negative report that raped the entire congregation of Israel. Joshua and Caleb came back with another spirit bearing the grapes of Eschol. They were bearing the tangible evidence that the land was everything God said it would be. Those grapes made the mouths of the Israelites to water. Even when they saw the evidence that the land was everything they said it would be, the firstfruits of the Spirit, they still did not go after it. When the ten spies only saw giants, Joshua and Caleb saw grapes.

Unbelief had taken hold of their hearts. Unbelief will keep us wandering too long in the wilderness. It will keep us from possessing the Promised Land. Unbelief was alive in their fathers in the wilderness and it was alive in the generation that the writer of Hebrews was writing to. Their unbelief was keeping them from entering into their rest. It was time for them to learn from the example of their fathers.

Unbelief will cause any heart to "depart from the living God" (Heb. 3:12). The word *depart* does not mean a total withdrawal from God. It is where we get our English word *apostasy* from. It just means that you go over and stand off to the side and no longer participate in the things of God. Standing off was the fruit of the problem while their unbelief was the root.[16] To stand off from the truth being revealed to them in the New Testament was proof that unbelief controlled the heart. No matter what they professed, their behavior proved them to be an active unbeliever. Many are content just to observe others experiencing the things of God and not get in there to experience the things of God for themselves. If the devil gets us to back away from the power, he has succeeded in his mission.

Chapter 15

Rebuilding Things That Calvary Once Destroyed

For if I build again the things which I destroyed, I make myself a transgressor. For I through the law am dead to the law, that I might live unto God. I am crucified with Christ: nevertheless I live; yet not I, but Christ liveth in me: and the life which I now live in the flesh I live by the faith of the Son of God, who loved me, and gave himself for me. I do not frustrate the grace of God: for if righteousness come by the law, then Christ is dead in vain.

—GALATIANS 2:18–21

WHEREAS JUDAISM WAS the cradle of Christianity, it was also its grave. Legalism needs to be torn down in the life of the church today. Legalism is when you base righteousness on anything other than the shed blood of Christ. Legalism is dangerous because it attempts to change the old nature and make it obey the law of God. In Romans chapter 7, Paul gives us a whole chapter to show us his frustration in trying to measure up to the law of God in his own strength.

When we abandon the Holy Spirit and the grace of God and think that through our works or self-effort we can serve God and be in right relationship with God, we are rebuilding the walls that Calvary once destroyed. Legalism will rob us of our spirituality, liberty, and spiritual wealth. We deliberately put ourselves into bondage and bankruptcy.

When Peter lived like a Gentile, he tore down the ceremonial Law. When he lived like a Jew, he tore down salvation by grace. If he sought to impose the law on Gentiles, which was abolished at the death of Christ, then He would rebuild again those things that were once destroyed. He would undo his justification by faith in Christ. One minute he was declaring the law to be null and void, and then he was declaring it valid again. The things that came crashing down around the apostle Paul on the Damascus Road because of Calvary would begin to live again if he abandoned the Holy Spirit and the grace of God and started trying to do it in his own strength.

Peter was a Christian Jew. He understood that the gospel which was meant for all people. It was based on Christ's work alone on the cross, not our works. Peter had been sent to speak and minister to the Gentile Cornelius (Acts 10). It was perfectly natural for Peter to eat with Gentiles. He would not shun them. He would participate fully in fellowship with them at meals because they were brothers and sisters in Christ.

There came a time in the church when Paul had to confront Peter (Gal. 2:11–21). Paul said, "You are a Jew, yet you live like a Gentile and not like a Jew. How is it, then, that you force Gentiles to follow Jewish customs?" (Gal. 2:14, NIV). He was saying, "Peter you are a Jew yet you live like a Gentile." He knew that following Jewish customs was not required for salvation. Yet Peter was a hypocrite, for he was forcing Gentiles to follow Jewish customs. By refusing to eat with them, Peter was behaving like he was trying to force them to change.

Paul reminded Peter of the gospel:

We who are Jews by birth and not Gentile sinners know that a man is not justified by observing the law, but by faith in Jesus Christ. So we, too, have put our faith in Christ Jesus that we may be justified by faith in Christ and not by observing the law, because by observing the law no one will be justified.

—GALATIANS 2:15–16

Peter was highly regarded as an apostle, but Paul confronted Peter because his behavior had changed. His behavior changed when certain men were sent by James from Jerusalem, and he felt that they would be critical of him associating with the Gentiles. He was afraid of those who belonged to the circumcision because they desired that all men, whether they are Jew or Gentile, should be circumcised. Peter, in the absence of the circumcision, had been eating with Gentiles. This would have been unusual for a Jew who was not a Christian. Table fellowship which was a sign of acceptance was a serious thing in Eastern countries, and for a Jew to share a table with a Gentile, much less to enter in under his roof, was never permissible according to Jewish Law, and it rendered him ceremonially unclean. Gentiles were considered to be unclean, and Jews would not associate with them. The Gentiles were not accepted as equals, and the Jews shunned them. When the circumcision was present, Peter would draw back and shun the Gentiles and did not desire to be seen with them, but when the circumcision was not present he did the opposite. This reminds us many times of those who whether or not they serve God are dependent on who is around. When I am in church I will do as the church, when I am in the world I will do as the world. This seems to be an attitude that abounds on every hand.

They were just like the Judaizers who felt that all the Jewish Old Testament customs were required for Christians. Other Jews joined him in his behavior, including Barnabas, Paul's companion. If Barnabas can be swayed and influenced by the Judaizers, then why do we consider it a strange thing that the Galatian believers were swayed by them? They were led astray and into hypocrisy. They believed in one thing, but behaved another way. Our behavior is a strong indicator for what we believe. They knew that they were not saved by works, but they behaved as if works were required to be saved. They adopted the mentality of the Judaizers who believed that they needed to follow the Jewish Law to be saved. The gang mentality took over, and Gentiles were being excluded.

Paul in his writings to the church kept coming back to the cross. The cross was a dominant theme in the Book of Galatians. Paul not only looked to the cross, he gloried in it. Paul knew the person who hung on that cross. Paul seemed to be captivated by Jesus Christ whom he mentioned forty-five times in the Book of Galatians. It was not a piece of wood but it was Christ who made the cross glorious to him. Paul said, "God forbid that I should glory, save in the cross of our Lord Jesus Christ, by whom the world is crucified unto me and I unto the world" (Gal. 6:14). Paul knew the power of the cross. It was there where Saul of Tarsus became Paul the Apostle. It was the cross that stood as a fence between Paul and the world. Lord, hide us behind the cross. Through the cross he was totally separated from his former habits and feelings. The cross ceased being a stumbling block to him and became the very foundation of his message.

Because of Calvary we have been delivered from this present evil age (1:4, NIV). The Greek word translated *evil* is *poneros*, which means this is a generation characterized by evil, active opposition against the good. The world knows that it is going down in corruption, but it is not content to know it is going down by itself; it wants to pull the child of God down right along with it. Christ gave Himself to die on the cross. Not only does the cross deliver us from the lordship, dominion, and control of sin, it will also deliver us in the future from any spiritual force or addiction that would seek to pull us down. Christ paid the price so that He might deliver us from this present, evil age.

"I have been crucified with Christ and I no longer live, but Christ lives in me" (2:20, NIV). At Calvary Christ died for sin, but at Calvary we died to sin's power, lordship, and control over our lives. Legalism may inflate the ego, flatter the flesh, and please the world, but the true Christian crucifies all three.

"Christ redeemed us from the curse of the law" (3:13, NIV). The curse of the law was sickness, disease, and poverty. Jesus was rejected that we might be accepted. He was cursed that we might be blessed. He was broken that we might be made whole. He died in naked shame that we might be clothed with His righteousness. He went to hell so we can go to heaven. Jesus became the ransom price to redeem us from the slave market of sin.

He died "to redeem those under law" (4:5, NIV). Jesus came up under the law and bore the penalty in our stead. The wrath that should have fallen upon us fell upon Him. Through His shed blood at Calvary, He satisfied justice and appeased God's divine wrath.

"They that are Christ's have crucified the flesh with [its] affections and lusts" (5:24). Christ has freed us from the bondage of the law. He has revoked our license to sin, placing us in a position of liberty. He has provided us with deliverance from the curse of sin, law, and self.

"The world is crucified unto me, and I unto the world" (Gal. 6:14). The cross became the barrier by which the world is fenced off from us and us from the world. The world is everything that is opposed to God, His kingdom, and His righteousness.

When the cross becomes our life, our glory, and our boast, the world with all of its standards, values, opinions, honors, and lifestyle is no longer cherished and loved. We cannot have a share in salvation and the glory of the cross without turning our backs on all that would draw us away from Christ and experiencing His nearness.

When we live by grace we are depending on the Holy Spirit. When we live by the law, we are depending on self and our own efforts. The efforts of the flesh can never accomplish what faith can accomplish through the power of the Holy Spirit.

The Judaizers tried to mix law and grace and released a satanic spirit of legalism into the life of the church. Paul told the Galatians, "You have fallen away from grace" (v. 4, NIV). The Galatians were setting aside the grace of God to go back to a flesh attempt to conform to the Law of Moses. For the Galatians to go back to Moses was to deny everything that God had done for them and through them. Peter in his own salvation had experienced the grace of God. In his own ministry he had proclaimed the grace of God. When the circumcision was present he would not fellowship with Gentiles. When the circumcision was absent he would fellowship with the uncircumcision. Paul confronted Peter and told him he was openly denying the very grace he had proclaimed (Gal. 2:11–13). Going back to the law nullified the cross. "If righteousness come by the law, then Christ is dead in vain" (2:21). Paul reminds them that "Christ shall profit you nothing" (5:2). Then he tells them they shall become "a debtor to the whole law" (v. 3).

We are saved by faith in Christ (He died for us). Either we die to sin or we will die in it. We live by faith in Christ (He lives in us). We are identified with Christ in His sacrificial death by the Spirit (we died with Him). This means that we are dead to the law.

I want to identify the losses that occur when we abandon the Holy Spirit and the grace of God for the law. First of all, to go back to Moses is to return to the graveyard. I am convinced that this is what has happened to many in the church. When they were first saved they were larger than life and very vibrant in the power of the Spirit. Now they have reached the place that they know how to do it. All that it has done is take us back to the cemetery and we have become dead to God all over again. We have been raised up with Christ to walk in newness of life (Rom. 6:4).

The yoke represents slavery, service, and control over someone else's life. It may also involve willing service and submission to someone else. When God delivered Israel from Egyptian servitude, it was the breaking of a yoke (Lev. 26:13).

Secondly, you become a slave and lose your liberty (Gal. 5:1), and we become slaves. Paul compared the law to a yoke of slavery. The yoke represented slavery, service, and control of a life by someone else. The farmer used the yoke to control and guide his oxen, because they would not willingly serve if they were free.

When the believers in Galatia trusted Christ, they lost the yoke of servitude to sin and put on the yoke of Christ (Matt. 11:28–30). The yoke of religion is hard, and the burden is heavy. Christ said, "My yoke is easy, and my burden is light" (v. 30). The word *yoke* implies a double yoke. If the weight of the entire yoke fell on us, it would crush us. The word *easy* means "kind and gracious." The yoke of Christ frees us to fulfill His will, while the yoke of the law enslaves us. The unsaved person wears the yoke of sin (Lam. 1:14, NIV) and the religious legalist wears the yoke of bondage (Gal. 5:1), but the Christian who depends on God's grace wears the liberating yoke of Christ.[1] The Galatians became like a bull that had become wrapped up in a net and couldn't get out. Paul tells the Galatians to take their stand for liberty.

Third, we become a debtor; we lose our wealth (vv. 2–6) and become a pauper. The believer living under the law becomes a bankrupt slave. It is bad enough when legalism robs you of your liberty, but it is just as bad when it robs you of your spiritual wealth in Christ.

It is Christ who set us free from the bondage of the law. He freed us from the curse of the law by dying on the tree (3:13). He was made poor that we might be made rich. The Christian is no longer under the law; he is under grace (Rom. 6:14). Christ died to set us free, not to make us slaves. To go back to the law is to become entangled with a maze of do's and don'ts and to abandon spiritual adulthood for a second childhood. It is like an adult climbing back into the crib.

Fourth, we become runners who have lost our direction (Gal. 5:7) and we have become runners on a detour. We don't run to be saved, we run because we are. Paul never used the image of a race to tell people how to be saved. He was always talking to Christians about how to live the Christian life. A contestant in the Greek games had to be a citizen before he could compete. In each race each runner had to stay in his assigned lane; some runners would cut in on their competitors to try to get them off course. This is what the Judaizers had done to the Galatians. They cut in on them and forced them to change their direction and go on a spiritual detour. God had called them to run faithfully in the lane that He marked grace. In short, we become losers; and the only way to become winners is to purge out the old leaven and yield to the Holy Spirit of God.[2]

Let's look at a few walls that are being built. Why have we come to a day when we believe that just because we observe the ritual and the formality of what we call church, that church and church alone can take care of our sin problem without us participating in the Holy Spirit?

The writer of the Book of Hebrews deals with our participation in the Holy Spirit. "How much more shall the blood of Christ, who through the eternal Spirit offered himself without spot to God, purge your conscience from dead works to serve the living God?" (Heb. 9:14).

This writer is making a contrast between the blood of animals and the blood of the Messiah. The blood of animals could cleanse from defilement and could set the body apart, so that the flesh could be purified, freed from defilement, and readmitted to public worship. It could free from the punishment of the law. It freed the outer man. The emphasis was on the external character. So long as the worshiper obeyed the regulations, he was declared clean. It was the purifying of the flesh but not the cleansing of the conscience. Old Testament sacrifices could not change the believer's heart. God said, "I will put my laws into their mind, and write them in their hearts" (Heb. 8:10). This is a work that had to be done by the Spirit of God. There was a day when the law was written on tablets, but now they are written on men's hearts.

> Forasmuch as ye are manifestly declared to be the epistle of Christ ministered by us, written not with ink, but with the Spirit of the living God; not in tables of stone, but in fleshy tables of the heart.
> —2 Corinthians 3:3

The Spirit could not have dwelt in us if Jesus had not paid for our sins. The cleansing of the conscience could not be done by external ceremony. It demanded an internal power. Every year the high priest had to go back in and offer the blood of another sacrifice so that mercy and pardon could be extended for another year. The blood could cover sin but could not take it away. If they could have made the believer perfect then, they would have ceased to be offered. Because Jesus was without spot, He was able to offer the perfect sacrifice.

While the blood of animals can cleanse the body, the blood of Christ can cleanse the soul and spirit and reconcile us to God. Only the blood of the Messiah can cleanse from actual sin. Jesus did not come just to cover sin but to take it away. That is why the blood of the Messiah was so much more effective. Christ became our Priest, altar, and sacrifice.

The writer of the Book of Hebrews makes a contrast between the limited value of the offerings under the law and the limitless value of the offering made by Christ at the cross. The Old Testament covenant was mediated by Moses and did not make the believer perfect, but the new covenant was mediated by Christ and produced the necessary righteousness.

The blood of Jesus Christ was central to the New Testament concept of redemption. He gave His blood to remove our sins and reconcile us to God.

THE BLOOD OF JESUS

1. Forgives the sins of those who repent and believe
2. Ransoms all believers from the power of Satan and his evil powers
3. Justifies all who believe
4. Cleanses the believer's conscience that he might serve God without guilt in full assurance
5. Sanctifies the people of God
6. Opens up a new and living way for believers to find grace and help in the time of need
7. Gives the guarantee of all the promises of the new covenant
8. Continues to cleanse from all sin those who continually draw near to God

How much more was the superiority of Christ's blood to the blood of bulls and goats and the ashes of the heifer! There is a quality to the blood of Jesus that was not found in the other sacrifices. The old transgressions are removed forever—not covered but taken away. Real sin is removed by a real Savior.

In the phrase "who through the eternal Spirit" (Heb. 9:14), the word *through* means "who through the instrumentality or by means of the Spirit." We were not there when God brought Israel out of 438 years of Egyptian bondage, but through the eternal Spirit we can participate and identify with their victory. We are living in a world full of divine surprises and supernatural visitations of the Holy Spirit. We are experiencing the tension of the world of the already and also the not yet. There is coming a day when every sickness and disease is going to be healed and even the dead are going to get up. There are times God takes what is getting ready to happen in our future and brings it into our present.

The Book of Revelation identifies Jesus as "Alpha and Omega, the beginning and the ending, saith the Lord, which is, which was, and which is to come, the Almighty" (Rev. 1:8). This means that God is not static, but active. God, who has been active in history, is continually breaking into our world. He was God in our past, He is God in our present, and He will be God in our future.

Christ "offered himself" (Heb. 9:14, NIV). The voluntary character of Christ's death is here emphasized. Animals had no will of their own. They were offered because the law demanded it, not by any consent of their own. No Old Testament sacrifice ever volunteered for the job.

Christ offered Himself with His own consent. His death was voluntary. He became our buyer and our price, our Shepherd and our Lamb, our High Priest, our offering, and our altar. By Him being willing to lay His life down, He empowered the sacrifice and made it effective. By the Messiah offering Himself voluntarily and by Him doing it as Deity, He made His blood effective. Jesus became man that He might suffer and die for the sins of the people.

Jesus was "without spot" (9:14). In His person He was absolutely spotless, holy, and perfectly righteous. There were requirements for Passover offerings and sacrifices. Animals that were offered under the Levitical system were to be unblemished according to the standards of the ceremonial law. There could be no blemish in His person and character. The Lamb that was sacrificed could not have any external flaws or defilement. He had to have moral integrity and perfection.

> Forasmuch as ye know that ye were not redeemed with corruptible things, as silver and gold, from your vain conversation received by tradition from your fathers; But with the precious blood of Christ, as of a lamb without blemish and without spot.
> —1 PETER 1:18–19

The word translated *precious* had two meanings: "costly value" and "highly esteemed" or "held in honor." Deity became incarnated into humanity. God holds the blood to be of great value.

There were three words in the New Testament for redemption: *agadazo*, *exagadazo*, and *luo*. Nothing was more nauseating than the slave market. *Agadazo* implies the scenario of when I was in a slave market on the auction block and the devil was the auctioneer. The world had come in with its silver and gold and tried to purchase me. I was slapped to check my temper and attitude. My teeth were inspected because they believed that the healthier the teeth, the healthier the slave. The devil said, "Who will make the first bid for this man?" Right when the world was ready to lay down its silver and gold to purchase me, in walked Christ who is the Light of the world. He declared, "I will make the first bid for this man." The devil asked, "What are your credentials?" Jesus said, "I am the buyer and price, the Shepherd and the Lamb, the High Priest, the Offering, and the Altar." And He went on to say, "I am willing to go to an old rugged cross and bleed and die that this man may go free."

Exagadazo implies that Jesus does not leave me in the slave market, but He takes me out. We have been saved *from* our sins, not *in* them. Matthew declared to us the words of Gabriel to Mary when he said, "[You] shall bring forth a son, and thou shalt call His name JESUS: for he shall save his people from their sins" (Matt. 1:21). The word *from* comes from the Greek word *apo*, which means "out from, away from." Jesus has come to take us out of the prison house of sin.

One of the compromises Pharaoh offered to Moses while in Egypt was to stay and worship his God. Moses knew that Molech, a favored Egyptian god, was in the form of a calf or an ox. If an Egyptian would have seen Israel sacrifice a bullock, they would have stoned them. So in order for Israel to worship, they had to come out of Egypt. They could not stay and worship; they had to go out to worship. We need to realize that we are going to become just like what we spend most of our time beholding. When Israel was at the foot of Sinai and Aaron took the jewelry off of Israel and made the golden calf, the moment that Israel looked at the golden calf everything that was alive in them in Egypt came back alive in them. It took one day to get Israel out of Egypt but forty years to get Egypt out of them.

Luo is a word that means "I wash you and set you free." Jesus took me out of the slave market of sin and set me upon a rock. He saw the chains and the shackles on my hands and feet. He declared: "I wash you and set you free." Then my chains fell from my hands and feet, and I knew that I was set free. So the word *redemption* covers my deliverance in, from, and out of the tyranny, lordship, and control of sin.

When Jesus raised Lazarus from the dead, Lazarus came forth bound with grave clothes from head to feet. He was alive physically but dead spiritually. Jesus used the word *luo* when He said to those who stood near, "Loose him, and let him go" (John 11:44). Jesus was not speaking to graveyard attendants. He was telling death and hell to get their hands off of Him. I am convinced that the grave clothes were more on his spirit than his flesh. I am convinced that whatever is going on in my spirit is battled through my mind, will, and emotions and is manifested through my flesh. When his spirit was free, his soul and body lined up. Then Lazarus went from the graveyard to the supper table.

Let's not forget the woman whom Satan had bound with a spirit of infirmity for eighteen years. She was in the synagogue and Jesus was there teaching on the Sabbath day. She was bowed over and could not make herself straight (Luke 13:10–16). This reminds me of so many in the church who have looked down for so long that it has begun to affect their posture. Jesus saw her, called her to Him, and said, "Woman, thou art loosed from thine infirmity" (v. 12). And Jesus "laid His hands on her: and immediately she was made straight, and glorified God" (v. 13). The religious leaders thought more of losing their ox and ass on the Sabbath day and leading them to water than they did this woman who was a daughter of Abraham receiving her deliverance. Jesus did not violate the law, but He did break their tradition. Jesus was a Sabbath day violator.

The Hebrews writer said that by our participation in the Holy Spirit, the blood of Christ will "purge [our] conscience." The Levitical system could only affect the external part of man, but left the inner man untouched. The sacrifices of the Messiah reached the center of the moral and spiritual being of each individual. He alleviated the guilt of our past and cleansed our conscience. Our inner man becomes renewed and made alive so that we can truly serve God. Old Testament ritual could never do this.

The sacrifice of Christ changed the character of the works done by the individual. Before salvation, the sinner did good works in the strength of his sinful nature. They were dead works. After the believer had been transformed by Christ's atoning death, his good works were motivated, empowered, and produced by the Holy Ghost. Now the believer has living works in his service to the living God. He is enabled to serve the living God. There is sanctification and renewal in his soul.

Only the blood of Jesus Christ can set the believer apart to the worship and service of God. We have been purchased by Christ for that purpose. Now we don't say prayers, we pray them. We don't sing from the words of a page but out of our experience. Church has taken on a brand-new meaning since the Holy Spirit has come. It is through the Spirit that the death, burial, and resurrection of Christ have come into our lives. It does not come through our works or our self-efforts.

If I leave the Spirit, I will return to the graveyard in my Christian experience. It is not the pastor's job to keep us swinging from the lights and to keep our heads in the clouds. People in the church are going to have to learn how to serve God. Renewal is going to have to become a day-by-day affair. We are going to have to recapture the walk of the Spirit and learn what it means to walk in the Spirit.

In the Old Testament God is the one who put the fire on the altar. He put it in the hands of the priests and told them to keep it burning. We are keepers of the flame. "Where no wood is, there the fire goeth out" (Prov. 26:20). When we see the fire burning low, we are going to have to learn to throw a log of holiness, consecration, prayer, praise, and worship on it. There are two ways to put out a fire: by smothering it and not letting it breathe or by neglecting it. A neglected fire always goes out.

If I leave the Spirit and the grace of God, I will return to the weak and beggarly elements (Gal. 4:9). The Galatians were giving up the power of the gospel for the weakness of the law. They were giving up the wealth of the gospel for the poverty of the law. The law never made anyone rich or powerful; on the contrary, the law could only reveal weakness and spiritual bankruptcy. Paul wept over the Galatians as He saw them abandon liberty for bondage, power for weakness, and wealth for poverty.[3]

If I leave the Spirit, I will return to a life of spiritual bankruptcy (5:2–6). When we trusted Christ, we became spiritually rich. We were wealthier beyond our wildest dreams and imaginations. We had a share in the riches of God's grace (Eph. 1:7), the riches of His glory (v. 18), the riches of His wisdom (Rom. 11:33), and the unsearchable riches of Christ (Eph. 3:8). In Christ we have "all the treasures of wisdom and knowledge" (Col. 2:3). We "are complete in him, which is the head of all principality and power" (2:10). In Him we are made full. There is no lack of efficiency on the part of Christ. Everything we need to become a well rounded, developing, enthusiastic Christian is found in Him. How can we discuss how dry and empty we are when we have been positioned in fullness?

Have we declared spiritual bankruptcy? Are we a church that is ignorant of our wealth? There is far more to be gained by staying with the Spirit and the grace of God than by going back to the law. Surely the Galatians had to know that something was missing in their spiritual bank account.

Everything that Calvary produced becomes destroyed. Every wall that came down, every addiction that was broken, and every sin that had a mortgage over our existence will slowly but surely revive. Egypt will once again look appealing, and we will return to a life of sin. Sin will revive what Calvary once destroyed. It was the Holy Spirit that kept us from going back to a life of sin because He suppressed our sin nature and placed our flesh under holy control. I have told many people in the church that I pastor to make sure you go all the way with God, or you will go back to a life of sin; it is only a matter of time. It was the Holy Spirit that made real the provisions of Calvary in our lives. Through Him we were made free.

If I abandon the Holy Spirit and the grace of God, I will become bewitched by a spirit of religion. Religion died in Paul's life the day he met Christ on the road to Damascus. He went from being religious to spiritual. It is our participation in the Holy Spirit that keeps us from being seduced by a spirit of religion. The Nicodemuses of the church are many. Nicodemus was religious but not born again. Judaism had become a bankrupt, religious system going down a dead-end road going nowhere—until Christ opened up a new and living way to bring us into the presence of God. Many believe that they have to be dead to be reverent. People know more about church than they know about God.

I need the Holy Spirit to come along and help me carry this heavy load. I need someone to put my flesh under holy control. Through the Spirit's control, I have a desire to live for others instead of myself and to be free from self-being at the center of my life (See Galatians 6.)

Chapter 16

Protecting Our Freedom in Christ

Stand fast therefore in the liberty wherewith Christ hath made us free, and be not entangled again with the yoke of bondage.
—GALATIANS 5:1

FREEDOM IN CHRIST is not only a privilege, it is also our responsibility. Our freedom is an fact because of what Jesus accomplished for us at Calvary. Jesus signed our declaration of independence at Calvary with His own blood. Freedom should be the goal of every born-again child of God. Many Christians know how to obtain it but do not know how to maintain it. Christ set us free to stay free and not to go back under the bondage of the law. Our freedom in Christ is not the result of efforts of the flesh. We have not been liberated by our own efforts. Once we have been set free it is our responsibility to maintain that freedom.

The fact that we were imprisoned by the law was a major theme in Paul's letter to the Galatians. Paul declared that "the scripture hath concluded all under sin, that the promise by faith of Jesus Christ might be given to them that believe" (Gal. 3:22). The word *concluded* is translated from the Greek word *sunkleio*, which means "to shut up or to confine."[1] The Scriptures, being divinely inspired, spoke of sin as a jailor who shuts all up in sin as in a prison. The function of the law was to convict us of sin so that we might turn to the Lord Jesus for salvation.

Then Paul says, "But before faith came, we were kept under the law, shut up unto the faith which should afterwards be revealed" (v. 23). Paul is referring to personal faith in the Lord Jesus Christ as Savior and Lord. It is a faith that looks back to the cross. Our salvation has now become an accomplished fact. Faith in the message of the cross has been the means of obtaining salvation ever since Adam.

The word *kept* comes from the Greek word *phroureo*, which means "to keep under a lock and key."[2] The law was a jailor who held in custody those who were subject to sin. During the 1,500 years that the law was in force, it was the means of convicting sinners of their sin and causing them to look ahead in faith to the atonement God would some day offer in the person of His Son, Jesus Christ. When faith came in the person of Christ, then the law was fulfilled. The law was given so that the sinner would see that sin was an actual transgression of God's law and that he might see the necessity of faith in the substitutionary offering of Christ as a sacrifice for sin. Then the sinner would be led to put his faith in the Christ, of whom it was prophesied that in the fullness of time would come and die for him.

Paul said, "The strength of sin is the Law" (1 Cor. 15:56). Paul declared that law intensified sin and made us aware of it. It makes us aware of what is right from wrong. It defines sin and condemns it. The law made no provision for mercy, pardon, or forgiveness. It was there to remind me of how much I had blown it. It could identify sin but leave me powerless to do anything about it. The law made no provision for victory, and it certainly did not offer to man the power to do good or shun evil.

We were shut in prison as long as we remained hostile toward God and His law. As long as we rebel we will remain in prison. No one comes out without repentance. It is faith in Christ that frees us from the jailhouse of sin. Faith lays hold of what Christ purchased for us at the tree. God places the obedience of Christ to the account of the believing sinner. The man who believes on Christ is no longer a debtor to sin.

The law bound men to the service of sin. Many have found it very hard to escape its grip as long as the law of God binds us. Sin had already conquered men before the law of God was actually given. Sin strengthened the enemy of our soul in its battle against us. God actually gave the commandment to help sin, who is our enemy overcome. In fact the law of God strengthened our enemy and did not give us any power against our enemy.

Those who have tried to break from the grip of sin realize how they were being held by a power that no one else could master. The law of God has given to sin power to enslave the lives of men. Apart from the law of God there can be no sin (Rom. 4:15; 5:13). "Where there is no law there is no transgression." Apart from the law of God sin would have no power to hold men in the service of sin.

The enemy of our soul has caused many people to embrace the law thinking that it will help them quit sinning. "Thou shalt not covet" (Exod. 20:17).

Why? Many times we want everything that we are not supposed to have. "Thou shalt not commit adultery" (Exod. 20:14). People that have never been tempted in that particular area will immediately began to lust after someone else other than their mate.

We need to be delivered from the law (vv. 4, 6). While we were held captive by our sin nature, our passions that were sinful were awakened by the law. They were at work within our members so that we would produce the fruit of death. It was the law that made sin alive in us (Rom. 7:9). We needed a Savior to redeem us. It is the gospel that is the power of God unto salvation (Rom. 1:16) and aids us in our battle against sin.

In Christ we have been set free from the law that held us captive. Sin has no power apart from the law. Sin goes to the law and asks permission to take possession of a man or woman. Sin asks, "Will you grant me permission to take possession of this man?" Yes! Says the law, you have my permission. Sin goes off with authority, takes possession of man and works in him every evil desire. Sin will get permission from the law to stir up all kinds of evil passions in him.

Sin, death, and the law go together. The law reveals sin. We know that the "Wages of sin is death" (Rom. 6:23). Jesus bore our sins in His own body on the tree (1 Pet. 2:24). He also bore the curse of the law (Gal. 3:13). It is through Jesus Christ that we have the victory and that we share that victory today. "Thanks be to God who keeps on giving us the victory through our Lord Jesus Christ."

The law cannot bring people to salvation. It offers to man a standard that we ought to reach but never do. It made sinners of us all and condemns us. The law has no power to condemn anyone that is clothed with the righteousness of Jesus Christ (Rom. 8:1).

When man rebelled against the law of God the law sentenced man to death. It became his jailor and threw man into prison. Man chose the service of sin. The law has put Him into prison and keeps him in prison. Justice has demanded that we stay in a debtor's prison without any hope of being acquitted. The only way he can be delivered from this place of misery and captivity is that he has to be delivered from the power of the law.

Justification by faith makes prisoners free. Jesus left the ivory palaces of glory to come and give His life a ransom for many. We were prisoners without hope (Gal. 3:22–24). We were indebted to the law. We could never be delivered by the efforts of the flesh. Through justification by faith we have been placed in a position of one who has never broken the law. Now we are no longer bound in prison. Sin has lost its legal rights over us. We do not have to serve it anymore or tremble at its power.

To believe the gospel is to believe that He paid a debt that He did not owe. The law is no longer our jailor. Sin has lost the right to keep us in its service. We proved this the day we left the prison house of sin. The law no longer binds the believer to the prison house of sin. The jailor sees that the debt has been paid. With the prison doors swung wide open we were free to pass from captivity to liberty.

Paul said that, "So also, when we were children, we were in slavery under the basic principles of the world" (4:3, NIV). Paul was saying that when we were immature under the law, we were under the slavery of the first principles of a world that was not Christian. To the Jew it referred to Judaism and its legal enactments. The Greek emphasized that we were under a permanent state of servitude. So Paul makes clear the very nature of slavery. We were condemned prisoners under the judgment of the law, due to live under its restrictions with no hope of earning freedom by observing its commands. All the law could do was point out how we had blown it. It could reveal sin and yet leave us powerless to do anything about it (3:19). Our imprisonment under the law not only separated Jews from Gentiles but also isolated them as prisoners in different cellblocks.

The Galatians had been placed in the family through adoption as adult sons. God the Father took the quill of his pen dipped in the blood of Calvary's Lamb, signed His name as the legal guardian of my life, stamped it with the seal of the Holy Spirit, and filed my adoption papers in the file cabinets of glory. All debts that I incurred while I was in sin have become sole property of God the Father. We were not placed in the family as babes but as adult sons. When the Old Testament was written, the revelation of God was in the infancy stages of revelation. Now that the light has come on in the fact that Jesus is the climax of God's revelation to man, the nursery needs to be left behind. The Holy Spirit enables us to live the Christian life. By the Galatians going back to the straightjacket of the law, it cramped their experience, it brought their actions as adult sons to a dead standstill, and it deprived them of the ministry of the Holy Spirit. Under the law a child has no more liberty than a child who is under a guardian. He had to move within a set of rules that were prescribed under the law. As adults they returned to the cradle, and as adult sons they returned to kindergarten 101. By them swinging back over to the law, they lost their freedom to act as adult sons.

Our release from the prison house of sin and from slavery under the law were basic themes in Paul's Galatian letter. We have been delivered from the judgment of the law of God. We are children of the free woman (Sarah) and we stand for the promise, not children of Hagar (bondwoman) who stands for the Mosaic commandments. Our lives are lived in the joyful freedom of knowing that in Christ, God has fulfilled His promise. This promise of God's blessing has led to a new community in which the divisions of race, class, and gender have been removed. "There is neither Jew nor Greek, there is neither bond nor free, there is neither male nor female: for ye are all one in Christ Jesus" (3:28). All believers have been raised to a higher life in Christ. All of us now have one heartbeat. The pulsating life of the Lord Jesus is the motivating power of the church. Ethic and racial distinctions have been wiped away. The mind of Christ guides us all. The life of the Lord Jesus is lived in all as it is made real by the Holy Spirit of God.

The redemptive act of Christ at Calvary has set us free and liberated us from slavery and imprisonment under the law. This is a major theme in Paul's letter to the Galatians. Through Christ's death on the cross, He took the curse of the law upon Himself (v. 13). When the Galatians believed the message of the cross, they received the Spirit (vv. 1–2). It was then that they participated in the death, burial, and resurrection of Christ. We now see ourselves as having been crucified, buried, and resurrected with Christ. Through the indwelling life of the Lord Jesus, we have been enabled to live unto God (2:19–20). By God sending forth the Spirit of His Son into our hearts, we can live together as one family.

Our slavery and freedom and Christ's liberating work are summed up in Galatians 5:1. When Paul said, "Stand fast therefore in the liberty wherewith Christ hath made us free," he is giving us a divine imperative. What we must do is always based on what God has already done. What God has accomplished through Christ gives us the opportunity and power to do what we must do. "For, brethren, ye have been called unto liberty; only use not liberty for an occasion to the flesh, but by love serve one another" (v. 13). We are not to use our Christian liberty as a license to do as we please, but to serve God and our fellow man. Because we are no longer under the bondage of the law does not mean that rules do not apply. It is then that the Holy Spirit takes the righteousness of the law and fulfills it in us as we walk after the Spirit.

Paul had often exhorted his readers to stand firm. When Paul addressed the church at Corinth, he told them to "be on your guard; stand firm in the faith; be men of courage; be strong" (1 Cor. 16:13, NIV). Paul was telling them that holiness produces stability. Paul was telling them to strike the roots of their faith deep into the soil of eternal truth. Sound doctrine must be combined with a vital experience, and both are necessary in order to have spiritual stability.

Grace is not a license to sin. Grace is God's power at work in us giving us the power and ability to overcome sin. "If we live in the Spirit, let us also walk in the Spirit" (v. 25). We are to be ordering our behavior by this life-giving principle of the Word and the Spirit. Paul is saying three things: God's gift of freedom must be defended (v. 1), God's gift of freedom must not be abused but must be used to serve (v. 13), and God's gift of life by the Spirit must be expressed through the Spirit (v. 25).

Christ died on the cross to liberate us from the bondage of the law. The Judaizers had to rely on their self-effort alone to conform to the Mosaic Law. The Galatians lived their lives in dependence upon the Holy Spirit. Their hearts were occupied with Jesus Christ. Their lifestyle was guided by the teaching of the apostles.

Paul wrote to the church at Philippi and said:

> Only let your conversation be as it becometh the gospel of Christ: that whether I come and see you, or else be absent, I may hear of your affairs, that ye stand fast in one spirit, with one mind striving together for the faith of the gospel
>
> —PHILIPPIANS 1:27

The most powerful weapon a child of God can possess from God's arsenal that can be used against the enemy of our souls is a consistent, godly life. God does not want us being up and down, on and off, in and out. I have met many that have told me that they just decided to take a break, but God has no part-time employees.

First of all Paul says, "Let your conversation be as it becometh the gospel of Christ" (v. 27). He is dealing with a political theme. We are to behave the way citizens are supposed to behave. Children of God are citizens of heaven. We are to conduct ourselves as citizens of heaven while we walk upon this earth. The church is a colony of heaven located on the earth. Our names are recorded in the city directory of heaven in a book called the Lamb's Book of Life. We need to realize that we are the only Bible that some people read. We are a love letter written by Christ to a world that is lost.

The church is to be the living embodiment of the Truth. In Ephesians 6 the first piece of weaponry that Paul identifies on the Christian soldier is having our loins gird about with truth (v. 14). Keep in mind that the breastplate of righteousness, shield of faith, and sword of the Spirit are connected to this belt (vv. 14, 16–17). It is truth that gives balance to the Christian soldier. We are to be living epistles, read and known of all men. The local church should be practicing the truth. Our behavior should be the mirror of what we believe. It is then that the devil will be defeated.

Secondly, Paul said, "You are to stand fast in one spirit" (Phil. 1:27). You are to stand firmly together in one Spirit. The church is to have one mind and one heart as we contend with the enemy of our souls. The church ought to have one prayer, one desire, and one determination: to stand fast until the end.

Thirdly, Paul says, "Striving together for the faith of the gospel" (v. 27). Paul is saying that there needs to be spirit of cooperation. Here Paul uses an athletic term *sunathleo*, striving together as athletes. The church is a team and it's teamwork that wins victories. Victories are not won by people who stand on the sidelines and tell others how it needs to be done. Neither is it one by someone on the sidelines criticizing the players on the field. We have players on the field needing the rest and fans in the stands needing the exercise. On this team we have the Word of God for the rulebook. Someone said the letters in the word *Bible* stand for Basic Instructions Before Leaving Earth. We have one goal and that is to honor Christ and do His will. If we work together, reach the goal, and win the prize, we will glorify Christ. If we break the rules and do not contend lawfully, stop training and quit developing spiritual muscles, and look to take the glory for ourselves, teamwork will begin to disappear and division and competition will set in.

Then Paul addresses the church at Philippi once again and says, "Therefore, my brethren dearly beloved and longed for, my joy and crown, so stand fast in the Lord, my dearly beloved" (Phil. 4:1). Every believer is to take his or her spiritual stance and stand firm in the freedom that was purchased for us by Christ at Calvary. False brethren had infiltrated the Galatian ranks to spy on their freedom that they had in Christ in order to make them slaves. "And that because of false brethren unawares brought in, who came in privily to spy out our liberty which we have in Christ Jesus, that they might bring us into bondage" (Gal. 2:4).

Paul used the term "false brethren" to describe the Judaizers from Corinth. They slipped in when they were not wanted. They came into the church and began to make a thorough investigation. Their purpose was to make them slaves again and take them back to the bondage of the law. This was a serious conflict. Will you stay with your spiritual liberty that Christ died to purchase or will you return to spiritual bondage? These false brethren were putting pressure on the Gentile converts to be circumcised and become identified with the Jewish people.

"Be not entangled again with the yoke of bondage" (5:1). The word *entangled* comes from the Greek *enecho*, which means held within, ensnared, held with a net.[3] They became like a bull wrapped up in a net again. They traded their liberty for bondage.

In Paul's day it was a common sight to see an oxen under a yoke tied to a heavy cart straining to pull a heavy load up a hill while being goaded with a sharp stick. The pressure under that yoke is almost exhausting. The crushing weight of the yoke is our obligation to keep the whole law. In Peter's address to the Jerusalem council, he reported, "Why do you try to test God by putting on the necks of the [Gentile] disciples a yoke that neither we nor our fathers have been able to bear?" (Acts 15:10, NIV). The yoke of the law was a yoke of slavery, because it placed the individual under the burden of commandments we cannot keep and under curses that we deserve for our disobedience.

God sent His Son, Jesus Christ, to lift this heavy yoke from our shoulders and take it upon Himself. He was "born under law" (Gal. 4:4, NIV) and kept all its demands for us; He died under the curse of the law for us (3:13). The curse that should have fallen on us fell on Him. The wrath that should have fallen on us fell on Him. Since Christ has set us free from this yoke of slavery, we must not take it on ourselves again. In contrast to the yoke of slavery under the law, Jesus said, "My yoke is easy and my burden is light" (Matt. 11:30). Too many times we are yoked up with people that enslave us instead of enriching us. The yoke that Jesus has is a double yoke. The burden is shared by two instead of having to carry the full load ourselves.

Paul gives us two negative consequences of submitting to the yoke of the law in Galatians 5:2–4. "Behold, I Paul say unto you, that if ye be circumcised, Christ shall profit you nothing" (v. 2). Paul is saying, "Mark my words, I, Paul, am telling you." So Paul comes as a representative of Christ and God the Father. When Paul mentions being circumcised it is in the present tense which means the process had just begun. Paul wants to stop the mutilation. In Paul's day it was the mark of belonging to the Jewish nation. By being circumcised the Gentile became a Jewish proselyte. Their motive was to try to be justified by the law. They thought they could gain God's approval by belonging to the Jewish nation. They did not consider their faith in Christ or the message of the cross to be the sole reason for justification before God. They had to be identified with the Jewish people and be circumcised.

If you start trusting circumcision, you have stop trusting Christ. If you do not trust in Christ, then Christ becomes of no value to you. They were putting their trust in their own position and in their own performance for God's blessing and approval. By doing this, any of us are indicating that who we are and what we have done has more value than who Christ is and what He has done. We have turned our backs on Christ.

"He is a debtor to do the whole law" (Gal. 5:3). The verse starts with "again, I declare to every man." The Galatians thought by identifying themselves as full members of the Jewish nation, they could secure God's blessing for themselves. Are you relying on yourself keeping the law to be the reason why God is blessing you? If you are relying on the law, then you are obligated to keep the whole law. If you offend in one point, you are guilty of breaking the whole law (James 2:10). James sees the law as a seamless garment that if it rips in one place it tears the whole garment. Paul says they have embarked on an impossible mission. You cannot base your relationship with God on your performance because you will not be graded on a curve. "Christ is become of no effect unto you, whosoever of you are justified by the law; ye are fallen from grace" (Gal. 5:4).

The Galatians had transferred their faith in Christ to a faith in legalistic observances of the law. When the law demanded, it gave me no hands or feet. Grace bade me to fly and gave me wings. Wings in scripture denoted supernatural power. When the law said "thou shalt" and "thou shalt not," it gave me no ability to live up to it. No man can be justified by faith in Christ and by his own efforts too.

You cannot mix grace and law. If you decide to live in the sphere of the law you cannot live in the sphere of grace. The way of the law makes salvation dependent upon human achievement. The man who takes the way of grace casts himself and his sin upon the mercy seat of God. The gospel of grace in Galatians is defended in chapters 1–2, explained in chapters 3–4, and applied in chapters 5–6. To live by grace means to depend on God's abundant supply for every need. To live by the law means to depend on our own strength and to be left without God's supply.

"Christ is become of no effect unto you" (5:4). Paul is saying, "You are severed from Christ." The tense of the verb is first aorist passive of the Greek word *katargeo*, which means "to make null or void and ineffectual."[4] Paul used it in the sense of being freed from a marriage contract. (See Romans 7:2.) So the vital bond of God's grace has been broken, and no other relationship with Christ is possible for the Christian. Paul is saying that their relationship with Christ had been completely severed. They were unaffected by Christ. They had been severed from growth or life, physical or spiritual.

The subject of the verb is the Galatian Christians. By putting themselves under the law, they put themselves in a place where they had ceased to be in relationship with Christ where they could draw spiritual benefits from Him. The ministry of the Holy Spirit would have enabled them to live a life pleasing to Him. There is not one of us that would be able to serve God if the Holy Spirit was not in our lives. The Judaizers had convinced the Galatians that by keeping the law they were not abandoning their faith in Christ. Christ had no effect upon their living a Christian life. The law was the way to attain perfection in the Christian life and come to the place of spiritual maturity. Those who regulate their lives by the law are removed from Christ reigning over their lives.

If you are trusting your own efforts to keep the law, then you are no longer trusting God's grace: "Ye are fallen from grace" (Gal. 5:4). Many who profess to be Spirit-filled feel that they can cool off spiritually and lose the baptism in the Spirit without losing their salvation. This is a biblical impossibility. The Holy Spirit is God's convicting agent of salvation. The believer was initiated into the Holy Spirit through God's grace. So the danger of apostasy, falling from grace, was very real or Paul would have never used such strong language. How can anyone rest in unconditional eternal security without ignoring Paul's warnings?

The Galatian believers had been bewitched by the Judaizers (3:1). They disobeyed the truth. They turned aside to another gospel (1:6–9). They turned back to the elementary things of the old religion (4:9). Then they became entangled again with that yoke of bondage (5:1). This led to their present condition where they had "fallen from grace" (v. 4). The tragedy of the fall is that they robbed themselves of the good things Jesus Christ could have done for them. When we deprive ourselves of the ministry of the Holy Spirit in the Christian life, we *will* fall from grace.

When the Galatians abandoned the Holy Spirit and the grace of God, there were many things that happened:

1. They fell from grace. The Greek word translated *fallen* is *ekpipto*, meaning they lost their hold on the grace of God. I realize that grace is hanging on a whole lot tighter to me than I am to it. Grace manifests itself in at least three ways:
    a. Justification
    b. Sanctification
    c. Glorification
2. Paul is talking about daily grace for daily living. They lost their hold on sanctifying grace. Paul has in mind a serious matter, substituting the law for Christ as the agent of salvation.
3. They lost the glow upon their countenance.
4. They lost the beauty of the lordship of Jesus Christ in their lives. Paul found himself having to travail all over in Zion until Christ be fully formed in them again until there was an outward expression of an inward relationship because they had been raped by the Judaizers.

Paul stated that they had fallen from grace. To fall from grace means to be alienated from Christ and to abandon the principles of Christ that bring us life and salvation. To fall from grace means to have our association with Christ nullified and to no longer abide in Christ.

Then Paul gives us a positive description of us maintaining our freedom in Christ. "We through the Spirit wait for the hope of righteousness by faith" (5:5). By faith in the gospel we received the Spirit (3:2). Now we live by the Spirit (5:16), are led by the Spirit (v. 18), and keep in step with the Spirit (v.

25). It is the presence of the Spirit that identifies us as the children of God (4:6). The power of the Spirit produces in us the character of Christ and the Spirit of holiness in the New Testament (5:22–23). By yielding ourselves to the Holy Spirit the yoke of the law is unnecessary (v. 18).

Paul says that a life of faith is a life of confident expectation of righteousness. Paul is speaking of future righteousness, which is ours when God completes His work in us by His Spirit. Through the Spirit we hope to reap the harvest of eternal life (6:8). Our Christian life began when we put our faith in Christ and the message of the cross. God credited His righteousness to our account (3:6–9). By the power of the Spirit, God produces righteousness in us. It has been placed on our account through justification, produced in us through progressive sanctification, and perfected in us by glorification.

Chapter 17

Returning to Slavery Again

Howbeit then, when ye knew God, ye did service
unto them which by nature are no gods.
—GALATIANS 4:8

PAUL DRAWS THE Galatians' attention again to the knowledge of God, which they now enjoyed in their new relationship with God (4:9). Through their conversion they went from paganism to Christ in their knowledge of God. Their knowledge of God has been communicated to them through their personal encounter with Him. Throughout biblical history the joy of God's people has come from the fact that God knows us, not that we know God.

People in today's society continue to worship and serve created things rather than the Creator. They have placed other things in the place of God. People, ancient or modern, do not know God. Paul is talking about an experiential knowledge of a personal relationship.

Human religions and philosophical efforts to know God are not going to lead us to an experiential knowledge of God. Paul wrote to the Corinthians and said, "In the wisdom of God the world through its wisdom did not know him" (1 Cor. 1:21, NIV). The wisdom of God's revealed message cannot be mixed with the wisdom of man. God has revealed His wisdom in the message of the cross of Jesus Christ. While the Jews stumble at the cross and the Greeks laugh at the cross, some are experiencing the power and wisdom of the cross. The message of the cross brought the Galatians out of paganism, superstition, and darkness. What has the message of the cross delivered us from?

Through the Galatians seeking to abandon the Holy Spirit and God's sanctifying enabling grace and seeking once again to attempt to observe the law, they were turning from their active, experiential, intimate knowledge of who God was and returning to the slavery of paganism they knew before they came to Christ. It was very important that the Galatians reexamine their relationship with the Holy Spirit (3:1–5). The Galatians had already begun to address God as "Abba, Father" (4:6). They were asked to compare their present knowledge of God as His children with their former ignorance of God as slaves. He rebukes their foolishness.

Paul is pointing out the great sin of idolatry, which is to worship a created thing rather than the Creator (Rom. 1:25). When the Galatians were without the knowledge of God, they were slaves to those things which by their nature were no gods. Now that they had come to know God, Paul is finding it to be strange how they are beginning to go back to powerless and limited practices of idolatry. Paul is asking them, "Do you want to become slaves all over again?" Paul seems to be afraid that he may have wasted his efforts on the Galatians. Paul did not deny the existence of these pagan gods. He did deny their deity. They belonged to a demonic world.

It seems like the Galatians were abandoning liberty for bondage. When they were lost in sin and had no knowledge of God they experienced the slavery of paganism. When they placed their faith in Christ as Lord and Savior they were delivered from superstition and slavery. Now they are departing from their liberty in Christ and going back into bondage. They were dropping out of the school of grace for the kindergarten of the law. They were destroying all the good things that the Lord had done for them through the ministry of the apostle Paul. They were going back to a stage that they had abandoned years ago.

Paul is pointing out the law was the elementary stage in this journey. He believes that the man who is mature will take his stand in grace. The law had been good in that it offered to them a standard of righteousness. It had served as a schoolmaster to bring them to Christ.

We need to understand that a legalistic spirit is one that will cause one to have a relapse. God has placed something in every man that gives him a desire to worship something. Because the Galatians were ignorant of the worship of the true God, they had many deities of their own. It is one thing for a heathen through his blindness and ignorance to worship idols, but when a Christian has received the knowledge of God and has been illuminated by the Holy Spirit to return to the weak and beggarly elements is a devastating thing. After they have tasted of the liberty that is theirs in Christ, why should they return to slavery?

When a legalistic spirit takes hold of the Christian it is an occasion for an alarm. Paul said, "I am afraid of you, lest I bestowed upon you labour in vain" (v. 11). Paul knew that the Galatians had been fickle. He was not prepared to see his work among them collapse. He had taken time to build it up with care and godly concern. For them to go back to paganism meant: 1) loss of advantages gained, and 2) loss of blessings that had been enjoyed since they came to Christ. Legalism suppresses all religious growth. It poses a constant danger to the holiest of men. It also reveals the necessity for earnest vigilant prayer.

In order for them to see how foolish they had been, Paul first of all reminds them when they were enslaved by pagan idolatry: "Formerly, when you did not know God, you were slaves to those by nature are not gods" (v. 8, NIV). They had set up graven images that were worshiped as gods. Craftsmen made idol gods of woods and stone. They worshipped beings like Zeus or Aphrodite. We must understand that graven images are imaginations manipulated by demons. Behind every idolatrous god stood a demon entity that enslaved those who worshiped these idols and mystical beings.

In the church at Corinth before they came to Christ, they worshiped idol gods. There were frenzies of enthusiasm, prophecy, and tongues, yet behind it all stood demonic activity. It did not matter to Paul if they were carved idols, mythical figures, or demons, he rejected their divine status. They did not have the essential attributes of God—omnipotence, omniscience, omnipresence, immutability, and His eternal being. They were finite, created things, not the infinite Creator. Paul wrote to the church at Rome and expanded his teaching on pagan worship: "They exchanged the truth of God for a lie, and worshiped and served the created things rather than the Creator" (Rom. 1:25, NIV).

Such was the case with Jeremiah when he said, "The word of the LORD came to me, saying, Before I formed you in the womb I knew you." (Jer. 1:4–5, NIV). The psalmist David said "O LORD, you have searched me and you know me." (Ps. 139:1, NIV). The worst tragedy of all is to *not* be known by the Lord. What could be more terrible than to hear the Lord say, "I never knew you: depart from me, ye that work iniquity" (Matt. 7:23). To be known by God is to be chosen and loved by Him. He chose to know us as His own, we know Him as our God. This personal relationship is initiated and sustained by God's grace.

Even though the Galatian believers had never read God's Word, they could delight in knowing God and being known by Him. This was knowledge of a love relationship. Paul said to the Corinthian church, "The man who loves God is known by God" (1 Cor. 8:3, NIV).

It must have come as a shock to the Galatian Christians to read these words. They had no intention of returning to their former life in paganism. They were attempting to make progress in their new spiritual life by learning to observe the Mosaic Law. The law itself taught that Israel was not to be involved with pagan idolatry. Paul is asking them, "How is it that you are turning back to those weak and miserable principles? Do you wish to be enslaved by them all over again?" (Gal. 4:9–10). Did the Galatians want to return to demonic worship?

By the phrase "all over again," Paul was saying that when the Galatians were ignorant sinners, they served false gods and had experienced pagan slavery. When they trusted Christ they were delivered from superstition and slavery. Now they were abandoning liberty in Christ and going back into bondage. They were dropping out of the school of grace and enrolling in the kindergarten of the law. Their pagan religious experience parallels the "basic principles of the world" (v. 3), which described their condition as Jews under the Law of Moses. Whenever the observance of the law takes the place of Christ as a basis of relating to God or being in right relationship to Him, it is just as detestable as pagan worship. They are weak because they do not have the power to overcome the guilt and power of sin; they are miserable, poor, and impotent because they cannot impart a new life. The Mosaic Law declares that the whole world is a prisoner of sin (3:22), but that law is powerless to set anyone free from the chains of sin. The Mosaic Law is not able to impart life (v. 21). To substitute the observance of the law for complete reliance on Christ is just as serious as returning to pagan worship.

Paul asked them why they are retuning to slavery by observing the law (vv. 9–10). Finally, Paul expressed his deep concern for them (v. 11). Paul treats the change in their spiritual direction as an extremely serious matter. He is deeply troubled and upset. He even wonders if all his efforts in planting these churches will prove to be in vain.

Are we as grieved as Paul was when our churches begin to put the observance of the law at the center of their lives and worship? Does it trouble us when we see Christians who put more emphasis on keeping certain traditions than on growing in their relationship with the Father through Christ in the power of the Spirit? There is one thing to many people in the church that is more powerful than the Word of God—tradition. In the time of Christ, the traditions of men were exalted above the truths of Scripture, and many could not distinguish between truth and tradition. Jesus told the religious leaders that they were "making the word of God of none effect through [their] tradition" (Mark 7:13). Do we feel a lack of concern for Christians who have become more law centered than Christ centered? Do we ever recognize that this shift has taken place?

Paul rebuked the Galatians for their disloyalty to the gospel (1:6–10). He gives them in detail his own loyalty to the gospel (1:11–2:21). His rebuke for their foolishness was followed by an explanation of the Galatians' conversion experience and an exposition of Scripture (3:2–4:11).

It is our freedom in Christ that has set us free. Christ has set us free. Paul does not appeal to his readers to fight to be free. Our freedom in Christ is not the result of our self-effort. We have not liberated ourselves by our own efforts. Because our freedom has been given to us in Christ, it is our goal and responsibility.

The declaration of our freedom is an accomplished fact and our goal to pursue. It is ours by the accomplishment of Christ at the cross. Paul tells us that our spiritual life found in the Holy Spirit (mentioned nineteen times) is freedom from condemnation. Romans chapter 8 is the declaration of the Christian's freedom.

Four Freedoms Because of Our Union with Christ

1. Freedom from judgment—no condemnation (vv. 1–4)

2. Freedom from defeat—no obligation (vv. 5–17)

3. Freedom from discouragement—no frustration (vv. 18–30)

4. Freedom from fear—no separation (vv. 31–39)

God has made provision for man to be holy. The experience has been made available to him by faith. Any attempt to achieve holiness by any other means is a violation of the doctrine of grace. As justification is by faith, so is sanctification. The Holy Spirit is the agent for the fulfillment of holiness in our lives. It is by living in the power of the Spirit and grace of God that holiness is fulfilled in the heart and life of the believer.

It is like a prisoner who is suddenly surprised to find out that he has been pardoned and set free. He did nothing to accomplish this. He was not even aware that it had happened. Now there he stands outside the prison walls, a free man. Now it is his responsibility to live as a free man.

One of the major themes of Paul's letter is our imprisonment in sin. Paul stated, "But the Scripture hath concluded all under sin, that the promise by faith of Jesus Christ might be given to them that believe" (3:22). He states in the next verse, "That before faith came, we were kept under the law, shut up unto the faith which should afterward be revealed" (3:23). "When we were children, were in bondage under the elements of the world" (4:3). In light of these scriptures there is no doubt about our slavery to sin, law, and the elements of this world. We were prisoners that were condemned by the law of God and doomed to live under its restrictions. The law offered us no hope of earning our freedom through our works. All the law did was to remind us of how we had blown it (3:19).

There are two themes parallel in Paul's letter to the Galatians: 1) our release from prison, and 2) our release from slavery. Jesus Christ "has redeemed us from this present evil age" (1:4). "Christ has redeemed us from the curse of the law" (3:13). "God sent His Son…to redeem those who were under the law" (4:4–5). "Brethren, we are not children of the bondwoman, but of the free" (v. 31). So the terms of our freedom are clear. We are not children of the bondwoman (Mosaic Law) but children of the free woman (promise). Our lives are lived in joyful freedom knowing that in Christ God has fulfilled His promises. This freedom from imprisonment under the law has led to a new community where the divisions of race, class, and gender are removed (v. 28).

The law made no provisions for mercy, pardon, or forgiveness. By the law merely came the knowledge of sin. This imprisonment under the law separated the Jew from the Gentile (v. 23); the law isolated its prisoners in different cellblocks according to their ethnic groups.

Another major theme of Paul's letter was the redemptive act of Christ at the cross that has liberated us from slavery and imprisonment under the law. It was by His death on the cross that He bore the curse of the law for us (v. 13). When we believed the message of Christ who was crucified, we received the Spirit (v. 1–2). Now we have been enabled by the Holy Spirit to participate in the benefits of the cross ourselves. We now see ourselves as crucified with Christ, set free from the curses and demands of the law. We are now enabled by the indwelling Christ to live for God (2:19–20). Through the indwelling Spirit we call God "Abba, Father" (4:4–7). We have been set free from living like slaves under the law; now we can live together as one family as the children of God.

"Stand fast therefore in the liberty wherewith Christ hath made us free, and be not entangled again with the yoke of bondage" (5:1). "Stand fast" is in the imperative indicative; Paul uses it again in verses 13 and 25. The whole layout of the chapter is based on these two verses. We are to take our stance in liberty (divine imperative) based on what God has already done (indicative). What God has accomplished for us in Christ is what has enabled us to stand firm. Freedom is not only privilege, it is our responsibility. By us allowing the Holy Spirit to order our behavior we will maintain our freedom over sin (v. 25); freedom must be defended (v. 1). Our freedom in Christ is not a license for us to go and do what we want, but God has set us free to serve not only Him but also our fellow man (v. 13).

Paul knew the problems that often arise within a Christian community. The best men would slip up (6:1). The word *fault* comes from the Greek word *paraptoma*, which does not mean a sin that was committed deliberately. It is like a man walking down an icy road or a slippery path.[1] Many times in this Christian life we will find ourselves being very harsh and judgmental toward those who have fallen into sin. Because of this attitude, people feel reluctant to come to a believer and confess their faults one to another. Who can they come to in order to confess their struggles? Our Christian duty is to get those who have fallen back on their feet. What defines us is not how we fall; it is how we get up after we have fallen.

In Paul's letters he often exhorts his readers to stand firm: He told the church at Corinth to "stand firm in the faith" (1 Cor. 16:13). He told the church at Philippi to "stand firm in one spirit" (Phil. 1:27) and to "stand firm in the Lord" (4:1). He commands them to stand firm in the freedom that Christ has given to them. Paul stood firm in his freedom against "false brethren, [who] had worked their way into the ranks of the church to spy on the freedom they had in Christ Jesus" (Gal. 2:4). It was their desire to place them back under the slavery of the law. He did not give in to their pressure to make Titus, a Gentile convert, a Jew by circumcision. Now other false brethren have infiltrated the church with the same demand. Paul says, "Do not let yourselves be burdened again by a yoke of slavery" (5:1).

In Paul's day oxen were placed under a yoke while they pulled a cart that was heavily loaded down as they strained to pull the cart up a hill, while they were being goaded with sharp sticks. The word *yoke* referred to the yoke of the law. In verse 3 Paul reveals that the crushing weight of this yoke is the obligation to keep and obey the whole law. Peter made the speech before the

Jerusalem council concerning this subject: "Why do you try to test God by putting on the necks of the [Gentile] disciples under a yoke that neither we nor our fathers were able to bear?" (Acts 15:10).

The yoke of the law is a yoke of slavery that places us under the burden of commandments that we cannot keep and under curses that we deserve for our disobedience. God sent His Son to lift that heavy yoke off of us and place it upon Himself. He was born under the law (Gal. 4:4) and kept all its demands for us; He died to bring us out from under that awful curse (3:13). Jesus has set us free from this yoke of slavery; we must not take it upon ourselves again. Now that the yoke of slavery under the law has been removed, Jesus has another yoke that He desires that we be submitted to. Jesus said, "My yoke is easy, and my burden is light" (Matt. 11:30). This is a yoke of learning. If we don't submit to the yoke that Christ has for us, the devil will form one for us that will fit us very well, and we will wear it.

Then Paul reveals the terrible negative consequences of submitting to this yoke of slavery.

> Behold, I Paul say unto you, that if ye be circumcised, Christ shall profit you nothing. For I testify again to every man that is circumcised, that he is a debtor to the whole law. Christ is become of no effect unto you, whosoever of you are justified by the law; ye are fallen from grace.
>
> —GALATIANS 5:2–4

His warnings are toward those who were getting circumcised. The present tense indicates that the process has just begun. Paul wanted to stop the slash of the knife. Here this is the first reference to the Galatian Christians being circumcised. Circumcision was the mark of belonging to the Jewish nation. In the Greco-Roman world it meant that Gentiles were becoming Jewish proselytes. They were trying to be justified by the law. They thought they could gain God's approval by belonging to the Jewish nation. They were giving no consideration that it was their faith in Christ that would produce God's approval. The Galatians were being convinced by the false teachers that it was not enough for them to have faith in Christ; they had to be identified with the Jewish people by observing the Law of Moses and by being circumcised.

Paul gives four negative consequences of adding such a supplement to faith in Christ.

1. "Christ will profit you nothing" (5:2). If you start trusting circumcision to gain God's blessing, then you have stopped trusting Christ. If you do not trust in Christ, then Christ is of no value to you. When you put your trust in your own performance to receive God's blessing, you are indicating that who you are and what you have done has more value than who Christ is and what He has done. You have turned your back on Christ.

2. You have placed yourself under the obligation to obey the whole law (v. 3). By getting circumcised, they were relying on keeping the whole law in order for God to bless them. This is an impossible mission. Once you have decided to base your relationship with God on your own performance, you will not be graded on a curve.

3. "Christ has become of no effect to you" (v. 4). The false teachers had assured the Galatians that by keeping the law they were not abandoning their faith in Christ. Instead, it was the way to obtain Christian perfection in the Christian life. They were removing the reign of Christ over their lives. If you are relying on your own efforts to keep the law, then you are no longer trusting in God's grace. Circumcision or Christ, law or grace: these are your two alternatives. You cannot have it both ways. You must choose.

4. "Ye are fallen from grace" (v. 4). Here the danger of apostasy, falling away from grace, must have been very real, or Paul would have never used such strong language. If we are resting in the doctrine of eternal security, we are ignoring Paul's warnings. People who ignore warnings are in great danger. It is like seeing the warning sign of a sharp curve and fifteen miles per hour speed limit but continuing to drive seventy miles per hour.

Paul then tells us how our freedom in Christ is maintained:

For we through the Spirit wait for the hope of righteousness by faith. For in Jesus Christ neither circumcision availeth any thing, nor uncircumcision; but faith which worketh by love.

—GALATIANS 5:5–6

Both verses focus on faith. Faith in Christ is the only way to protect our freedom in Christ.

First of all, living in the Spirit is living a life of faith. "For we through the Spirit wait for the hope of righteousness by faith" (v. 5). It is by faith in the gospel we received the Spirit (3:2). We now live by the Spirit (5:16). We are led by the Spirit (v. 18), and we keep in step with the Spirit (v. 25). The presence of the Spirit marks and identifies us as the children of God (4:6). It is the power of the Spirit that produces the character of God (5:22–23). The control of the Spirit in our lives makes the yoke of the law unnecessary (v. 18).

Second, there is an expectation of righteousness. Paul's focus is future righteousness, which is ours when God completes His work in us by the Spirit. By depending on the Spirit, we can expect the harvest of eternal life in the future (6:8). When we first put our faith in Christ, righteousness was credited to us (3:6–9). In the present, by the power of the Spirit, God produces righteousness in us (5:13–25). Our righteousness—credited to us by justification, produced in us by sanctification, and perfected in us by glorification—is always a gift received from God by faith.

Third, what matters in this life is our union with Christ, not our union with Jews or Gentiles or any other racial or social group. The world's divisions between Jew and Greek, slave and free, male and female have been obliterated in our union with one another in Christ.

Fourth, our life is a life of loving one another because "faith worketh by love" (v. 6). Freedom from the law does not leave our lives without moral direction. Faith in Christ not only gives us moral direction but also the moral dynamic to fulfill the true intent of the law by serving one another (vv. 13–14). The evidence of faith will be genuine love, for true faith in Christ is expressed through love.

Chapter 18

Wolves in Sheep's Clothing

L UKE THE APOSTLE, the first century historian, quoted Paul in his farewell address to the Ephesian elders:

> *For I know this, that after my departing shall grievous wolves enter in among you, not sparing the flock. Also of your own selves shall men arise, speaking perverse things, to draw away disciples after them. Therefore watch, and remember, that by the space of three years I ceased not to warn every one night and day with tears.*
> —ACTS 20:29–31

Ephesus was the most prominent city in Asia Minor when it came to commerce and culture. In the times of the New Testament, it was a major seaport. Asia Minor contributed to much of the commercial and economic success of Ephesus. We know that Paul preached there for more than two years (19:8–10). He ran into trouble with silversmiths who made statutes of the goddesses Artemis or Diana. Ephesus contained a major temple to Artemis.

The church at Ephesus was begun by the apostle Paul on his second missionary journey. It was considered to be the largest church in the times of the New Testament. It was located in a wicked city that was given over to the worship of the goddess Diana. Ephesus means "desired one." It was characterized by fervent evangelism.

Paul had warned them over a period of three years, and his prophetic word came to pass. Paul is bringing his farewell message to a close, and here in this text he is warning the Ephesian leaders of the dangers that they had to recognize and things they were going to have to be willing to confront if they were going to protect and lead the church in the right paths. Even though Paul is looking forward to the future, things are not looking too promising for the Ephesian church. Paul had given a charge to the elders at Ephesus that they were to care for the flock of God. They were going to have to guard the church with continual watchfulness. They were to be faithful to their pastoral work. They were to be concerned about spiritual welfare. They were appointed by the Spirit. The Spirit had given them spiritual gifts that equipped them for their ministry as shepherds of the church.

When Paul used the word *remember* (v. 31), it involved more than simply the mental act of recalling; it meant to give heed and to be encouraged. The elders at Ephesus drew strength and guidance from Paul's example.

In Acts chapter 19 we see how effective Paul's revival was in Ephesus. Twelve disciples of John's baptism received the Holy Ghost (vv. 1–7). The exorcists were put out of business, through a demon's confession the fear of the Lord fell on the Jews and Greeks at Ephesus, through the power of the Holy Ghost the occultic world was shut down, and they burned their books of spells and incantations in the streets (vv. 13–19). "So mightily grew the word of God and prevailed" (v. 20).

CHARACTERISTICS OF THE CHURCH

- Owned by God
- Redeemed by Jesus Christ
- Ruled by the Holy Ghost
- Served by Christian elders
- Assailed by false teachers
- Betrayed by insincere friends

Paul exalted the character of the church to which they belonged and to which they bore the office of an elder. The church was purchased as a possession through and by Jesus' precious blood. Their appointment came from the Holy Ghost and they were representatives of Jesus Christ. They were not to lord over the church (1 Pet. 5:3). They were to feed it with spiritual nourishment (John 21:15–17). The word *feed* meant to lead them into pastures where they can be fed proper nutrition. It also spoke of governing, counseling, and advising the flock. The tender lambs and babes were to be fed the sincere milk of the Word (1 Pet. 2:2). Those who had reached the age of maturity were to be fed solid Christian doctrine—strong meat (Heb. 5:14).

First of all Paul warned them of dangers around them. He warned them of wolves that desired to prey on the flock of God. These were the Judaizers and false teachers who were counterfeit brethren who desired to exploit the church for personal gain.

These false prophets and teachers traveled from community to community, peddling their religious teachings, seeking monetary support from those of the community who were religiously gullible. These charlatans were well known in the ancient world, both within Christian circles and without.

There are also dangers among us (Acts 20:29). There are people in the church who are ambitious for position and power. Church history is filled with people who want to bask in the popularity of leaders whom God has raised up, but they do not want to submit to authority. In his third Epistle, John addressed "Diotrephes, who loveth to have the preeminence" (3 John 9–11). It is astounding to see within the pages of God's holy Word, how more than one false prophet got their start within the Christian church.

Then Paul tells us that there are dangers within us (Acts 20:30). He says, "Take heed therefore unto yourselves" (v. 28). Paul list three things of which Christian pastors should take heed: to themselves, lest when they have preached to others they should themselves become castaways (1 Cor. 9:27); to the flock, lest any of them be lost; and to the wolves, lest any should rise within the fold or break into it from without. One pastor was asked his philosophy on ministry. He said, "I feed the sheep, milk the goats, and shoot the wolves."

In Revelation 2:1 we are told that Ephesus had left her first love. They had cooled off in their love for Christ. They were at one time the fastest growing church in the first century era. They treated the most wonderful relationship in the world as though it was commonplace. It only took sixty years after Pentecost for this to happen. How long has it taken us to fall out of love with Christ? We need to get back to our first love, first obedience, and our first commitments. This is no time to cool off in our love for Christ. If we will return to our first love, the church will rediscover its healing, families will be strengthened, there will be wholeness in the church, and the joy of our salvation will be restored.

The Scriptures tell us about a general revolt against Paul's teaching throughout Asia, a continent which heard the Word of the Lord in just two years. There was no TV or mass media, just word of mouth. Now the whole continent was rejecting Paul.

Having looked through a telescope of divine inspiration and divine truth, and already seeing these trends, Paul urges the elders of Ephesus to be watchful and to follow his example. They were to remember how he had shown such careful and tearful concern for his converts during those three years as he pointed out to them the right path for their feet to walk in day and night.

A wolf in sheep's clothing is a very dangerous animal. Many times we feel that they are safe just because they are in the church. When their true character is revealed, we find ourselves to be totally unprepared for the attack. They are dangerous persons who pretend to be harmless. Their plans are bad while they pretend to do good in innocence. Wolves have the reputation of being wild and dangerous as they hunt or kill sheep. They would speak "perverse things" (Acts 20:30), which means twisted, distorted, or bending. False prophets and false teachers don't come with a brand new message, but rather a perversion or distortion of the old.[1] Their teaching would be a threat to the life of the flock of God. They would pervert the truth and lead people away from the faith. The word *remember* comes from the Greek word *menmoneuw*, which means more than a simple act of recalling; it means "to give heed and to be encouraged."[2]

In the writings of Peter, he warns us:

> There were false prophets also among the people, even as there shall be false teachers among you, who privily shall bring in damnable heresies, even denying the Lord that bought them, and bring upon themselves swift destruction. And many shall follow their pernicious ways; by reason of whom the way of truth shall be evil spoken of.
>
> —2 PETER 2:1–2

Keep in mind that you never find the word *prophet* being used in the New Testament outside the context of being under a pastor. The most dangerous people today in the life of the church are prophets or teachers who have no pastor. Why have so many become enemies of the cross of Christ? Why do the occult and cults have one thing in common? They all attack the deity of the Lord Jesus Christ. Why have these false prophets and false teachers obtained such a following? Did you ever think you would live to see the day when the way of truth would be held in contempt by so many? Jesus declared, "I am the way and the truth" (John 14:6). He is Truth personified. To reject the truth is to depart from Christ.

In John 10 we have the parable of the good shepherd. Within that chapter

John contrasts true pastors of the flock with false teachers, who are described as wolves because of the trouble and the havoc that they cause. False prophets are described as wolves in sheep's clothing in Matthew 7:15.

In exposing the false teachers, Paul gave six identifying marks that can guide us to discern the presence of wolves in sheep's clothing in our midst today:

1. False Christians distract Christians from obeying the truth of the gospel.

The day we became born again we entered into the race of the Christian life. The running of the race became one of Paul's favorite metaphors. We are exhorted in the Scripture that we are to train like athletes. Because the Galatians remembered passing Calvary they knew they had gotten off to a grand start. By the gospel being proclaimed to them they found the course that was laid before them. Their commitment to the gospel of Jesus Christ was made evident through and by their obedience. They knew the truth, they had heard the gospel, they had heard the facts, and they had heard it straight. Salvation was by grace through faith and there was nothing to be added.

Having entered into this race with every intention of obtaining the prize, they learned the importance of not getting distracted, tripped up, or hindered. In the running of this race it is very easy to become distracted, allowing someone or something to block your pathway. Each runner is required to remain in his/her own lane lest they be disqualified. We need to watch out for those who desire to cut into our lane with the intentions of tripping us. This can become a great frustration to someone who intends on finishing the race.

2. False teachers replace the call of God with their own deceptive persuasions.

When Paul preached the message of the cross, the voice of God was clearly heard (1:11–12). Even though the Judaizers were skillful in their speech, claimed to be God's messengers, and claimed to share a message that was backed by Scripture, all that was heard by the Galatians was the harshness of the law with their message of works. Their message stood in opposition to the "One who called them by the grace of God" (v. 6).

3. False teachers gain control over the whole church.

The influence of false teachers is negative because they seek to gain control over the direction of the life of the church.

4. False teachers will cause confusion and discouragement.

Through and by the Spirit they had learned to call God, "Abba, Father." The false teachers had begun to threaten them with the judgment of God if they did not seek to keep the law of God. This caused the Galatians to become confused and discouraged.

5. False teachers spread false reports about spiritual leaders.

Because Paul was zealous for the traditions of Judaism (1:14) he preached circumcision before his conversion. The false teachers bore fraudulent letters claiming that they had Paul's support to circumcise the Galatians. After His conversion on the Damascus Road, he preached that the cross of Christ was the only way to salvation. The blessing of God and the removal of the curse were accomplished by Christ's sacrificial atoning death (3:13–14). From that point on Paul resisted any notion of trying to force the Gentiles to be circumcised (2:14).

Ever since the cross he has been persecuted for not preaching circumcision (5:11). Many of the Jews, Christian and non-Christian, were opposing him because he did not require it. He did not go along with their idea that the Gentiles had to belong to the Jewish nation to belong to God's covenant people.

If Paul preached circumcision the Jews would have never persecuted him. The offense of the cross would have ceased. The message of salvation by the cross would have been denied.

When Peter wrote to the church to warn them about the false teachers who were peddling damaging doctrines, he stated, "But chiefly them that walk after the flesh in the lust of uncleanness, and despise government. Presumptuous are they, self-willed, they are not afraid to speak evil of dignities. Whereas angels, which are greater in power and might, bring not railing accusation against them before the Lord" (2 Pet. 2:10–11). False teachers do not hesitate to bring accusation against their superiors. Angels would not dare to do this, unlike false teachers who are careless of the lordship of Christ and are free with their insults. Angels revere the Lord as they live their lives in His presence. No insulting language is allowed to pass from their lips. When Moses died, God took him and buried him in a place where the devil himself could not find him. If Israel would have found out where Moses was buried, they would have built a monument to him and would have gone no further into the Promised

Land. When Moses died, Israel wept over him for thirty days in the plains of Moab (Deut. 34:8). The church today is very busy erecting memorials to our past instead of erecting monuments to our future. Even when Michael and Lucifer disputed the over the body of Moses, Michael did not bring a railing accusation against Lucifer, but said, "The Lord rebuke thee" (Jude 9). Not even Michael would speak in a degrading manner to a fallen angel. Unlike the behavior of angels, these false teachers, wolves in sheep's clothing, were not afraid to attack the spirituality of their leaders (pastors and shepherds) of the flock. This was a common mark of a false teacher.

6. False teachers emphasize sensational rituals.

Paul was saying that all these false teachers wanted to do was to put on a sensual show. They tried to deceive the church by the belief that if they are circumcised they would be brought into fellowship with God. Paul said in Christ Jesus, "Neither circumcision or uncircumcision have no value" (Gal. 5:6). Paul totally discredited circumcision being imposed on the Galatian believers. They wanted to make a good impression outwardly (6:12) while they boasted in their ceremony (v. 13).[3]

In Acts 20 Paul lists five sins that are destructive to the life and ministry of spiritual leaders in the church:

1. *Carelessness* (v. 31), failure to stay alert and forgetting the price that others have paid so that we might have the Word of God. Here Paul exhorts them to "watch and remember." He is reminding every leader that they should take their responsibility seriously.

2. *Shallowness* (v. 32). We cannot build the church unless God is building us individually. The Word of God is able to build up and enrich our lives before a world that is lost. The spiritual leaders of the church must spend time on a daily basis in the Word and prayer.

3. *Covetousness* (v. 33). It means to have a consuming and control-ling desire for what others have or for more of what we already possess. The last of the Ten Commandments is "thou shalt not covet" (Exod. 20:7). If we covet we will find ourselves breaking the other nine commandments. If we covet, we will find ourselves stealing, telling lies, and murdering to get what we want. We will

even go as far as to dishonor our own parents. Covetousness is idolatry (Eph. 5:5; Col. 3:5). When Paul laid down the conditions for leadership among the elders, he instructed the church not to be guilty of covetousness (1 Tim. 3:3).

4. *Laziness* (v. 34). Paul labored at Corinth as a tent maker, so that he would not become burdensome to the Corinthian church. There is nothing wrong with a Christian worker receiving a salary from the church where he ministers. "The worker deserves his wages" (1 Tim. 5:18, NIV). We should be certain that we are earning those salaries (Prov. 24:30–34).

5. *Selfishness.* We who are in the body of Christ should be busy giving ourselves away and not saving ourselves for ourselves. We should be investing our lives into the lives of others.[4]

These wolves would not come just from without but would arise within the church. It is not just from intruders such as false teachers, but from the ranks of the leaders within the church itself; some will arise to seduce the followers of Christ into heresy. This development did take place and is evident from Paul's writings.

> Holding faith, and a good conscience; which some having put away concerning faith have made shipwreck.
> —1 TIMOTHY 1:19

Faulty beliefs will lead to moral disaster. Here Paul is giving us a warning about neglecting our consciences. The verb translated "put away" implies a violent and deliberate rejection. The Christian teacher must be a good soldier and a good sailor too.

> The Spirit speaketh expressly, that in the latter times some shall depart from the faith, giving heed to seducing spirits, and doctrines of devils.
> —1 TIMOTHY 4:1

> All they which were in Asia be turned from me: of whom are Phygellus and Hermogenes.
> —2 TIMOTHY 1:15

And their word will eat as doth a canker: of whom is Hymenaeus and Philetus; Who concerning the truth have erred, saying that the resurrection is past already; and overthrow the faith of some.
—2 Timothy 2:17–18

Renner made the statement that even though the spirit of Gnosticism was growing and had become very dangerous to the Christian faith, the apostles countered their efforts with strong teaching of Scripture and apostolic doctrine. The apostles remained busy in their writings of the New Testament. They were busy with church planting, and many local congregations were coming into being. Halfway through the first century, Gnosticism was taking hold in many places, which caused a great disturbance within the life of the church.

In A.D. 170, there was a group called the Montanists who had a genuine love for the Lord and operated in the gifts of the Spirit. They impacted the church by believing that a man should be filled with the Holy Ghost and led by the Spirit of God.

Tertullian, a third-century preacher, affirmed and embraced the doctrines of the Montanists. Their doctrine stated the following:

1. They believed in the millennial reign, the fact that Christ would reign on the earth for 1,000 years.

2. They believed the Bible was the inerrant Word of God, that it was absolutely true.

3. They believed in baptizing in the name of Father, Son, and Holy Ghost (Trinitarian formula for water baptism).

4. Their teachings were confirmed by prophetic utterances that sounded like barking dogs. They claimed that this was the beginning of a fresh move of God.

5. Even though they had a great start, they fell into perversion because they embraced teachings that were not found in God's Holy Word.

6. They relied on sensationalism to hold and attract the crowd's attention.

7. They believed in the operation of Spiritual gifts. They rejected the idea that the gifts of the Spirit ceased with the apostles (first century).

8. They believed in the priesthood of all who believed.

9. They experienced ecstatic worship, visions, and prophecies.

10. Only the born again were offered church membership.

11. They were accused and slandered that they themselves were the Holy Spirit.

Dr. William R. Williams, in his *Lectures on Baptist History: 1877*, said, "It was hard to find any doctrinal errors in their views. They saw the power of the Holy Spirit as the great conservator and guardian of the life of the Christian church. They were a Spirit-filled people who opposed a church structure that moved in fleshly power and human manipulation rather than the power of the Holy Spirit."[5]

Many Christian's in today's church are like the Sadducees who were deniers of the supernatural. They did not believe in angels, spirits, or the resurrection. To them the canon was closed, and they were not open to believe that God could do anything new. That is why they were sad you see. Much of today's church resists being identified with these fiery heroes of the past. They not only deny God's power to work, but also the existence of the manifestations of the gifts of the Spirit. They would rather be identified with those who persecuted them. If they had lived in Jesus' day, they would have been in opposition to Jesus' ministry.

Around A.D. 200, the power and gifts of the Holy Spirit that had characterized that first century church began to fade and slowly began to disappear. Many of the early church's fathers believed that they were not witnessing the gifts of the spirit as the previous generation had seen. In the year A.D. 260 there was only a small trace of the operation of the Spirit in operation in the life of the church. Soon the gifts of the Spirit had seemed to vanish altogether.

What happened to the life of the Spirit? Did the gifts of the Spirit pass away with John, who was the last apostle? Absolutely not! Many within the life of the church want to believe this. It is easier for people to believe this blatant lie than for them to fast and pray and lay hold of a fresh move of God in their generation. In just 160 years after the death of John there is historical data that tells us that the gifts of the Spirit were still in operation.

During the first century, when the apostles were alive and were ministering, they placed heavy emphasis on apostolic teaching. These teachings became the writings of the New Testament. Accompanying that teaching were signs, wonders, miracles, and gifts of the Holy Spirit.

Toward the end of the first century into the middle of the second century, after the death of John, Paul had given a prediction that grievous wolves would enter among the flock, and his prophecy became true. Gnosticism got a foothold into the life of the church. After the death of John and with the strong leadership of the apostles out of the way who took a strong position in the Scriptures, false teachers began to make their way into the church at an alarming rate of speed.

Through the efforts of false teachers the respect for the Word of God began to deteriorate. This brought a rapid change into the spiritual atmosphere of the church. The people began to depart from the teaching of the apostles to follow after teachings that were not founded by the Word of God. The foundation that gave them the ability to know right from wrong and good from evil was being totally forgotten. People began to move away from the foundation of the apostles to follow after teachings were not based on Scripture.

Renner states that if we remove the Word, we remove the power.[6] In the beginning the departure took place very slowly. In the first century, when the apostles were alive and were proclaiming the Word of God in power, their message was being confirmed with miracles, wonders, and signs. Eventually, as the church began to drift away from the teachings of the apostles and prophets, there was not enough Word being preached for the Holy Spirit to confirm the message. Church history reveals that when the teaching of the apostles was replaced by the message of the gnostics, ecclesiastical structures, and legalism, which had usurped the place of the Word of God, by A.D. 260 the gifts and power of the Holy Spirit ceased to function in the life of the Church.

We need to understand that the Spirit and the Word agree. The presence of the Holy Spirit is attached to the strong teaching of Scripture. When the Word was gone, the Spirit's power was gone too. The tendency of the time was not toward the Word but away from the Word. We have too many people chasing signs and wonders instead of signs and wonders chasing those who believe. Many are departing from churches where there is strong biblical teaching, and they fail to understand the power of God that is operating in their lives is attached to the revelation they are under. If it took you sitting under strong doctrinal teaching to bring you out of sin, then it is going to take strong doctrinal teaching to keep you on the straight and narrow until you get home.

The departure from the faith in pursuit of greater spiritual experiences will eventually rob you of God's power. When the teaching of the Word of God began to be replaced with other things, the power and gifts of the Holy Spirit disappeared, and spiritual darkness began to settle into the church. Then the church was ushered into the Dark Ages.

From time to time there would be occasional revivals of supernatural power. When there is a return to the teaching ministry of the Word of God, it will bring the gifts and power of the Holy Spirit back into the church. The Word and the Power are inseparable.[7]

Paul also warned us about being turned aside to fables:

> For the time will come when they will not endure sound doctrine; but after their own lust shall they heap to themselves teachers, having itching ears; And they shall turn their ears away from the truth, and shall be turned into fables.
> —2 Timothy 4:3–4

When Paul said, "Men shall be lovers of their own selves" (2 Tim. 3:2), he used the Greek word *eimi,* which means "I am," and it describes a self-centered, self-seeking attitude within the church. We have come to a time when people are no longer concerned about the Word or the lost of our generation. They are only concerned about themselves and being entertained. We have got a lot of spiritual entertainment today. Our chief concern seems to be to have a good time. We don't care about substance. Many say, "Don't give me the meat of the Word, give me cake!"[8]

Paul said, "They will not endure sound doctrine" (v. 3). The word *endure* comes from the Greek word *anechomai,* which means "to put up with, to bear with, to tolerate." The word *sound* is from the Greek *hugiaino,* which refers to something healthy. The time will come when they will no longer tolerate healthy doctrine.[9] *Doctrine* is the wholesome teaching of the Word of God. It comes from the word *didaskolia,* which means "good teaching." There is going to come a time when people will be so self-centered that they will no longer tolerate food that is good for them.[10]

If we lack foundation we will lack discernment. God will allow us to have the desire of our heart whether it is good or bad. The word translated *lust* is *epithumia,* which refers to a strong, deep-rooted desire. It describes people who are doubled over with passion.[11] Because of itching ears they will turn their ears away from the truth and be turned into fables. They had the truth but turned from it. They are going to find someone to preach it like they want to hear it being preached and tell it like they want to hear it being told.

The phrase "turn away" speaks of a radical character change that will take place right inside the church. Silliness will replace seriousness. Then Paul said they will be turned unto fables. Here Paul uses the word *ektrepomai* or "turned unto fables" (v. 4). Paul then uses a medical term, which refers to a bone that out of joint. Some of these people are out of joint with the rest of the church. Or they are out of joint with solid Christian teaching. [12] I believe that it is very safe to say today that there are many that have gotten out of joint with the rest of the body and with solid New Testament truth. When a bone is out of joint it hurts. It hinders the movement of the body. It slows down its activity. It hinders development. When error is in the church it hurts the church. The word *fables* comes from the Greek *muthos* where we get the word mythology from.[13] There are many that would rather hear stories than truths from the Scripture.

Throughout the history of the church there have been many that have refused to love sound doctrine, which was the wholesome teaching of the Word of God. As we draw closer to the end, we are going to see the situation grow worse. While many profess Christianity, even though they attend a local church and give all indications that they have a reverence for God, there will be no toleration for sound doctrinal teaching. They will conform to a religious system that makes them feel comfortable without any demands for righteousness or personal holiness. People are looking for churches that will make them feel comfortable in their sin, instead of them forsaking their sin. They will desire sermons that demand less than the gospel demands. Many think they should leave church feeling good. What they do not understand is that it is more important that we leave church living good. If we leave living good we can leave feeling good. We can know that it is well with our soul.

They will not accept God's Word when it speaks of repentance, sin, damnation, and the necessity of holiness and separation from the world. They will not seek pastors who adhere to the standards of God's Word. They will find a preacher that reassures them that they can still be a Christian while living according to the flesh. Many do not believe that through their behavior they can forfeit their position in the kingdom of God.

The Holy Spirit has warned us that all who remain faithful to God and submit themselves to His Word can expect persecution and suffering for righteousness sake (Matt. 5:10–12). We must separate ourselves from people, churches, and institutions who deny the power of God in salvation and who preach a compromising gospel. We must be faithful and loyal to New Testament gospel and to God's faithful ministers who proclaim it. By doing this we can be assured of close fellowship with Christ (Rev. 3:20–22). There will be seasons of refreshing from the presence of the Lord (Acts 3:19–20). We must remember that the foundation stones of the true church are the apostles and prophets (Eph. 2:13). Unless we are teaching what the prophets foretold, the teachings of Christ, and what the apostles proclaimed, we are not the church.

The only protection that we have is that an awareness comes through a deep desire in the believer's heart to do the will of God (John 7:17). There must be a desire to walk in righteousness and the fear of God (Ps. 25:4–5).

The faithful must not think that because apostasy is prevalent on every hand that an authentic revival cannot occur or evangelism cannot be successful. God has promised that in the last days God will save those who call upon His name and separate themselves from this perverse generation.

> But there were false prophets also among the people, even as there shall be false teachers among you, who privily shall bring in damnable heresies, even denying the Lord that bought them, and bring upon themselves swift destruction.
>
> —2 Peter 2:1

First of all Peter said within the life of the church there were self-appointed prophets. While they were teaching the true doctrine, they would bring in false doctrine right along with it. False teaching would be brought alongside the truth. The heresies they would usher in would lead people to ruin and destruction that would lead to a loss of eternal life along with eternal misery and perdition.

He warned us of false teachers with destructive heresies, by covetousness exploiting with deceptive words (2 Pet. 2:1–3). According to Peter, the false teachers within the church were "denying the Lord that bought them" (v. 1). The word *denying* comes from the Greek *arneomai,* which means "to renounce or disown." They were denying the substitutionary death of our Lord. The word *bought* comes from the Greek *agorazo,* which is one of the three words used in the New Testament for redemption. He purchased us in the slave market of sin. He became our buyer and our price, our Shepherd and our Lamb, our High Priest and our offering, and our offering and the altar. Our Lord's precious, outpoured blood was the ransom needed to redeem slaves from the prison house of sin. His death satisfied the just demands of the high court of heaven. He paid a penalty for the sinner so the believer can stand justified in the sight of God.[14]

As a result they "have forsaken the right way" (v. 15). The Greek word for *forsaken* is *kataleipo*. It is in the present tense where Peter emphasizes the habitual action of abandoning.[15] They have left the straight road.

They had become "wells without water" (v. 17). The word *well* comes from the word *spring*. It speaks of an ever-leaping, living fountain. The phrase "without water" is an Oriental expression where a mirage excites the traveler's hope of water, only to have it disappointed. It is where one looks for a clear spring of water, the living Word of God, but there is a spring gone dry.[16] At one time they had escaped the wickedness of the world through Jesus Christ, but were now entangled again in sin (v. 20). These warnings clearly confirm the danger of being bewitched and befooled.

Dangers are clearly present. We are beleaguered by the traditions of men. We are assaulted by the philosophies of men—humanism, secularism, post-modernism. We are allured by false teachers who appeal to greed. We are challenged by false doctrines who deny God and the deity of Christ. We are assailed by changing trends—easy divorce, same sex marriages.

We need to remember how we received the Spirit. It was through the hearing of faith (Gal. 3:2). It was promised to those who believe, repent, and are baptized (John 7:37–39; Acts 2:38). It is given to those who are children of God. (Gal. 4:6). We don't need to forget that our spiritual life began in the Spirit (3:3). We are born of the Spirit (John 3:5). We are strengthened by the Spirit in the inner man (Eph. 3:16). There is no other means by which we can grow as Christians (Rom. 8:9–14).

We need to remember who supplied the Spirit and worked miracles. It was God (Gal. 3:5). He poured out the Spirit abundantly through Jesus Christ our Savior (Titus 3:6). He bore witness through signs, wonders, miracles, and gifts of the Spirit (Heb. 2:4). It was God who bore witness to Christ and the apostles (2:3). Miracles confirmed they were sent by the Lord (Mark 16:19–20). Beware of lying signs and wonders that would lead us astray. There is no way to know the will and Word of God other than through the apostles of Jesus Christ (1 John 4:5–6).

The gnostics of the second century and modern theologians are in agreement that grace and works should be mixed together to effect salvation. There are new movements occurring today claiming that we must have works added to grace to affect our salvation. This is blasphemy because there are no works that anyone can produce to affect our salvation. They are saying the sacrifice of Christ for His elect was insufficient to affect salvation alone. The idea that anyone needs works to complete salvation is totally a false teaching and must be rejected. Whereas works do not produce salvation, we do believe from the Scripture that they are the result of salvation.

Sweeping doctrinal changes were blowing through their midst causing great havoc. As a result there was rebellion against leadership and insubordination, revolt, and defection in the life of the church.[17]

Paul told Timothy to "charge some that they teach no other doctrine" (1 Tim. 1:3). The doctrine that Paul had entrusted to the Ephesian elders was now being distorted, twisted, and perverted. The phrase "other doctrine" was from a compound word in the Greek language, *heteros*, which is something of a different kind. It is where we get the word *heterosexual* meaning different sexes. The word *didaskalos* speaks of teaching. So Paul was referring to teaching of a different kind or of a different nature. These false teachers will bring about a new distorted, twisted, perverted message.

To be justified means being put in right relationship with God. It is not a process but it is an act. It means to be acquitted of our sins, to be put in the position of one who has never broken the law. God now looks at us as He would look upon His own Son. He declares us to be righteous in His sight. Our works could not have produced this.

Present day Judaizers still want us to conform to the Law of Moses in order to be saved. While I agree that we are not under the law but under grace, grace does not give us a license to do as we please. Grace is no license to sin, neither is it a cover-up for a fallen condition. Now that we are born again, rules are part of our nature. According to Romans chapter 8, it is the Holy Spirit who takes the righteousness of the law, and fulfills it in us as we walk not after the flesh but after the spirit (v. 4).

If we abandon the Holy Spirit and the grace of God and return to a flesh attempt to serve God, we have placed a roadblock in front of ourselves which causes us to go on a detour and we build up the requirements of the law, after Christ tore down the middle wall of partition. It proves that all that we are is lawbreakers.

If we build up requirements of the law while seeking justification with God, we are rejecting Christ. We are setting aside the grace of God. We are rejecting Christ and trying to do it in ourselves and measure up to the law of God in our own strength. What good is Jesus to us? "If righteousness could be gained through the law, then Christ died for nothing" (Gal. 2:21). If we can be justified through our works, then we don't need Christ, He died for nothing, and we can get to heaven on our own.

Paul points out to Peter that his behavior is silly. We cannot be justified by the law. Our works will not produce salvation because salvation cannot be earned. We are completely dependent on Jesus Christ. Jesus did not die and suffer for nothing. He died and gave His life for the sins of humanity. It was through His sacrifice that we obtained eternal life. We have become dead to the law. Because we were unable to satisfy the law's demands we cling to Jesus Christ who through His sacrifice on the cross satisfied the demands of the law. We will go to the judgment bar of God clinging to Jesus Christ.

Paul wrote to the church of Colossians and told them, "The Head, from which all the body by joints and bands having nourishment ministered, and knit together, increaseth with the increase of God" (Col. 2:19). Jesus is the Head of the body, the church. Every member is under the control of the Head, just as every part of the body is obedient to our brain. It is no time to be losing your hold on Christ lest our connection to spiritual life be severed. It will prevent us from growing at all and there will be no increase. The source of our spiritual life is Christ Himself. We need to stay solid, healthy, and efficient in the faith, not allowing ourselves to be seduced by a spirit of religion.

Paul wrote to the church at Ephesus and said:

> From whom the whole body fitly joined together and compacted by that which every joint supplieth, according to the effectual working in the measure of every part, maketh increase of the body unto the edifying of itself in love.
>
> —EPHESIANS 4:16

Whenever there is nutrition and structural unity, the result will be growth in the body. Joints and bands have two functions: to supply nutrition and for the compacting of the frame. They communicate life and energy to the body and preserve unity and order. Whenever there is proper nutrition and we maintain an atmosphere that is free from disease, growth is automatic. We are to spread nutrition not poison to the body.

There is increase when there is a dependency on the Holy Spirit to live God's Word. He is the One that prepares me for works of service. He enables me to use my gifts to the fullest. There is increase in the body when we begin to ride high on the tide of each other's experiences. There needs to be gifted leadership. There need to be men and women who are embracing discipleship. Their needs to be a cooperate maturity in the body. We need to be speaking the truth in love.

The Father continues to supply the Spirit in power and blessing. This is done by faith through grace not by works of the law. The word that was used for the *giving* of the Spirit was *epichoregon*, which means to grant freely, support to help. This is a word that Paul used to describe the gift of the Holy Ghost, *Paraclete*, given to the believer. He is the Holy Ghost, the Paraclete, the Comforter, the One who is called to stand by our side, our Counselor for our defense, our attorney in the court of law. He is the one that aids and assists us as I attempt to live this Christian life.

Chapter 19

When Sheep Become Pigs and Dogs

For if after they have escaped the pollutions of the world through the knowledge of the Lord and Savior Jesus Christ, they are again entangled therein, and overcome, the latter end is worse for them than the beginning. For it had been better for them not to have known the way of righteousness, than, after they have known it, to turn from the holy commandment delivered unto them. But it happened unto them according to the true proverb, The dog is turned to his own vomit again; and the sow that was washed to her wallowing in the mire.

—2 PETER 2:20–22

ALSE TEACHERS ARE the main subjects of this whole chapter. They had denied the doctrine of the atonement and the substitutionary death of the Lord Jesus Christ. "But there were false prophets also among the people, even as there shall be false teachers among you, who privily shall bring in damnable heresies, even denying the Lord that bought them, and bring upon themselves swift destruction" (2:1). Many of the false teachers that Peter was addressing were at one time saved, under a God-called pastor and operating in spiritual gifts. They became entangled with the sins of the world and were overcome and came into a worse condition than they were before.

Peter had already emphasized the new birth (1 Pet. 1:3, 22, 25). He had already told them that they were partakers of the divine nature (2 Pet. 1:4). In his first Epistle, Peter had already described them as sheep (1 Pet. 2:25, 5:1–4). Jesus used this metaphor of sheep when He reinstated Peter into a leadership position of the apostolic band after Peter had denied three times that he even knew Him. Jesus had charged him that he was to feed His sheep.

Note the language that Peter uses in this text of 2 Peter:

1. "After they have escaped the pollutions of this world" (v. 20)

2. They had "knowledge of the Lord and Savior Jesus Christ" (v. 20).

3. "They are again entangled again therein, and overcome" (v. 20). They talked a great deal about liberty but knew nothing of its practice.

4. They had "known the way of righteousness" (v. 21). They had sinned against knowledge. They were personally acquainted with the way of righteousness. They called darkness light and bondage liberty.

5. They had "turn[ed] from the holy commandment delivered unto them" (v. 21). The law itself was God's gift of love to them. The holy commandment is delivered to man for his good by God. The Book of Deuteronomy stresses: "I command thee this day for thy good" (Deut. 10:13). Rejection of God's law is the first step to rejection of God.

6. "The dog is turned to his own vomit again" (v. 22).

7. "The sow that was washed to her wallowing in the mire" (v. 22).

Many times in the local church we mistake a person having good morals for the new birth or saving grace. Many have appeared to be sons of God when their hearts and their lifestyle have proven them to be nothing more than sons of Belial. Jesus knew the difference. When the Jews said that they were the descendants of Abraham, Jesus said, "Ye are of your father the devil, and the lusts of your father ye will do" (John 8:44). John knew that nature was determined by birth. John the Baptist knew the difference when the Pharisees and Sadducees, who could never get along, dropped their petty differences and came out to hear a man sent from God whose name was John. Even though they were dressed in religious attire, he referred to them as a "generation of vipers" (Matt. 3:7). John was telling them that their nature was not changed; they were still producing the behavior of a serpent.

Many times false Christians offer false freedom, false promises, and false experiences. It is not a profession of spirituality that marks true believers but a possession of the Spirit of God within. Reform can clean a person on the outside, but only regeneration can clean them up and change them on the inside. Reform can cleanse but it cannot fill. Temporary reformation without true repentance and a new birth can lead to greater sin and judgment. Many feel today that if they change the name of their church and the times of their services that they have had revival. Though many experience reform that cleanses, we still have to fill the house with God. Sinful tendencies do not disappear when a person reforms, they only get stronger. Holiness is not simply refusing to do evil things. True holiness is more than just conquering temptation; it is conquering the very desire to disobey God.

"Escaped the pollutions of this world" (2 Pet. 2:20). Peter uses the aorist tense, which means it was an actual event that took place in the past. *Escape* is from the Greek compound word *apo-phuego*; *apo* meaning marked off dissociation, breaking away from a former association and *phuego* meaning to turn away, to seek safety by flight, to escape completely.[1] They had escaped the moral contaminations of this world. Peter addressed this exodus when he said, "Having escaped the corruption that is in the world through lust" (2 Pet. 1:4). They had made their exodus and their departure from the pollutions of this present evil world system. Have we escaped the defilement and the decay of this present evil world system? The world is a society that is alienated from God by rebellion. Through the influence of the Word of God, the Word served as a detergent and a deterrent that keeps our lives pure.

Corruption is much deeper than defilement on the inside. It is decay on the inside. The word *defilement* comes from the Greek word *miasma*, which means filthy contaminations on the outside.[2] It proceeds from a person that is infected with a terrible disease. From a dead and corrupt body flows stagnant and putrid waters that destroy and infect our health. It is one big putrid marsh that corrupts the body. It sends off its destructive effects in every direction so that no one can escape. The only thing that can heal it is the power of God. The word *corruption* means "decay on the inside."

Augustine said, "The whole world is one great diseased man, lying extended from North to South, East to West. To heal this sick man the Almighty Physician descended from heaven."[3]

If we feed the new nature with the nourishment of the Word of God, then we won't be interested in the garbage of this world. If we make provision for the flesh, our sinful nature will lust after the old sins (2 Pet. 1:9). We will disobey God. Godly living is the result of cultivating a new nature.

"They are again entangled therein and overcome" (2 Pet. 2:20). The word *entangled* comes from the word which means "inner weaving, a braiding, noosed and fettered." Going back to their former life of sin is a gradual process, not an act of a moment.[4] As many of these false teachers persisted in their false teaching that grace became a license to sin, they became entangled in their former way of life that took them captive again. They were once set free from this lifestyle, but they became intertwined with their former way of life. The word *overcome* from the present, passive, indicative Greek word *hettaoo*, which means that they became conquered by the very sins that they were once delivered from.[5]

Then Peter tells them that the latter end is worse than the first. This same idea is posed in Matthew 12:43–45 and Luke 11:26. Jesus knew that Israel had gone through many different types of reform. He also knew that reform could cleanse, but it could not fill.

> When the unclean spirit is gone out of a man, he walketh through dry places, seeking rest, and findeth none. Then he saith, I will return to my house from whence I came out: and when he is come, he findeth it empty, swept and garnished. Then goeth he, and taketh with himself seven other spirits more wicked than himself, and they enter in and dwell there: and the last state of that man is worse than the first. Even so shall it be also unto this wicked generation
>
> —MATTHEW 12:43–45

Jesus was not referring just to a man, but also a nation, even a generation. He was describing a demon of idolatry that walked out of Israel during the time of the Babylonian captivity. He was not cast out; he walked out like a man leaving his house to go for a walk. He returned to the house during the time of Christ. Israel at this time was more wicked than any generation before them. He found them going through reform, but they had not filled the house with God. This spirit of idolatry found the house empty, swept, and garnished like a house that was ready for the new tenant to move right in. The devil, who makes house calls, has returned with company. He had brought with him seven spirits more wicked and powerful than himself. Our only hope is that we have filled our house with God so the Holy Ghost will answer the door. Jesus said the last state of that man is worse than the first.

Peter then says, "For it had been better for them not to have known the way of righteousness, than, after they have known it, to turn from the holy commandment delivered unto them" (2 Pet. 2:21). The word *known* implies experience and acquaintance, to know fully. The Word of God has served as a deterrent and a detergent that had caused their lives to become pure. They were once in the realm of the holy commandment. These men had known the way of righteousness; they had escaped the world's defilements. For a period of time, they seemed to have lived in victory.

To those who have known righteousness, apostasy can become a real possibility. Their experience at one time was true. Satan is a counterfeit. He has a false gospel (Gal. 1:6–9). He has false ministers. Paul talked about being "in perils among false brethren" (2 Cor. 11:26). He has a false righteousness, and a false church one day will produce a false Christ. The phrase "delivered unto them" spoke of the law of morality that Jesus gave in the Sermon on the Mount. It was the oral tradition of Christian teaching. If those who have been gifted to sit under the purity of the gospel should turn away from it, they are not worthy to be called Christians and they are not fit for heaven.

They seem to have knowledge of salvation and they could probably speak the language of the church, but they lack a real experience with the Lord. They received the Word of God and turned from it. They went from being sheep to dogs and pigs.

"The Way" was an early name for Christianity. Jesus said, "I am the way" (John 14:6). Peter speaks of it as "the way of truth" (2 Pet. 2:2). Peter then speaks of those who "have forsaken the right way" (2 Pet. 2:15). Peter spoke of it as the "way of righteousness" (2 Pet. 2:21). Jesus used the term when He said, "For John came unto you in the way of righteousness, and ye believed him not" (Matt. 21:32).

"But it is happened unto them according to the true proverb" (2 Pet. 2:22). Here Peter is using the perfect tense and is telling us what is certain to befall these apostates. Peter is giving us his stamp in what is going to manifest. The word *proverb* comes from a compound word *paroimia*. 1) *para* means "by," and 2) *oimos* means "a way or highway." Peter is pointing out that the examples he is giving are the same. Dogs are going to act like dogs, and pigs are going to act like pigs. The actions of the false teachers are reflections of what they have been all along. This proverb is well known among rabbis, and the actions that are being described are well known among pagans. Dogs and pigs were considered to be unclean animals according to the Jews. They represented the unholy, filthy, rejected. They were the scum of the animal world.

In both Old and New Testaments dogs and pigs were used to describe the greatest of sinners. Proverbs declares, "As a jewel of gold is a swine's snout, so is a fair woman which is without discretion" (Prov. 11:22). "As a dog returneth to his vomit, so a fool will return to his folly" (Prov. 26:11). Goliath asked David, "Am I a dog?" (1 Sam. 17:43). When Abner expressed his disgust with Ishbosheth he said, "Am I a dog's head?" (2 Sam. 3:8). Mephibosheth said, "What is thy servant, that thou shouldest look upon such a dead dog as I am?" (2 Sam. 9:8). Hazael said, "Is thy servant a dog?" (2 Kings 8:13).

Jesus gave a command not to give "that which was holy to a dog." Could you imagine a priest who served at the temple taking a piece of meat that belonged to the Lord and feeding it to a dog? He said, "It is not meet to take the children's bread and give it to the dogs" (Matt. 15:26). Paul called trouble-makers dogs (Phil. 3:2).

Peter is referring to Proverbs 26:11: "As a dog returneth to his vomit, so a fool returneth to his folly." Peter is telling us that it is possible for a sheep to become a dog. "The dog is turned to his own vomit again" (2 Pet. 2:22). The Jews expressed their hatred for Gentiles by calling them dogs. Dogs represented the immoral and those who rejected God (Deut. 23:18). Dogs were filthy scavengers who ran in packs and lived on garbage. To call anyone a dog was to place him in the lowest possible class. Dogs will bite and devour one another (Gal. 5:15), many times without warning. They will in a greedy fashion receive filth. Many church members today have itching ears for filthy gossip. They love to hear filthy jokes. Dogs are often liars. They will bark when there is nothing to bark at. The only thing they will not bark at is a parked car. Why do Christians who are parked in their faith and have their foot on the brake instead of the accelerator think that the devil would ever bark at them? Dogs will keep people awake by senseless barking. Peter likened habitual sinners to dogs (2 Pet. 2:22) Those who are excluded from the eternal city of God are called dogs (Rev. 22:15). He is describing the false teachers who had known the truth and had turned from it. It was not a title of respect or endearment. Dogs get rid of corruption on the inside by vomiting it up. For a period of time the dog feels better. The dog is clean on the inside but remains a dog. He cannot leave well enough alone.

Peter says, "They return to their own vomit" (v. 22). Here the word *return* comes from the word *epistrepho*, which means "to return to a point or area where one has been before." In the case of these false teachers they are returning to their own regurgitated gastric contents. They will go sniffing around the vomit again. It is to their own ruin. If their nature had been changed, they would not have desired to go around what they once threw up, much less eat it. So the dog is still a dog.

The word *vomit* comes from the word *exerama,* that which has been thrown up. What Peter is portraying is not that the dog just returns to sniff the vomit, but that the dog actually laps up what which has been vomited. The actions of the dog reveal his true nature. There are many dogs that eat and swallow again what they just threw up.

Then Peter said sheep can become pigs. "And the sow that was washed to her wallowing in the mire" (v. 22). A pig was an unclean animal according to Jewish Law (Deut. 14:8). It was not to be eaten by a Jew. They were forbidden by Jewish Law to even touch the carcass of a hog. It was considered to be an abomination to eat swine's flesh (Isa. 66:17). A hog was incapable of appreciating beauty (Prov. 11:22; Matt. 7:6). Being a pig farmer was considered to be a lowly occupation (Luke 15:15). Hogs were hypocritical and unredeemed sinners (2 Pet. 2:22).

Hogs are dangerous creatures in the fact that they can't: 1) appreciate the beauty of pearls, 2) are only interested in satisfying their gluttonous appetites, 3) thrive on what clean creatures reject, and 4) if they don't get their slop they will rend you.

They are filthy creatures. They wallow in the mire. They thoroughly enjoy it. How many church members enjoy wallowing in the mire of sin, and drinking from the slop buckets of this world? We act like pigs and dogs when we show no appreciation for the riches and beauty of the things of God.

Jesus told us that we are not to cast our pearls before swine (Matt. 7:6). Pearls represent that which is good, holy, and of value. They represent something of great worth. They are highly prized by the commercial world (Rev. 17:4; 18:12); they were prized jewels of the ancient world. There are some things that are worth more than pearls: 1) wisdom and the fear of God (Prov. 1:7), 2) a godly woman, adorned with modest apparel (1 Tim. 2:9), 3) the gospel message (Matt. 7:6), and 4) gates of the New Jerusalem were as one pearl (Rev. 21:21).

A sow that has been washed has reformed himself. Many within the life of the church have went through this same reformation. They will wash themselves when they go to Church on Sunday morning but by nightfall they will wallow in the mud holes of this world. A washed pig can return to a mud hole.

Here we have outward cleansing but not one that was inward. The pig can go through a good scrubbing, yet they cannot resist rolling around the mudhole or manure again. The pig was washed on the outside but remained a pig. The pig looked better and the dog felt better, but neither one had their nature changed. Like the sow, the followers of the false prophets wanted to go back and wallow in the gross forms of sins from which they were once delivered by the cleansing action of God's Word. The false teachers had been exposed to the gospel but had internally remained "full of dead men's bones and all uncleanness." The outward cleansing was undone by the pigs desire to find relief by returning to the mire. A pig can only to stay clean for a short period of time then they must head to the nearest mud hole. We don't condemn a pig for acting like a pig because it is his nature. If we saw a sheep heading for the mire we would be concerned.

Peter is saying that to just make a religious profession or even a temporary outward change does not change one within. They professed to have experienced salvation, but in due time went from being a sheep to a pig and drifted back to a life that suited their nature. The false teachers made a profession of faith and one of spiritual renewal. Their teachings and practices revealed that they were no more than apostates that were lost in sin.

How does a born-again Christian give that which is holy to the dogs, and cast his or her pearls before swine?

- When we hang out dirty laundry before the world.
- When we take our brothers and sisters to court (1 Cor. 6:1–8)
- When we as the church take on a worldly attitude
- When we try to clean fish before we catch them
- When we try to get the old nature to obey the laws of God

Sinners must repent before they can go from being dogs and pigs to sheep. It is only then that they can appreciate the pearls of truth from the Word of God.

What are our choices today, this past week or this past year? We loudly proclaim what we really are through our behavior. A false faith can be characterized by the absence of good fruit (2 Pet. 1:8–10). Ignorance to spiritual things causes one to indulge in fleshly behavior. Unsaved people are ignorant and are destroyed for a lack of knowledge (Hosea 4:6). Since we are born into a world of sin and have a fallen nature it is only natural that we live sinful lives. A sinner is going to be a sinner. A dog and a pig behave differently because they have different natures. Nature determines appetites and actions.

These false teachers never were what they professed to be. Here they were returning to what they had been all along. Dogs and pigs can get scrubbed up but not be clean. By their very nature they will return to unclean living. Now these apostates are in deeper bondage. They are farther from the truth. They are more in spiritual filth than they have ever been. If one is going to be true to his new nature he is going to have to persevere in the area of his faith. We only receive a new nature by being born again through repentance toward God and faith in the Lord Jesus Christ.

The godly are here warned of both dangers and warned not to be included in the ranks of pigs and dogs. It is a portrait of mankind out of touch with God. Both animals were unclean according to the Jews. Jesus warned the Jews in the Sermon on the Mount, "Give not that which is holy unto the dogs, neither cast ye your pearls before swine" (Matt. 7:6). Here Jesus is giving reference to those who are opposed to God's and His Word. As God's people we are privileged to handle the holy things of the Lord. No dedicated priest would throw meat from the altar to a filthy dog, and only a fool would give pearls to a pig. Even Jesus refused to talk with Herod (Luke 23:9). Paul himself refused to argue with people who resisted the Word of God (Acts 13:44–49).

In the second century b.c., there was a Syrian story of Ahikar. "My son, thou hast been to me like the swine that had been to the baths, and when you saw a muddy ditch, you went down and washed in it, and cried to your companions, come and bathe."[6]

Believers have received a new nature, a divine nature, and different appetites and desires. They have been transformed from pigs and dogs into sheep. Nature determines appetite. Pigs want slop and can't stay out of mud holes. Dogs will eat their own vomit. A pig and a dog can rise no higher than their nature.

If nature determines appetite we ought to have the divine nature of God. We ought to have an appetite that is pure and holy. If God is our Father, we ought to live in the kind of environment that suits our nature. We ought to be traveling and associating with those who are true to our nature.

We can rise no higher than our divine nature. True freedom must come from within. Sheep desire green pastures. David said, "He maketh me to lie down in green pastures" (Ps. 23:2). In order for sheep to lie down they must be free from torment, friction, hunger, and pestilence.

Nature determines behavior. An eagle will fly, dolphins will swim. Nature determines environment. Squirrels climb trees, moles burrow under ground, and trout swim in the water. Nature determines association. Lions travel in prides, sheep in flocks, and fish in schools.

That is why Paul wrote to the church at Corinth and admonished them, "Be not unequally yoked together with unbelievers" (2 Cor. 6:14). In the Old Testament it was contrary to the law of God to place an ox and a mule under the same yoke. Jeremiah warned us "not to become as the mule that has no understanding." Their natures were different. The ox had the strength to stomp someone in the ground. By the ox submitting to the yoke it represented strength under submission. The ox was stronger than the mule and many times wound up pulling the mule around the pasture by the neck. The mule by nature became stubborn. Many times that is the reason why we stay tired and burned out. It is because we are yoked up with people that exhaust us. We cannot be afraid to cut people loose from us who have a different nature, that don't share our passion and are going a different direction.

Paul goes on to say, "What fellowship hath righteousness with unrighteousness? And what communion hath light with darkness? And what concord (agreement) hath Christ with Belial (Satan)? And what part hath he that believeth with in infidel (some one who refuses to believe the gospel)? And what agreement hath the temple of God with idols? For ye are the temple of the living God; as God hath said, I will dwell in them, and walk in them; I will be their God, and they shall be my people. Wherefore, come from among them, and be ye separate, saith the Lord, and touch not the unclean thing; and I will receive you. And I will be a Father unto you, and ye shall be my sons and daughters, saith the Lord Almighty " (2 Cor. 6:14–18).

Chapter 20

Works of the Flesh

Now the works of the flesh are manifest, which are these; Adultery,
fornication, uncleanness, lasciviousness. Idolatry, witchcraft,
hatred, variance, emulations, wrath, strife, seditions, heresies,
Envyings, murders, drunkenness, revellings, and such like: of the
which I tell you before, as I have told you in time past, that they
which do such things shall not inherit the kingdom of God.
—GALATIANS 5:19–21

DOES YOUR BEHAVIOR betray your profession? While many in our country profess the name of Christ, their behavior seems to betray their profession. When a person is truly born again their profession will be mirrored through their morality. We cannot separate what we believe from how we live. Our lifestyle is our doctrine. A survey was recently done that stated that there was little difference between the church and the unchurched on a wide range of issues including lying, cheating, and stealing. On one poll from Roper Organization (*National & International Religious Report*, 1990), stated that moral behavior actually deteriorated after the born-again experience for many people.[1] The question is will we stand upon God's Word, or will we cave in to the prevailing attitudes of our culture? Will we demand if we profess the name of Christ to live out our profession, or will be tolerate immoral behavior?

Do we make a distinction between those who profess the name of Christ and non-believers? Does a mere profession constitute a true conversion without one repenting of his sins, turning his back on a life of sin, and setting his face toward heaven like a flint? The whole epistle of Galatians demands that such a distinction be made. Those who have met Jesus Christ and Him who is crucified are changed. If we are truly in Christ we will produce the fruit of the Spirit. Those who are not in Christ will produce the works of the flesh. The evidence that one is truly a Christian is the fruit of the Spirit, not his or her religious profession.

Paul has assured his readers that the Spirit will enable them to resist the desires of the flesh. What the law could not do for them, God would do by the work of the Spirit in them. The Galatians were attracted to the law because it gave them specific moral guidelines that they could apply day-to-day situations. The Judaizers were renowned for their ability to develop applications of the law for every conceivable situation.

Paul's command to "live by the Spirit" (v. 16) left everything up in the air. How can they know they are gratifying the desires of their sin nature if it is not defined? How can they know what life in the Spirit is like if it is not defined? We are bound to repeat the mistakes of the Galatians if we are not careful. We must be careful not to live under the law but rather live by the direction of the Spirit.

After Paul described the believer's victory over the sin nature, he defines specific acts of the sinful nature (vv. 19–21) and then lists the fruit of the Spirit (vv. 22–23). They provide us an evaluation to determine whether we are living to gratify the flesh or living in the Spirit.

No man was ever more conscious of the tension between the flesh and the spirit than Paul. To Paul, Christian freedom was to walk in the life of the Spirit and to not indulge in the flesh. The Galatian believers were not to use their liberty from the law as a base of operations from which they were to cater to the flesh, but their lives were to be ruled by love and by the operation of the Holy Spirit. The Christian is going to have to learn how to cooperate with the Holy Spirit in His sanctifying work. Progressive sanctification is the way to the life and the power of God.

"The works of the flesh are manifest" (v. 19). Paul's use of the word *works* connects this list with the works of the law. Paul has already established that by the works of the law no flesh could be justified or to stand in a right relationship with God. Paul knew that unless a man's nature is changed he can only produce the fruit of his nature. The Galatian believers in their attempt to obey the law were actually producing works of the flesh, which were the acts of the sinful nature. The law has no power (but the Spirit does) to overcome or change the destructive influence of the sinful nature. When a person is under the control of the Holy Spirit, having received justification by faith in Christ, his whole nature is bent in a godly direction. A change has taken place through and by the work of the Spirit so the believer walks in the Spirit rather than carrying out the dictations of the flesh (5:16).

The word *deeds* refers to the moral character of a person that issues forth from his life. It is what you are when no one else is around. Character is what you are when the Lord comes and knocks at your door and you don't have to change the channel of the TV before you let Him in. These are deeds that issue from the flesh. They represent the outworking of human behavior apart from grace.

The works of the flesh are dependent on no one but ourselves. Even though a person may seek to be religious and attain righteousness through the law, he is still in dependence upon himself. This is the essence of a lost condition.

The word *flesh* is the essence of a man's life apart from Christ. The flesh represents his natural birth. If you want to know what he is, you can cut through the façade he portrays and know that his life is characterized by a life that is bent and going away from God in defiance to the law of God. Sin has dominated his heart and the way he lives his life.

John Stott in his book on the *The Message of Galatians* states, "When man is in control of his own destiny his spirit will be in opposition of God. He may make a religious profession, but his focal point will be himself. He wants to rule his own life. He rejects any dependence upon Christ-saving work or the Holy Spirit. All that he is he is by nature. He is an expression of his fallen condition, not a life that is transformed by the grace of God."[2]

John MacArthur, *MacArthur NT Commentaries,* states that Paul's whole contention was that the flesh and the Spirit cannot co-exist (5:17). You cannot be a believer and an unbeliever at the same time. You cannot be a recipient of grace and be one who lives in dependence of the law at the same time.[3] We need to ask ourselves the question, "Where are we more at home? With the works of the flesh or the fruit of the Spirit?"

The word *manifest* comes from the Greek word *phraneros*, which means that the works of the flesh are evident and they can be seen. The desires of the sinful nature may be hidden from the eyes of man, but the acts produced by those desires are public and are plain for all to see. These works of the evil nature are active not passive. It needs to be kept in mind that works glorify man but fruit glorifies God.

Paul is dealing with the contrast between the natural life and the spiritual life. Paul gives us a list of the vices of paganism that were prevalent among the

Greeks and Romans of his day. Pagan philosophers often gave a list of vices and virtues. Even pagans who were considered to have good morals regarded these with horror. They were contrary to the natural results of man's true nature. What human nature produced was plain for all to see.

The Galatians did not need the Mosaic Law to define the nature of evil. He had already told them that they were not under the supervision of the law (v. 18); why would the Galatians turn to the Law of Moses for instruction in their morality? Paul describes the acts of the sinful nature as transgressions of the law. Paul is telling us that we already know evil when we see it. The chaos caused by these vices is contrasted with the wholeness and unity of the fruit of the Spirit. Life in the Spirit is both active (walking) and passive (being led). Love and goodness are fruit of the Spirit, so Paul then urges the believer to work at loving and doing good (5:6, 13–14; 6:4–5, 9–10).

Even in the Book of Corinthians we see how Paul had to fight against these vices in the Gentile church. Because of the floodtide of immorality in the Gentile life, the Judaizers felt that the law was necessary. Jewish churches were not usually exposed to gross vices of this sort.

Paul lists fifteen acts of the sinful nature and divides them into four categories:

1. Illicit sex, which covers all kinds of immoral sexual relationships

2. Religious heresy

3. Social conflict or sexual perversions. The art and literature of Paul's day provide ample evidence for the widespread practice of sexual immorality. The sexual life of the Greek-Roman world of New Testament times was a lawless chaos. In the two millenniums since the Roman Empire, our generation has come closer than any previous generations to the blatant prevalence of sexual perversions that characterized the Roman Empires. A study of the Roman Empire shows that any society that tolerates the unchecked promotion of such perversions will inevitably fall apart from the rottenness within.

4. Drunkenness

There were breaches in sexual laws, which included sexual immorality, impurity, and debauchery. All churches seem to be plagued to some degree with sexual immorality. Paul knew that most of the Jewish church would quickly condemn those who were guilty of sexual immorality while considering themselves to be safe, since they had performed the works of the law by getting circumcised (5:2) and observing special days (4:10).

Paul then turned to these law-keeping Christians and gave them a long list of acts stemming from the sin nature. Like the story of the woman caught in the act of adultery (John 8:3–11), the teachers of the law were ready to stone her. Jesus said, "He that is without sin among you, let him first cast a stone at her" (v. 7). Then He began to write on the ground. The teachers of the law were convicted of their own sin and dropped their rocks and went home because of what Jesus wrote in the ground.

When Paul confronts law teachers who are ready to stone law breakers, he lists acts and attitudes that come from the sin nature. No one can find any safety in their selective observance of the law. They too are enslaved by sin. Only Christ can set them free; only the Spirit can make them free.

Adultery is sex with someone outside the marital relationship with someone other than your spouse. The believer is not to be unfaithful by stepping out of the boundaries of his own marriage to gratify his sexual desires. When a person fulfills his sexual desires outside the bonds of marriage, if he persists in such practices with no desire to repent, then he will bring himself under the judgment of God.

Fornication is sex outside the covenant relationship of marriage. Fornication comes from the word *pornia*, which is where we get the word pornography from—taking pleasure in pornographic pictures, films, or writings; the engagement of any form of illicit sexual behavior. It was a sin that was characteristic of the Graeco-Roman world. The Jerusalem council said that believers were to abstain from fornication (Acts 15:20, 29). Fornication was a problem among the Thessalonians, and Paul called for progressive sanctification (1 Thess. 4:3). Paul calls for believers to exercise personal discipline over their desires. The believer is not to follow the ways of the world in their animalistic desire for sex. In the Old Testament it spoke of idolatry, which was a spirit of being unfaithful to God. Baal worship involved sexual immorality as part of the fertility cult. It was a characteristic of the pagan world.

Paul is speaking of prostitution in a Greek society. Extramarital affairs were more common then than in our own day. Female slaves were often purchased for that purpose. When a person became involved in sexual immorality they were considered to be prostituting themselves.

Uncleanness is the pus of an unclean world. When we engage our minds and indulge our eyes in immoral scenes and activities, then we have fallen into impurity. It is when an unregenerated person becomes subject to his natural desires. It is when you let yourself go and engage your mind on impure fantasies and place your eyes on what God has forbidden. It speaks of a tree that has never been pruned, material that has never been sifted. It speaks of sexual impurity. Uncleanness comes from the original Greek word *katharos*, an adjective meaning "purity." It was commonly used in contrast to describe a house that is left clean and in good condition. It also referred to ceremonial cleanness, which entitled a man to approach his gods. Impurity is anything that makes a man unfit to come before God and anything that separates man from Him.

Lasciviousness is readiness for any pleasure. The man or woman who practices it knows no restraint; it speaks of an appetite that knows no shame. It means unbridled behavior that would shock the public. Ancient Greece would use this term to express someone who lives like a dog, or acts like a goat. He gives himself to desires without restraint. He loses his mind to the pursuit of sexual appetites. All of these sins were rampant in the Roman Empire. Josephus described it as an act of Jezebel who built a temple to Baal in Jerusalem. It describes a man who is so far gone in desire that he ceases to care what people think or say.

Idolatry is the worship of gods that are made by the hands of man. It is not merely worshiping the image of a god but also participating in the temple feasts (1 Cor. 10:7, 14) and even being greedy for possessions (Col. 3:5). The power behind graven images is imaginations that are manipulated by demons. It is when we give anything equal or greater authority in our life to something other than God or His Word. It is when the material takes the place of God. We are supposed to worship God, love people, and use things. Often we use people, love self, and worship things. It is when anything takes the place of your love and devotion to Christ. False religion is the worship of other gods (whether images in temples or shopping malls) and dependence on other powers (drugs or occult practices).

Look at any nation that has crumbled and you will find greed, idolatry, and immorality have gnawed away at their foundation. It happened to Israel, Judah, and the Greek and Roman Empires.

Witchcraft is the use of drugs for sorcery of which the ancient world was full. The original Greek is where we get the word *pharmacy* from. When Paul was at Ephesus in (Acts 19:19), they burned the books of charms and spells at Ephesus. Magicians in Paul's day often used drugs to bring about their evil effects and to poison the people. Orthodox Jews regarded these with horror.

Then Paul listed eight social sins—attitude and actions that destroy personal relationships. Christians were "biting and devouring one another" (Gal. 5:15) and "provoking and envying each another" (v. 26, NIV). The letter that Paul wrote to the Galatians indicates that theses conflicts were caused by the false teachers' campaign to enforce the observance of the law in the churches. The curse on "all who rely on observing the law" (3:10) was already being experienced in the breakdown of relationships between Christians. While they were concentrating on performing "works of the law" (2:16), their lives were being characterized by the "works of the flesh" (5:19).

Hatred is when a man is hostile toward his fellow man.

Variance is contention, strife, fighting, discord, quarreling, or wrangling. It is when we try to make someone look bad so that we can look good in the eyes of others. It is the struggle in the church for superiority.

Emulations are the desire to obtain nobility when we see it—the desire to have what someone else has.

Wrath is uncontrolled temper. It is an outburst of temper. It not only describes anger that lasts but anger which flames up and then dies.

Strife is when we canvass for political office, not because our motive is for service, but for what we can get out of it.

Seditions are an attitude that says, "I am here to undermine the authority of my pastor." It is when people insist that people are to follow them instead of the Lord.

Heresies is a term that comes from a philosopher's school of followers or any band of people who share a common belief. It is a body of men who separate themselves from others and follow their own tenets. It is cliques which destroy the unity of a church.

Envy is the greatest disease among men. It is the desire to have what someone else has. You hold a grudge over the fact that others have such things, and you want to take them from them. It leads to an embittered mind.

Murder is not just when we take a life but we can murder someone else's reputation with our mouth and destroy their influence. Gossip is murder's first cousin.

Drunkenness in the ancient world was a common vice. Here Paul refers to wild drinking parties held in honor of pagan gods, particularly the god Bacchus. Drunkenness and orgies were part of pagan culture; they still are. There were drunken orgies of festivals to pagan gods. Alcohol and wild parties of teenagers may be equivalent to this. Such abuses crept into the Lord's Supper in Gentile churches.

Revellings speaks of a band of men who accompanied a victor of the games after their victory. They danced, laughed, and sang praises. It was unrestrained revelry.

The Jews had charged Paul of teaching freedom from moral restraints (Rom. 3:8). Paul said those who practiced these things "shall not inherit the kingdom of God" (Gal. 5:21). Paul is not talking about the act of sin, but the habit of it. He is referring to the habitual practices of such things.

By practicing and engaging in these activities we can bar ourselves from the kingdom of God and forfeit our position in the kingdom of God. One can literally shut himself out of the kingdom. Is it your desire to deny yourself entrance into the kingdom of God by practicing the works of the flesh? By adopting this lifestyle we show that we do not possess saving faith. The Christian through identification with Christ at the cross has died to these vices already and has made a clean break from the works of darkness. If we are slaves to such passions, we reveal by our behavior that we are not true born-again sons of the King.

The Judaizers in their attempt to obey the law may have been what blinded them to their own sins. They were intent on establishing for themselves a secure place in the kingdom of God, but by doing so they were destroying the people of God. Those who are so concerned about securing their own place that they would deny any place for others will lose their own place in the end.

The evidence of justification by faith was the presence of the Spirit. His presence is the evidence of conversion. They had received the Spirit by believing in the gospel, not by observing the law—just as righteousness had been placed on Abraham's account on the basis of His faith (3:1–6). Their lives were transformed and empowered as they were indwelt and directed by the Spirit. They could not have claimed spiritual transformation if there was no change in the morality. They could not have claimed justification by faith if there was no presence of the Holy Spirit. If this were the case, they would not inherit the kingdom of God.

The Galatians were declared by God to be righteous because of their faith in Christ's sacrificial atoning death. God, through sanctification of the Spirit (instantaneous and progressive) made them righteous through and by the work of His Spirit. Those whose lives are characterized by the works of the flesh are demonstrating that they have never been born again.

Chapter 21

Fruit of the Spirit

But the fruit of the Spirit is love, joy, peace, longsuffering, gentleness, goodness, faith, Meekness, temperance: against such there is no law.
—GALATIANS 5:22–23

THE PRODUCTION OF fruit in the life and heart of a believer is the result of the life of the Spirit within. The fruit of the Spirit is the character of Christ and the spirit of holiness as it is reproduced in the heart and life of the believer. It was the desire of the apostle Paul to see Christ formed in the lives of the Galatian believers (4:19). There was to be an expression of something happening on the outside because something was happening within. In a day when fire is considered to be more important than fruit, we need to understand unless the character of Christ is formed within us the fire will mean nothing. Fire will attract a crowd but it will take fruit to keep them. Fire must issue forth from the fruit not fruit out our fire.

Paul's image of the fruit of the Spirit is drawn from the imagery of Old Testament and the teachings of Jesus. "Until a spirit from on high is poured out on us, and the wilderness becomes a fruitful field, and the fruitful field is deemed a forest, then justice will dwell in the wilderness, and righteousness abide in the fruitful field, the effect of righteousness will be peace, and the result of righteousness, quietness and trust forever" (Isa. 32:15–17, NRSV). The promise of the Spirit and the promise of moral fruitfulness in God's people are connected in the Old Testament.

Jesus taught that the genuineness of His followers would be demonstrated by good fruit from their lives (Luke 13:6–9). Because of the presence of the Spirit and through our communion with Him, it would cause us to go from bearing fruit, to more fruit to much fruit.

According to Leviticus 19:23–25 it was the law of the fruit-bearing tree that no fruit was eaten from it the first three years. God took Israel and planted her in fertile soil, drove a stake next to her to support her growth, and made every provision for her fruitfulness. He built a hedge about her to keep the goats and weeds out of the vineyard. On the fourth year their crops belonged to the Lord. It was not until the fifth year that the harvester would take any figs for himself. It needs to be remembered that God is longsuffering and gracious toward His people. He goes to the utmost to see us repent and bear fruit. He has every right to cut us down, but in His mercy He spares us. God waited three years during our Lord's earthly ministry, but the nation of Israel produced no fruit. Then forty years later the Romans came under Titus and destroyed Jerusalem and the temple. Finally, the tree was cut down.

In verses 22–23 Paul focuses on the believer's expression of righteousness, which fulfills God's promises for His people.

Paul is warning us that it is important that there be a right atmosphere before fruit can grow. Fruit has to have a certain climate to be able to grow. Fruit will not grow in just any kind of climate. Heaven's fruit will not dangle from the branches of a believer's life whose atmosphere is charged with strife and contention. The Judaizers were anxious for the praise of men and vain glory. This attitude led to competition and division. The fruit of heaven will not grow in just any kind of climate either. The fruit of the Spirit will not grow in every individual's life or in every church.

The legalist might be able to boast that he is not guilty of adultery or murder (Matt. 5:21–32), but he will never see the graces of the Spirit in his life. Fruit grows out of the life of the Spirit. The evidence of the Spirit is life; and the by-product of life is fruit. Fruit grows out of life. Fruit is the unfolding of life by the Spirit of God. When you think of works, you think of effort, labor, strain, and toil. When you think of fruit, you think of beauty, quietness, and the unfolding of life.

The flesh produces dead works (Heb. 9:14), but the Holy Spirit produces living fruit. Freedom in Christ means freedom to produce the fruits of righteousness through a Spirit-led life. The fruit has seed in it to produce more fruit (Gen. 1:11). Jesus is very concerned about whether or not we produce fruit. The flesh cannot produce the fruit of the Spirit.

In order for heaven's fruit to grow in the believer's life they must maintain an atmosphere that is charged with the presence of the Holy Spirit and the Word of God. The holy place in the Old Testament tabernacle was known as heaven's greenhouse. It is where the atmosphere of heaven is recreated in the earth. It is where our spiritual lives go from buds to blossoms to fruit to fire.

The fruit of the Spirit is the character of Christ and the Spirit of holiness in the New Testament. It is single-minded lifestyle. It is produced in the life of the children of God as they allow the Spirit of God to direct and influence their lives to destroy the power of indwelling sin and walk in fellowship with God.

The Holy Spirit will produce living fruit. Love begets more love; joy helps to produce more joy. Jesus wants us to go from bearing fruit, to more fruit, to much fruit (John 15:2, 5, 8). It is the way we glorify Him. The old nature cannot produce the fruit of the Spirit. Only the new nature can do that.

Fruit is produced to be eaten; not put on display. People around us are starving. Fruit is to be produced so that others may be fed and helped. When people find spiritual fruit in our lives, they will know that we have something they lack. We don't bear fruit for our own consumption; we bear fruit so that others may be fed and helped and so that Christ may be glorified. The flesh can bring results that bring praise to us, but it cannot produce fruit that brings glory to God. Fruit takes patience, an atmosphere of the Spirit, walking in the light, the seed of the Word of God, and a sincere desire to honor Christ. It is then that we will go from buds to blossoms to fruit to fire. Many times in the church our fire has drawn people; but our lack of fruit is the reason why we lost them. The fire comes out of the fruit (character), not fruit out of our fire. God is much more concerned about our character than He is our fire.

We must distinguish the gift of the Spirit, which is salvation; and the gifts of the Spirit, which have to do with power for service. The graces of the Spirit speak of our Christian character. Gifts of the Spirit have been so overemphasized that they have led some Christians to neglect the graces of the Spirit. The building of Christian character takes precedence over displaying special abilities. If you were sitting in your house watching television and the Lord came and knocked at your door, would you not have to change the channel on the television before you let Him in? Character is what you are when no one else is around.

If we are saved the fruit of the Spirit is present. It does not mean that we are perfected. If we are saved the fruit of the Spirit is present but has to be developed as we grow in grace and progress in the walk of the Spirit. Christians ought to practice these virtues over and over again. The fruit of the Spirit is the spontaneous product of the presence of the Spirit within the heart of the Christian. It has deep roots in the soil of the Old Testament. It was a metaphor that was natural to an agricultural people like Israel. Jesus said that you can tell a tree by the fruit it bears (Matt. 7:16).

The old nature can counterfeit the fruit of the Spirit. The flesh can never produce the fruit of the Spirit. When the Spirit produces fruit, God gets the glory and the Christian is unaware of his spirituality. When the flesh is at work, a person inwardly becomes proud and pleased when others compliment him. The work of the Spirit is to cleanse and purify us and make us less and less like this world and more and more like Jesus Christ—for His glory, not for the praise of men.

Paul's list of moral qualities produced by the Spirit provides the assurance that those who live by the Spirit will actually fulfill God's requirements for His people. The Spirit will produce those moral qualities that God requires. Let us look at some.

GODWARD ASPECTS OF THE CHRISTIAN LIFE

Love comes from the New Testament Greek word *agape*. It is a world that speaks of unconquerable benevolence. Even when people try to insult, injure, or humiliate us, we will seek their highest good. It is when we seek only the best for those who seek the worst for us. It is when we care for and seek for their highest good without personal gain. The other fruits of the Spirit are outgrowths of love. It is God's gift to us (Rom. 5:5); we must cultivate it and pray that it will increase (Phil. 1:9).

We serve one another in love (Gal.5:13). Love fulfills the law (v. 14). Love is the expression of faith (v. 6). Love is demonstrated in a tangible way in the sacrificial love of Christ (2:20) and the service of other Christians (5:13). All the other moral qualities flow from love.

Joy is an attitude of the heart that comes from being in right relationship with God and doing those things that are pleasing in His sight. The foundation of it is God. It is an inward peace that is not affected by outward circumstances. It is a holy optimism that keeps us going in spite of difficulties. Love and joy produce peace.

Joy is the result of a life that is yielded to the Holy Spirit. When relationships fall apart because of broken commitments, there is a loss of joy (4:15). When there is conflict and bitterness, as there was in the Galatian churches, there was no joy. The renewal of joy in relationships is the first result of true love.

Peace means to bind back together that which has been separated. The Old

Testament Hebrew word was *shalom*, which means wholeness, completeness, and prosperity. It means the tranquility of heart. It is when we realize that the times and seasons of our lives are in His hands. The peace of God is on patrol in the town of man's soul and stands outside the door of our hearts and minds and won't let anything in that will upset us. Instead of hatred, discord, dissensions, and factions, there is harmony in our relationships. Many are not at peace with one another because they have no peace with God.

MANWARD ASPECTS OF THE CHRISTIAN LIFE

Longsuffering is endurance, patience, and being slow to anger. It is the opposite of fits of rage or short temper. It is courageous endurance without quitting. It is the quality of putting up with people when our patience has been tried. It is the quality of staying with people when you have been constantly wronged or irritated by them. It has been said that if God had been a man, He would have wiped out this world long ago. God has patience and suffers long with sinners and will not cast them off. In our dealings with our fellow man, we must reproduce this loving, forbearing, patient, forgiving attitude of God toward others. When we are longsuffering we will not seek to avenge ourselves or wish difficulties on those who oppose us. We will be kind and gentle even with the most offensive.

Gentleness is when we do not want to hurt someone or give them pain. This word speaks of kindness. The Greek word translated *kindness* is *chrestotes*, which refers to sweetness. Gentleness and kindness reflect a sweet disposition and doing good toward people (v. 10); and that it is the way to continue with them in love. Christ's yoke is *chrestotes* where Jesus said, "My yoke is easy, and my burden is light" (Matt. 11:30). Jesus showed this virtue when he was kind to the sinner woman who anointed His feet.

Goodness is love in action. It is when a zeal for truth and righteousness and a hatred for evil are expressed in acts of kindness, especially when having to rebuke evil. The Greek word used is *agathosune*, which rebukes and disciplines. Jesus showed this virtue when He cleansed the temple and drove out the money changers.

Faith is faithfulness, firm, unswerving in loyalty. It is reflected in those united by a promise, committed, trustworthy, and honest. Faithfulness is the quality of keeping commitments in relationships. The Galatians had proven to be fickle in their attitude toward Paul (4:13–16). Only the Spirit could produce the quality of loyalty kept no matter the cost. It was used in secular Greek language for trustworthiness. It is characteristic of man who is reliable.

Meekness in the New Testament has three meanings: 1) submissive to the will of God (Matt. 5:5, 11:29; 21:5), 2) teachable, not too proud to learn (James 1:21), 3) considerate (1 Cor. 4:21; 2 Cor. 10:1; Eph. 4:2). It speaks of strength under submission. It is like an animal that has been tamed and brought under control. It is not weakness. Jesus said, "I am meek and lowly in heart" (Matt. 11:29). Moses was very meek (Num. 12:3). The meek Christian does not throw his weight around or assert himself. Meekness is the right use of authority and power.

Temperance is self-control or mastery of our own desires and passions. It is the opposite of self-indulgence. It is being faithful in marital vowels, purity, and chastity. It is when we have mastered the desires of our flesh and its love for pleasure. Those who are Spirit-led will not indulge in the sinful nature (v. 13), not characterized by sexual immorality, drunkenness, or orgies. They do not use other people to gratify their own appetites. They have the strength to say no to themselves, to the desires of the sin nature. It is the mastery of self. It is used when an athlete disciplines his body (1 Cor. 9:25). It is when the Christian masters his sexual desires (1 Cor 7:9). Paul believed that when the Christian identified with Christ's death, burial, and resurrection, he rose to a new kind of life. The evil things of the old self were gone and the lovely things of the Spirit had come into view.

"Against such there is no such law" (v. 23): Paul is directing his comments toward those who want to be under the supervision of the law. Paul assures them that if they are being led by the Spirit, they are not under the law (v. 18), because the Spirit produces all the qualities that fulfill the requirements of the law (vv. 14, 23). There is no rule in the Mosaic Law that can be cited against such character qualities. The Spirit-led life is a life that fulfills the law. The way to fulfill the law is to live by the Spirit as God's children, not under the law like slaves.

Paul concludes these admonitions to the Galatians with a statement about putting to death the sinful nature and encourages them to walk in the Spirit: "And they that are Christ's have crucified the flesh with the affections and lusts. If we live in the Spirit, let us also walk in the Spirit" (vv. 24–25). Galatians 2:19 and 6:14 say that Christians have been crucified with Christ, but Galatians 5:24 says they have put to death the sinful nature. The goal of warfare against my sin nature is not a negotiated peace but final execution. This statement of crucifixion describes an absolute and irreversible renunciation of evil. The past tense was used and referred to the time of baptism, when the Christian publicly identified himself with Christ. The death of the sin nature opens the door for the life of the Spirit. Death has been followed by a new life.

Repentance and renunciation of evil means that we have said an absolute, unconditional No! to all of our sinful desires and passions. The renunciation of evil is not only a baptismal vow, it is practical everyday discipline. When my sinful nature suggests glancing at a *Play Boy* magazine, I shout a defiant No! to my sinful nature. When I hear a juicy bit of gossip and desire to repeat it, I close my mouth and say No! Instead I say, "Lord, set a watch upon my mouth." When another Christian criticizes me unfairly and my flesh screams for revenge, I say No! to my sinful passion.

The continuous war against the sinful nature and the absolute execution of the sinful nature must be kept ever before us. The Christian perfectionist who talks as if the sinful nature has been or can be totally conquered in this life has lost sight of the need to fight the war everyday. The pessimist is halfhearted in battling the flesh because he never expects victory and he has lost sight of the victory that is his through identification with Christ on the cross. Christ died *for* sin, while we die *to* it. We must realize that either we die *to* it, or we will die *in* it.

Chapter 22

Restoration

Brethren, if a man be overtaken in a fault, ye which
are spiritual, restore such a one in the spirit of meek-
ness; considering thyself, lest thou also be tempted.

—GALATIANS 6:1

I T WAS THE belief of the apostle Paul that when one is led by the Holy
Spirit, relationships in the life of the church that have been broken by
sin will be restored. Divisions along hostility came into the church when
the Judaizers tried to force the Gentiles to become Jewish. There were Jewish
Christians standing for circumcision and for the Gentiles to keep the Law
of Moses. While some Gentile believers were pursuing being identified with
the Jewish community, other Gentiles were resisting living according to the
Law of Moses. This led to many within the church biting and devouring one
another (5:15) and provoking one another to envy (5:26).

First of all, the Spirit-filled believer has a responsibility to restore those
who have been taken captive by sin. Biblical spirituality is living in the world
with God. It involves walking with God, talking with God, and breaking
bread together with God. Paul in many places throughout this epistle has
emphasized that all the converts of Galatia had received the Spirit (3:2–5, 14;
4:6, 29; 5:5, 16–18, 22–23, 25). Paul addressed his new converts as *brethren*
(6:1). Here he used the word *adelphos*, which means we are members of the
same family, born of the same womb, washed in the same blood, fighting for
the same cause, headed for the same destination. Each believer in the body
of Christ has received the same indwelling of God through and by the Spirit.
Paul is giving a call to arms to every believer that has received the message
of the cross and has been a recipient of the Spirit to be actively engaged in a
ministry of restoration.

One way of keeping in step with the Spirit is to restore someone who
has been trapped in sin. The Spirit-led Christian thinks of others and how

they can minister to them. This is an illustration of spirituality in the New Testament. Only those who are spiritual can bring healing and unity into a church that has been torn apart by division. There are corporate responsibilities to one another and individual believer's accountability before God, which involve our integrity in our walk with God. Those who are led by the Spirit are aware that they were sinners saved by grace; now through the grace of God, they are saints redeemed from the power of sin and raised up to live above the grip of sin.

The first responsibility of those who are spiritual is the restoration of those who have sinned. "If anyone is overtaken in a fault" (v. 1): the word *overtaken* comes from the Greek word *paralambano,* which means ambushed, seized by sin, or trapped or taken unawares. Sin had always had a domino effect in lives. The consequence of immoral failure can be multiplied very quickly. The moment the Galatians abandoned the Holy Spirit and the grace of God and returned to a flesh attempt to serve God, sin took them by surprise. Sin often appeared in their lives before they were aware of its presence. They became easy prey to the tempter of men's souls.

There were people within the life of the church who had become trapped by sin. Paul is indicating the highest probability that members in the church can and do sin. Sin in the church is a reality. In John's Epistle to the church, he said, "If we say we have no sin, we deceive ourselves, and the truth is not in us" (1 John 1:8). John was not writing to the sinner but to the church. Paul did not specify what the sin was. Due to them abandoning the Holy Spirit and departing from God's sanctifying enabling grace it could have been the one of the acts of the sinful nature (5:19–21). Paul is more concerned about the manner in which sinners in the church are treated than he is the sin itself.

The word *fault* in verse 1 comes from the Greek word *paraptoma,* which means to fall beside, a false step, a blunder, or a failure to achieve.[1] Here sin is willfully stepping beyond the limits of the law. Transgressions are a willful step beyond the limits of the law—knowing where the boundaries are but still going beyond it. In Romans chapter 7 Paul shows his frustration of trying to measure up to the law of God in his own strength. In Romans chapter 6 and 8 he found the way of victory.

The church has been broken and torn by divisions. In this first verse of Galatians 6, the word *restore* means to repair, to restore to a former good condition, to equip. It is a verb that is a medical term, which would signify the resetting of a broken bone by a physician so that a broken member of the body can once again work properly and perform its vital function for the benefit of the whole body. Paul is giving a command for the restoration in the plural, which means He is addressing everyone.

We would expect a doctor to be gentle while setting a bone, how much more should we be gentle when we seek to restore a life that has been broken by sin. It can refer to a fisherman mending a net that has been torn (Matt. 4:21; Mark 1:19). It is also used as manning a fleet or supplying an army with provisions.[2] Spiritually, it means to perfect in spiritual maturity and to equip the saints for service (2 Cor. 13:11; Eph. 4:12; 1 Thess. 3:10; Heb. 13:21). Paul used the same verb to express his desire that the divided church in Corinth be perfectly united.

> Now I beseech you, brethren, by the name of our Lord Jesus Christ, that ye all speak the same thing, and that there be no divisions among you; but that ye be perfectly joined together in the same mind and in the same judgment.
>
> — CORINTHIANS 1:10

It takes a great deal of love and courage to approach a brother that has erred from the faith to seek to help him. Jesus compared it to eye surgery in Matthew 7:1–5. Jesus gave us instruction on reconciliation.

> Moreover if thy brother shall trespass against thee, go and tell him his fault between thee and him alone: if he shall hear thee, thou hast gained thy brother. But if he will not hear thee, then take with thee one or two more, that in the mouth of two or three witnesses every word may be established. And if he shall neglect to hear them, tell it unto the church: but if he neglect to hear the church, let him be unto thee as an heathen man and publican.
>
> —MATTHEW 18:15–17

Jesus said you were to go to him not for the sake of winning an argument, but to win your brother.

As long as any member of the body is broken by sin, the whole body suffers. If a broken member of the body gets amputated, the whole church will suffer loss. A ministry of restoration is needed for the recovery of the fallen who were ambushed by sin so that the community of the church can be healthy and productive in the cause of Christ in the earth. This is biblical spirituality.

Many times it is fatal in the life of the church for one of its own to fall into moral failure. In the Old Testament it took greater sacrifice to atone for sins of a leader than for the average lay person. The fall of a leader brought great shame on a nation, and it took great sacrifice to atone for that sin. One of the hardest people to restore is a fallen minister. At first it is everyone else's fault but his, and then he vents his bitterness on the one who is trying to restore him. Many times he weeps, not because he is ashamed of his sin, but because he was caught. The healing does not begin until he acknowledges that he has done wrong. What is important is how the church responds when such failure occurs.

In the Galatian churches, the Judaizers had no compassion for those who were taken captive by sin. Because of their desire to place the Gentiles under the law (4:21), they became like spiritual watchdogs who were ready to pounce on someone anytime they got out of line. Because they were anxious for praise and vain glory, this led to competition and division (5:26) along with their outburst of anger (5:20), They did not see these things as being as serious as a sin that they were busy condemning in the lives of others. When the church responds with harshness and comes across with a condemning attitude, many times it crushes the sinner, and many times it will divide the body. In our attempt to hit the nail on the head, we wind up bruising the wood. The occasion of sin is the opportunity of a Spirit-led people to display the fruit of the Spirit in order to bring healing to the sinner and to restore the unity within the life of the church.

Having a compassion for those who have erred is essential if we are going to be used by the Holy Spirit to bring healing. It is has been said that sin will take you further than you want to go, and cost you a price far greater than what you want to pay. Many feel that their relationship with God is a private affair, and what they do is no one else's business. Remember when Adam sinned, death passed on to all his descendants, for all had sinned. His first son, Cain, was the first murderer. Abel was the first martyr. Under Seth the fires of true worship began to burn again. When someone sins in the church, people get hurt because they become victims of that sin. Sin takes dominion, lordship, and control over them. Sinners themselves are sometimes victims of that sin. They have been overtaken, ambushed, and seized by sin.

Even so, too many in the life of the church today have a victim mentality. Paul is not excusing the sinner of personal responsibility. It must be understood that no one makes us sin. We sin because we want to. There is pleasure in sin, but it is only for a season. Jesus recognized the terrible force of sin: "Whosoever commiteth sin is a servant of sin" (John 8:34). He who practices a habitual lifestyle of sin is a servant of sin. Jesus knew that it was only the son that had the future in the Father's house not the slave. He knew the slave could be transferred out at any given time. Paul is saying that everyone who sins is trapped by that sin. They are moral offenders who are enslaved and entrapped. We are to have a compassionate attitude toward them.

The fallen brother is to be restored in "a spirit of meekness" (Gal. 6:1). What Paul is saying is that we are to restore one in a spirit of gentleness. A Spirit-filled believer approaches the matter in a spirit of meekness and love. The legalist approaches it in a manner of condemnation and pride. Gentleness is a fruit of the Spirit (5:23). Meekness is not weakness. It is strength under submission. It is strength under control. We are not to react in emotions of anger or in an arrogant spirit, as if this could have never happened to us. We are not to categorize sin as we often do. The only difference between us and the sinner is the grace of God. The Spirit-filled community is to see the person overtaken in a fault restored and on their way to recovery. This is going to quire us having our emotions under control of the Holy Spirit and our hearts filled and saturated with His love. With we are to love them all the way on their road to recovery.

The Spirit-filled community needs to help break the bondage of sin over their life. Where is the Spirit-filled church that carries an anointing to destroy every yoke of tyranny and oppression in the lives of men?

"Considering thyself, lest thou also be tempted" (Gal. 6:1). Paul offers a command for self-examination, in the singular, addressed to each individual. The legalist because of his self-righteousness pretends that he would never commit such a sin. Anyone who is dependent on the Holy Spirit and relies on God's sanctifying, enabling grace knows that no one is beyond the possibility of falling. "Let him that thinketh he standeth take heed lest he fall" (1 Cor. 10:12). When someone is truly walking in the Spirit, their walk will be characterized by a genuine spirit of humility that will enable them to recognize their own weakness as well as their dependency upon the Holy Spirit for victory. They will come to the understanding that if it had not been for the grace of God, it could have been them. If we as the church are going to be in the restoration business it will require the integrity of each member.

Paul is commanding them to watch their personal lives and take spiritual inventory of their walk before God. . There is not one of us that is immune to temptation. If we had fallen into open sin, how would we want to be treated when we came back into the church? Would we want someone to point the finger at us or seek through the love of God to restore us? This warning not only makes me guard myself against temptation but also enables me to respond with a spirit of meekness to someone ambushed by sin. It is not time to react with anger and self-righteousness toward a fellow believer who has been ensnared by sin. There must be a consciousness of our own weakness and a total dependency on the love of God being shed abroad in our hearts by the Holy Ghost, in order for us to respond in a correct manner toward those who have been taken captive by sin.

Jesus says that the church is going to have to emphasize three things if it is going to be effective:

- Prayer (Matt. 18:19–20)
- Forgiveness (Matt. 18:21–35)
- Spiritual discipline

A legalist has no interest in lost souls. He will always come across in a condemning and condescending manner. How many times have I heard it said, "I knew that they did not have what it took to hang in there." They never realized their role when it came to restoration. Instead of approaching their fallen brother, they share the sad news with others.

Paul is telling the Spirit-filled community that they have a responsibility that is corporate. "Bear ye one another's burdens" (Gal. 6:2). Paul was issuing a command that if we are going to fulfill the law of Christ we are going to have to carry each other's burdens. Where is the spirit of discernment in the life of the church that enables us to be able to detect when a brother or sister is under a heavy burden; when they seek to hide behind a smile; when their hearts are actually breaking? As a community of priests, we have the responsibility of bearing the burdens of a people before the presence of God. Paul seems to be recalling the onyx stones that were placed on the shoulders of the high priest, which contained the names of the twelve tribes of Israel. Bearing the burdens of a people is the work of a servant. Many of these burdens come in different categories and have a crushing effect (physical, emotional, financial, spiritual, mental, death of a loved one, or a family member that has recently gone through a divorce).

The legalist adds to the burdens of others and is never interested in bearing the burdens of their fellow man. This was the sin of the Pharisees in Jesus' day. "For they bind heavy burdens and grievous to be borne, and lay them on men's shoulders; but they themselves will not move them with one of their fingers" (Matt. 23:4). The legalist is always harder on other people than they are on themselves. The Spirit-filled Christian will demand more of himself than he does others.

A legalistic spirit will always be detected when someone has been taken captive by sin. The Pharisees dragged a woman who was found in the act of adultery (John 8), and the Jewish mob almost killed Paul because they thought he had defiled the temple by bringing in Gentiles (Acts 21:27). Legalists do not depend on facts; all they need is suspicions and rumors, and their imaginations will take them there. There is a big difference in how a legalistic mentality would deal with a brother who had erred with the way a Spirit-filled community would deal with a fallen brother.

When the church is filled with the Spirit they will realize in their attempt to restore a fallen comrade in the faith that it will require a love that will cover a multitude of sins. Legalists will find it easier to make an example out of their brother. Legalists will attempt to tear down their brother to make themselves look good. They thrive on competition and by comparing themselves to their fellow man in order to make themselves look good. They will actually rejoice when a brother falls—like the spirit of the elder brother who speaks loud about the sins of his brother while he ignores his own sin (Luke 15:28–30). That is why the publican went home more justified than the Pharisee (18:9–14).

Paul said, "Let us not be desirous of vain glory, provoking one another, envying one another" (Gal. 5:26). The word *provoke* means "to challenge to a contest or to combat, to call forth, to compete one with another."[3] The believer who has captured the walk of the Spirit-filled man or woman has no desire to sit around and compare himself with other Christians. While the Spirit-filled community in a spirit of meekness will approach an erring brother, the legalist takes an attitude of pride and condemnation. When Jesus sought to be a physician to sinners, He was severely criticized by the Pharisees

(Mark 2:13–17). The Spirit-filled community even today will be criticized by those who have legalistic mindsets. If your church grows, it is because you are liberal. We have never learned the lesson that Peter learned on the rooftop of Simon the Tanner's house: "What God has cleansed you don't call common or unclean" (Acts 10:15).

If we are going to compare ourselves with anyone, let's compare ourselves with Christ. The Judaizers were busy bragging on themselves and their achievements. They bragged many times about their converts (Gal. 6:12–14). Many times their comparisons made them look better than what they really were. It is easy to look around the church and find someone that is less fortunate than we are. When the Spirit-filled community is filled with the love of God for their fellow man, they will not expose one another's failures or weakness in order to make themselves look good.

By carrying the burdens of our fallen brothers and sisters, we "fulfil the law of Christ" (v. 2). There is a difference in fulfilling the law of Christ and keeping the Law of Moses. The keeping of the Law of Moses was by the Judaizers and all who followed their message. By them observing the Mosaic Law, it separated God's people (Jewish nation from Gentile sinners). Circumcision, purity and dietary laws, and Sabbath and feast regulations were boundary markers that were established by the law to preserve the identity of the Jewish people. By doing so they were fulfilling the purpose of the Law of Moses. If they lived observed these traditions, they would enjoy the blessings of God; anyone living outside these boundaries were believed by the Jews to be under a curse. The law taught that Gentiles had to conform to Judaism to be a part of the people of God. Because of the Jews' zeal for the Law of Moses they took on a spirit of intolerance toward those who did not wish to conform to Judaism.

By Paul being zealous for the traditions of his fathers it shows us how destructive a zeal for the law could become (1:13–14). Through his conflict with false brethren in Jerusalem (2:4–5) and with Peter in Antioch (2:11), it becomes easy to see how one having a zeal for the law could divide the church especially when you start referring to Gentiles who have been saved by grace through faith as sinners. It was the law that excluded them from the people of God by the Judaizers' influencing believers to bite, devour, provoke, and envy each other. Even though they were attempting to keep the Mosaic Law, they were not fulfilling the law of Christ to love their neighbor as yourself (Matt. 19:19).

The church fulfills the law of Christ when we bear the burdens of men and women who have fallen prey to sin. It is the love of Christ that is produced in the heart and life of a believer by the Spirit. Christ manifested His love for the lost when He died, was buried, and resurrected. It was the greatest demonstration of love. Paul said the only thing that counts is "faith which worketh by love" (Gal. 5:6). The call is not to drive sinners from the church, but to serve those who have fallen prey to sin. By serving one another in love and by carrying each other's burdens, there is a service that is performed. It is in this that the entire law is summed up. This was revealed in the death and resurrection of Christ. Christ loves sinners and gave Himself for us (Gal. 2:20). On the cross He bore the curse of the law on our behalf (3:13). Christ set us free from the yoke of slavery under the law (5:1).

There were three kinds of people that the law said to put outside of the camp: 1) lepers (Num. 5:2), 2) those who came in contact with the dead (Num. 15:35); 3) those who had issues (Lev. 15:25–30). It is amazing to me that the very people that the law said to put out of the camp, Jesus came and restored back to community life. He cleansed the lepers. He raised the dead. He healed those who had issues. Why are we so quick to drive men away instead of seeking to restore them?

If we are indwelt with the Spirit of Christ, we will fulfill the law of Christ and reflect the love of God that was established through His life, death, and resurrection. Like Christ who bore our griefs (sicknesses and diseases) and carried all of our sorrows (pains) (Isaiah 53:4), as we serve one another in love we will also fulfill the law of Christ. Many feel that because we are not under the law, but under grace, rules and regulations do not apply. Paul, in his writings to the church at Rome, made it clear "that the righteousness of the law might be fulfilled in us, as we walk not after the flesh, but after the Spirit" (Rom. 8:4). Now that we are born again, rules are a part of our nature.

Many have never understood that it still takes the righteousness and holiness under Moses combined with the worship of God under David to produce the glory in Solomon's temple. Many have a passion for sanctification and holiness but they do not have passion for worship. Some have a passion for worship but not a passion for righteousness and holiness. It takes both to ride the train. You cannot have war in your house and have worship. There was not one iron tool used on Solomon's temple. Iron was symbolic of war. It is the Holy Spirit that takes the righteousness of the law and fulfills it in us. As we love our neighbor as ourselves, not only are we being Christ like but the love of God that is in our hearts that has been prompted by the Holy Ghost is fulfilling the law of Christ.

Paul said, "Let every man prove his own work, and then shall he have rejoicing in himself alone, and not in another" (Gal. 6:4). The word that Paul uses for *test* means "to examine for the purpose of determining its worth." As a jeweler examines a precious stone under a magnifying glass under a bright light to determine its worth, so each Christian should put himself to the same test under the search light of the Word of God to determine his true worth before God. Because people are so prone to being deceived, we are to do spiritual inventory on ourselves to evaluate whether our faith in Christ is being expressed in Christ's actions and love. We must make a careful examination of our own work. We are not to compare ourselves with others (v. 4). There is no place for competition within the body today.

How many are entering into a state of depression because they have looked in the focus papers from the state office in order to compare themselves with others. We should "rejoice with them that do rejoice, and weep with them that weep" (Rom. 12:15). If one member is blessed, the whole body gets blessed. The legalist lives by competition and comparison, and tries to make himself look good by making a fellow brother look bad. Through this evaluation our God-given mission in life should come into focus.

Paul said it is then that we should have rejoicing in ourselves and not in another (Gal. 6:4). It is then that we can take pride in our own work without comparing ourselves with others. It is then that we will have a reason to boast in ourselves and in the Lord for His goodness to us and feel no need to compare ourselves with others.

There are two kinds of boastings: 1) Verse 13 of chapter 6 tells us that the Judaizers "want you to be circumcised that they may boast about your flesh" (NIV). The Jews were the circumcised faithful people of God. Because the Gentiles were uncircumcised they were despised and shut out. Comparisons when it comes to national identity and religious practices that had nothing to do with right standing before God. "For in Christ Jesus neither circumcision nor uncircumcision has any value" (5:6, NIV). After his conversion Paul did not boast of being a member of Jewish nation, bearing Jewish identity, or in his zeal to devote himself to Jewish traditions. He counted them as loss that he may win Christ. The boasting of the Christian community is not an issue of the flesh, "that they may glory in your flesh" (6:13), when it comes to racial superiority and religious practices. Our boast is in the Lord.

2) Paul boasted in the cross of Christ. "God forbid that I should glory, save in the cross of our Lord Jesus Christ, by whom the world is crucified unto me, and I unto the world" (v. 14). The cross stands as a fence between the believer and the world. Through the cross I am alienated from all my former habits and feelings. "Lord, hide me behind the cross." How can we embrace the cross without dying to sin? The cross was God's ultimate display of His love for sinners. When we are identified with the death, burial, and resurrection of Christ, it is then that the love of God for sinners can be revealed in and through us by the power of the Holy Spirit.

For Paul to make his boast may be considered to be foolish by the standards of the world. To the Jew it was weakness (1 Cor. 1:25), "for the Jews require a sign" (v. 22). For their Messiah to come and die on a cross was a weakness to the Jews. They were looking for a military leader to come to deliver them from the bondage and tyranny of Rome, but Jesus came to deliver from the lordship, control, and dominion of sin. So Jesus did not fit their image of a Messiah.

"The Greeks seek after wisdom" (v. 22). They sought for a world filled with beauty, intellectualism, and harmony. The cross with all its bloodshed had no place in their endless discussions. I am still amazed at the professing Christians who still don't want to talk about the cross.

Paul said:

> But we preach Christ crucified, unto the Jews a stumbling block, and unto the Greeks foolishness; But unto them which are called, both Jews and Greeks, Christ is the power of God, and the wisdom of God. Because the foolishness of God is wiser than men; and the weakness of God is stronger than men.
>
> —1 CORINTHIANS 1:23–25

For Christians to bear one another's burdens in Christian service may seem shameful to the world. But, when the love of Christ that was demonstrated at Calvary is seen in the actions of Christians, there is a reason to boast. Because the power of Spirit makes real what happened to Jesus at the cross, it should be an occasion for Christians to love God and serve their fellow man.

"Every man shall bear his own burden" (Gal. 6:5). The word *bear* comes from the Greek word *phortion*, which speaks of a soldier's pack. It speaks of the work given to us by our Master, before whom we will give an account at the Day of Judgment of how we used the opportunities and talents He gave us to serve Him. No one else can bear this burden for us. It is a task for which we are personally responsible. Each of us has been called by God to carry our own load. The word *bear* in verse 2 came from *baros*, expressing the need to come to the aid of others who cannot carry the crushing burden of the consequences of their sin. As we learn how to bear one another's burdens in this way, we began to fulfill our mission in this life.

Paul is addressing the need to support those who are fulfilling their ministry by teaching the Word of God. "Let him that taught in the word communicate unto him that teacheth in all good things" (v. 6). The word *goodness* is a fruit of the Spirit. When the Spirit-filled community is empowered by the Spirit they will share good things with those who teach them.

The word *teacheth* comes from the Greek word *catechist* meaning instructor. The word *catechumen* refers to those who receive instruction. The Church of Galatia was receiving biblical instruction from those who had the ability to teach. Christian growth is dependent on sound biblical teaching. Paul saw the need for this and encouraged it. There is a real need in the church today for men and women to have a teachable spirit.

Being a teacher in the church was a full-time occupation. Paul believed that teachers in the church should work hard at their job of imparting Christian knowledge and should get paid well for it (1 Cor. 9:14; 1 Tim. 5:17). "Even the Ox remains unmuzzled while they tread out the corn" (1 Cor. 9:9). Many have tried to make pastors and teachers feel inferior and say they don't have a real job. Paul placed great value on teaching the Word, which is necessary to produce strong and healthy churches and Christians. Today we have faulty conversions because we have a faulty gospel.

Paul felt that because these teachers have sowed into us, we need to sow back into them. When we do, there is unity in the church. The phrase "must share" (Gal.6:6, NIV) comes from the Greek word *koinonia*, meaning fellowship, partnership, joint participation. Do we consider ourselves to be a partner with someone who his sowing the precious seed of the Word of God into the lives of men and women? Paul was encouraging partnership with the Word. As a teacher gives out the treasure of what God has deposited into him, we must give out of our material treasures to the one that has made a deposit into us. Why should the Christian teacher make a deposit if he cannot make a withdrawal?

If a church is going to be strong and unified in the faith, then they are going to have to give the teaching ministry of the Word of God its rightful place. We are going to have to have men and women who know how to rightfully divide the Word. Because of their efforts to teach the Word, they need to receive enthusiastic and generous support. Because Paul did not want to become a stumbling block to the unsaved, he worked as a tentmaker (Acts 18:3), but he repeatedly taught that spiritual leaders in the church were to be supported by the gifts of the people.

The Book of Proverbs tells us "buy the truth, and sell it not" (Proverbs 23:23). What kind of value do we place on sitting under the Word of God? If we place value on it then we need to purchase it when it is made available to us. If you have the privilege of sitting under this glorious gospel, you need to value it. If you value it and see it's worth then you want mind purchasing it. When it comes to the truth, there is a cost to sitting under it's contents. The enlightenment that we receive is priceless.

By you sowing seeds and sharing with the one that has taught you the Word of God you are sowing into the Spirit and will reap a reward that will come back to you many times over in the form of many types of different blessings.

Paul has contrasted two ways of life: life in the Spirit and life according to the flesh. Now is the time for a decision. We cannot remain neutral. We are going to have to decide whether or not we are going to walk in the Spirit or gratify the desires of the sin nature. We are going to have to deal with the consequences of our decisions.

When Paul says, "Be not deceived; God is not mocked" (Gal. 6:7), he gives us an agricultural metaphor while issuing to us a warning. Many feel that they will not have to reap what they have sown. They want a righteous harvest without sowing righteous seed. Many feel they can sow whatever kind of seed they want and still expect a good harvest. When we feel that we will reap something different than what we have sown, we are deceiving ourselves and trying to make a fool out of God. No one can mock God and get away with it.

Paul says, "The one who sows to please his sinful nature, from that nature will reap destruction; the one who sows to please the Spirit, from the Spirit will reap eternal life (v. 8, NIV). We are faced with a decision that determines our destiny. Our destiny is determined by our decision to sow to the Spirit or sow to the sin nature. Paul looks on our material possessions as seed. He sees two kinds of soil: the flesh and the Spirit. Once we have sown, we cannot change our harvest.

Money that is sown to the Spirit will produce life, and in that harvest those seeds can be planted again for another harvest. We need to understand that everything we do is either an investment to the flesh or to the Spirit. We will reap in proportion to what we have sown. "He which soweth sparingly shall reap also sparingly; and he which soweth bountifully shall reap also bountifully" (2 Cor. 9:6). If we walk in the Spirit and sow into the Spirit, we will reap a spiritual harvest. If the sowing has been generous, the harvest will be bountiful. The old proverb is true: Sow a thought and you reap an act; sow an act and you reap a habit; sow a habit and you reap a character; sow a character and you reap a destiny.[4]

The Judaizers did not have this attitude toward giving and receiving. Paul sacrificed and labored that he might not become burdensome to the churches. The false teachers used the churches to promote their own schemes and fill their own coffers. This happened in the church at Corinth (2 Cor. 11:20).

One who sows to the flesh (sin nature) will destroy relationships by back biting, devouring, provoking, envying others (5:15, 26). Sowing into the sin nature will always produce a harvest of destruction. The battle between the flesh and the Spirit will go on until the day God calls us home. Those who continue to grow spiritually in these relationships through the power of the Spirit will experience the fullness of eternal life.

Sowing into the Spirit involves:

- Restoring those who are ensnared in sin (6:1)
- Bearing one another's burdens (6:2)
- Give back to those who have deposited into us (6:6)
- Doing good to all (6:9)
- Building strong lasting relationships with fellow believers that enrich but do not enslave.

We will not be able to fulfill the law of Christ unless we take an active participating role in the pain and suffering of our generation. It means that we must become unselfish in our service. We must realize that we do not grow in isolation and alienation but only in the context of relationships. To come into church late and leave early just to avoid contact with one another is not the way to go.

Growth in our relationships will require efforts on our art. Broken relationships will not healed without hard work and strenuous efforts. Paul encouraged the Galatian believers to keep on working at building their relationships, when he said, "Let us not be weary in well doing" (v. 9). One of the greatest obstacles in rebuilding relationships is that it is easy to lose heart and become fatigued. We hear in the apostle Paul this same fatigue when he said, "I am afraid of you, lest I have bestowed upon you labour in vain." (4:11).

Paul was aware that fatigue and discouragement can cause us to give up when we grow weary serving others in love. "In due season we shall reap, if we faint not" (6:9). When we sow acts of love, we reap a harvest of love in return. When we give generously and sacrificially to the needs of others, we reap a harvest of gratitude. When we sow God's Word into the lives of people, we reap a response. We must never give up, because our Lord will return and reward those who have been faithful in His service.

Paul is calling upon the church to persevere in the service of the Lord as he reminds us that we are a part of the family of God. It should motivate us to do good to our brothers and sisters in Christ. "As we have therefore opportunity, let us do good to all men, especially unto them who are of the household of faith" (v. 10). The priority of the church is to serve the family of God. This has been a central theme in Paul's letter to the Galatians:

All believers are the spiritual children of Abraham by faith in Christ (3:6–29).

All believers are entitled to equal rights and privileges (4:4–7).

All believers are children of the free woman; the heavenly Jerusalem is our mother (4:21–31).

Chapter 23

God Is Not Mocked

Be not deceived; God is not mocked: for whatsoever a man
soweth, that shall he also reap. For he that soweth to his
flesh shall of his flesh reap corruption; but he that soweth
to the Spirit shall of the Spirit reap life everlasting.

—GALATIANS 6:7–8

IN VERSE SIX, Paul exhorts the Galatians to continue in fellowship with the teacher who taught them about salvation by grace through faith. The Galatian believers had turned to the Judaizers and their teachings, having deserted the grace of God for the fleshly efforts of law observance. By doing so they were depriving themselves of the ministry of the Holy Spirit. Now Paul is exhorting them to get up under the ministry of teachers who led them into grace, and if they failed to do so they would reap a harvest of corruption.

John addressed this in his second Epistle when he said, "If there come any unto you, and bring not this doctrine, receive not into your house, neither bid him God speed: For he that biddeth him God speed is a partaker of his evil deeds" (2 John 1:10–11). So the believer is not to give encouragement or financial support or remain under the ministry of such teachers. For them to do this is to come into opposition to God and His Word and under the same condemnation as these false teachers.

A believer's love and loyalty to Christ and the Word of God must lead him to reject and count as an enemy of the Gospel of Christ anyone who is not committed to the doctrine of Christ and that of the apostles. If we have it wrong about Christ, we have it wrong about God.

All false religions are an appeal to the fallen nature of man. While they seek to attempt to satisfy a man's desire for worship, there seems to be a tolerance for allowing them to continue in sin. The Judaizers catered to the fallen condition of the Galatians. They made no demand for regeneration, which was the recreation of the new nature, nor did they demand faith in the atoning sacrifice that paid for sin. Their teaching stressed salvation by works, which glorified man not God, allowing man to go on in his sin. They attempted to seek the favor of God by their good works and deeds. There are many that desire to go to churches that make them feel comfortable in their sin instead of them forsaking their sin.

This only led to corruption in their lives. In chapter five of Galatians, we see the corruption had already started. The Galatians were already being led astray by the Judaizers. He reminded them that they were not going to make a fool out of God; it led to a disaster in their lives and it brought about chastening from the hand of God. There is a saying that he who furnishes the seed is responsible for what grows.

When Paul said, "Be not deceived" (Gal. 6:7), he used the present passive imperative. He was issuing a command. Paul was giving a prohibition which forbade the continuance of an action going on.[1] Paul was them to top being led astray! The Galatians, like many of us today, had the attitude that it is not important what teachers we listen to. They were deceiving themselves.

"God is not mocked" (v. 7). Paul used the word *mukterizo*, which means to turn the nose up, to ridicule, ignore, and sneer. It was an expression of contempt[2] toward God and is never without punishment. God is not going to be fooled. It is vain to think we can outwit God by reaping a harvest that is different from what we have sown. Spiritual insanity is doing the same thing over and over again, expecting different results. If we want to go somewhere we have never been, we are going to have to do something we have never done. If we keep doing what we have always done, we will continue to get the same results we have always gotten.

"Whatsoever a man soweth" (v. 7) implies the metaphor of the grain harvest that was used by the Lord in many of the parables. We can sow our wild oats if we want to but we may not realize that we have set some things in motion in the realm of the spirit that will soon manifest in the natural. God can and does forgive sin, but not even He can wipe out the consequence of sin. If you sin against your body, sooner or later your health will fail. Origen believed that all though men would be saved, the marks of sin would remain. Solomon believed that no man can cast his bread upon the waters without it returning home to him some day (Eccles. 11:1).

Make no mistake about it, you cannot turn your nose up at God. A man will reap exactly what he sows. If he sows to his own nature as it bids him, he will reap a harvest of trouble that he is not ready to deal with.

Those who claim to be born-again followers of Christ and possess the Holy Spirit, while at the same time consciously sowing to the flesh, are guilty of mocking and despising God. Paul was telling them to let there be no deception; such persons would not reap everlasting life but corruption (v. 8) and eternal death. God has told us to be careful how we sow and where we sow. The basic principle of sowing and reaping is found throughout the Bible. God has ordered that we reap what we sow.

God looks upon material possessions as seeds. He sees two kinds of soil: the flesh and the Spirit. All that we do is invested in the flesh or in the Spirit. Once we have finished sowing we cannot change our harvest. We will reap whatever we have sown, and we shall reap in proportion to what we have sown. Paul said to the church at Corinth, "Whoever sows sparingly will also reap sparingly, and whoever sows generously will also reap generously" (2 Cor. 9:6, NIV).

"He that soweth to his flesh shall of the flesh reap corruption" (Gal. 6:8). He has chosen a course of conduct that will gratify the cravings of his depraved nature. Paul is speaking of the physical and moral decay of rottenness that follows the sins of the flesh. Human nature writes in our bodies the penalty of sin. If a man allows the lower side of his nature to dominate him, in the end he can expect a harvest of trouble.

Paul said, "He that soweth to the Spirit shall of the Spirit reap life everlasting" (v. 8). When you share money with those who preach the Word, that is money that is sown in the Spirit. If a minister is sharing eternal truths, we can share with him the material things that we possess. This will produce life. There will be seeds in that harvest that can be planted again into another harvest. God gives seed to the sower (2 Cor. 9:10). If believers plant it properly, there would be no lack in the work of the Lord. Much of our seed is wasted on carnal things that never will bring glory to God.

The only influence we have over our future is the seeds that we have sown today. We cannot go where we have not sown. If we want a righteous harvest we need to sow some righteous seed. If we don't like our harvest, the only person we need to be mad at is ourselves; after all we are the ones who sowed it.

A believer who walks in the Spirit and sows in the Spirit is going to reap a spiritual harvest. If his sowing has been generous, the harvest will be bountiful. If a believer chooses a course of conduct that pleases the Holy Spirit, he will reap the blessing of eternal life. So we should never lose heart and give up doing what is good. We should not give up because of weariness. Eternal life is knowing God for ourselves. It is the life of God within our spirit man.

Chapter 24

Perversions of the Serpent

*As ye have therefore received Christ Jesus the Lord, so walk in him:
Rooted and built up in him, and established in the faith, as ye have
been taught, abounding therein with thanksgiving. Beware lest any
man spoil you through philosophy and vain deceit, after the tradition
of men, after the rudiments of the world, and not after Christ. For
in him dwelleth all the fulness of the Godhead bodily. And ye are
complete in him, which is the head of all principality and power.*

—COLOSSIANS 2:6–10

THE BOOK OF Ephesians deals with the church of Christ and the exalted position of the body of Christ. The Book of Colossians deals with the Christ of the church and the exalted position of the Head. In all things Christ must have the pre-eminence. The Christian life should reflect that priority. Colossians is the most Christ-centered Book of the whole Bible. In Colossians there are two major topics: The supremacy of Christ (chapters 1–2) and submission to Christ (chapter 3–4).[1]

In the Book of Colossians the believer is portrayed as being rooted, grounded, settled, established, alive, hidden, and complete in Christ. The believer is prepared to make Christ first and foremost in every area of his life. The believer is spoken of as being clothed in God's love with the peace of God ruling in his heart and equipped to make Him first. In this Epistle provision has been made for the believer to live a life of power in Jesus Christ.[2]

In "as ye have received Christ Jesus the Lord" (Col. 2:6), the word *received* is translated from the second aorist, active indicative of *paralambono*. Here Paul uses a compound word: *para* means beside, to take to one side and *lambano* means to appropriate to one's self. This word speaks of the decisive character of that reception.[3] Their faith had laid hold of the person of Christ and His fullness. Here Paul is speaking of the doctrines regarding the person and work of the Lord Jesus Christ. [4]

William Barclay, in his book on "Letters to the Philippians, Colossians and Thessalonians" deals with marks of the faithful church.[5]

The true church must have the power to resist seductive teaching. It must reach a level of maturity whereby men cannot beguile it with enticing words. The phrase "enticing words" came from the court of law. It spoke of the persuasive power of a lawyer's arguments that would enable a criminal to escape his just punishment. The true church must have a grip on the truth so that it is unmoved by seductive arguments.

A true church must have a soldier's discipline. Paul spoke of the order and the firmness of the faith of the Colossians. These words are military terms. The word *order* comes from the Greek *taxis*, which speak of rank or ordered arrangement. The church should be like an ordered army, with every man in his appointed place. They are to be ready and willing to obey the word of command.

The word *firmness* comes from the word *stereomai*, solid bulwark. It speaks of an army that is not able to be broken up. They are solidly immovable against the shock of the enemies charge.

The true church's life must be in Christ. Its members must walk in Christ. Their whole lives must be lived in His presence.

A true church will hold fast to their faith which they have received. It never forgets the teaching about Christ that it has been taught.

A true church is abounding and overflowing with gratitude.

In Colossians there were two forms of gnostic teaching that were confronting the church. The doctrines of Christ's person and work were being perverted by the Judaizers (false teachers): doceticism—Christ only seemed to have a body; and cerinthianism—Christ came on Jesus at His baptism and departed from Him while He was on the cross. This made Christ and Jesus two different individuals. Paul moves quickly from the metaphor of a growing plant and building under construction to give an illustration of a growing Christian life.

"So walk ye in him" (v. 6). The same way you received Him was the same manner they were to order their behavior. Paul was saying, "You were taught right, now go on walking in Him. Walk in dependence upon Him."[6] Stick to your first lessons in Christ. The way they accepted the gospel was to be a pattern of continual faithfulness. The Colossians were to keep the doctrines pertaining to Him which they learned when they were first instructed by Paul.

Christ was the sphere of spiritual growth and development and the believers were to go on walking in Him. When men looked at Christ, they saw in Him a

Savior. He came from heaven to earth to show us how the Christian life could be lived, so that one day we could go from earth to heaven. Paul said He was "Made in the likeness of men: and being found in fashion as a man, he humbled himself, and became obedient unto death, even the death of the cross" (Phil. 2:7–8). Jesus stooped to our level by becoming man and bearing our guilt and sin. Through faith we can now acknowledge Him to be Lord and Savior.

Paul goes from the metaphor of walking to that of growing a tree (v. 7). It was Paul's desire that the Colossians get rooted in Christ. The word *rooted* is a perfect participle of the Greek word *rizo*, which expressed abiding results.[7] The more original rendering might be: having been rooted with the present results that you are firmly anchored. Paul is saying, get rooted and stay rooted. It is an action that took place in the past with its effects persisting in the present.[8] It speaks of a tree whose roots are deep in the soil.

We need to remember that the life of a tree comes from its root system. We need to make sure that our roots are planted deeply in the soil of Jesus Christ, wrapped around the Rock of Ages. Christ is the very life of the plant. We are living in such a transient society. How many times can we dig up a tree and plant it somewhere else without killing it altogether? If you destroy a tree's root system you kill the tree. We need to remember that if there are no roots there are no fruits.

Then Paul turns to the metaphor of building a building and the steady growth of the structure (v. 7). Jesus is the binding force of the building. Paul uses the phrase "built up," which is a present participle emphasizing continuous action being constantly built up.[9] Christ is the sphere in which the building is going on. It speaks of a house that is erected on a firm foundation. The whole construction of the church comes from Christ's personality, life, and power. Paul is emphasizing the steady growth of the structure. In the change of metaphors that Paul is using, we find that Christ is the inspiration of the walk, life of the plant, and the binding force of the structure. It is an organic union with Christ.

Then Paul emphasizes the need for them to be "stablished in the faith" (v. 7). The word *stablished* is a present participle from the word *bebaio*, meaning to make firm, stable, constantly being strengthened and established.[10] It is one thing to be in the church but another thing to be established in the faith. The hardest thing there is to do when it comes to the convert is to get him established. The Open Bible records "in chapters 1–2 Paul lays down doctrinal truth. In chapters 3–4 truth bears fruit in our everyday conduct and lifestyle.

Not only are they to increase in their knowledge of the faith, but they are to experience the power of it in their lifestyle."[11]

"Abounding therein with thanksgiving" (v. 7). The word *abounding* comes from the Greek word *perrisseuo*, having abundance to that of excellence.[12] We need to realize that our ability to give thanks is the true barometer of spirituality in the Christian's life. The more spiritual we become, the more we will abound with thanksgiving. A spirit of being unthankful always leads to a spirit of unholiness. Thankfulness will direct our thoughts toward God, from whom all growth has been made possible; therefore, praise and glory belong to Him.

Paul warned us of being cheated through philosophy and principles of the world "Beware lest any man spoil you through philosophy and vain deceit" (v. 8). When Paul used the word *beware*, it was the Greek word *blepete*, which means to watch out, be on your guard, or look out![13] Right from the start Paul hit them hard and strong. The warning is introduced by a call to vigilance. The present tense suggests a constant watchfulness on their part. Paul is not warning them of the possibility of but actually warning them of impending danger. He wanted them to be aware of the spiritual hazardous condition that was growing right inside the church. False prophets and false teachers were making inroads to this church at an alarming rate of speed. Spiritual deception had become so bad that they had actually begun to worship angels.

Paul had already spoken of a mighty deliverance which had come to them through the gospel (1:12–13). For them to revert back to a man-made religious system after knowing the liberating power of Christ would be nothing else but a return to bondage.

The word *spoil* comes from the Greek word *sulogogeo*, where Paul describes the violent behavior of a hostile army invading an innocent and unsuspecting land. When the enemy takes over a geographical area, they immediately rape women, kill children, burn down homes, rob people of their possessions and destroy everything in their path as they march along.[14] They take delight in capturing the young and make them their own personal slaves in a foreign country.

We are to beware of anyone who would carry us off as his spoil. The word that is used in the original speaks of a slave dealer carrying away the people of a conquered nation into slavery. Paul had already told the Colossians that they had been liberated (v. 12–14). Now he finds the Colossians submitting to a new and disastrous slavery.

Paul is telling them to slap the saints awake out of their spiritual stupor.

They need to realize that evil is lurking in their midst. If they don't deal with the problem bravely, they will soon become ravaged.

The Colossian church was an innocent church and was genuinely spiritually hungry. But the church was in great danger of being exploited, abused, and scandalized by false prophets and false teachers who wanted to plunder the saints for their own personal gain.

The word *philosophy* (v. 8) comes from the word *philosophia* which is a compound word. *Philos* is where we get the word *love* and *sophia* is where we get the word *wisdom* from. When these two words are combined it means the love of wisdom.[15] Gnostics were in the habit of claiming that their teachings were things that Jesus never told the crowds. They were only communicated to a chosen few. Just as the serpent tempted Eve with the fruit of the tree, they were telling the saints that these vain philosophies would make them wise (Gen. 3:6). These men offered a philosophy which they declared was necessary in addition to the teachings of Christ.

Then Paul spoke of "vain deceit" (v. 8). The word *vain* is used eighteen different times in the New Testament. It always stands for something empty, hollow, or wasted. The word *deceit* comes from the Greek word *apate*, and it refers to delusion or a hallucination.[16] What these false teachers have labeled as wisdom, Paul calls empty, hallow, wasted, delusions, and nightmares. The false prophets and false teachers were nothing more than spiritual hallucinators, who were dreaming up stories and feeding delusions to the church in the name of a new, God-given revelation.

Paul warned us to be on our guard against all philosophies, traditions, and religions that emphasize man functioning independently from God and His written revelation. Today one of the greatest philosophical threats is secular humanism. It teaches that man has not been created by God but has evolved through evolution. It rejects the belief in a personal, infinite God and denies that the Bible is God's inspired revelation to man. Biblical values and morality are rejected. The philosophies of humanism began with Satan's lie to Eve in the Garden that man can become as God (Gen. 3:5). The scripture identifies the humanist as those "who changed the truth of God into a lie, and worshipped and served the creature more than the Creator" (Rom. 1:25).

Barclay states that the false teachers wished the Colossians to accept additions to Christ. They were teaching that Jesus Himself was not sufficient, that He was not unique. He was one among many of the manifestations of God.

They taught that it was necessary to know and to serve other divine powers in addition to Him.[17]

Paul deals with the dangers and perversions of the serpent in the second chapter of Colossians:

Enticing words (Col. 2:4) are theories that spring from faulty reasoning and persuasive arguments—speech that is adapted to persuade. It is discourse that leads others into error. These are words that are full of trickery, and because men are gullible they are easily caught by their tactics. Remember the Judaizers were great persuaders.

Philosophies of men (v. 8) are empty because they are void of real truth. The simple trust preached about Jesus that was preserved in the gospel is not enough.

Traditions of men (v. 8) are handed down from generation to generation. There are some things in the local church that are more powerful to our people than the Word of God, and that is tradition. Remember the Rabbis of Jesus' day exalted traditions of men above Scripture.

Legalism (vv. 16–17) is when righteousness is based on any other thing than the shed blood of our Lord Jesus Christ.

Mysticism (v. 18) was embraced when Gentile converts embraced Judaism and became circumcised. It was believed to have triggered the activity of the powers and authorities in the heavenlies. Gnostics prided themselves on special visions of secret things which were not open to the eyes and ears of ordinary people. The danger seems to be that men often will not see what God sends to them, but only what they want to see. It opened up a mystical passage into a covenant community. When they died with Christ at Calvary, they were delivered from the control of spiritual powers of evil.

The mystics taught that the stars and planets were elements of this world. False teachers taught that they were still under their influences and needed special knowledge, beyond what Jesus could give to be liberated.

Idolatry (v. 18) was angelic worship. It represented a heresy that taught that God's rule over the church was mediated by angelic agents. They were teaching that Jesus was only one of the many mediators between God and man and that angels must receive worship. Don't worship angels; worship the One who made the angels. The false teachers substituted angelic mediators for the divine Head Himself.

Asceticism (vv. 20, 21) is relying on rituals and ascetic observances for a foundation of moral teaching. The false teachers wished to introduce all kinds of rules and regulations about what men and women could eat and drink or what days they must observe (festivals and fasts). Christian freedom comes from the death of evil desires and the springing to life of the good desires by virtue of Christ being in the Christian and the Christian in Christ.

The goal of the perversions of the serpent was to devalue the person of Christ. There is a strong form of legalism going through the church world today. It states that Jesus Christ's victory over Satan at the cross and the blood that was shed to defeat sin was not enough to purchase our freedom. It teaches that we have to do additional things to gain freedom from the grip of Satan. This is blatant legalism. The teaching implies that the cross is no longer necessary. The shed blood of Christ has no place in their discussions.

I believe though many profess that they have been to Calvary, that they do not know Calvary. Through pluralism we are being told that Jesus Christ is not the only way to the Father. I believe that through the cross the wisdom of men was brought to naught. Jesus' sacrifice on the cross did what no other power was able to do. It also accomplished what the wisdom of men was not able to accomplish. I believe at the cross every sin was defeated and every chain and fetter was snapped asunder. He did not save us from some sins but *all* sin. We need to come to terms with what Jesus accomplished for us at the cross. To those who are perishing the preaching of the cross is foolishness. To those of us who are saved it is the power of God (1 Cor. 1:18). The power of the cross is still transforming lives today. Thank God, Calvary is still enough to change a Saul of Tarsus to Paul the Apostle!

There are four steps to counteract this heresy.

1. Know who Jesus is (Col. 2:3, 9).

When Jesus was at Caesarea, Philippi, He asked His disciples, "Whom do men say that I the Son of Man am? And they said, some say that thou art John the Baptist: some, Elias; and others, Jeremias, or one of the prophets. He saith unto them, But whom say ye that I am?" (Matt. 16:13–15). This is no time to be going on what others have said. We don't need to rely on second hand information.

"And Simon Peter answered and said, Thou art the Christ, the Son of the living God" (v. 16). For three years Peter had walked, talked, ministered, and ate with Jesus. About that time the Holy Spirit pulled back the veil and said,

"Peter, take a good look." Peter stepped forward to make a definite declaration that Jesus was the Christ.

Know that in Him "are hid all the treasures of wisdom and knowledge" (v. 3). Know that in Him "dwelleth all the fulness of the Godhead bodily" (v. 9).

2. Know what He has done for you (Col. 2:13, 15).

"And you, being dead in your sins and the uncircumcision of your flesh, hath he quickened together with him, having forgiven you all trespasses" (v. 13).

We were dead in our trespasses, unregenerate, uncircumcised, and unforgiven. We have no more power than a dead man has to overcome sin or to atone for it. Christ has done all that can be done and all that needs to be done.

"And having spoiled principalities and powers, he made a shew of them openly, triumphing over them in it" (v. 15).

3. Know who you are (Col. 2:10, 12).

"And ye are complete in him, which is the head of all principality and power" (v. 10). You are "buried with him in baptism, wherein also ye are risen with him through the faith of the operation of God, who hath raised him from the dead" (v. 12).

4. Know what you are to be doing for Him and get with it (2:6–7).

"So walk in him. Rooted and built up in him, and established in the faith, as ye have been taught, abounding therein with thanksgiving" (vv. 6–7).

Worship is due to Christ and Christ alone. If Christian worship and witness is based on anyone else or anything other than Christ, then we will fail to produce a congregation that participates with Christ in God's salvation. (It can't be based on church membership, water baptism, or the rituals of church). Only the finished work of Christ at Calvary can take the sinner to heaven. Anything less demotes the work of Christ and its results. The only condition for Gentile membership, when it comes to being the new Israel of God, is faith in Christ.

Peter made the statement concerning Jesus: "Neither is there salvation in any other: for there is none other name under heaven given among men, whereby we must be saved" (Acts 4:12). God's salvation is by Him and through Him alone. Christ is the Head over God's creation, the church. "He is the head of the body, the church" (Col. 1:18). The word *head* speaks of source and origin. Every power, angelic and demonic, is under His lordship. He is "the head of all principality and power" (2:10). He is completely sufficient for every spiritual need of the church.

When our focus is removed from His lordship, the formation of authentic Christianity becomes impossible. The church becomes decapitated. It is then that the church is rendered spiritually dead. The church loses its hold on Christ and growth becomes impossible because it is has severed itself from the very channel of spiritual life. All life comes from the head and flows to the body. What good is a body without a head?

Paul said that "in [Christ] dwelleth all the fullness of the Godhead bodily" (v. 9). The word *dwelleth* comes from the compound Greek word *katoikeo*. The word *oikeo* means to be at home and *kata* means down, showing permanence. It speaks of a permanent residence instead of a transient community. The verb is in the present tense, showing durative action.[18] "In Him there is a continuous and permanently at home all the fullness of the Godhead in bodily fashion."[19] Permanently at home in the person of Christ dwells the fullness of the Father, Son, and Holy Ghost. Christ is the fountainhead of all spiritual life. Don't seek it through the worship of angels.

The word *fullness* comes from the Greek word *pleroma* meaning fullness, plentitude—the entire fullness of the Godhead. The believer shares the fullness that is in Christ. This has a profound consequence for His people. The church experiences *pleroma* because of the gracious energies that are communicated to her by the Head. In Christ we find the satisfaction for every spiritual need. This is the purpose for which we were created. In Christ the believer has already attained a share of that fullness. "And of his fulness have we all received, and grace for grace" (John 1:16).

He has made us efficient and adequate for every good work. We are complete in Him, which means that in Him we are made full. There is no lack of efficiency on the part of Christ. Everything I need to become a well-rounded, growing, eager, enthusiastic, developing Christian is found in Him. How can so many complain about how spiritually empty and barren they are when they have been positioned in fullness? We been made partakers of that divine nature. Christ has already imparted to us the life of God. We don't need angelic mediators to attain our spiritual goals. Christ is the Head of all principality and power and every angelic being. The One born in Bethlehem took on our human nature, and now in heaven He still retains His glorified humanity and in Him the very essence of deity has its eternal dwelling place.

Paul refutes the Docetic Gnosticism that Jesus had no human body as well
as the Cerinthian Gnosticism that said Christ came on Jesus at His baptism
and departed from Him while He was on the cross—making Christ and Jesus
two different personalities. Paul here makes known his belief in the deity and
humanity of Jesus Christ.

The fall of man placed us in a state of incompleteness. The man who is dead
in his trespasses and sins is in a state of incompleteness. He is out of touch
with God. He is not concerned about the will of God. He is not concerned
about the dynamic of God, which is the indwelling of the Holy Spirit. Sin has
affected his reasoning so that he cannot understand spiritual truth.

Regeneration brings us into union with Christ. It is then that we partake of
the life of God. When we are reconciled to God, it is then that we are made
complete. We are once again in fellowship with our Creator. Everything the
devil stole from Adam in the Garden we get back at the cross. The will of God
is now the final authority in our life. We are experiencing the energizing of
God's Holy Spirit. It is a foretaste of perfection that will accompany our glorification. Our mind is now enlightened by the Spirit of God to discern that
which is holy from that which is profane; that which is good from that which
is evil. Now we are no longer spiritually blind.

When Paul wrote to the church at Corinth, he said, "But I fear, lest by any
means, as the serpent beguiled Eve through his subtilty, so your minds should
be corrupted from the simplicity that is in Christ" (2 Cor. 11:3). In the church
at Corinth many were being deceived by false teachers who were bringing in
a distorted gospel (v. 4). They appeared to be ministers of righteousness, yet
their teaching was a distortion of the Word of God. It led many of Paul's
followers into a spiritual disaster. By them accepting the teaching of these
deceitful workers (v. 13), they were in danger of having their minds led astray
from the wholehearted devotion to Christ. In the verse 6 of chapter 6, Paul
referred to the morality and the blameless life a gospel minister and church's
devotion that should be marked an undivided loyalty and a lifestyle of purity.
When Paul spoke of the simplicity that is in Christ, he was speaking of a
devotion that was whole and undivided. The bride is to be wholly focused on
her spouse. The church is to be undivided in its devotion to Christ.

Paul felt a holy jealousy for the church when it came to their purity of
doctrine and their manner of life. He felt deeply concerned about their spiritual progress. He feared that they would transfer their loyalty from him to

his enemies as they were being led away from the Christian faith that he had taught them. The Corinthians were being led away by rival ministers and were not even aware they were being led astray. They were welcoming a new gospel that was nothing more than a mixture of law and grace. They were receiving it with open arms. It was a satanic spirit seeking to restore a spirit of legalism into the church.

In the scripture "As the serpent beguiled Eve" (1 Cor. 11:3), Paul used the word *exepatesen* for *beguiled*, which means to be completely, thoroughly, and utterly deceived.[20] By the craftiness of the serpent, these false apostles who were satanic in their methods were doing the devil's work. For the Corinthians to be influenced by them would violate their pledge to Christ.

The person behind this departure was Satan, who is pictured as a serpent. Paul had a great deal to say about the adversary, the devil, to the Corinthians. Satan had several devices for attacking believers:

- Burdening the consciences of believers who had sinned (2 Cor. 2:10–11)
- Blinding the minds of unbelievers (4:4)
- Beguiling the minds of believers (11:3)
- Buffeting the bodies of God's ministers (12:7) [21]

Believers in Corinth were behaving as Eve did in the Garden of Eden. The focus is on the mind. Satan is a liar. It is his job to get us to feel that the lie is more real than the truth. If he can get us to ponder those lies and then to believe them, he has succeeded in his attempt. Such was the case with Eve. First, he questioned God's Word: "Yea, hath not God said?" (Gen. 3:1). Then he denied God's Word: "Ye shall not surely die" (v. 4). Then he substituted his own lie for the truth: "Ye shall be as gods, knowing good and evil" (v. 5). It was here that the New Age movement came into being.

Satan is crafty. In the New Testament it refers to someone using their ability to distort through trickery and slyness. He knows that believers will not immediately accept a lie. So the enemy has to bait the hook—make it easy for us to accept what he has to offer. Satan is an imitator; he copies what God does and then tries to convince us that his offer is better than God's. He does it by using counterfeit ministers who pretend to serve God, but who are really the servants of Satan.

We need to watch out for ministers who present a different message. Satan has a counterfeit gospel. It involves another gospel, another Jesus, and another Spirit. This different gospel being preached by false apostles led to a gospel that was void of reconciling power. It introduced a different spirit into the life of the church. It was not the Holy Spirit leading to liberty, but a satanic spirit leading to legalism. A different gospel produces a different kind of religious experience, which is not the Holy Spirit.

Paul presents a three-fold summary of Christianity: 1) Jesus, the author of this new creation, 2) the Spirit, providing the new kind of life that was to be lived through this new creation, and 3) the gospel, the instrument for spreading this life in this new creation.[22]

Through the teachings of these false apostles, they attempted to strip Jesus of His saving grace and establish a religious system that was based and merited through fleshly efforts of men. They saw Jesus as a miracle worker and a teacher, but they felt that Jesus was nothing more than a social reformer. It was the rejection of Jesus as the crucified Lord.

Their motive was not to glorify God. Their methods were deceitful. (See 2 Corinthians 2:17 and 4:2.) The word *deceitful* implies using a bait to catch a fish. They offered church members a Christian life that is superior to the one described by the apostle Paul in the New Testament. It was the unbiblical mixture of law and grace. Their attempt was to win the church away from Christ. They were missionary intruders who were inspired by Satan (11:13–15). They were wooing the Corinthians to abandon the Christ who Paul preached.

The preachers of this false gospel are with us today. They claim they have authority as God's servants, but their authority is bogus. They claim they are the true servants of God, but in reality they were imposters. They claim to be on a higher level spiritually than Paul. Their clever oratory amazes and astounds ignorant believers. What a tragedy it is when unstable believers, at the mercy of every wind that blows, are swayed by false doctrine and persuasive speech of Satan's ministers, instead of standing firm on the basic truths of the gospel that have been taught to them by faithful pastors and teachers.

Chapter 25

Angel of Light

For such are false apostles, deceitful workers, transforming themselves into the apostles of Christ. And no marvel; for Satan himself is transformed into an angel of light. Therefore it is no great thing if his ministers also be transformed as the ministers of righteousness.

—2 CORINTHIANS 11:13–15

SATAN IS NOT only a deceiver, he is an imitator. He copies what God does and tries to convince us that his offer is better than God's. Jesus was careful to draw the line between the physical (because they were his physical offspring) and spiritual descendants of Abraham because of their faith. Jesus said to the Jews, who were claiming special insight because they were the physical descendants of Abraham:

> Ye are of your father the devil, and the lust of your father ye will do. He was a murderer from the beginning, and abode not in the truth, because there was no truth in him. When he speaketh a lie, he speaketh of his own: for he is a liar, and the father of it.
>
> —JOHN 8:44

Jesus had told them that the devil was their father and they had his very nature. Nature is determined by birth. If Satan was their father they would share his nature. They were behaving just like their daddy. The Jews at that time were on the outside very religious, but inwardly they were followers of Satan. John the Baptist referred to the Pharisees and Sadducees as a generation of vipers. (Matthew 3:7). Even though they were dressed in religious attire, they still had serpent like behavior. Satan often offers to mankind a false righteousness that will never grant a person admission into the Kingdom of God. The Jews at this time did not have the nature of Abraham neither did they conduct themselves like Abraham.

The religious leaders of Israel were giving off characteristics of the children of the devil: 1) they were rejecting the truth (John 8:40), 2) they tried to kill Jesus because He spoke the truth, 3) they did not love God (v. 42), and 4) they could not understand what Jesus was trying to teach them (vv. 43, 47). A person can be well informed when it comes to religious tradition, but they have no understanding of the Word of God. They were spiritually deaf to the voice of God. They refused to hear and understand. Cain was of the offspring of Satan himself (1 John 3:12). He was both a liar and a murderer. He murdered his brother and then lied about it (Gen. 4). It should not be hard for us to understand how the religious leaders could lie about Jesus, hire false witnesses, and then have Him killed. The devil himself loves falsehood. His lies and deceptions are always contrary to God's truth and always seek to destroy it. When Jesus and the Jews met, the false met the One was true and tried to destroy the One who was truth personified (John 14:6). Anyone who seeks to do away with the truth is performing the very behavior of the devil himself.

Satan has a counterfeit gospel that involves a different savior and a different spirit. Here Paul used two different words to describe *another*: 1) *allon*, which means "one not of the same kind or quality," 2) he also identified by the use of the word *heteron,* which means "strange."[1] We must understand that for us to preach another gospel (one void of real reconciling power), we will produce another Jesus—not one that is crucified, buried, and resurrected and coming again the clouds of glory. They were presenting a Jesus who was nothing more than a miracle worker, not a Jesus of reconciling grace. It is then that we will release a satanic spirit of legalism in the life of the church, a mixture of law and grace; not the Holy Spirit whom Paul refers to as being a Spirit of liberty, but a satanic spirit who would seek to usher in the shackles of legalism.

Having felt a godly jealousy for his brethren, Paul had expressed his concern for the Corinthian church. They were being corrupted from single-minded devotion to Christ and to the gospel. The word *corrupted* comes from the word *phtheiro,* which is a verb that means "to destroy, to seduce, to ruin." Satan literally was seducing their minds. The minds of the Corinthians were being seduced by the Judaizers. Nothing will cause Paul to take on a spirit of holy jealousy any more than to know that the Corinthians were departing from a single-hearted devotion to Christ and the gospel. This proves that Paul had the very heart of God for the Corinthians. It was like God's desire for His people's single-hearted devotion. It expresses Paul's affection for their welfare. Paul considered himself to be a father to the Corinthian church. He had arranged the marriage of his daughter to a choice bridegroom. He had betrothed the Corinthians and pointed them to one Husband. He felt that it was his responsibility to guard the bride with a godly jealousy until the time came to present her in marriage as a pure virgin to the Bridegroom which is Christ. It was Paul's intention that his converts were pure and blameless for the day of Christ (Phil. 1:10). The Corinthians and the church today are to live as an eager bride with a lifestyle that is characterized by loyalty and purity. The Corinthian church was to be totally focused on her spouse. The church was to be totally undivided in their commitment to Christ.

In Eastern countries, it was the parents that chose the wife for their son. Legal contracts were drawn up, and the marriage was arranged. It was the responsibility of the father of the bride to protect the virginity during the betrothal period. In Jewish tradition, the betrothal was just as binding as marriage itself. A couple that was betrothed would address each other as husband and wife (Deut. 22:23–24). During this time it was expected for them to abstain from sexual relations. A bloodstained cloth was given as proof of virginity on the wedding night.[2]

In the Old Testament Yahweh was betrothed to Israel. God was jealous for Israel's reputation as a people among the nations. In the New Testament the church is the bride, and the groom is Christ. As Corinth's spiritual father he feels a great responsibility to see to it that Corinth maintains their faithfulness to Christ and the gospel. He knows that one day Christ will return, and it will be the time when the marriage will be consummated.

According to French Arrington, in his book on the *Ministry of Reconciliation*, the problem was that in Corinth they were not content or satisfied with one husband. They had taken on an attraction to another one. Their devotion to Christ was being in placed in a dangerous position. A real danger existed in them continuing to be faithful to Christ.

He was fearful that their minds may be corrupted and led away from the sincerity that is in Christ (2 Cor. 11:1–3). The danger of leaving the simplicity that is in Christ was very real. The Corinthians were in danger of having their minds led astray from wholehearted devotion to Christ. Being single minded and living a life of purity before God is the attitude that should have characterized their relationship to Christ. For the Corinthians to be influenced by the Judaizers would violate their betrothal to Christ. Within modern-day

Christianity, there are ministers who appear to be righteous, yet their teachings contradict the Word of God, and they are leading their followers into spiritual disaster. Paul could not believe that they were willing to put up with these false teachers who were presenting another Jesus, another spirit, and another gospel (2 Cor. 11:4). Here he is referring to the Judaizers who were teaching that the Gentiles needed to be circumcised and had to keep the Law of Moses.

This problem was not only common in Paul's day but it is also very prevalent in the day and time we live in. There are those who are teaching a different kind of Jesus than the one that is presented in Scripture. Many who are claiming to be led by the Holy Spirit are giving place to another spirit. What is being proclaimed from many of our pulpits across America has been altered, watered down, diluted, and is a different gospel than what was preached by prophets, Christ, and that of the apostles.

There seems to be a strong emphasis on the part of our religious world to define the following: 1) who is Jesus Christ? The true Jesus is the One that was preached by the apostles. 2) How does the Spirit reveal His truth to us? That truth is revealed in the pages of the Word of God (both in Old and New Testament). 3) What is the gospel of Jesus? It is what was preached by the apostles and received by the early church.

Satan would love to deceive us the same way that he did Eve in the Garden of Eden (Gen. 3). His method is threefold: 1) He will challenge the Word. "Yea, hath not God said, Ye shall not eat of every tree of the garden" (Gen. 3:1). 2) He will deny the Word. "Ye shall not surely die" (Gen 3:4). 3) He will substitute the truth of the Word with his own lie. "You shall become as gods knowing good and evil" (3:5). The first Calvinistic message was preached by the serpent in the garden and is still being preached in many of our pulpits today. It is going to cause millions to be plunged into hell because of it. It is the doctrine of unconditional eternal security. It is a doctrine that teaches permissive sin.

Millions of people are placing their eternal destiny in the hands of men, and they are accepting as gospel anything that comes out of their mouth. They do not feel any responsibility to study behind them to make sure what they are proclaiming is truth. Seducing spirits and doctrines of demons are going across America, even the world, and producing a form of Christianity that does not even resemble the Word of God. A word of prophecy should never come to us as revelation but conformation. What is being preached should be confirmed to us by what God has already declared to us in His Word.

Paul said, "For if he that cometh preacheth another Jesus, whom ye have not preached, or if ye receive another spirit, which ye have not received, or another gospel, which ye have not accepted, ye might bear well with him." (2 Cor. 11:4).

The Corinthians welcomed the message of this new gospel, a mixture of law and grace with the same zeal they received Paul's message of the cross. No wonder Paul was so shocked by their behavior. Paul had proven his love for the church by protecting it from the attacks of the false teachers, yet Corinth still fell prey to the Judaizers and let them come in. Corinth had left their first love and no longer were they giving single-hearted devotion to Christ. It was not just that they turned away from Paul; the greater sin is that they had turned away from Christ.

Are we presenting another Jesus today? While Judaism teaches that He was a good man and a teacher, Islam says that Jesus was a prophet. Jehovah's Witnesses say that Jesus was a created being. They believe that Jesus being the Son of God was just a title and that He was not equal with the Father. Mormons declare Him to be the god among many gods. They are proclaiming that Jesus Christ, who is the Creator, and Lucifer (created angel) are brothers. Every occult and cult all have one thing in common: they all attack the deity and the Lordship of Jesus Christ. Many are trying to redefine who Jesus was. They are stripping Him of many of His attributes—omnipotence, omnipresence, omniscience, immutability, and His eternal being. They are attempting to strip Him of many of His teachings while seeking to explain away His miracles.

The apostles were eyewitnesses of Jesus' ministry and were qualified to give testimony to who He was. In fact, the only reliable historical record that we have of Jesus is the New Testament. It was written by men who knew Jesus intimately and who were personally acquainted with His apostles. Their testimony that is recorded in Scripture tells us who Jesus was. Matthew tells us that Jesus is the Christ, the Son of the Living God (Matt. 16:16). John tells us that He was the Word that was in the beginning, who was with God and was God (John 1:1–2). Colossians tells us, "In Him dwells all the fullness of the Godhead bodily" (Col. 2:9–10). Corinthians tells us that He is the One that died for our sins and rose from the grave and that it was foretold in the Scriptures (1 Cor. 15:1–4).

Peter said, "We were eyewitnesses of His majesty" (2 Pet. 1:16). John said, "That which is from the beginning, which we have heard, which we have seen with our eyes, which we have looked upon, and our hands have handled, of the Word of life: (For the life was manifested, and we have seen it, and bear witness, and shew unto you that eternal life, which was with the Father, and was manifested unto us); That which we have seen and heard declare we unto you, that ye also may have fellowship with us, and truly our fellowship is with the Father, and with His Son Jesus Christ" (1 John 1:1–3). What John is saying is that if we are going to have fellowship with the Father and with His Son Jesus Christ we are going to have to hear Jesus with John's ears, see Jesus through John's eyes, and handle Jesus through John's hands.

John in his second epistle declared, "Whosoever transgresseth, and abideth not in the doctrine of Christ, hath not God. He that abideth in the doctrine of Christ, he hath both the Father and the Son" (2 John 9). The word *transgresseth* means "to run away too far, to pass beyond the assigned limits."[3] When this is done it is false progress. Many false teachers want to make us think that they are progressing in revelation while the church is in a rut. They want the church to join up with their efforts because they have something to offer our converts that is new and exciting while they are abandoning the very doctrine of Christ that teaches that Jesus Christ is the Son of God who came in the flesh. The truth of the matter is if we have it wrong about Christ we have it wrong about God. If we do not abide in true doctrine then we do not have the Father or the Son.

John declared, "That all men should honor the Son, even as they honor the Father which hath sent Him" (John 5:23). You cannot honor the Father if you are not going to honor the Son. Jesus is equal with the Father and is worthy of the same worship that is due to the Father. The verb *timosi* is a present active subjunctive which means "may keep on honoring the Father."[4] Jesus is calling on us to worship Him with the same honor as they would the Father. So worship not only includes the adoration of the Son but also putting Him first in every area of our lives. A gospel that professes to be progressive theology that is in denial of Christ is not progressive at all. Just the opposite is true; it is actually a gospel that will cause one to go backwards.

Many people are professing that they are being led by the Holy Spirit. First of all the Holy Spirit would never lead you to do anything that is contrary to Scripture. The Spirit and the Word are in agreement. John said, "Beloved, believe not every spirit, but try the spirits whether they are of God: because many false prophets are gone out into the world" (1 John 4:1). Any doctrine that does not line up with the Word of God needs to be rejected. The greatest need in today's church is the need for discernment.

We need discernment for the following reasons: 1) The devil hates the Word of God and its truth. 2) Man has a nature that has been corrupted by the fall. 3) The world that we live in is in the grip of the evil one and it's very antagonistic to all spiritual truth. 4) Genuine Christians are not immune to the deception of the enemy. 5) Nothing delights the enemy of our soul any more than to know that he has taken control of a local church. 6) Because God is being glorified through the church, the devil wants to take the worship off of God and place it upon himself.

Many times we are careless in the area of discernment of the spirit that motivates a religious teacher or preacher. There is a big difference in being religious from being a Christian. God has placed within the heart of every man a desire to worship something. Man was created to worship God. Because man is depraved, their religious thinking has become distorted and confused.

The words *religion and religious* appear only seven times in the New Testament. Only one time was it used in good way. "Now when the congregation was broken up, many of the Jews and religious proselytes, followed Paul and Barnabas: who, speaking to them, persuaded them to continue in the grace of God" (Acts 13:43). Here the word *religious* comes from the word *sebomai* which means "to worship and be devout." The context of the passage shows to us that it was not a true religion.

Then in Galatians 1:13–14 Paul makes reference to a religion system called Judaism (which appears twice) that he was in prior to his conversion. In Acts 26:5 the other references refer to religious observance to whatever or whomever one deemed as a god (Acts 26:5). James declared, "If any man among you seem to be religious, and bridleth not his tongue, but deceiveth his own heart, this man's religion is in vain. What is pure religion and undefiled before God and the Father is this, to visit the fatherless and widows in their affliction, and to keep oneself unspotted from the world" (James 1:26–27). Only in these verses is it used in a good sense.[5]

The word *try* comes from the word *diokimazo* means "to determine whether or not something passes the test; to approve it if it does."[6] A local church must always judge those who seek to have an impact or influence upon it. If we don't do that, it is spiritual suicide. Satan and his subjects delight to get into a church to murder and rape the souls of men with false doctrine.

There is a test to determine whether or not a believer is being led by the Holy Spirit: 1) Do they deny that Jesus Christ has come in the flesh? 2) Do they believe in the deity of Christ? 3) The message that is carried by a false teacher will be pleasing to the world; it will glorify the flesh and inflate the ego. Their message will ignore the depravity of man. Salvation is then turned into nothing more than a course in self-improvement. Jesus said He will guide you into all truth (John 16:12–13). It is the work of the Spirit to point the believer back to the Word of God. Feelings and emotions are unreliable guides when it comes to faith.

Then we have the problem of another gospel. Christianity is the only religion that believes and teaches that one cannot be saved by their works. This was contrary to the message being preached by the Judaizers. If we seek to attempt to change this gospel it will only lead to perversion.

The Gospel the apostles proclaimed taught:

1. Jesus Christ was nailed to an old rugged cross for our sins (1 Cor. 15:1–3).
2. He was raised from the dead (1 Cor. 15:4).
3. He was exalted as Lord and Savior (Acts 2:33–36).
4. He is coming again to execute judgment and be glorified in His saints (2 Thess. 1:7–10).
5. Jesus is the Christ, the Son of God (Acts 8:35–37).
6. Confess that Jesus is Lord (Rom. 10:9–10).
7. That we are to repent of our sins (Acts 2:38).
8. Remain faithful until He returns (Rev. 2:10).
9. Their message told us that we could receive eternal life (Rom 6:23), gift of the Holy Spirit (Acts 2:38), and the remission of sins (Acts 2:38).

Wherever you find the genuine, the counterfeit is not far behind. We never heard of a fallen angel until we read about the angels that did fall from their first estate. We never heard about false prophets until the prophets of God took their rightful place and began to function in their office. We never heard about false shepherds until God gave Israel shepherds after His own heart that fed them with knowledge and understanding. We never heard about false teachers until teachers took their rightful place and began to flow in their gift. We never heard about false brethren until we knew what it was like to be a part of the family of God. We never heard about another gospel until the good news had come to us in power in the Holy Ghost with much assurance. We never heard about the Antichrist until Christ, the Anointed One came on the scene. We never heard about false righteousness until we knew what it meant to be the righteousness of God in Christ Jesus. We never knew what false apostles were until the real apostles were sent by Christ Himself.

In the Scripture we read of the contrast between the wheat and the tares, the chaff and the wheat, the sheep and the goats, and the righteous and the wicked. When Paul wrote to the Corinthian church, he had several questions for them:

> Be ye not unequally yoked together with unbelievers: for what fellowship hath righteousness with unrighteousness? and what communion hath light with darkness? And what concord hath Christ with Belial? or what part hath he that believeth with an infidel? And what agreement hath the temple of God with idols?
> —2 CORINTHIANS 6:14–16

Have you ever taken the time to look at our archenemy by the name of Lucifer (Isa. 14:12)? Lucifer's name means "Son of the Morning" or "Light Bearer." It is actually the first and last time it appears in the Old Testament. It means the following: 1) to shine, 2) to be foolish, 3) to boast, 4) to glorify, 5) to praise, 6) to be insane and crazy. We know from the scriptures that Satan shines as an angel of light. He was so foolish that he thought that he could overthrow God from His throne. Satan loves to boast. He glories in his wisdom and power. He wants to receive praise as a god. We know that in Jesus' wilderness temptation, a created angel tried to get the Creator to bow down and worship him.

He was one of the most prominent angels mentioned in Scripture. He was a created angel (Col. 1:16). He is not omnipotent, omniscient, omnipresent, immutable, or eternal. He does not possess the attributes that belong to God. He was an exalted angel of the highest order (Ezek. 28:12–14). As an anointed

Cherub he covered the creation of God. He was praise and worship leader in heaven. He was one of the most beautiful angels that God had ever created. He was perfect before God until the day that pride led to his fall. Pride turned an angel into a devil. Lucifer knew how to take music and move people. It was the message of the cross that led Satan to his doom. That is why he hates it so much.

Isaiah said, "How art thou fallen from heaven, O Lucifer." Isaiah saw him as a bright and morning star. It was common in Scripture to compare monarchs to the sun or other heavenly bodies. He was an angel of worship (Ezek. 28). He walked in the glory. Every precious stone was his covering, and He glistened as He stood in the light of the presence of God. Now he has fallen to the earth like a fallen star. His glory has been diminished. His brightness has been quenched. Somewhere between Genesis 1:1 and Genesis 1:2, he fell and ruined creation. "The earth was without form, and void; and darkness was upon the face of the deep. And the spirit of God moved upon the face of the waters" (Gen. 1:1–3). God brought order out of chaos and beauty out of confusion through His spoken Word.

What was it that led to his downfall? He asserted his will against the will of the Creator. He stood in opposition to the will of the Creator. This led to an angel becoming a devil. He was cast down from his place of power that he once enjoyed. He became an enemy of God and man. From the beginning of time itself, he has used every device to ruin mankind and rob God of the glory that is due to His name.

Lucifer was evil in the following ways:

- Liar (John 8:44)
- Murderer (John 8:44)
- He did not abide in the truth (John 8:44).
- He was an apostate in that he fell from the position that he once enjoyed.
- Proud (1 Tim. 3:16)
- Deceiver (Rev. 12:9)
- Thief (Matt. 13:19)
- He sought to devour (1 Pet. 5:8).

Jesus said, "I have come in my Father's name, and you do not receive me; but if another comes in his own name him you will accept him" (John 5:43, NIV). Many of the Jews claimed to love God, but their attitude toward Christ proved that their love was not real. They did not honor Jesus. They rejected the Son of God who came in His Father's name. They would one day accept a false messiah, the Antichrist, who would come in his own name. If we reject what is true, we will settle for the false. How prone we are to follow the false prophets today.

There were many accusations that were made by the Judaizers against Paul: 1) He was bold while he was absent but meek when he was present (10:1). 2) He had acted in a fashion that they considered to be worldly (10:2). 3) When he was off at a distance he used to frighten people with his letters that were considered to be stern, but when he was present among them he lacked a demanding presence, and his speech was not impressive (10:9–10). 4) They said his apostleship was inferior to theirs (11:5–6). 5) They attacked his integrity when it came to financial matters. 6) Because he would not receive financial support from the Corinthians they said he really did not love them (11:7–11).

The language in the Greek seems to be harsh. Paul called them "*false pseudos*" The phrase "false apostle" does not appear anywhere else in the writings of the apostle Paul. It is believed that Paul possibly coined this word in the heat of the debate with the false teachers. They claimed to have been sent by Christ. The same false teachers that Paul confronted in Galatia he is now confronting in Corinth. They were once again demanding that Gentile converts take upon themselves the yoke of the law and submit to the right of circumcision.

Many of those in Corinth gave the following characteristics to describe the ideal apostle: 1) impressive, 2) demanded attention when he walked into a room, 3) the ability to be a good speaker (10:10), 4) exercising authority over those who are under him (11:20–21), 5) have visions and revelations (12:1), 6) ministry accompanied with signs and wonders (12:11–13), 7) spokesman for Christ with manifestations of the power of God accompanying his ministry (13:2–4), 8) has Jewish connections (11:21–22), and 9) bears letters of recommendation from the church at Jerusalem. Those who were false apostles stressed only manifestations and power without any place for human weakness or sufferings. They preached a different gospel than the one Paul preached (11:4). They took great pride in their speaking ability (11:6). They claimed they carried out their mission the same way Paul did (11:12). They imposed their authority on the church (11:19–21). They were proud of their heritage as Jews, and they professed that they were the servants of Christ (11:21–23).

Then Paul in defense of his ministry pointed out that his ministry was not without commendation (3:2–3). He possessed the knowledge (11:6) and the authority (11:21–22). Paul had also experienced visions and revelations from God (12:1–5). He told them that his ministry was confirmed with miracles, wonders, and signs (12:11–13). He believed that he could reveal the evidence that Christ had spoken through him (13:3–4) while he emphasized power and authority. He emphasized God's power in his life as it rested upon God's servants in their weakness.

Paul marked genuine apostolic ministry by their fruits (3:2–3), not by the success of their ministry. By the character in which that ministry is conducted as it possesses the gentleness and meekness of Christ (10:1–2), a true apostolic ministry will bear the sufferings of Christ (4:8–12: 11:23–28).

Paul dealt with the subject of a false Christ and false prophets when he said, "For such are false apostles, deceitful workers, transforming themselves into the apostles of Christ" (2 Cor. 11:13). The word *deceitful* speaks of using bait to catch fish to lure or ensnare.[7] These false apostles would put out the bait to catch their victims. The word deceitful describes someone that is dishonest and treacherous with others. Paul could tell by their mannerisms that they were deceitful workers. It was their deception that brought destruction. While they took on the name of being an apostle, the Corinthians never realized that Christ had not sent them. They were not only counterfeits but also they were referred to as sham apostles. The Bible speaks of these deceitful ministers and Paul referred to these leaders and fraudulent ministers as being energized by Satan. It was not enough to appear to accomplish great things for God or that they preached an attractive gospel. They gave all the appearances that they were righteous. "They had a form of godliness but denying the power thereof" (2 Tim. 3:5). They offer church members a Christian life that is superior to the one that is described in the New Testament.

The word *workman* comes from the word *ergates* where the word is used as a noun. It describes a worker who is employed in the service of Christ. They claimed that their reason for coming to Corinth was to serve Christ, when all they cared about was serving themselves at Corinth's expense. They were wolves in sheep's clothing as they masqueraded themselves as apostles of Christ.

French Arrington in his book on *Ministry of Reconciliation*, stated "They expended every energy to discredit Paul and destroy his influence and ministry. They had a love for power, success, prestige that was behind the religious mask that they wore. Paul was able to discern their master and the source of their inspiration."[8]

In Corinthians chapter 11, Paul said "For Satan himself transforms himself into an angel of light." (v. 14) Paul used the word *transformed* three times (vv. 13–15). It means to disguise, to masquerade. There is a change on the outside but not on the inside.[9] The garments that they were wearing on the outside did not truly reflect what they were within. Satan's workers, like Satan himself, never appear in their true character; they always wear a disguise and hide behind a mask. Satan, in order to conceal his true identity, would step into angelic attire. These false teachers bear the family resemblance of Satan who was their master. Satan dwells in a realm of darkness, never comes in his true identity. He always comes in the garments of light. How else would he get his lies across? His opponents dressed up as the apostles of Christ and servants of righteousness. They were ministers of Satan and advocated righteousness through works of the law rather than faith in Christ.

"For Satan himself masquerades an angel of light" (v. 14). When angels appeared they are described as being like lightning (Matt. 28:3). "Two men stood by them in shining garments" (Luke 24:4). When the shepherds were abiding in the fields, "An angel of the Lord came upon them, and the glory of the Lord shone round about them" (Luke 2:9).

They were pseudo apostles. They claimed a category that did not belong to them. Not only was their message false, but also the spirit they spread and the gospel they offered had not truth in it. They attempted to mix law and grace. Their gospel produced another Jesus, that released a Satanic spirit of legalism into the life of the Church. They were sham apostles. Their activities in Corinth were deceitful, treacherous, and cunning.

They claimed to have divine endorsement as God's servants, but their authority was bogus. While claiming to be the true servants of God they were actually imposters and false teachers. The Corinthians were blown away with their oratory. Unstable believers were heavily influenced by their speech, instead of standing firm on the truths of the Gospel that had been preached to them by the faithful pastors and teachers. They said Paul was not a gifted speaker (2 Cor 11:6; 10:10).

Somehow these intruders lacked the marks of true servants of Christ. While they were appearing to do the work of Christ they were taking on the identity of an apostle that had been sent by Jesus Christ. They made every effort to discredit Paul and destroy his influence and ministry. They were motivated by dishonesty and selfishness. They desired to promote themselves and capitalize on the gospel. Behind their religious mask was a love for power, success and prestige. Paul discerned their master was Satan and that he was their source of inspiration.

"Therefore it is not great thing if his ministers be transformed as the ministers of righteousness" (v. 15). Can you imagine the agents of Satan selling themselves as agents of the righteousness of God? Paul labeled their gospel as satanic.

These intruders have disguised themselves as the ministers of Satan They are not just Paul's opponents but enemies of the cross of Christ. Paul said, "And no marvel; for Satan himself transforms himself into an angel of light" (2 Cor. 11:14). At the fall Satan he lost his ability to manifest himself in physical form. He appeared to Eve in the Garden in the form of a serpent. Goodness will never pretend to be evil. Evil is no dress to be worn openly. Satan himself masquerades and disguises himself as an angel of light. How else could he get his lies across? He may come in the appearance of something that resembles holiness. "Therefore it is no great thing if his ministers also be transformed as the ministers of righteousness; whose end shall be according to their works" (v. 15).

We must be careful of false teachers who disguise themselves as the apostles of Christ and ministers of righteousness. They imitate real ministers of Christ. They will put the form of godliness into their message. Their gospel is based on human reasoning and not one that has it's source and origin in the Scriptures. Their message is not based New Testament apostolic doctrine. (See 1 John 4:1.)

Paul in 2 Corinthians 11:20 gave us a list of five crimes the false teachers had committed against the church: 1) They made slaves out of them. They literally took them captive as birds in a trap. 2) They devoured them.[10] The word *devour* means "to eat down resources like parasites." 3) They took advantage of them. 4) They exalted themselves at the expense of others. 5) They spiritually struck them on the face. In the phrase "to strike you in the face," Paul used the verb *dero,* which meant "to flay or skin like an animal." It was a picture of violence and contempt. Paul's opponent had become so opinionated that they were actually slapping in the face those they brought under their authority.[11] These troublemakers bullied the church and would do whatever they could do to get their way.

Jesus said, "For false Christs and false prophets shall arise, and shall shew signs and wonders, to seduce, if it were possible, even the elect" (Mark 13:22). The "elect" is in reference to Israel and the Gentiles who would be saved during the tribulation period. Miracles from the false Christs will be the drawing card, but miracles are not a proof of divine calling or approval. The test is the Word of God.

Jesus warned His disciples fourteen different times in the gospels to be aware of leaders (false apostles, false teachers, and false brethren) who would lead you astray. All ministers must measured by the teachings of Christ Himself. We are exhorted to examine preachers and leaders in the church. There are always false teachers and false brethren who, with the help of Satan, will remain undetected until God reveals them for who they are. The apostle Paul gave qualifications for leadership to protect the integrity of the ministry. We must not be deceived by their charisma, oratory, education, miracles, philosophy, or popular message.

We must remember the foundation of the prophets and apostles and the foundation stone of the true church. Paul said to the church at Ephesus, "And are built upon the foundation of the apostles and prophets, Jesus Christ himself being the chief corner stone" (Eph. 2:20). We are to believe that only the blood of Christ can bring about the remission of sins.

Believers today must be aware that within the church there may be preachers, pastors, and ministers of God's Word who are of the same spirit and life as the corrupt teachers of God's law in Jesus' day (Matt. 24:11, 24). They will outwardly appear righteous to men (23:28). They are wolves in sheep's clothing. "Beware of false prophets, which come to you in sheep's clothing, but inwardly they are ravening wolves" (7:15). They are like the Pharisees of old. Away from the crowds and in their hidden lives, they are given over to extortion and excess (23:25). They are "full of dead men's bones, and of all uncleanness" (v. 27). They are "full of hypocrisy and iniquity" (v. 28). Behind closed doors they are full of lust, immorality, adultery, greed, and self-centered indulgence. Their aim is not to serve Christ, but to promote themselves. They have a love for power, success, and prestige behind their religious masquerade.

Paul said, "Their end will be what their actions deserve" (v. 15). We are going to have to give an account of what we have done before God. It is the belief of many of the Jewish people that their works will determine their destiny. These false teachers have done Satan's work and they will share with Satan in his doom. Paul stated that the enemies of the cross of Christ will face eternal destruction and will be banished from the presence of the Lord and from the majesty of his power (Phil. 3:19).

EXAMINING FALSE TEACHERS OR FALSE PROPHETS

Discern their character. Do they have a diligent prayer life and manifest a sincere and pure devotion to God? Do they manifest the fruit of the Spirit and a love for the lost? Do they hate evil and love righteousness? Do they cry out against sin?

Discern their motives. True Christian leaders will seek to do four things:

1. Honor Christ.
2. Lead the church into sanctification. (Don't tell them it's OK because the world is doing it.)
3. Have a desire to win the lost.
4. Proclaim and defend the gospel of Christ and the apostles.

Test the fruit of their life and message. Are their converts totally committed to God's Word, no displaying allegiance to them and their teachings?

Discern their level of reliance on Scripture. Do they teach the original message and writings of both Old and New Testament as fully inspired by God?

Test their integrity with respect to the Lord's money. Do they seek to promote the work of God in ways that are consistent with the New Testament standards for leadership?

There is a great danger of the church falling into spiritual boredom. Whenever there is information with no application, spiritual boredom is always the result. Knowledge without application always becomes boring and unfulfilling. James said, "Be ye doers of the word, and not hearers only, deceiving your own selves" (James 1:22). When James uses the phrase "hearers only," it comes from the Greek word *akroates*. It speaks of people who attend a class for audit, not for credit. They were only present for the lecture.[12]

James confronts us with two important questions: 1) Are we serious about God's word and its application in our lives? 2) Are we simply hearers who have no intention of doing the word? The word *doers* comes from the Greek word *poietes*. It is where we get the word *poet* from. The word carries with it a sense of creative ability of a poet. We are to find creative ways to apply the word to our lives. James said the result is that we are "deceiving our own selves." The word *deceiving* comes from a word that means "miscalculation, misjudge, and misreckon."[13] The test of whether or not we have heard the Word is whether or not we are willing to apply it. When there is information without application spiritual boredom will often settle in. Many times when believers are in this state they will be more susceptible to open the door to seducing spirits and doctrines of demons.

We have become a generation of sermon tasters. We have allowed the Word to go in one ear and out the other. We have not allowed the Word to get down into our spirit and become translated into actual deeds and behavior. Because of this many have become bored with church, prayer, worship, and the Word. The wrong response to spiritual boredom will put us in a worse condition than we are already in. The only way out is to begin to find fresh, new ways to apply the Word of God to our lifestyle. It is the doing of the Word that removes the boredom. It is sad to say that we have come to a time that the Word is not enough for some people. They have begun to turn to other things to keep their excitement going. I believe the stage has already been set for the Antichrist who will come with lying signs and wonders.

Paul views his opponents as instruments of Satan, who disguise themselves as servants of righteousness. Paul labeled their self-seeking approach as satanic. They imitate the real ministers of Christ. They want to be known as gentlemen of the cloth, but it is nothing but cloth. They are not empowered by the Spirit but energized by Satan.

They are like their master, Satan, whose realm is a realm of darkness. He never comes as Satan, but always in the garb of light. The prince of darkness puts on the garb of light and sets the fashion for his followers in the masquerade to deceive the saints. Paul called them false brethren (Gal. 2:4).

Barclay gave us a test by which a man can examine his own Christianity.[14]

1. Do you know salvation through the cross of Christ?

2. Are you growing in the power of the Holy Spirit, in prayer, and knowledge of God?

3. Is there a great desire to spread the gospel of the kingdom by example and by preaching and teaching to others?

4. Are you bringing others to Christ through your witness?

It is neither strange nor surprising that men who are really agents in the realm of Satan would attempt to sell themselves as agents of righteousness. Paul labeled their self-seeking approach as satanic.

In conclusion, we must beware that we do not become bewitched in these last days. As long as we remain passionate for Christ and His Word, we will be able to recognize our adversary, even though he is disguised as a child of God, even a minister of righteousness. Beware, do not be deceived.

To Contact the Author

pastormiller@mebtel.net

Bibliography

Arrington, French. *The Acts of the Apostles*. Peabody, MA: Hendrickson Publishers, 1988.

———. *Encountering the Holy Spirit*. Cleveland, TN: Pathway Press, 2003.

———. *Maintaining the Foundations: A Study of 1 Timothy*. Grand Rapids, MI: Baker Book House, 1982.

———. *The Ministry of Reconciliation*. Grand Rapids, MI: Baker Book House, 1980.

Barclay, William. *The Gospel of John*, vol. 1. Philadelphia, PA: Westminster Press, 1986.

———. "The Letters to the Corinthians." In *Daily Study Bible*. Edinburgh: Saint Andrews Press, 1954.

———. *The Letters to the Galatians and Ephesians*. Philadelphia: Westminster Press, 1976.

———. *The Letters to the Philippians, Colossians and Thessalonians*. Louisville, KY: Westminster John Knox Press, 1975.

Barlow, George. *Preachers' Complete Homiletic Commentary*, vol. 28. New York: Funk & Wagnalls Company, 1978.

Barnes, Albert, *Notes on New Testament,* Baker Book House, Grand Rapids, Michigan, Galatians, 1884.

Bicket J. Zenas, *The Spirit Helps Us Pray,* A Biblical Theology of Prayer, Logion Press, Springfield, Missouri, 1993

Carson, Herbert M. "Colossians and Philemon." In *Tyndale New Testament Commentaries*. Grand Rapids, MI: Eerdmans Publishing Company, 1960.

Carver, G. Frank. *Beacon Bible Commentary*. MO: Beacon Hill Press of Kansas City, 1968.

Dake, Finis. Dakes Annotated Reference Bible. Lawrenceville, GA: Dake Publishing, 1961.

Full Life Study Bible. Grand Rapids, MI: Zondervan Publishing House, 1992.

Gallagher, Steven. "Denying, Resisting, Disdaining the Power of God," by Pure Life Ministries, Dry Ridge, KY, spring 2008.

Gause, R. Hollis. *Living in the Spirit: The Way of Salvation*. Cleveland, TN: Pathway Press, 1980.

Gibbon, Edward, *Historian's Assessment of Ancient Christianity,* Decline and Fall of Roman Empire, New York: the Modern Library, Volume I, 2010.

Giordano, Connie, *There Is No Such Thing as a Lazy Christian,* Series of "All about God." (October 31, 2009. 2010.)

Greek, Michael. "2 Peter and Jude." In *Tyndale New Testament Commentaries*. Grand Rapids, MI: Eerdmans Publishing Company, 1968.

Horton, M. Stanley. *What the Bible Says About the Holy Spirit*. Springfield, MO: Gospel Publishing House, 1976.

Meredith C. Roderick, *Faithless Generation,* Volume IV. Issue I, Salad Bar Christianity, August 7, 2000.

New Open Bible: Study Edition. Nashville: TN: Thomas Nelson Publishers, 1990.

Phillips, John. *Exploring Hebrews*. Chicago: Moody Press, 1977.

Smitters, David, *Charles G. Finney & His Intercessors,* Lectures on Revival, Autobiography by Charles Finney.

Renner, Rick. *Dressed to Kill*. Tulsa, OK: Rick Renner Ministries, 1991.

———. *Dynamic Duo: The Holy Spirit and You*. Lake Mary, FL: Creation House, 1994.

———. *Merchandising the Anointing: Developing Discernment for These Last Days*. Tulsa, OK: Albury Publishing, 1990.

———. *Seducing Spirits and Doctrines of Demons*. Tulsa, OK: Pillar Books, 1988.

Rice, John, *The Power of Pentecost*. Murfreesboro, TN: The Sword of the Lord Publishers, 1949.

Robertson, A. T. *Word Pictures in the New Testament*, vols. 1–6. Nashville, TN: Broadman Press, 1930–31.

Stone, Perry. *Breaking the Jewish Code*. Lake Mary, FL: Charisma House, 2009.

Wiersbe, Warren W. *Be Alert*. Wheaton, IL: Victor Books, 1984.

———. *Be Confident*. Wheaton, IL: Victor Books, 1973.

———. *Be Daring*. Wheaton, IL: Victor Books, 1988.

———. *Be Encouraged*. Wheaton, IL: Victor Books, 1984.

———. *Be Free*. Wheaton, IL: Victor Books, 1975.

Willmington, H.L. *Willmington's Guide to the Bible,* Tyndale House Publishers, Wheaton Illinois, 1986.

Wuest, Kenneth. *Word Studies in the Greek New Testament: Romans*, vol. 1. Grand Rapids, MI: Eerdmans Publishing Company, 1950.

———. *Word Studies in the Greek New Testament: 2 Peter*, vol. 2. Grand Rapids, MI: Eerdmans Publishing Company, 1950.

Notes

CHAPTER 1

1. John R. Rice, *The Power of Pentecost* (Murfreesboro, TN: Sword of the Lord Publishers, 1949), 23.

2. R. Hollis Gause, *Living in the Spirit: The Way of Salvation* (Cleveland, TN: Pathway Press, 1980), 69.

3. Kenneth Wuest, *Word Studies in the Greek New Testament*, vol. 1 (Grand Rapids, MI: Wm. B. Eerdmans Publishing Co., 1961).

4. Quote from Nicene Creed found at http://en.wikipedia.org/wiki/English_versions_of_the_Nicene_Creed_in_current_use (accessed May 29, 2010).

5. Wuest, *Word Studies*, vol. 1, 128.

6. Frank G. Carver, *Beacon Bible Commentary* (Kansas City, MO: Beacon Hill Press, n.d.)

7. Wuest, *Word Studies*, vol. 1, 116

8. Ibid.

9. Ibid., 117.

10. Ibid.

11. Ibid., 105.

12. Rick Renner, *Merchandising the Anointing: Developing Discernment for These Last Days* (Tulsa, OK: Albury Publishing, 1990), 31–32.

13. Full Life Study Bible (Grand Rapids, MI: Zondervan Publishing House, 1992), 272–273.

14. French L. Arrington, *The Acts of the Apostles: An Introduction and Commentary* (Peabody, MA: Hendrickson Publishers, 1988), 35.

15. Renner, *Merchandising*, 12.

16. Edward Gibbon, *Historian's Assessment of Ancient Christianity,* Decline and Fall of Roman Empire (New York: The Modern Library, 2010), 407.

17. Roderick C. Meredith, *Faithless Generation,* Volume IV. Issue I, Salad Bar Christianity, August 7, 2000.

18. Wade Clark Roof, *Spiritual Marketplace: Baby Boomers and the Remaking of American Religion* (NJ: Princeton University Press, 1999).

19. Charles Coleson, "Salad-Bar Christianity," *Christianity Today*, August 7, 2000, http://www.christianitytoday.com/ct/2000/august7/31.80.html (accessed May 29, 2010).

CHAPTER 2

1. Wuest, *Word Studies*, vol. 1.

2. Ibid., 162.

3. C. S. Lewis quote from *Mere Christianity* accessed at http://www.biblegateway.com/resources/commentaries/IVP-NT/Gal/Freedom-Moral-Transformation (May 29, 2010).

4. "Freedom for Moral Transformation," *IVP New Testament Commentaries: Galatians 5* found at http://www.biblegateway.com/resources/commentaries/IVP-NT/Gal/Freedom-Moral-Transformation (accessed May 29, 2010).

5. Wuest, *Word Studies*, vol. 1, 179.

6. Ibid.

7. Ibid., 153.

8. Ibid.

9. Warren Wiersbie, *Be Free: Galatians* (Wheaton, IL: Victor Books, n.d.), 130.

Chapter 3

1. H. L. Willmington, *Willmington Guide to the Bible,* Roman Poet Ovid 43 B.C. (Wheaton, IL: Tyndale House Publishers, n.d.), 381.

2. Wuest, *Word Studies*, vol. 1, 11.

3. Ibid., 13.

4. Albert Barnes, *Barnes Notes on the New Testament,* An Introduction to the Book of Galatians (Grand Rapids, MI: Baker Book House, n.d.), 278.

5. Ron McKenzie, *Being Church Where We Live* (Christchurch, New Zealand: Kingwatch Books, 2004).

6. Paul Barnet, *Jesus, the Rise of Early Christianity: a History of New Testament Times* (Downers Grove, IL: Intervarsity Press, 2002), 21.

7. William Barclay, *The Letters to the Galatians and Ephesians*, (Philadelphia, PA: Westminster Press, 1976), 9.

8. Ibid.

9. Wuest, *Word Studies*, vol. 1, 33.

10. Ibid. 34.

11. Ibid.

12. Elmer Towns, *The Gospel of John: Believe and Live* (Chattanooga, TN: AMG Publishers), 124.

Chapter 4

1. A. T. Robertson, *Word Pictures in the New Testament*, vol. 4 (Nashville, TN: Broadman Press, 1960), 276.

2. Warren W. Wiersbe, *Be Free* (Wheaton, IL: Victor Books, 1975), 15.

3. Wuest, *Word Studies*, vol. 1, 86.

4. Robertson, *Word Pictures*, vol. 4, 276.

5. Wuest, *Word Studies*, vol. 1, 36–37.

6. French Arrington, *The Ministry of Reconciliation* (Grand Rapids, MI: Baker Book House, 1980).

7. Wuest, *Word Studies*, vol. 1, 36–37.

8. Renner, *Merchandising*, 92.

9. Wuest, *Word Studies*, vol. 1, 40.

10. Martin Luther quote found at http://thinkexist.com/quotation/here_i_stand
-i_can_do_no_other-god_help_me-amen/255741.html (accessed May 31, 2010).

11. Finis Dake, *Dakes Annotated Reference Bible* (Lawrenceville, GA: Dake
Publishing, 1961), 202.

12. "Understanding the Law," *IVP New Testament Commentaries: Galatians
3*, found at http://www.biblegateway.com/resources/commentaries/IVP-NT/Gal/
Understanding-Law (accessed May 31, 2010).

13. Barclay, *Letters to the Galatians and Ephesians*, 31–32.

14. Ibid., 32.

15. Wiersbe, *Be Free*, 84.

16. Barclay, *Letters to the Galatians and Ephesians*, 32.

17. H. L. Willmington, *Willmington's Guide to the Bible* (Wheaton, IL: Tyndale
House, n.d.), 400.

18. "Moving from Slavery to Freedom," *IVP New Testament Commentaries:
Galatians 4* found at http://www.biblegateway.com/resources/commentaries/IVP
-NT/Gal/Moving-Slavery-Freedom (accessed May 31, 2010).

19. Barclay, *Letters to the Galatians and Ephesians*, 33.

20. Ibid.

21. Ibid., 36–37.

CHAPTER 5

1. Robertson, *Word Pictures,* vol. 4, 279.

2. Wuest, *Word Studies*, vol. 1, 49.

3. Ibid., 33.

4. Ibid., 34.

5. Rick Renner, *Dressed to Kill* (Tulsa, OK: Rick Renner Ministries, 1991).

6. Wuest, *Word Studies*, vol. 1, 206.

7. Ibid., 50.

CHAPTER 6

1. Barclay, *Letters to the Galatians and Ephesians*, 5–6.

2. Perry Stone, *Breaking the Jewish Code* (Lake Mary, FL: Charisma House,
2009).

3. H. L. Willmington, *Willmington's Guide to the Bible*, 403.

4. Rick Renner, *Living in the Combat Zone*, (Tulsa, OK: Pillar Books and
Publishing, n.d.), 40–41.

5. Wuest, *Word Studies*, vol. 1, 38.

6. George Barlow*, Preachers' Complete Homiletic Commentary*, vol. 28 (New York:
Funk & Wagnalls Company, 1978), 9.

7. Wuest, *Word Studies*, vol. 1, 142–143.

8. Ibid., 177.

9. Ibid.

10. Warren W. Wiersbie, *Be Daring* (Wheaton, IL: Victor Books, 1988), 21–22.

11. Barclay, *Letters to the Galatians and Ephesians*, 4.

CHAPTER 7

1. Wuest, *Word Studies*, vol. 1, 84.

2. J. H. Thayer, *Greek English Lexicon of the New Testament*, (New York: American Book Company, n.d.), 318.

3. Wiersbe, *Be Free*, 65.

4. Wuest, *Word Studies*, vol. 1, 85.

5. Ibid., 87.

6. Wiersbe, *Be Free*, 67.

7. Ibid., 7.

8. Rick Renner, *The Dynamic Duo: The Holy Spirit and You* (Lake Mary, FL: Creation House, 1994), 119.

9. David Smitters, *Charlest G. Finney & His Intercessors,* Lectures on Revival, Autobiography of Charles Finney.

CHAPTER 8

1. Wiersbe, *Be Free*, 81.

2. Wuest, *Word Studies*, vol. 1, 84.

3. Wiersbe, *Be Free*, 65.

4. Wuest, *Word Studies*, vol. 1, 84–85.

CHAPTER 9

1. Stanley M. Horton, *What the Bible Says About the Holy Spirit* (Springfield, MO: Gospel Publishing House, 1976), 84–85.

2. William Barclay, *The Gospel of John*, vol. 1 (Philadelphia, PA: Westminster Press, 1986), 84.

3. French Arrington, *Encountering the Holy Spirit* (Cleveland, TN: Pathway Press, 2003),

102.

4. Barclay, *John*, 83.

5. A. T. Robertson commentary on Luke 12:49 found at http://www.godrules .net/library/robert/robertluk12.htm (accessed June 2, 2010).

6. Robertson, *Word Pictures*, vol. 2, 182.

7. Robertson, *Word Pictures*, vol. 4, 37.

8. Ibid., 404.

9. Wuest, *Word Studies*, vol. 1, 214.

10. Connie Giordano, *There Is No Such Thing as a Lazy Christian,* Series of "All About God," October 31, 2009.

11. Wuest, *Word Studies*, vol. 1, 215.

CHAPTER 10

1. Dake, *Annotated Reference Bible*, 403.

CHAPTER 11

1. Zenas J. Bicket, *The Spirit helps us Pray,* Logion Press, Spring Field, Missouri, 40.

CHAPTER 12

1. F. J. May, *The Book of Acts & Church Growth* (Cleveland, TN: Pathway Press, n.d.), 20.

2. Wuest, *Word Studies*, vol. 1, 87.

CHAPTER 14

1. Renner, *Merchandising*, 29.

2. Robertson, *Word Pictures*, vol. 1, 62.

3. Renner, *Merchandising*, 50.

4. Ibid., 26.

5. Ibid., 27.

6. Ibid., 28.

7. Ibid., 28–29.

8. French Arrington, *Maintaining the Foundations: A Study of 1 Timothy* (Grand Rapids, MI: Baker Book House, 1982).

9. Ibid., 96–97.

10. Renner, *Merchandising*, 43–44.

11. Rick Renner**,** *Seducing Spirits and Doctrines of Demons* (Tulsa, OK: Pillar Books of Publishing, n.d.), 37.

12. Ibid. 37

13. Robertson, *Word Pictures*, vol. 4, 623.

14. Steven Gallagher, "Denying, Resisting, Disdaining the Power of God," Pure Life Ministries, Dry Ridge, KY, spring 2008, 6–7.

15. Ibid., 37. 37–38.

16. Rick Renner, *Seducing Spirits and Doctrines of Demons* (Tulsa, OK: Pillar Books,

1988),

17. Warren W. Wiersbie, *Be Confident* (Wheaton, IL: Victor Books, 1973), 40.

18. John Phillips, *Exploring Hebrews* (Chicago: Moody Press, 1977), 53.

CHAPTER 15

1. Wiersbe, *Be Free*, 116.

2. Ibid., 121.

3. Ibid., 94.

Chapter 16
1. Wuest, *Word Studies*, vol. 1, 108.
2. Ibid., 109.
3. Ibid., 137.
4. Ibid., 140.

Chapter 17
1. Barclay, *Letters to the Galatians and Ephesians*, 53.

Chapter 18
1. Renner, *Merchandising*, 87.
2. Arrington, *Acts*, 210.
3. Headings for points one through six from "Exposing the False Teachers," *IVP New Testament Commentaries: Galatians 5*, found at http://www.biblegateway.com/resources/commentaries/IVP-NT/Gal/Exposing-False-Teachers (accessed June 9, 2010).
4. Wiersbe, *Be Free*, 90–91.
5. William R. Williams, *Lectures on Baptist History: 1877* (White Fish, MT: Kessinger Publishing, 2009).
6. Rick Renner, *Merchandising the Anointing: Developing Discernment for These Last Days*, (Tulsa, OK: Rick Renner Ministries, n.d.), 105.
7. Renner, *Merchandising*, 105–106.
8. Renner, *Seducing Spirits*, 76–77.
9. Ibid., 77.
10. Ibid., 78.
11. Ibid.
12. Ibid., 80.
13. Ibid., 81.
14. Wuest, *Word Studies*, vol. 2, 46.
15. Ibid., 57.
16. Ibid., 58
17. Renner, *Merchandising*, 89.

Chapter 19
1. Wuest, *Word Studies*, vol. 2, 22.
2. Warren W. Wiersbie, *Be Alert* (Wheaton, IL: Victor Books, 1984), 73.
3. Michael Greek, *Tyndale Commentary, 2 Peter and Jude*, (Grand Rapids, MI: Eerdman's Publishing Company, n.d.), 121.
4. Wuest, *Word Studies*, vol. 2, 62.
5. Robertson, *Word Pictures*, vol. 6, 170.

6. Michael Greek, "2 Peter and Jude," Tyndale New Testament Commentaries (Grand Rapids, MI: Eerdmans Publishing Company, 1968), 121.

CHAPTER 20
1. Flesh or Spirit, Galatians 5:19-21, October 4, 1998. Sermons from the Epistle to the Galatians. Page 1.
2. John Stott, The Message of Galatians, 146.
3. John MacArthur, MacArthur NT Commentaries, 160

CHAPTER 22
1. Wuest, Word Studies, vol. 1, 165.
2. Ibid.
3. Robertson, Word Pictures, vol. 4, 314.
4. Samuel Smiles quote found at "The Results of Generous Giving," IVP New Testament Commentaries: 2 Corinthians 9, http://www.biblegateway.com/resources/commentaries/IVP-NT/2Cor/Results-Generous-Giving (accessed June 10, 2010).

CHAPTER 23
1. Wuest, Word Studies, vol. 1, 171–172.
2. Ibid., 172.

CHAPTER 24
1. New Open Bible: Study Edition (Nashville: TN: Thomas Nelson Publishers, 1990), 1346–1347.
2. Ibid., 1346.
3. Robertson, Word Pictures, vol. 4, 489.
4. Herbert M. Carson, "Colossians and Philemon," Tyndale New Testament Commentaries (Grand Rapids, MI: Eerdmans Publishing Company, 1960), 59.
5. William Barclay, The Letters to the Philippians, Colossians and Thessalonians (Louisville, KY: Westminster John Knox Press, 1975).
6. Robertson, Word Pictures, vol. 4, 489.
7. Ibid.
8. Carson, "Colossians," 60.
9. Ibid.
10. Robertson, Word Pictures, vol. 4, 490.
11. New Open Bible, 1347.
12. Carson, "Colossians," 61
13. Robertson, Word Pictures, vol. 4, 490.
14. Renner, Merchandising, 109.
15. Ibid., 111.
16. Ibid.
17. Barclay, Letters to the Philippians, Colossians and Thessalonians.

18. Wuest, *Word Studies*, vol. 1, 201.

19. Ibid.

20. Frank G. Carver, *Beacon Bible Commentary* (MO: Beacon Hill Press of Kansas City, 1968), 602.

21. Warren W. Wiersbie, *Be Encouraged* (Wheaton, IL: Victor Books, 1984), 122.

22. Carver, *Beacon*, 604.

William Barclay, *The Letters to the Philippians, Colossians and Thessalonians* (Louisville, KY: Westminster John Knox Press, 1975).

CHAPTER 25

1. Bible Gateway.com, *Paul Unmask His Opponents,* 2 Corinthians 11, IVP, 4.

2. Wright 1982, 743–744. Wiersbie, *Be Encouraged*, 123.

3. Warren W. Wiersbie, *Be Alert: Be Aware of Religious Impostors* (Colorado Springs, CO: Victor Books, n.d.), 112–113

4. Elmer Towns, *The Gospel of John: Believe and Live* (Chattanooga, TN: AMG Publishers, n.d.), 52.

5. *Try the Spirits,* Sermons to Baptist Churches, Baptist Trumpeters Publications, 2.

6. Ibid, 3.

7. Frank G. Carver, *Beacon Bible Commentary* (Kansas City, MO: Beacon Hill Press of Kansas City, n.d.), 608.

8. French Arrington, *Ministry of Reconciliation: Study of 2 Corinthians* (Grand Rapids, MI: Baker House, n.d.), 156.

9. Bible Gateway.com, *Paul Unmasking His Opponents,* 2 Cor. 11, IVP, 11.

10. Frank G. Carver, *Beacon Bible Commentary* (Kansas City, MO: Beacon Hill Press of Kansas City, n.d.), 610

11. Colin Kruse, *Tyndale New Testament Commentaries: 2 Corinthians* (Grand Rapids, MI: William B. Eerdmans Publishing Company, n.d.), 193.

12. Rick Renner, *Merchandising the Anointing* (Tulsa, OK: Rick Renner Ministries, n.d.), 40.

13. Ibid., 41.

14. William Barclay, "The Letters to the Corinthians," *The Daily Study Bible* (Edinburgh: Saint Andrews Press, 1954), 279.